D1557824

Analysis Techniques
for Racecar
Data Acquisition

Other SAE books of interest:

Hands-On Race Car Engineer
By John H. Glimmerveen
(Product Code: R-323)

Kinetic Energy Recovery Systems for Racing Cars
Edited by Alberto Boretti
(Product Code: PT-159)

**Engine Failure Analysis—Internal Combustion
Engine Failures and Their Causes**
By Stefan Zima and Ernst Greuter
(Product Code: R-320)

For more information or to order a book, contact SAE International at
400 Commonwealth Drive, Warrendale, PA 15096-0001, USA;
phone 877-606-7323 (U.S. and Canada only) or 724-776-4970
(outside U.S. and Canada); fax 724-776-0790;
email CustomerService@sae.org;
website http://books.sae.org.

Analysis Techniques for Racecar Data Acquisition, Second Edition

By Jörge Segers

Warrendale, Pennsylvania, USA

400 Commonwealth Drive
Warrendale, PA 15096-0001 USA

E-mail: CustomerService@sae.org
Phone: 877-606-7323 (inside USA and Canada)
            724-776-4970 (outside USA)
Fax: 724-776-0790

ISBN 978-0-7680-6459-9
SAE Order Number R-408
DOI 10.4271/R-408

Segers, Jörge.
   Analysis techniques for racecar data acquisition / by Jörge Segers. — Second Edition.
      pages cm
   Includes bibliographical references and index.
   ISBN 978-0-7680-6459-9
   1. Automobiles, Racing—Dynamics—Data processing.   2. Automobiles, Racing—Performance—Measurement.   3. Automobiles, Racing—Testing.   I. Title.
   TL243.S43 2014
   629.28'2—dc23
                                                       2013037907

Information contained in this work has been obtained by SAE International from sources believed to be reliable. However, neither SAE International nor its authors guarantee the accuracy or completeness of any information published herein and neither SAE International nor its authors shall be responsible for any errors, omissions, or damages arising out of use of this information. This work is published with the understanding that SAE International and its authors are supplying information, but are not attempting to render engineering or other professional services. If such services are required, the assistance of an appropriate professional should be sought.

To purchase bulk quantities, please contact:

SAE Customer Service
E-mail: CustomerService@sae.org
Phone: 877-606-7323 (*inside USA and Canada*)
            724-776-4970 (*outside USA*)
Fax: 724-776-0790

Visit the SAE International Bookstore at
books.sae.org

Dedicated to Daan and Savitri

Contents

Contents

Preface to the Second Edition

When the first edition of this book was first published in 2008, my goal was to create a book presenting up-to-date techniques to analyze data collected from onboard data logging systems in race cars. Since the first edition, I have received a great deal of feedback from people all over the world indicating that I was successful in obtaining this goal. I am extremely happy that this book has been able to fill a void in this ever-developing area.

However, since 2008 my personal understanding of this subject has evolved. First of all, the technology has developed, making it possible to obtain more advanced and accurate data regarding the performance of race cars at less cost. There are a number of observations that have led me to write this second edition.

Some race series have actively restricted data logging to decrease the team's running budgets. In these cases, it is extremely important that a maximum of information be extracted and interpreted from the hardware that is at hand. Although I do not agree with the philosophy of limiting data acquisition by sporting regulations, it does level the field, as everybody will have access to the same information. This means that a team that uses the data more efficiently will have an edge over the competition.

The opposite is also true. The ever-decreasing cost of electronics makes advanced sensors and logging capabilities more accessible for everybody. With this comes the risk of information overload. There will be a point where a team will no longer be able to process all the available data. Therefore, techniques need to be provided that will help in drawing the right conclusions quickly from very large data sets.

I wanted to include newly gained knowledge since the first publication. Experience is a continuous process, and I felt that the time had come to upgrade the book. There were some items in the first edition that needed to be addressed, explained better, or with more examples. The book contains three new chapters. The first (chapter 8) covers the techniques that are available to analyze tire performance. The second (chapter 17) gives an introduction to metric-driven analysis, a technique that is used throughout the book. Finally, a chapter was added to explain what kind of information the data contains about the track being driven on (chapter 18).

Preface to the First Edition

A proven way for athletes to be successful in any sporting discipline is for them to record their performance, analyze what has happened, and draw conclusions from the factors that influence that performance. Marathon runners log their running speed and distance along with their heart rate to optimize their training schedules. Football players record their games on video to evaluate techniques, performance, and tactics. Chess players write down every move in a game to replay and analyze it afterward. They measure something, learn from it, and try to use it to their advantage the next time.

In motor racing, sophisticated recording devices are used in conjunction with numerous sensors to record what the car and its driver are doing. Engineers often are employed full-time to maintain the system, analyze the recorded data, and draw the correct conclusions from it.

Motor racing is known for high-end technology, and this technology changes every day. Ten years ago, race car data acquisition was somewhat limited to well-funded teams in high-profile championships. Nowadays, the cost of electronics has decreased dramatically. Powerful computers are available for very little expense. Data acquisition systems are now sold for the price of a single racing tire. This means data acquisition has become accessible to everyone.

Whatever the price of the data acquisition system, it is a waste of money if the recorded data is not interpreted correctly. This book contains enough information to prevent the investment in a data acquisition system from being a waste of money.

Whether measuring the performance of a Formula One race car or that of a road-legal street car on the local drag strip, the dynamics of the vehicles and their drivers remain the same. Identical analysis techniques apply. This book contains a collection of techniques for analyzing data recorded by any vehicle's data acquisition system. It details how to measure the performance of the vehicle and driver, what can be learned from it, and how this information can be used to your advantage the next time the vehicle hits the track.

Acknowledgments

When I began working in motor racing in 1998, I soon learned that this business is a team effort. The sum of the qualities of each member determines the team's success. Eight years later, when I wrote this book, I learned this also is a team effort, very similar to running a successful racing team. That is why I would like to begin by appropriately crediting "my" team.

First, I would like to thank everyone at SAE International for guiding this project in the right direction. Special thanks go out to Martha Swiss, intellectual property manager, Heather Slater, product developer, Terri Kelly, administrative assistant, and Terry Wilson for artwork.

A big contributor to this book was Josep Fontdecaba I. Buj, engineering director at Creuat S.L.; not only for writing chapter 12 but especially for the many discussions we had about suspension setup and data analysis. His input added immeasurable value to this book.

David Brown and Andrew Durant at Race Technology gave me detailed insight about GPS-based data acquisition techniques. I would like to thank them for providing me with the hardware that was used to create much of the data traces used throughout this book. Their company is proof that data acquisition can be affordable for all motor racing disciplines.

I am proud to have Cosworth Electronics support the creation of this book. The information and analysis files supplied by this company were invaluable. Thanks go out to Thomas Buckler, Robert Kirk and Michael de Cock.

The following people deserve credit for taking the time to evaluate the manuscript and for providing me with invaluable feedback: Peter Wright (consultant to the FIA), Dr. Wolfgang Ullrich (head of Audi Sport), John Glimmerveen (author of the book *Hands-on Racecar Engineer*), Doug and Bill Milliken (authors of the book *Racecar Vehicle Dynamics*), and William C. Mitchell (head of Mitchell Software).

This book addresses what I know about race car data acquisition, and what I know is influenced greatly by the people I had a chance to work with. Therefore, my great respect goes out to all the engineers, mechanics, and team owners that were there to teach me. I hope I can repay these debts when they read this book.

Every graph in this book was created by a race car driver. Many of these graphs resulted in successful track performance, pole positions, race victories, and championships. I thank all of these drivers for providing me with data to analyze.

Henrik Roos of the Simbin Development Team is the person that triggered my interest in technical writing. He gave me the idea to write a book on this little-documented subject in the first place.

Special thanks for this second edition go out to Pierre-Alain Aucouturier and Philippe Leuwers at Texys Sensors for their support and detailed supply of information on the latest sensor technologies. Also Giuseppe Callea of BHAI TECH srl. deserves special mention for his contribution in chapter 3 on the evaluation of sensor reading accuracies and the interesting discussions on simulation techniques.

I would like to thank Tony Gardner and David Tucker of iRacing.com for their help with the chapter on simulation. The first edition of this book proved quite popular in the online racing community. It surprised me to find out how close something—that is often wrongfully considered as a computer game—resembles real racing. I am sure that this interest group will find a lot of useful information in this book.

Jörge Segers

Chapter 1
Introduction

One of the most important weapons for a race car team is information. The more information it can gather (and process), the better its judgment will be in making key decisions. Data acquisition provides engineers with the information they and the team require to evaluate vehicle performance.

1.1   What Is This Book All About?

First of all, the question of why data acquisition is necessary should be answered. Why do we need to measure information? When it comes to performance in motor racing, the stopwatch is the most important measurement instrument. It all comes down to minimizing lap times or to maximizing the distance covered in a given time frame. The stopwatch gives a measure for the performance of the total of the vehicle and all its subsystems, the driver, and the tires. An activity that is not measured cannot be controlled nor managed. The measurement of performance and subsequent analysis of the results leads to better performance and a higher rate of improvement. This is why we need data logging!

Nowadays, almost every race car is equipped with a data logging device that can measure almost every performance parameter of the vehicle and its driver. These measurements can be used to examine the effects of setup changes or changing track conditions, driving style, and causes of performance variations or component failures.

This book covers the use of electronic data logging systems in race cars. It is not a how-to manual for installing a data logger, selecting different components, or choosing the most appropriate configuration, although these topics are discussed briefly. This book is primarily about analyzing the endless data streams produced by the system. It is also about using this information to evaluate and optimize a given race car's setup.

The data logging system provides information about how a car/driver combination is performing at a particular location on a racetrack. This book takes the analysis a step further and tries to determine why the car/driver is performing in this particular way at this particular place on the track. Upon completing the book, the reader will have the insight to effectively use competition car data acquisition.

Useful literature addressing race car data acquisition and data analysis has been published previously. However, in this work a mathematical approach to data analysis is emphasized, with the primary intention being to show the reader how even a limited amount of data can provide useful information about race car dynamics.

In the early days of motor racing, many of the engineer's decisions were based on intuition and experience. The stopwatch, tire pressure gauge, pyrometer, and driver's comments served as the data logging system. Nowadays, the electronic data acquisition system can provide almost everything the engineer needs to know about the car's behavior (Figures 1.1 and 1.2).

Figure 1.1 Race car data logging systems record user-defined parameters while the car is in motion (Courtesy of GLPK-Carsport)

As the degree of competition increases, costs of racing and testing increase. Because of this, there is a greater demand for understanding the race car dynamics to increase testing efficiency, educate drivers, and provide them with the tools to educate themselves. It is also important to provide the parameters to simulate the dynamic behavior of the car. This more than justifies the use of data acquisition, and in the past this was indeed only possible at the higher echelons of motor racing. However, times have changed: the cost of electronics continues to decrease and data acquisition is now a common technique, used in Formula One and Indy cars to club sport championships and karting.

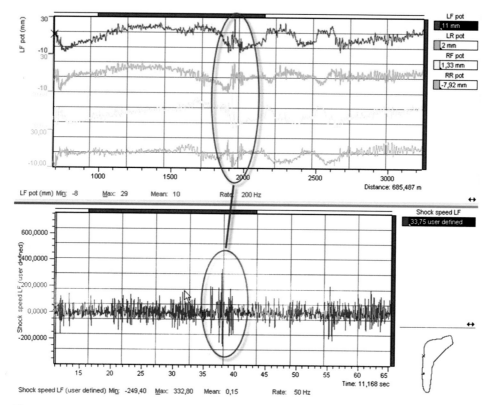

Figure 1.2 This graph shows the signals recorded from four potentiometers mounted on the suspension as well as the damper acceleration of the left front wheel. The area indicated shows what happened to the wheels when the photograph in Figure 1.1 was taken.

The configuration of the book is as follows:

Chapter 1: This chapter is an introduction to data acquisition. What is data acquisition's purpose? What should one measure? What are the hardware requirements? What are the latest developments in data acquisition?

Chapter 2: What is required from the analysis software? In what different ways can data be displayed? How can one manipulate the data channels?

Chapter 3: During race weekends or test sessions, time limitations require the engineer to quickly find what is needed in the logged data. Developing the ability to read the graphs is required.

Chapter 4: In this chapter, straight-line acceleration is analyzed, as well as the ability of the race car to overcome the external resistances acting upon it.

Chapter 5: Acceleration usually is followed by braking. This chapter covers the performance analysis of the car's braking system.

Chapter 6: Most race cars carry a gearbox to adapt the vehicle torque to a wide range of velocities. This chapter discusses shifting techniques and the choice of the proper gear ratios for a given racetrack.

Chapter 7: How can the car's cornering balance be evaluated? How does one diagnose oversteering and understeering?

Chapter 8: How can the data be used to understand the behavior of the race car's tires?

Chapter 9: In this chapter, methods to quantify the roll stiffness and its distribution on the front and rear axles are covered.

Chapter 10: This chapter addresses how the loads at the tires' contact patches are calculated and investigates the effects of lateral and longitudinal load transfer.

Chapter 11: The shock absorbers determine the transient behavior of the race car. This chapter focuses on analyzing the damping characteristics of the vehicle.

Chapter 12: This chapter explains how to evaluate suspension performance using frequency domain analysis techniques.

Chapter 13: A car traveling through air is subject to aerodynamic forces. The various methods used to measure these forces from logged data are covered in this chapter.

Chapter 14: Data logging is very often used to analyze what the driver is doing. How can data analysis help improve the driver's performance?

Chapter 15: Lap time simulation is a recent technology that has found its way into almost all levels of motor racing. With the data logging system, this is a valuable and cost-effective tool for vehicle development. This chapter illustrates how the logged data helps tune the vehicle simulation model.

Chapter 16: Data logging can be an invaluable help in selecting the right tactics for the race or practice session. This chapter shows how to use the data logging system as a predictive tool for race strategy.

Chapter 17: Metrics and run charts analysis of a large dataset can accelerate interpretation and decision making from the logged data significantly. In this chapter the techniques to develop vehicle specific metrics and their analysis are covered.

Chapter 18: The logged data can reveal some interesting information from the race track. This information can help the engineer to better prepare the setup of the car.

Chapter 19: The last chapter introduces sensor technology. Usable data must be measured correctly. To ensure this, a basic knowledge of measurement technology is required.

1.2   What Is Data Acquisition?

Put simply, a race car data acquisition system is an electronic memory unit that stores user-defined parameters as a function of time while the car is on the track. The stored data can be downloaded to a computer where it can be analyzed, often with specialized software packages.

1.2.1   Data Acquisition Categories

This analysis can be broken down into the following categories:

1. **Vehicle Performance Analysis**
   Logged data forms an objective measurement of vehicle performance that can be used with the (subjective) comments of the driver to evaluate what is going on with the car. The engineer can pinpoint more easily any handling problems and the locations on the racetrack where they occur. From this analysis, the engineer decides which setup changes should be made to the car before the next driving session.

2. **Driver Performance Analysis**
   Logging the cockpit activities of drivers sheds some light on their driving style. Data acquisition makes it possible to analyze different laps by a driver or to compare the differences in style and performance among multiple drivers. This type of analysis is particularly useful in championships where more than one driver uses the same car. A more statistical analysis of the data gives the driver a more profound idea about his or her driving style.

3. **Vehicle Development**
   Data logging is an invaluable tool in a race car development program. Purpose-driven measurements aid in decision making with regard to what direction development should be focused.

4. **Reliability and Safety**
   By recording vital channels such as engine oil pressure and temperatures as well as battery voltages, reliability problems can be discovered before more damage is done to the car. Safety is another factor in play here (e.g., tire pressure monitoring systems). In case of damage, the logged data can point to the cause of the problem.

5. **Determining Vehicle Parameters**
   Race car simulation software is becoming more popular and is an important add-on for any data logging system. To develop a simulation model of a given race car, all relevant parameters of the car should be known by the programmer to guarantee sufficient model accuracy. Model parameter examples include vehicle suspended and unsuspended mass, track width, wheelbase, center of gravity height, and roll center locations. Some parameters can be measured on the static vehicle or

calculated; others should be measured under racing conditions and can be extracted from the data.

6. **Running Logs**

   A data logging system records the active history of a race car. It records how long the car runs and what happens to it during this time. When this information is coupled with the vital parts of the car, a running log of component lifetimes can be created. The system keeps track of when a part should be replaced and rebuilds performed.

1.2.2 Data Categories

Although many of the signals often are interrelated, the data that the system measures can be divided generally into the following categories:

1. **The Vital Functions of the Car**

   These signals include the important engine and driveline-related channels such as engine oil pressure and temperature, water temperature, fuel pressure, gearbox and differential temperature, and battery voltage. Basically, in this category are included all channels that tell us something about the reliability of the car. Engine revolutions per minute (RPM) is a signal that also falls into this category.

2. **Driver Activity**

   Driver activity parameters are those over which the driver has direct control. They include throttle position, steering angle, brake pressure and pedal position, and gear position.

3. **Chassis Parameters**

   These are the vehicle dynamics-related signals such as vehicle speed, lateral and longitudinal *g*-force (Gs), steering angle, damper position, brake line pressure, tire temperatures and pressures, ride height, and suspension loads.

1.2.3 Basic Data Acquisition Signals

Depending on the budget available for acquiring a data acquisition system, the possibilities are almost infinite. Data acquisition systems exist for almost any application. A traditional configuration for data acquisition starters consists of a suitable logging unit that measures the following signals for chassis and driver performance analysis:

- Engine RPM
- Wheel speed
- Throttle position
- Steering angle
- Lateral acceleration
- Longitudinal acceleration

In addition to these channels, the vital functions of the car (e.g., fluid pressures and temperatures, battery voltage) should be logged. A beacon channel should be provided to indicate the beginning and end of a lap. Measuring the six basic signals already gives the engineer a massive amount of data to analyze.

1.2.4   Supplemental Data Acquisition Signals

Extended vehicle dynamics analysis can require more sensor signals to be recorded, the most important probably being suspension travel. Next to the six signals previously mentioned, the following channels are recommended:

- Suspension (shock absorber) movement
- Brake line pressure
- Tire temperatures (infrared)
- Clutch pressure
- Gear position
- Speed of each wheel
- Front and rear axle lateral acceleration
- Vertical acceleration
- Tire pressures
- Ride height
- Suspension loads (strain gauges)
- Brake disc temperatures
- Yaw speed (gyroscope)
- Propshaft torque
- Aerodynamic pressures (pitot tubes)
- Gear lever force

This list can go on, and of course engineers should always ask themselves what exactly they want to measure. Specific needs require specific channels to log. Most teams start data-logging the six basic channels and then extend the system step by step as they gain more experience in analyzing the data. Analysis often provides as many answers as it does new questions. However, brake pressure, suspension movement, and infrared tire temperature is usually the next logical step. When investing in a system, keep in mind that the number of signals may be extended in the future, which impacts the wiring harness, available memory, and other hardware.

The engine electronic control unit (ECU) often features its own data logger that records engine-specific data. This system should be capable of communicating to the external data acquisition unit logging the chassis-related parameters. In this way, the signals from the engine ECU can be transferred and overlaid with lap-timing beacons. For engine performance analysis, the most important signals are engine RPM, throttle position, lambda, and air box pressure.

1.2.5   Example of Parameters

Table 1.1 provides an overview of the parameters logged from GLPK Racing's Dodge Viper during the 2004 Belgian GT season. The system used was a MoTeC advanced dash logger (ADL) with an internal memory of 10 Mb, communicating with the engine ECU to receive all engine-related channels.

Table 1.1 Logged channels on GLPK's Dodge Viper GTS-R	
1	Engine RPM (Measured by engine ECU)
2	Engine Oil Temperature (Measured by engine ECU)
3	Engine Oil Pressure (Measured by engine ECU)
4	Air Inlet Manifold Pressure (Measured by engine ECU)
5	Throttle Position (Measured by engine ECU)
6	Lambda Left (Measured by engine ECU)
7	Lambda Right (Measured by engine ECU)
8	Engine Water Temperature (Measured by engine ECU)
9	Air Temperature Before Throttle (Measured by engine ECU)
10	Battery Voltage at Engine ECU (Measured by engine ECU)
11	Internal Temperature Engine ECU (Measured by engine ECU)
12	Lateral G-Force at Center of Gravity
13	Longitudinal G-Force at Center of Gravity
14	Vertical G-Force at Center of Gravity
15	Lateral G-Force at Front Axle
16	Lateral G-Force at Rear Axle
17	Steered Angle
18	Brake Pedal Position
19	Brake Line Pressure Front
20	Brake Line Pressure Rear
21	Damper Position Front Left
22	Damper Position Front Right
23	Damper Position Rear Left

Table 1.1 Logged channels on GLPK's Dodge Viper GTS-R (Continued)	
24	Damper Position Rear Right
25	Tire Temperature Rear Right Inside
26	Tire Temperature Rear Right Center
27	Tire Temperature Rear Right Outside
28	Tire Temperature Rear Left Inside
29	Tire Temperature Rear Left Center
30	Tire Temperature Rear Left Outside
31	Tire Temperature Front Right Inside
32	Tire Temperature Front Right Center
33	Tire Temperature Front Right Outside
34	Tire Temperature Front Left Inside
35	Tire Temperature Front Left Center
36	Tire Temperature Front Left Outside
37	Battery Voltage at Dashboard
38	Differential Oil Temperature
39	Gearbox Oil Temperature
40	Internal Temperature Dashboard
41	Traction Control Wheel Speed Front Left
42	Traction Control Wheel Speed Front Right
43	Traction Control Wheel Speed Rear Left
44	Traction Control Wheel Speed Rear Right
45	Lap Time Beacon
46	ABS Wheel Speed Front Left
47	ABS Wheel Speed Front Right
48	ABS Wheel Speed Rear Left
49	ABS Wheel Speed Rear Right
50	Gear Position (Measured by Engine ECU)
51	Gear Lever Force (Measured by Engine ECU)

Most engine parameters are recorded by the engine management system and sent to the data logger through a serial link. The logging unit measures and stores gearbox and differential temperatures as additional vital channels.

The six basic channels are all present: engine RPM, vehicle speed, throttle position, steering angle, and lateral and longitudinal acceleration. There are five different *g*-force channels. Lateral, longitudinal, and vertical acceleration are measured by a three-axis *g*-force sensor located near the car's center of gravity. In addition, two lateral *g*-force sensors are located on the front and rear axle. These are convenient for analyzing understeering and oversteering.

There are eight wheel-speed signals recorded by the logging unit. This might seem a bit excessive, but this particular car was equipped with an engine-controlled traction control system (TCS) and, completely separate from this, an antilock brake system (ABS). Because the team uses separate wheel-speed sensors for both systems, a failure in one does not affect the other. All eight signals are logged for analysis as well as diagnostic purposes.

Three sensors indicate what occurs in the braking system. The amount of pedal travel by the driver is recorded by a linear potentiometer. Brake line pressures are logged as well. In addition to being useful for analysis, brake line pressure readouts make it easier to adjust the brake balance.

Suspension travel is measured by four potentiometers mounted on the shock absorbers. Three locations per tire measure tire surface temperature, which accounts for another 12 sensor signals.

Table 1.1 already represents 51 channels that are directly logged. From these, the analysis software calculates another 73 math channels, which brings the total to 124. Getting lost becomes a potential risk. In this case, the investment in such a system and all the sensors was justified by several reasons:

- The championship consisted of seven races on three different racetracks. To continuously improve the vehicle and driver performance, more data was required.

- During the 2004 season, the team was developing a semi-active hydraulic suspension system. Vehicle dynamic parameters were measured to compare with those measured using the conventional suspension.

- Traction control and the ABS required four wheel speed sensors anyway, so those signals (in this case, eight) were wired to the data logger as well for analysis and diagnostics.

- The team implemented lap time simulation software and used the data acquisition system to help build a virtual model of the race car.

More signals measured means more accurate conclusions, but it often requires more analysis skills as well. Getting the most out of the available channels is explored in this book.

1.3 Hardware

Data acquisition systems are available in various configurations, but they always have the main components in common (Figure 1.3).

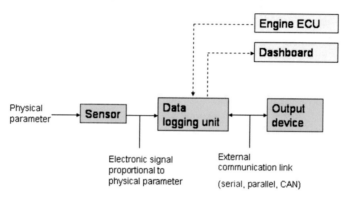

Figure 1.3 General configuration of a data acquisition system

A physical parameter (e.g., pressure, temperature, speed, force) of interest is captured by a sensor that transforms the measurement into an electronic signal proportional to this parameter and understandable to the data logging unit. The most important property of the data logging unit is that it stores the measured parameters in an electronic memory. An output device (computer or laptop) can communicate with the data logger via an external link. This link is very often bidirectional because most systems offer some parameters to be configured by the user. Controller area network (CAN) communication links are becoming more popular as a replacement for serial or parallel links because of the communication (downloading and uploading) speed and the much easier addition of different devices to the system.

Via this or a separate communication link, an external display can be added to the system to visualize sensor readings to the driver. Some current systems on the market include dashboards with an integrated memory. In this case, the dashboard and data logger form one unit. Most engine ECUs offer the possibility to transfer engine-related sensor signals to an external data logger.

Figure 1.4 gives an example of a possible configuration. It concerns an engineering system from STACK Ltd. built around a CAN. The system starts from a display system with eight possible inputs (RPM, water and oil temperature, oil and fuel pressure, lap beacon, lateral G and speed). The dashboard measures these values but does not store them. Through a connection to a CAN, the measured signals are transferred to a recording module (the logger). To allow more inputs to be recorded, additional input modules can be added to the network (only one is pictured). With an interface cable, the user can link a computer to the network to download data and configure the system.

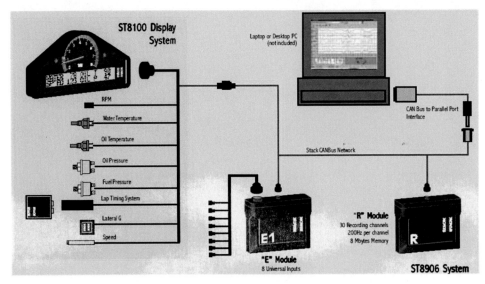

Figure 1.4 An example of a possible data acquisition hardware configuration

1.4   Recent Hardware Trends

During the last three decades, data acquisition systems have come a long way and basically followed the advances in microcontroller technology. The three areas of primary importance are the available memory to store data from increasing numbers of sensors, the number of possible sensor inputs, and the speed at which the data can be downloaded to an external computer.

Available logging memory is expressed in megabytes or gigabytes, and microcontroller manufacturers are able to store more available memory on an ever-decreasing microchip area. Increasing logging memory results in longer recording times or the possibility to increase the number of measured channels. A complete 24-hour race can be recorded while logging a reasonable amount of channels.

The use of external memory cards, such as secure digital (SD) or compact flash (CF) cards, is becoming more popular. These come in memory capacities of up to 64 Gb, and using them as logging memory makes long download times a thing of the past (Figure 1.5).

Modern data acquisition devices often are incorporated into a CAN within the vehicle. The CAN is a serial bus system suited for networking devices, sensors, and actuators within a system and was developed by Robert Bosch GmbH. It is easier to add devices to the network (e.g., external dashboards, input expansion boxes) and make them communicate with each other. Data transfer rates between these devices are far greater, compared with parallel or serial connections.

Figure 1.5 Race Technology's DL1 data logger uses a CF memory card as logging memory

The classic download cable plugged into a serial or parallel port has been replaced by USB cables, allowing vast amounts of data to be downloaded to an external computer within seconds. The latest developments include communicating with the system in the car and downloading data from it through a wireless network. Typical transfer rates of a Wi-Fi network are 7 to 30 Mb/sec which produce acceptable download times.

A more popular feature of modern data acquisition techniques is the synchronization of video images, audio channels, and logged data. Figure 1.6 shows an example in which the images (and sounds) recorded by an in-car camera are synchronized with the channels logged by the data acquisition unit. These types of systems are primarily intended to register driver action in the cockpit, but basically a camera can be aimed at almost anything, including the car's suspension and rotating shafts. The example in Figure 1.6 shows a camera aimed at the left-rear tire to register sidewall movement of the tire construction. An audio channel makes the system even more powerful and puts the engineer much closer to what actually happens in the car. A missed gearshift can be detected immediately from the recorded engine sounds, but also wheel spin or clutch slip can be diagnosed without filtering out the problem from different signal traces.

The accuracy of track maps can be improved greatly by adding global positioning system (GPS) measurements to the data logging system. Race Technology's DL1 data logger uses a 5-Hz GPS to measure position and speed. GPS position accuracy depends on various factors, but combining it with inertial corrections (integration of lateral and longitudinal acceleration) can significantly improve it.

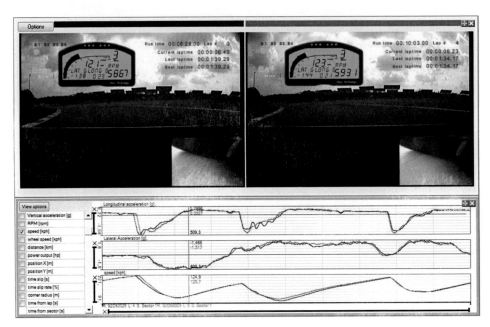

Figure 1.6 Video logging

GPS integration has two major advantages. The quality of track maps is much better than when only inertial sensor signals are used to calculate the map (Figure 1.7). A closed circuit is not required, making this technology suitable for rallying and power-boat racing. For motorcycling, it greatly facilitates the generation of a track map. Infrared timing beacons that define the beginning and end of a lap are no longer required. The second advantage of using GPS is the higher speed accuracy, which is typically within 0.1–0.2%. This is far better than that obtained with a magnetic pickup sensor measuring wheel speed. Speed accuracy is of vital importance to calculate the lap distance, and improving it increases the quality of lap segment calculations and lap overlays.

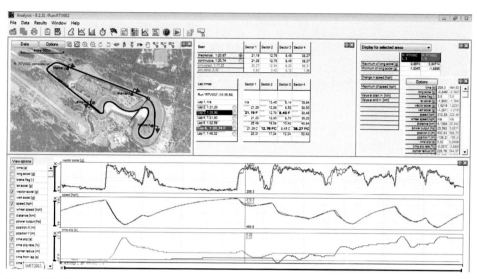

Figure 1.7 Track map created with GPS

Chapter 2

Data Analysis Software Requirements

To do a good job, the right tools are required. The most important tool for data acquisition engineers is the software used to analyze data. This chapter acts as a guide for selecting a suitable software package, and tips are given on using this package effectively.

2.1 General Requirements for Data Acquisition Software

Everything a data logger does is storing numbers. And even at modest sampling rates, a single lap's data forms a very long list of numbers. We need a tool to help us visualize this list in a way that helps us understand easily what is happening with the car. On a racetrack during a race event or test session, the time available to analyze data from the onboard logger is limited. The data acquisition engineer must provide clear answers in a very short time. The analysis software used is an important factor in this. Therefore, choosing the right software package for the job is absolutely essential (Figure 2.1).

Figure 2.1 The software used for analysis of the logged data should enable the user to visualize the data in a way that makes drawing conclusions from it easy and less time-consuming (Picture courtesy of Rachel Loh)

2.1.1 Software Features

Software preferences can vary from person to person, but the most important question to be answered is, "Does the software let you customize the way the system displays the data to suit your needs?" Look for the following features:

- User-definable graph limits
- Multichannel display
- Multilap overlays and plot of time difference between compared laps
- Zooming
- Predetermined display templates
- Cursor functions (e.g., cursor data point values, set markers, distance, and time location)
- Plot data versus time or distance, *X-Y* graphs, histograms
- Track mapping
- Statistical data per lap and lap sections
- Data file organization
- Adding session notes to the data
- Switching between units
- Capability of creating mathematical channels
- Data filtering
- Data export to other software packages
- User friendliness, software support, and updates

2.2 Different Ways of Displaying Data

A race car data logger will be able to generate megabytes of data within the time frame of a practice session or race, depending on the amount of sensor signals and their sampling rates. This is basically a huge series of numbers. For efficient analyses of these numbers we need to be able to reduce the amount of data into something that makes sense quickly. We can do this by either visualizing the data graphically or summarizing it by the means of statistics.

The following excerpt is taken from the book *The Visual Display of Quantitative Information* by Edward R. Tufte [2-1]:

At their best, graphics are instruments for reasoning about quantitative information. Often the most effective way to describe, explore and summarize a set of numbers—even a very large set—is to look at pictures of those numbers. Furthermore, of all methods for analyzing and communicating numerical information, well-designed data graphics are usually the simplest and at the same time the most powerful.

Most data analysis software packages provide different ways of presenting data graphically. Each way has its own advantages and puts the data in a different daylight. The most important are time and distance plots, *X-Y* graphs, histograms, and run charts.

The second tool available to facilitate the analysis of logged data is statistics. Statistics can be used to summarize or describe a collection of data. By using statistics, the original data set can be reduced in size to a collection of information that is easier to interpret.

The following section explores the most important tools available to present data.

2.2.1   Time and Distance Plots

The time plot is the most frequently used form of graphic design. A random sample of 4000 graphics drawn from 15 of the world's newspapers and magazines published from 1974 to 1980 found that more than 75% of all the graphs published were time plots [2-1]. In a time plot, each event registered by a sensor is displayed as a consecutive list of points.

Figure 2.2 shows the speed signal of a lap around Zandvoort—the upper versus time, the lower versus distance. Compared with the time plot, the distance plot expands fast sections of the track and compresses slow sections.

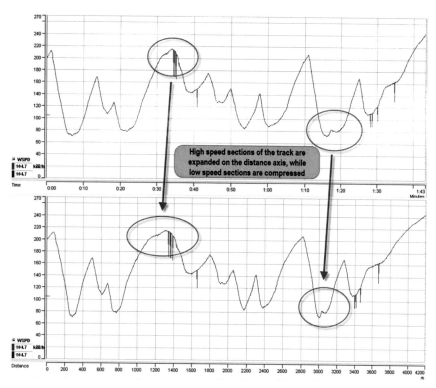

Figure 2.2 Speed traces from one lap around Zandvoort—the first against time, the second against distance

The distance graph indicates where an event occurred, whereas the time graph shows when an event occurred. Graphs are plotted against distance because a certain track location remains reasonably constant over different laps and correlating an event to a certain place on the racetrack is desired. Distance plots will be used to answer questions such as "what is the location of the braking point?" or "where is the location of the apex the driver took in a particular corner?" Time plots are used to determine the duration of an event or the rate of change of a signal.

The engineer often wants to investigate more than one channel at a time. This can be achieved by opening multiple graphs on the computer screen or by placing the required channels in one graph. The first possibility (Figure 2.3) has the advantage of separating all signals from each other to make patterns easily recognizable. If all the channels in Figure 2.3 are placed in one graph, it becomes virtually unreadable, as illustrated in Figure 2.4.

However, placing multiple channels in one graph has the advantage in that the *y*-axis is stretched to its maximum, while the time (or distance) axis remains the same. Variations in the signal are much more visible. Figure 2.5 provides an example in which speed and throttle signals are displayed from the same lap in Figures 2.3 and 2.4. Most software packages offer the user the capability to manually scale the signal axis to fit the data on the screen.

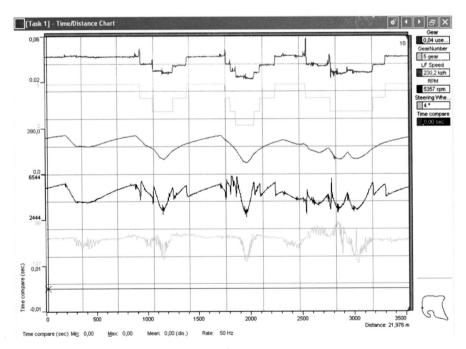

Figure 2.3 Multiple traces pictured separately

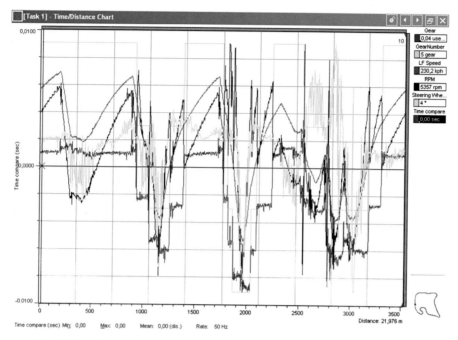

Figure 2.4 Multiple traces in one graph

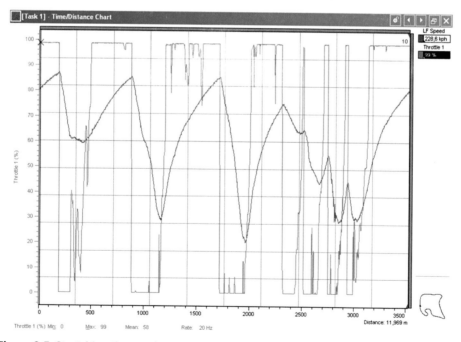

Figure 2.5 Stretching the graph's *y*-axis can make signal variations easier to detect.

2.2.2 Track Maps

The track map is a graphical representation of the trajectory of the car. Its primary use is to navigate the user around the track. When you put your mouse cursor in any time or distance chart or a scatter plot, the track map will reveal the location on the track you're looking at (Figure 2.6).

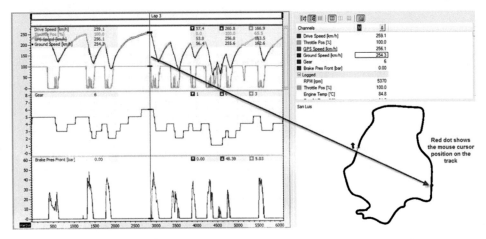

Figure 2.6 Track map of the San Luis circuit; the red dot corresponds with the location of the mouse cursor in the distance chart.

We can, however, use the track map to visualize our data in a specific way as well. For instance, we can superimpose the chosen gear ratio on top of a track map or indicate where the driver brakes, is at full throttle, or where he's coasting. The four maps in Figure 2.7 have the derivative data of shock potentiometers (heavily filtered to take out any high-frequency content) superimposed. When the map color is blue, the damper is in rebound, whereas red indicates a damper in bump.

The advantage of superimposing channel data on a track map is that it gives a very clear reference to *where* on the track something happens.

2.2.3 *X-Y* Graphs

When the correlation between two signals is investigated, plotting them in an *X-Y* graph can be useful. A very popular example of this feature is given in Figure 2.8. This represents the vehicle's traction circle by plotting the lateral against the longitudinal *g*-force.

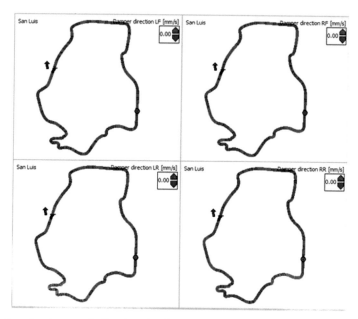

Figure 2.7 Four track maps indicating the direction of damper travel on the four suspension corners

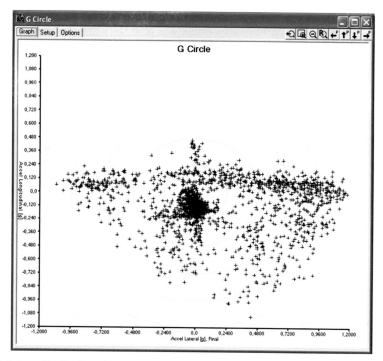

Figure 2.8 Longitudinal against lateral *g*-force data from a rally cross heat around Circuit Duivelsberg at Maasmechelen in an Opel Corsa

2.2.4 Histograms

Histograms represent the distribution of a set of data points into several ranges. Popular histograms used for race car data analysis are RPM, throttle position, and shock velocity. Figure 2.9 shows a histogram of the vertical chassis movement of a race car. This graph was created to analyze the effects of friction on the vertical stability of the car.

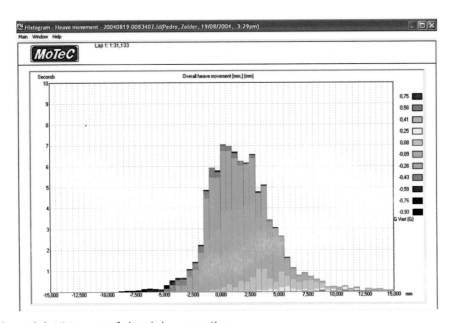

Figure 2.9 Histogram of chassis heave motion

2.2.5 Run Charts

Very often comparative analysis is limited to looking at single laps. It is useful to look at the complete data from a wider angle in order to spot trends or abnormal situations. Run charts are time-based charts in which the unit of time is a single lap. Each point in the chart represents a statistic taken from its specific lap. Simple examples of these statistics include top speed, average throttle position, minimum oil pressure, average tire temperature, and average understeer angle. Run charts can also pinpoint data that's worth having a closer look at.

Figure 2.10 is an example of a run chart where the average understeer angle value (see chapter 7 for more information on this channel) is shown for each lap of a race with three drivers on the same car. The graph clearly shows a trend toward more oversteer (lower understeer angle average) for Driver 1 and Driver 3, while Driver 2 develops toward more understeer over time.

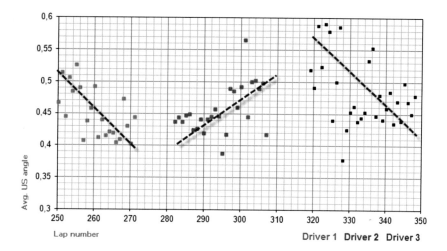

Figure 2.10 Example of a run chart showing the average understeer angle per lap for a complete race

Run charts can be used to visualize data of a complete practice session, test day, race weekend, or even a complete racing season. By combining different channels in run charts, correlations between these channels can be found. Run charts are generally created outside the data analysis software in a spreadsheet or through a mathematical software package by exporting the contents of a statistics table.

The example in Figure 2.11 shows how a driver modified the brake balance of the car as the weather conditions during a test day changed from wet to dry conditions.

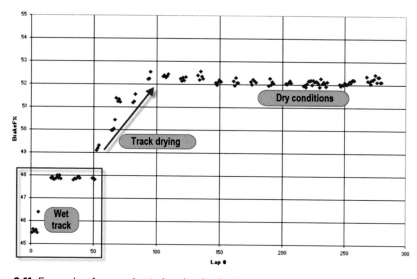

Figure 2.11 Example of a run chart showing brake balance variation during a test day where the track went from being wet to dry

2.3　Keeping Notes with Data Files

The number of data files created during a race weekend or test session can be quite substantial. On top of that, the vehicle's configuration probably did not remain constant. Even if this were the case, environmental conditions were probably different. To avoid confusion, an effective system of relating the recorded data to the car's configuration is required. The simplest solution is to note the file names for each session on the vehicle's setup sheet. The analysis software also may feature an editor to add notes to the respective data files.

Some software packages allow a specific setup sheet to be appended to each data file. This can be very useful, as various items on the sheet are probably necessary to perform specific mathematical operations with the data. Table 2.1 is an example of a setup sheet

Table 2.1 MoTeC session constant setup sheet						
			Date	Initial	12/10/2004	12/10/2004
			Time	Initial	13:00	13:17
Long Name	Short Name	Channel ID	Units		Test Spa Outing 1	Test Spa Outing 2
Vehicle General						
Wheelbase	Wbase	20400	Mm	2418		
Wheelbase–Left	WbaseL	20442	Mm	2418		
Wheelbase–Right	WbaseR	20443	Mm	1418		
Track–Front	TrackF	20401	Mm	1654		
Track–Rear	TrackR	20402	Mm	1722		
Total Weight–Front	TWghtF	20403	Kg	577		
Total Weight–Rear	TWghtR	20404	Kg	697		
Static Ride Height–Front	RHStatF	20409	Mm	58	56	
Static Ride Height–Rear	RHStatR	20410	Mm	97		
Static Weight–Front Left	WstatFL	20426	N	2894		
Static Weight–Front Right	WstatFR	20427	N	2766		
Static Weight–Rear Left	WstatRL	20428	N	3502		
Static Weight–Rear Right	WstatRR	20429	N	3335		
Ackermann Factor	AckFact	20444	%			

Table 2.1 MoTeC session constant setup sheet (Continued)						
Suspension Constants						
Roll Bar Rate–Front	RBR F	20405	Kg/mm	60.21		
Roll Bar Rate–Rear	RBR R	20406	Kg/mm	21.57		
Spring Rate–Front Left	SR FL	20407	Kg/mm	28		32
Spring Rate–Front Right	SR FR	20408	Kg/mm	28		32
Spring Rate–Rear Left	SR RL	20440	Kg/mm	32		
Spring Rate–Rear Right	SR RR	20441	Kg/mm	32		
Static Roll Center Height–Front	RCH F	20430	Mm	46.19		
Static Roll Center Height–Rear	RCH R	20431	Mm	50.49		
Motion Ratio–Front Left	MR FL	20434		1.373		
Motion Ratio–Front Right	MR FR	20435		1.373		
Motion Ratio–Rear Left	MR RL	20436		1.725		
Motion Ratio–Rear Right	MR RR	20437		1.725		
Motion Ratio Roll Bar–Front	MRRollF	20438		1.495		
Motion Ratio Roll Bar–Rear	MRRollR	20439		1.550		
Front Anti-dive	AntiDive	20423	%	36.7		
Rear Anti-squat	AntiSQ	20424	%	73.8		
Driveline						
Diff Ratio	DiffR	20411		4.10		
Gear Ratio 1	Gear1	20412		8.57		
Gear Ratio 2	Gear2	20413		5.94		
Gear Ratio 3	Gear3	20414		4.64		
Gear Ratio 4	Gear4	20415		3.74		
Gear Ratio 5	Gear5	20416		3.14		
Gear Ratio 6	Gear6	20417		2.78		
Gear Ratio 7	Gear7	20418				
Aero Constants						
Rear Wing Angle	RWPos	20425	Deg	0		
Splitter Height Front	HSplitter	20432	Mm	65		
Splitter Angle Front	Asplitter	20433	Deg	0.6		
Ambient Conditions						
Static Ambient Temperature	Tair	20419	C	15		
Static Ambient Pressure	Pair	20420	kPa	100		
Track Temperature	Ttrack	20422	C	17		

created in a spreadsheet. The data analysis software reads the values in the table and relates them to the correct data file using the time noted in the columns, storing them as session-dependent constants. These constants then can be used in mathematical expressions (Figure 2.12).

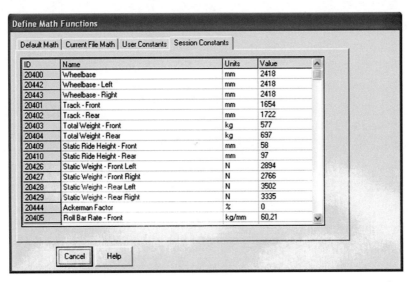

Figure 2.12 The setup constants in Table 2.1 can be used in the MoTeC analysis software in mathematical expressions

Suppose calculation of the front dynamic ride height from the shock motion signals is desired. The equation incorporates constants for the front static ride height and motion ratio. At the start of the test, the front static ride height is 58 mm. Before the car's next outing, this is modified to 56 mm. The time at that moment is 13h00, as noted in the setup sheet. The analysis software modifies the appropriate session constant and recalculates the dynamic ride height channel for all files recorded after 13h00.

Occasionally, old data files need to be referenced. Maintaining a qualitative record of the car configuration and ambient conditions helps with quickly finding information.

2.4   Mathematical Channels

A software feature that is mentioned throughout this book is the creation of mathematical channels. Calculations are performed on the logged data so that the results can be plotted and analyzed as separate channels. The way these channels are created can vary between different software packages, but the following operations should be possible:

- Add/subtract

- Multiply/divide

- Sine/cosine/tangent

- Differentiate/integrate

- Average

The software often features the capability to include constants that can be used in the math expressions (Figure 2.13).

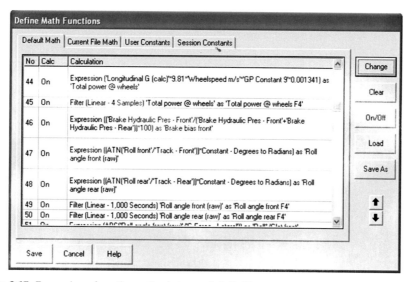

Figure 2.13 Examples of mathematical channel definitions

2.5   Data Overlays

One of the most powerful features of data analysis software is overlaying graphs from separate laps. If a software package does not support this option, buy another system! Ninety-five percent of all analysis work consists of comparison. This technique is useful in analyzing setup changes, driver consistency, and performance changes due to varying ambient conditions. In multicar teams or in endurance racing where multiple drivers share the same car, data overlays can indicate differences in driving style.

In Figure 2.14, speed traces are overlaid from two laps around Silverstone Circuit. When comparing two laps, begin with the speed traces because the intention of every change in setup or driver activity is to influence the vehicle speed. First find where the gains and losses are (indicated in the graph by the time compare channel), and then find out why they occur.

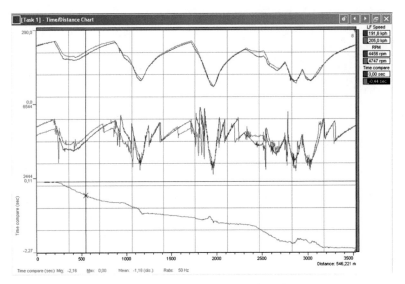

Figure 2.14 Overlay of two laps around Silverstone Circuit

When different traces are overlaid, it is preferable to plot them against covered distance. When the *x*-axis is time, the two traces tend to diverge over the duration of the lap. Different lap times mean different times were measured to get to a given point on the racetrack.

The software usually calculates the time difference between the two laps being compared. The Pi Toolbox software from which Figure 2.14 was taken calculates the cumulative time difference between two laps. (More information about lap overlays can be found in chapter 3.)

2.6   Filtering

Data filtering or, more appropriately, smoothing is a process in which data points are averaged over a given time interval. This suppresses the higher frequencies in the signal and enhances the lower frequencies. Filtering removes noise from the signal or conditions the signal for the analysis of slower movements. Filtering is a useful but sometimes dangerous tool because the risk exists that relevant high-frequency events are removed from the signal. In general, use filtering as little as possible.

Figure 2.15 shows a damper signal logged at 50 Hz (dark gray-colored trace). The lighter trace represents the same damper signal filtered at four samples. This means that every data point is replaced by the average of this point and the four samples at either side of it.

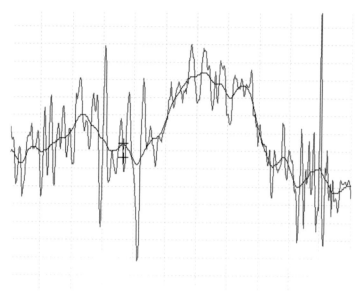

Figure 2.15 Raw and filtered signal

The filter time t_{filter} can be calculated using Equation 2.1. In this equation, n is the number of samples in the filter interval and f_s the sampling frequency. The filter time in the example is 8/50 Hz = 0.16 s.

$$t_{filter} = \frac{2 \cdot n}{f_s} \qquad \text{(Eq. 2.1)}$$

The lighter trace has the advantage in that the slow movement of the damper (induced by chassis movement) is much clearer. On the other hand, information dealing with high-speed movement, such as road irregularities or nonsuspended mass effects, is lost. The maximum deflection of the damper also seems smaller. Preferably, display filtered graphs as shown in Figure 2.15, with the filtered signal in a light color and the original trace in a darker background color to view what is occurring at the higher frequencies. If channels are included in mathematical expressions, use the raw channel instead of the filtered one. Afterwards, the math channel can be filtered if necessary.

2.7   Exporting Data to Other Software Packages

Sometimes the data logging software does not handle every analysis requirement. It may be required to export data into other software packages such as spreadsheets, mathematical software, and lap time simulations. Most software packages can export logged data in ASCII (American Standard Code for Information Interchange) or CSV format (comma-separated values). These are essentially text formats that can be read by basic text editors, spreadsheets, or mathematical analysis software.

Applications for data export can deal with fuel strategy, running logs for the car, Fourier analyses on shock absorber motion, and lap time simulation reference laps. Table 2.2 is an example of how the MoTeC Interpreter software exports the wheel speed and throttle position signals of a lap segment to a CSV file.

Table 2.2 Example of how data is exported into a CSV file
FormatMoTeC CSV File"
Venue,"Spa"
Vehicle,"Dodge Viper GTS/R"
User,"Anthony"
Data Source,"MoTeC ADL 2222"
Comment,"R LSB+1 HSB+1 Reb+2 RARB H/S"
Date,"17/03/2004"
Time,"14:56:21"
Sample Rate,"10.240"
Duration,"14.648"
Segment,"Lap 1 - 2:19.941"
WSpd FL,"TP",
Wheel Speed - Front Left,"Throttle Position",
km/h,"%",
170,"2",
211.0,"80.8",
211.1,"79.8",
210.9,"79.5",
212.5,"80.1",
212.9,"95.2",
212.6,"100.0",
212.0,"100.0",
212.6,"100.0",
214.0,"100.0",
214.6,"100.0",
214.9,"100.0",
215.9,"95.9",
215.9,"92.7",
217.1,"91.4",..

2.8 Getting Organized

Most popular software packages provide a number of ways to configure the software to suit different needs. This configuration should be done before arriving at the racetrack. A good impression is not made when the display templates still need to be organized when a printout of speed, throttle, and RPM data is needed. Preparation is everything.

2.8.1   Channel Grouping

Display templates are often preprogrammable, allowing users to choose which channels they want to display together. This is a matter of preference, but all signals related to the same type of analysis should be grouped together. The following list can be used as a guide:

1. **Vital Functions**
   Engine RPM, engine water and oil temperature, oil pressure, gearbox and differential temperature, battery voltage

2. **Gearing**
   Vehicle speed, engine RPM, throttle position, gear ratio

3. **Fuel Consumption**
   Fuel pressure, fuel level, fuel used, fuel per lap

4. **Engine Performance**
   Speed, engine RPM, manifold air pressure, air temperature inlet manifold

5. **Lambda**
   Engine RPM, throttle position, lambda

6. **Driver Activity**
   Speed, throttle position, steering angle, brake pedal position

7. *G*-force
   Speed, *g*-force lateral, longitudinal, vertical, combined *g*-forces

8. **Braking**
   Speed, *g*-force longitudinal, brake pedal position, brake line pressures

9. **Damper Position Raw**
   Speed, damper position channels

10. **Roll and Pitch Angle**
    Speed, lateral and longitudinal *g*-forces, roll angle, pitch angle

11. **Wheel Load**
    Speed, lateral weight transfer, longitudinal weight transfer

12. **Understeer/Oversteer**
    Speed, throttle position, front lateral *g*-force, rear lateral *g*-force, steering angle, understeer angle

13. **Open Template**
    Use when putting signals together that do not fall under the preprogrammed display templates or to quickly group some channels of interest for fast analysis.

2.8.2 Channel Colors

Assign specific colors to specific channels. For example, all sensor signals related to one wheel share the same color. A channel that comes back in different display templates should have the same color. Choose appropriate background colors. Make things easy.

2.8.3 Sensor Prep

Before arriving at the track, make sure that all sensors are properly calibrated, the dashboard programmed, and the correct sampling frequencies set. Suspension potentiometers, strain gages, steering angle sensors, accelerometers, and brake pressure sensors should be zeroed when the car is on the setup pad. Also, remember that the development of mathematical functions is not a trackside job!

2.8.4 Example Checklist

Figure 2.16 is a checklist that was duplicated from the Pi System 6 software manual. With the exception of a couple of items, it can be used for any data acquisition system.

Typical procedures: Version 6 Professional

	Procedure	when	section
Setup engineer	Set PC communication	first time	Server
	Name data logging system	first time	Setup
	Set track and driver details	first time / each track	Setup
	Set download directories	first time / each track	Setup
	Choose Junction boxes	first time	Setup
	Calibrate sensors and channels	first time / change sensors	Setup
	Set System wheelspeed and RPM	first time / change sensors	Setup
	Choose LCU channels and logging criteria	first time / each track	Setup
	Choose MRC channels and logging criteria	first time / each track	Setup
	Set driver display	first time / each track	Setup
	Set alarms and telltales	first time / each track	Setup
	Set end-of-lap and real-time telemetry	each track	Setup
	Set microwave telemetry	first time / each track	Setup
	Create spreadsheet or database setup sheet	each track	(Excel or Access)
	Set fuel strategy	each track	Setup
	Reset Engine Log Book	first time / new engine	Setup
	Send setup to logging system	each track / change sensors	Server / Setup
	Test sensors	each track / change sensors	Setup
	Copy setup and calibrations	first time / change sensors	Setup

Log data

	Procedure	when	section
Data analyst	Download data	each outing	Server
	Make and adjust Map	each track	Analysis
	Define and adjust beacons	each track	Analysis
	Create and edit Math channels	first time / each track	Analysis
	Create and edit User Math Functions	first time / each track	(C++) / Analysis
	Integrate vehicle dynamics information	each track	Analysis
	Define global constants in Excel or Access	each track	Analysis
	Produce reports and graphs	each outing	Analysis
	Export data for engine and chassis experts	each outing	Analysis
Engine technician	Analyse Engine Log Book data	dependent on engine performance	Analysis
	Analyse end-of-lap telemetry data	each outing	Telemetry
	Analyse microwave telemetry data	each outing	Analysis / Telemetry
	Analyse Engine Manufacturers' channels	each outing	Analysis

Figure 2.16 Trackside checklist for Pi System 6 software (Courtesy of Cosworth Electronics)

2.8.5 Pit Box Setup

Set up the computer equipment in the pit box at a location where it does not disturb the mechanics (Figures 2.17 and 2.18). A table with a couple of chairs in a corner of the pit box is just fine for preparing analysis work and holding discussions with the drivers. Mainly as a matter of preference and budget, the following equipment is recommended:

- Laptop with an external mouse
- Color printer
- Data download cable
- Installation CD of the data acquisition software
- A USB drive (convenient to transfer data between different users)
- A digital weather station

Figure 2.17 Try to find separate space in the pit box to do analysis work (Courtesy of GLPK Racing)

Figure 2.18 Nicely organized pit box area for the engineers with a constant view on the car area and a large TV screen used to display telemetry data

2.8.6 Basic Tips

When transporting a car to the racetrack, it is normal to take spare parts. The same goes for the data acquisition system. Not only should critical sensors be within reach in case of failure but so should cables, connectors, and other spare equipment. Budgets have a say in this, but it is always better to have backup solutions.

Download the data logger every time the car enters because even engine warm-ups and rollout laps can provide relevant information. When analyzing the data, begin with the vital channels: engine and driveline temperatures, pressures, and battery voltage. Ensure that no strange things are happening before addressing the performance data, even if the driver is standing nearby, shouting that the car is not drivable!

Listen to the driver; it makes it much easier to know what to look for. Then, observe what the car is doing (e.g., speed, acceleration, driver activity) before trying to understand why it is doing this (e.g., shock data, strain gages). Remember that the speed trace is where it all happens. A stopwatch determines whether a lap is a slow or quick one, but the speed graph tells where time is gained or lost.

Do not focus only on the fastest lap in a session; analyze all laps and look for consistencies and inconsistencies. Remember that traffic on the racetrack can have a considerable influence on lap time. Statistics and run charts are a very effective way of looking at the data at a wider angle.

One last tip: Look for the obvious first. Determine which channels are expected to show differences after a setup change. The effects of aerodynamic changes most likely show up in the speed and wheel load traces.

Chapter 3
The Basics

Much of the workload for the data acquisition engineer consists of comparative analysis. Comparing data from different laps or runs with previously collected data reveals the effect of setup changes or driver performance. Most data analysis packages offer similar techniques for comparing different data sets. This chapter covers these techniques and provides a basic interpretation of the patterns showing up in the sensor signals most often used.

The last section in this chapter covers the evaluation of how much confidence can be allocated to certain sensor readings for the analysis of the dynamic behavior of a vehicle. This text was contributed by Giuseppe Callea, Head of Vehicle Dynamics at BHAI TECH, an Italian company with expertise in the research and development of performance programs for manufacturers, motorsport organizations, and racing drivers.

3.1   Check the Car's Vital Signs

The primary function of a data acquisition system is to diagnose problems. Monitoring of the vehicle's vital parameters (oil pressure, fluid temperatures, voltages, etc.) will enable the team to discover mechanical problems at an early stage, which will hopefully result in the prevention of expensive failures. In the event that a failure does occur, the recorded data might point the engineers to the cause of that failure.

When analyzing data, reliability and safety are the first priority. There is not a lot of performance in a car that's standing still when compared with one on the racetrack! Make sure all pressures, temperatures, and voltages are safe before analyzing performance. A deficiency in these signals may explain a lack of performance.

The most important channels to check are engine oil pressure, engine water and oil temperatures, transmission oil temperatures, battery voltage, fuel pressure, and (maximum) engine RPM. To these, reliability indicators such as tire pressures, brake pressures, clutch pressures, and engine knock signals should be added.

An easy way to check the vehicle's vital signs is by using a tabular report as the one shown in Figure 3.1. This table shows the minimum, maximum, and average values for each logged channel for the duration of the run or a single lap. Some software packages can highlight values when they exceed a user-defined alarm value.

Statistics - 20040821-0083405.ld(Bert, Zolder, 21/08/2004, 6:39pm)

Burst Logging - 2 | Diagnostic and Status Summary | Lap Report | Engine Log - 1
Engine Log - 2 | Engine Log - 3 | Engine Log - 4 | Tell-tales | Version Details
Normal Logging | Fastest Lap Logging | Burst Logging - 1

Name	Min	Max	Avg	Freq	Sets	ID	Units
Wheel Speed - Front Left	0,0	228,6	133,1	10	48840	170	km/h
G Force - Lateral	-1,72	1,74	-0,23	2	9768	15	G
Lap Distance	0	4782	2332	1	4884	125	m
Engine RPM	0	6522	4444	10	48840	1	rpm
Engine Oil Pressure	-0,142	6,500	5,360	5	24420	14	bar
Engine Temp	54,0	91,0	78,0	1	4884	5	C
Fuel Pressure	2,360	8,400	7,991	5	24420	12	bar
Throttle Position	0,0	100,0	41,3	5	24420	2	%
Battery Voltage at ADL	12,53	14,14	13,98	2	9768	7012	V
Engine Oil Temp	35,6	102,6	93,0	1	4884	13	C
Air Pressure - Manifold	82,0	106,0	98,4	5	24420	3	kPa
Fuel Used per Lap	0,00	2,92	2,10	1	4884	7410	l
Brake Pedal Position	-51,7	34,3	2,1	5	24420	3911	mm
Steered Angle	-262,2	240,3	29,9	5	24420	4605	deg
Fuel Used	0,11	104,71	50,11	1	4884	7088	l
Diff Oil Temp	23,8	95,4	83,8	1	4884	3080	C

Checksum | Preferences | Close

Figure 3.1 Statistics table with minimum, maximum, and average values for each channel

Some care must be taken when interpreting the values in this table. In Figure 3.1, the minimum value for engine oil pressure is zero, but this value was obtained when the car halted in the pits at zero engine RPM. This is a pretty straightforward conclusion, but these values may be hiding another problem in the data. That is why one cannot rely solely on a statistics table to check vital signals. The graphs must be examined to ensure that everything is working like it should.

To check for deficiencies in the signals, begin with a graph covering the complete run (Figure 3.2). The data was obtained from the first stint of a 24-hour race in Zolder, Belgium, from a Dodge Viper. This example shows engine RPM, oil and fuel pressure, engine oil and water temperature, gearbox and differential oil temperature, and battery voltage. The advantage of examining a complete run is that trends in the signals can be recognized easily. In Figure 3.2, all fluid temperatures rise to a maximum value, after which they stabilize. Engine oil pressure is slightly higher at the beginning of the stint when the engine has not reached operating temperature. After that, it stabilizes to around 5.5 bars. Everything seems to be working fine here. When something abnormal is discovered, focus on the specific event and investigate the problem.

In Figure 3.3, a graph shows the results of a qualifying run around the Silverstone Circuit. The alternator belt fails on this car and as a result the battery voltage gradually

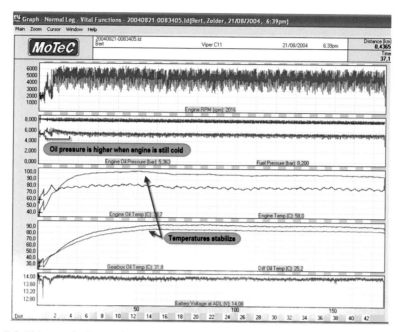

Figure 3.2 This graph shows the car's vital signs for a complete run.

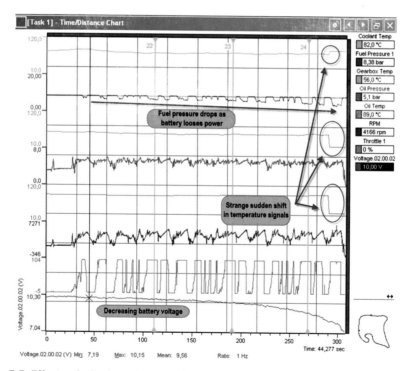

Figure 3.3 Effects of a broken alternator belt

drops. At the beginning of the run, the battery voltage is approximately 10 volts, which is already too low. Investigations of the previous run indicate that the problem began there (and that it should have been dealt with already!).

The decreasing power of the battery had some side effects that become clear from this graph as well. The fuel pumps cannot maintain the desired fuel pressure. The more the battery voltage drops, the bigger the drop in the fuel pressure signal.

At the end of the run, there is a sudden change in the three pictured temperature channels (engine oil, water, and gearbox temperature). They change to default values that the ECU uses when a sensor is not working. Obviously, the drop in battery voltage causes the sensors to malfunction.

The problem in this example was easily detectable. Sometimes it is not that obvious, and the diagnostic signs are much more subtle and hidden in the data. The data engineer should develop a feel for the normal patterns of the car's vital signs so that potential problems can be detected early. The car in this particular example halted next to the track, meaning there were two problems:

- The data acquisition engineer did not notice the problem in the data from the previous run.
- The driver did not notice the problem during driving or did not get a warning.

Mathematical channels can help visualize alarm values in the car's vitals. Conditional expressions can be created to give a value of one if a vital channel exceeds or drops below a predetermined value. For instance, a low oil pressure alarm channel assuming a value of one as soon as oil pressure drops below three bar while the engine RPM is greater than 3,000 can be defined as shown in Equation 3.1.

$$\text{Low OP} = (\text{Oil Pressure} < 3.0) \cdot (\text{Engine RPM} > 3000) \qquad \text{(Eq. 3.1)}$$

The resulting channel is shown in Figure 3.4.

Sometimes it is also quite useful to display one channel in relationship to another in order to detect any potential problems. When the relationship between these two channels is not as expected, something might be wrong. The example in Figure 3.5 shows an engine oil pressure problem. The data was taken from a GT3 car, during a race in the rain (which explains the low lateral G values). The graph shows a scatter plot of engine oil pressure against lateral acceleration. There are a number of data points that fall below 4.8 bars (which seems to be the lower boundary of "normal" pressure values). These values occur exclusively in right-hand corners (positive lateral acceleration) and decrease with higher lateral acceleration. This effect can have different causes, including too low an oil level or a bad scavenge tank design.

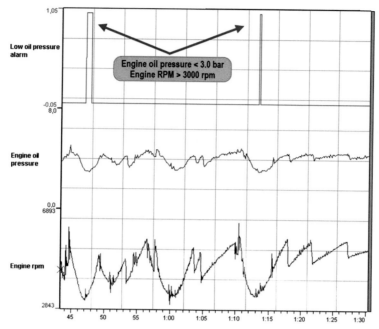

Figure 3.4 Low oil pressure alarm channel

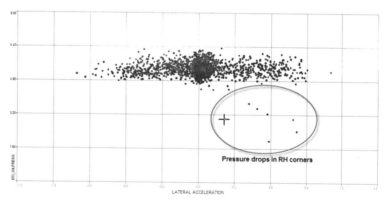

Figure 3.5 Engine oil pressure versus lateral acceleration revealing a problem in right-hand corners

Most race car data acquisition systems can configure the driver display by adding alarm messages in case of a problem or sending an output signal to a warning light. Make sure that if something goes wrong, the driver gets a clear warning. Also think about priorities when determining the right alarm values. In the example shown in Figure 3.3, the driver gets a fuel pressure alarm that overrides the low-battery warning.

The result of an alarm might be a message on the dashboard screen or the activation of an alarm light, or both. The trick is to warn a driver who is trying to concentrate on staying on the asphalt and probably has other things on his mind than looking at a dashboard.

The example in Figure 3.6 is the configuration screen for the AIM MXL dashboard logger. The green rectangles show the possibilities to program six warning LEDs on the dashboard. In this case it's nothing fancy, as the lights can only be switched on when the channel allocated to a specific LED exceeds a user-definable value.

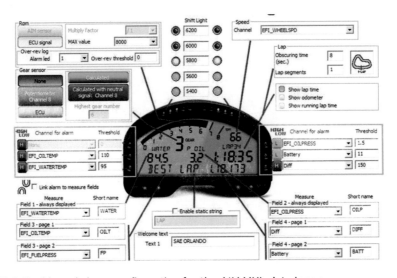

Figure 3.6 Dashboard alarm configuration for the AIM MXL data logger

In Figure 3.7 an alarm is programmed into the MoTeC ADL2. In this case the user has the option to build more complex alarm conditions. The alarm can be displayed on the dashboard as a text message, or one of the dashboard electrical outputs can switch on a warning light.

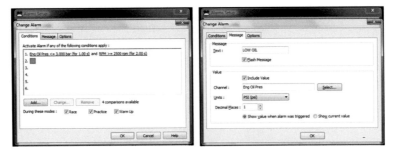

Figure 3.7 Programming an oil pressure alarm with multiple conditions

In the configuration screen in Figure 3.7, an alarm condition will be signaled as a flashing text message when engine oil pressure drops below three bars (for one second) *and* the engine RPM exceeds 2500 for more than 2 seconds.

Correct alarm configuration gives the driver the right information about what is happening to the car, and he can then inform the team accordingly. The driver should also be aware of what the alarm means and at what value it is triggered. Finally, the driver should know how to offset the alarm, because in many cases an alarm message hides other data values on the dashboard.

The engineer should also be well aware about the parameters that trigger an alarm. Sometimes the decisions taken from this information will decide on the outcome of the race.

3.2   Lap Markers and Segment Times

Performance analysis usually begins with figuring out where on the track time is gained or lost before actual events are investigated. A quick way to assess this is to investigate lap segment times.

Lap times are determined by the analysis software measuring the time it takes for the car to pass the lap beacon. This beacon represents the location on the track where a lap ends and the next one begins. It can be an infrared pulse logged by the data system or a manually entered beacon point in the data. Most data analysis packages offer the option of placing additional virtual beacons around the track at certain distances from the start/finish beacon. Lap segment times are determined by measuring the elapsed time between two consecutive beacons. Placement of these beacons depends on what needs to be analyzed. Engine performance can be evaluated best on a straight track segment where the car is accelerating. Corners can be defined as separate segments, but the corner itself can also be divided into *entry*, *apex*, and *exit* to investigate cornering performance.

In Figure 3.8, an example is given from the Istanbul Grand Prix track. The track was divided in seven segments, separated by six manually entered segment beacons and an infrared lap beacon.

The tabular report in this example gives segment times for all covered laps for each track sector. The fastest and slowest segment times are highlighted in the table. The last column gives the difference in lap time to the fastest lap in the outing.

The software calculated two performance indicators from this table—the theoretical fastest lap and the fastest rolling lap, which attempt to indicate the true performance potential of a given configuration. As often happens during a lap, the driver was delayed by a slower car on the track or a mistake was made by the driver. In this case, the

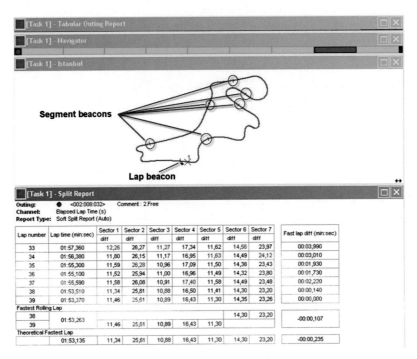

Figure 3.8 Segment times report using "virtual" beacons

Within the figure:

[Task 1] - Tabular Outing Report
[Task 1] - Navigator
[Task 1] - Istanbul

Segment beacons

Lap beacon

[Task 1] - Split Report

Outing: ●   <002:008:032>   Comment : 2.Free
Channel: Elapsed Lap Time (s)
Report Type: Soft Split Report (Auto)

Lap number	Lap time (min:sec)	Sector 1 diff	Sector 2 diff	Sector 3 diff	Sector 4 diff	Sector 5 diff	Sector 6 diff	Sector 7 diff	Fast lap diff (min:sec)
33	01:57,360	12,26	26,27	11,27	17,34	11,62	14,58	23,97	00:03,990
34	01:56,380	11,80	26,15	11,17	16,95	11,63	14,49	24,12	00:03,010
35	01:55,300	11,59	26,28	10,96	17,09	11,50	14,38	23,43	00:01,930
36	01:55,100	11,52	25,94	11,00	16,96	11,49	14,32	23,80	00:01,730
37	01:55,590	11,58	26,08	10,91	17,40	11,58	14,49	23,48	00:02,220
38	01:53,510	11,34	25,81	10,88	16,50	11,41	14,30	23,20	00:00,140
39	01:53,370	11,46	25,61	10,89	16,43	11,30	14,35	23,26	00:00,000
Fastest Rolling Lap									
38	01:53,263						14,30	23,20	-00:00,107
39		11,46	25,61	10,89	16,43	11,30			
Theoretical Fastest Lap									
	01:53,135	11,34	25,61	10,88	16,43	11,30	14,30	23,20	-00:00,235

concerned segment time was slower. The theoretical fastest lap is the sum of the fastest sector times in an outing and represents the time that could have been achieved in an ideal lap. In the example shown in Figure 3.8, this ideal lap would have been 0.235 sec quicker than the fastest lap. Very good drivers should get close to their theoretical fastest lap time.

Great care should be taken in placing importance on the theoretical fastest lap because a slower time in one segment can result in a faster time in the next. The driver may take a driving line through one corner that is faster in the particular corner but compromises speed in the next one. Missing braking points also can cause inconsistent segment times. The confidence level of this performance indicator also depends on the location of the segment beacons. Segment times in areas bordered by beacons placed at the apex of a corner are more sensitive to inconsistencies than those bordered by beacons placed at the middle of a straight.

The fastest rolling lap is the lap time achieved between beacons that are not necessarily at the end of a lap—an indication of the performance potential when there is heavy traffic on the track. It is a lap time the driver actually achieves. In the example, if the end-of-lap beacon was the split between segment five and six the fastest lap time would be 0.107 sec faster than the fastest lap in this outing.

Another issue that requires attention when calculating the theoretical fastest lap is the number of track segments. The more track segments incorporated, the faster the ideal lap is. There must be an optimum number of segments that provide a realistic theoretical fastest lap. Sound judgment is necessary here, both in choosing the right number of segments and having confidence in this performance indicator. The following example illustrates the effect of the number of track segments on the theoretical fastest lap.

This example discusses a run in a Porsche 996 around Spa Francorchamps recorded with a Race Technology DL1 GPS data logger. The fastest lap by this vehicle in this run was 2′43″67. First, the track was divided into seven segments, and the segment times for the full run were calculated by the analysis software. The results are given in the table in Figure 3.9; the fastest sector time per segment is highlighted. The sum of these fastest segment times resulted in a theoretical fastest lap of 2′42″25 or a difference of 1.42 sec compared to the fastest performed lap.

In Figure 3.10, the same run was taken, but the track was only divided into three segments. The difference is obvious, with a theoretical fastest lap time of 2′43″25. The difference here compared to the fastest real-life lap is only 0.42 sec.

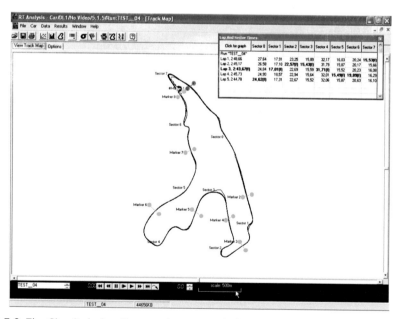

Figure 3.9 The Circuit de Spa Francorchamps track divided in seven track segments

Figure 3.10 The Spa track divided into three segments

In most cases, begin with fewer segments. Variation in segment time may be greater with fewer sections because there is much more potential for mistakes or other problems in longer sectors. If that happens, increase the number of segments when it is necessary to pinpoint problem areas.

3.3   Comparing Laps

The most powerful tool in any data acquisition software package is overlaying and comparing different laps. Most analyses performed on race car data are comparative. When something is changed on the car, comparing a run to previous ones indicates the difference of that change.

By overlaying two traces as a function of distance, the performance of the vehicle and the driver can be compared at the same point on the track. Overlaying against time does not bring any meaningful conclusions because events at the same time probably happen at other locations, and the traces tend to diverge over the length of the lap.

Figure 3.11 shows an example of two overlaid laps around the Nürburgring. It illustrates how the vehicle speed can be compared directly for every location on the track. Comparing speed is often the first step in the analysis of logged data because this channel contains the ultimate result. An increase in speed inevitably decreases lap time.

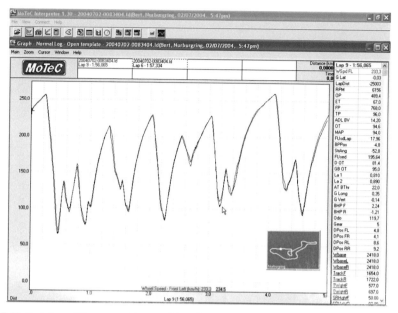

Figure 3.11 Overlay of the speed trace of two laps around the Nürburgring

The respective lap times in this example are:

Lap 6 (Black trace)   1'57"334
Lap 9 (Red trace)   1'56"065

This is a difference of 1.269 sec between the two laps. Try to find in Figure 3.11 where this difference in lap time was created. Once the locations where time was gained or lost are pinpointed, they should be further investigated to find out what exactly happened and where the speed difference originated.

To pinpoint more efficiently areas on the track where time is gained or lost, mathematical functions can be created. These are created automatically by the analysis software. Some subtle differences between software packages are possible, but the idea is always the same.

Continuing with this example, Figure 3.12 shows the same speed trace overlay with two extra graphs that determine the difference in lap time between the two laps. The MoTeC analysis software calls this variance that can be graphed either as instantaneous or cumulative. Instantaneous variance is defined in Equation 3.2.

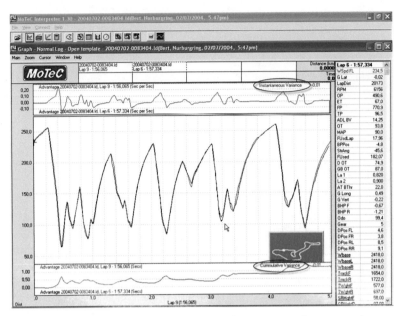

Figure 3.12 Instantaneous and cumulative variance between two laps around the Nürburgring

$$\text{Variance}_{\text{Inst.}}(s) = t_{\text{LAP1}}(s) - t_{\text{LAP2}}(s) \quad\quad \text{(Eq. 3.2)}$$

with s = distance, going from zero to the length of the track measured between 2 beacons (lap distance)

$t_{\text{LAP1}}(s)$ = running lap time of Lap 1 as a function of distance

$t_{\text{LAP2}}(s)$ = running lap time of Lap 2 as a function of distance

This is the difference in running lap time plotted against the distance of both laps. In Figure 3.12, instantaneous variance is shown as the upper trace. When this channel is less than zero, it means an advantage for the lap in which the black speed trace was recorded. This gives the user the opportunity to locate areas where variations between the two laps occur.

Cumulative variance can be expressed mathematically as Equation 3.3.

$$\text{Variance}_{\text{Cumm.}}(s) = \int_{0}^{\text{lap distance}} \text{Variance}_{\text{Inst.}}(d) \cdot ds \quad\quad \text{(Eq. 3.3)}$$

This is the sum of the time differences between the two laps. The last sample in this graph is the total difference in lap time. The lower trace in Figure 3.12 shows the cumulative variance for the example. A positive value indicates an advantage for the lap in which the gray trace was recorded. Cumulative variance shows how a difference in lap time developed over the duration of the lap. Effects of corner exit speed, changes in gearing, and braking points on lap time can be determined easily from the graph.

Because speed equals distance per unit of time, variance calculated by the subtraction of the two speed signals gives the same result. As an example, Race Technology's analysis software calculates two similar variables: time slip rate and time slip.

Time slip rate is the difference in vehicle speed, expressed as a percentage. If in one corner the car is doing 100 km/h during the reference lap and in the next lap it is doing only 80 km/h, it is 20% slower. Time slip rate at that point on the track is 20%. Therefore, the higher the time slip rate, the slower the car is at that point. A negative time slip rate means the speed at that point is higher than that of the reference lap.

Time slip is the sum of all time slip rates. Multiplied by the elapsed lap time, it provides exactly the same result as the cumulative variance. Figure 3.13 gives an example of two laps around Circuit Zolder. At the end of the lap, the time slip value is exactly the difference between the two lap times.

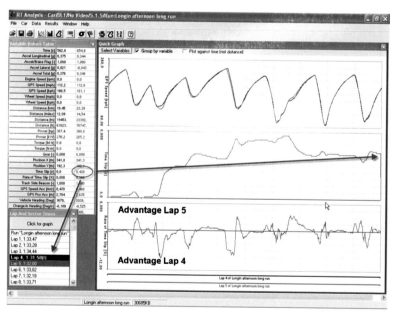

Figure 3.13 Time slip rate and time slip between two laps around Zolder

Distance usually is calculated by integrating the speed signal. Therefore, by using this speed signal directly to calculate the difference between two lap times as a function of distance, the accuracy is a bit better.

In Figure 3.14 a comparison between two drivers is shown around the French Nogaro track. At the cursor point (1) the speed of the black lap is 134.1 km/h, while in the red lap it is 128.2 km/h. At this point the time slip rate is:

$$100\% \cdot \frac{134.1 - 128.2}{134.1} = 4.40\%$$

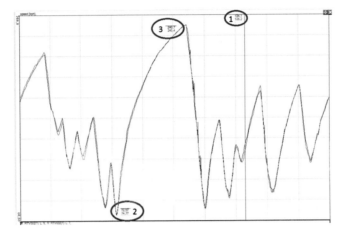

Figure 3.14 Comparison between two drivers around Nogaro

Consider the speeds of the black and red lap at points (2) and (3). At point (2) the car accelerates out of a second gear corner onto the main straight. Point (3) is the point where the top speed is achieved just before braking for the next corner. Assume the speed difference between the two laps to develop linearly. The elapsed time between the two points is 13.3 seconds. For how much of this period of time has the red lap the advantage? How much time in total will the red lap gain on the black one on this straight?

$$100\% \cdot \frac{74.77 - 72.57}{74.77} = 2.942\%$$

At cursor point (3) the time slip rate is:

$$100\% \cdot \frac{240.4 - 240.7}{240.4} = -0.128\%$$

This is graphically presented in Figure 3.15. We assume the difference in speed to develop linearly so we can assume the same linearity for the time slip rate. Mathematically we can define this as:

$$\text{TSR}(t) = -\frac{2.942 + 0.128}{13.3} \cdot t + 2.942 = -0.231 \cdot t + 2.942$$

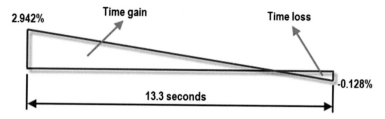

Figure 3.15 Time slip rate along the straight

Now we simply calculate the time after which the time slip rate will reach zero:

$$t_0 = \frac{-2.942}{-0.231} = 12.736 \text{ seconds}$$

The time gained during this period is:

$$\frac{2.942 \cdot 12.736}{2 \cdot 100} = 0.187 \text{ seconds}$$

The time lost afterwards is:

$$\frac{0.128 \cdot (13.3 - 12.736)}{2 \cdot 100} = 0.0004 \text{ seconds}$$

This means that the red lap gains 0.1866 seconds on the black lap on the straight.

The quality of an overlay and the variance function depend greatly on the accuracy of the distance calculation. Most of the time, distance is determined by integrating the wheel-speed signal and, therefore, is subject to a number of potential errors. Locking brakes and wheel spin may alter the relationship between the RPM of the wheel and the vehicle speed temporarily. The rolling radius of the tire changes as a function of the load put on it. The accuracy of the timing beacon also can be a source of error. Finally, the path the driver follows differs somewhat from lap to lap, so the lap distance also varies as a result.

All of this means care with overlays is required because it might mean events that occurred at the same location are not being compared. Most modern qualitative software packages incorporate algorithms to reduce the effect of wheel lockup by comparing wheel speed to the longitudinal g-force channel. When the values of the speed channel change too much with reference to the integrated longitudinal g-force channel, these values are corrected by interpolation.

Measuring suspension travel helps evaluate the error in the distance channel and even can serve to align two sets of data. As long as the car follows the same line around the track, the road profile creates an enormous amount of small peaks in the suspension potentiometer data, and this serves as a fingerprint of the track. The bigger the offset between these peaks, the larger the error is in the distance function. Suspension travel is typically measured at a high sampling frequency, so it is an ideal channel to align the distance function of two overlaid laps. An example is illustrated in Figures 3.16, 3.17, and 3.18.

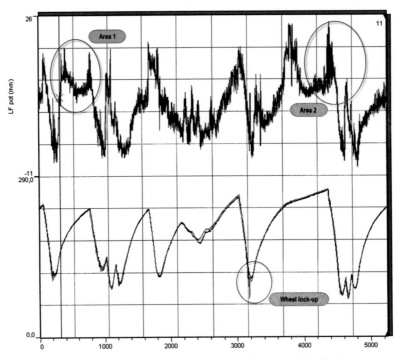

Figure 3.16 Overlay of two laps around the Istanbul Park Racing Circuit. The upper trace shows the left-front suspension potentiometer channel. The lower trace is the left-front wheel speed.

Figure 3.16 shows an overlay of two laps around the Istanbul track. Speed trace and left-front suspension potentiometer data are pictured. On first glance, this looks like a clean overlay. Two areas are indicated in the graph. Area 1 is situated at the beginning of the lap, while Area 2 is more to the end of the lap, with the preceding corner showing a wheel lockup event in one of the laps under comparison.

Figure 3.17 zooms in on the potentiometer data in Area 1. The spikes in the data created by road surface irregularities are synchronized for the two laps. At this point during the two laps, there is no significant difference in the distance function, and the overlay can be considered aligned.

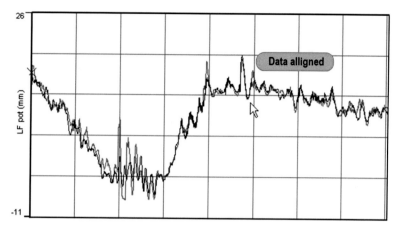

Figure 3.17 Zoom of left-front suspension potentiometer signal on Area 1. At this point in the lap, there was no significant offset in road profile data.

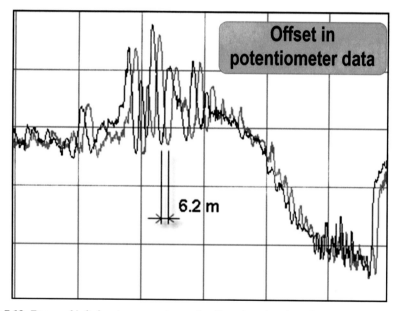

Figure 3.18 Zoom of left-front suspension potentiometer signal on Area 2. The signal shifted 6.2 m.

Figure 3.18 takes a closer look at Area 2. As shown in Figure 3.16, this area was preceded by a corner where in the red trace a wheel lockup event occurred. This means that at this point, measured wheel speed is much lower than the true vehicle speed. As a result, the potentiometer data is not synchronized after this event. The red trace lags the black one by 6.2 m. At this point, the accuracy of the overlay was compromised, which could lead to wrong conclusions.

55

Most software packages can offset the timing beacon with a certain distance or time interval, allowing a manual correction to be performed on the data. This does, however, change only the starting point of the lap and has no influence on the distance errors created during the lap. If one is zooming in on a specific area, the data must be checked to ensure it is aligned at that location and the beacon is offset as necessary.

Some software writers use algorithms in their software to align data using the track pattern. This method was developed by William. C. Mitchell [3-1] and produced effective results.

Measurement of the road surface also can help when a beacon is missed or when the signal is not present at all. If the software allows the user to insert beacons manually, the peaks in the potentiometer signal can serve as reference points to place beacons into the data.

In Figure 3.19, a speed trace recorded around Zolder is shown. Because a beacon channel was not recorded, lap time data is not present. The arrows in the illustration indicate where the beacon normally would be recorded if it had been present, which was somewhere at the start/finish straight in front of the pits. A quick look at the graph shows that during this run the car did six laps.

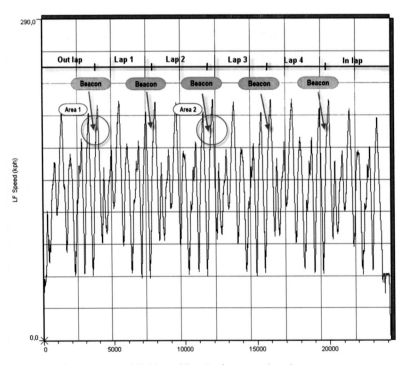

Figure 3.19 Speed trace around Zolder without a beacon signal

When a suitable suspension position peak can be found near the locations indicated by the arrows, this peak can serve as a virtual beacon. Figures 3.20 and 3.21 provide two examples for the Zolder speed trace. The first graph shows speed and left-front potentiometer traces for the location indicated in Figure 3.19 as Area 1. The road profile is evident from this signal, and a distinctive peak in the trace was selected as the location for the beacon. As a reference, the distance to the next braking point is 150 m.

The same was done in Figure 3.21 for Area 2. The same distinctive peak returned in this trace, now at 155 m from the next braking point.

This procedure is followed for every required beacon, and at the conclusion the following lap times were achieved during this run:

Out Lap	2'20"065	Lap distance = 3763 m
Lap 1	1'52"835	Lap distance = 4000 m
Lap 2	1'52"725	Lap distance = 4004 m
Lap 3	1'51"730	Lap distance = 4000 m
Lap 4	1'50"450	Lap distance = 3991 m
In Lap	2'28"655	Lap distance = 4363 m

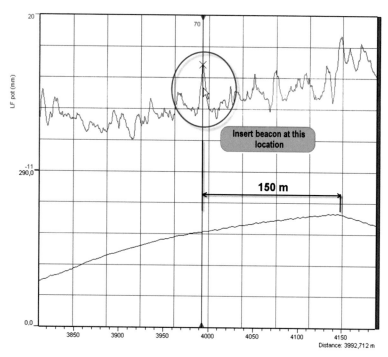

Figure 3.20 Area 1 zoomed in

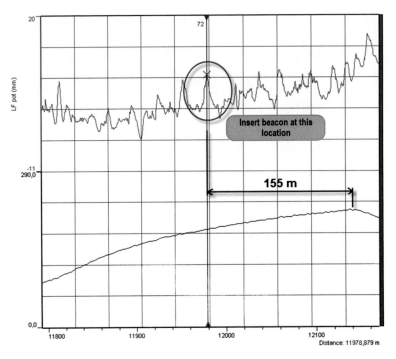

Figure 3.21 Area 2 zoomed in

To validate the quality of the manually inserted beacons, two laps from this run can be overlaid and the road profile compared. Figure 3.22 illustrates an almost perfect fit in the area just after the start/finish beacon for laps three and four.

The previous example used a run that did not have a beacon signal. When a run only misses part of the required beacons, the distance from a recorded beacon signal to a distinctive peak in the road profile can determine where a missing beacon should be inserted, as illustrated in Figure 3.23.

3.4   Track Mapping

Track maps are graphical representations of the location at which logged data was recorded. It is a helpful software feature for lap navigation and a visual aid for drivers and engineers that can be used while analyzing the data. To draw a track map, three signals should be present: wheel speed, lateral acceleration, and a lap beacon. Wheel speed integration gives the covered distance; combined with lateral acceleration, the heading of the vehicle can be calculated. The lap beacon indicates the start and finish point of the lap. This technique is called inertial mapping.

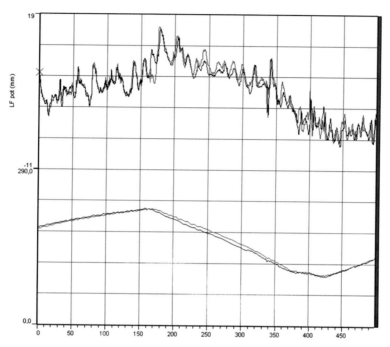

Figure 3.22 Overlay of laps three and four at the area just after the manually inserted beacon

It is, however, just a graphical representation of the racetrack and has its limitations. It can offer a clear and quick illustration of events occurring on the track, as shown in Figure 3.24. In this example, braking and acceleration zones are indicated by different colors. Top speeds on the straights and minimum cornering speeds are given with their corresponding engine RPM. Accuracy limitations, however, mean that it is no more than that—a visual aid.

With the GPS use becoming more popular in race car data acquisition, the accuracy of track maps generated by analysis software packages has increased significantly. Maps now offer some interesting features.

By combining the GPS position and velocity signal with lateral and longitudinal acceleration, track maps that are accurate to within 1 meter can be generated. This makes it possible to overlay track maps of different laps and compare the driving lines (see chapter 14).

Inertial mapping does not work on tracks that are not closed (e.g., a special stage in a rally). For motorcycles, special algorithms are necessary to calculate a track map often detrimental to accuracy. Also for boats, inertial mapping is not an option. GPS mapping

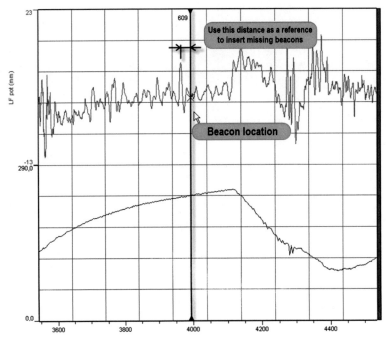

Figure 3.23 Use the distance from a recorded beacon to a distinctive road surface irregularity as a reference to insert missing beacons in the data

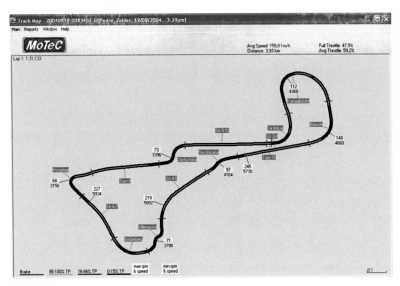

Figure 3.24 Track map of Zolder indicating top speeds, minimum cornering speeds, and corresponding engine RPM

gives excellent results here. GPS in itself does not produce highly detailed track maps, but in combination with inertial mapping the results increase in quality.

Another advantage of GPS mapping is that a trackside beacon is not necessary. A coordinate beacon can be defined in the software, which is more accurate than using an infrared beacon. How many times are beacons not placed before a session or left out on the track after the day is finished?

Figure 3.25 shows a track map of Spa generated by Race Technology's DL1 GPS data logger. The graph covers a complete outing. Zooming in on separate corners reveals the driving lines taken during this outing, as the boxed section (the Raidillon corner; here the driver came very close to the concrete wall!) clearly illustrates. Even an off-road deviation due to a missed braking point is recorded, making it easy to determine where the grass in the radiator came from.

GPS does not increase only the accuracy of track maps. Speed measurement by GPS is not influenced by wheel spin, lockup, or changing a tire radius due to load or wear. This means that the distance function becomes more accurate, thereby increasing the quality of lap overlays. More confidence can be put in the lap time variance calculation.

Segment beacons are determined coordinates created in the analysis software. They are not dependent on any distance calculation, which increases the segment time calculation accuracy, and, therefore, offer a more accurate theoretical fastest lap and fastest rolling lap.

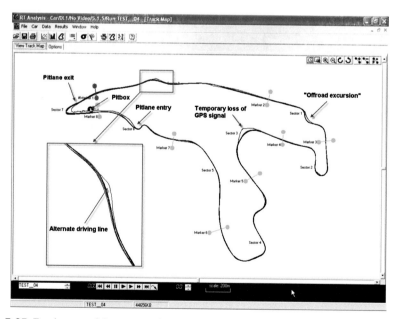

Figure 3.25 Track map of Spa created using GPS

3.5   The Beginner's Data Logging Kit

As mentioned in chapter 1, any data logging system intended for the analysis of race car and driver performance should log at least the six basic signals: engine RPM, vehicle speed, throttle position, steering angle, and lateral and longitudinal acceleration. These signals already contain a vast amount of information to analyze. Even in a state-of-the-art data acquisition package with numerous sensors, these six signals remain the most important and most used data resource for the engineer. The next logical step is to add suspension potentiometers to the system. In this section, the traces created by these sensor signals are explored and a feel for reading the graphs developed.

3.5.1   Logging Engine RPM

Engine RPM often is recorded from a magnetic sensor placed near a teethed trigger wheel on the engine's crankshaft. This sensor counts the pulses generated by this trigger wheel and converts them into the number of crankshaft revolutions per unit of time. The produced graph typically resembles the one in Figure 3.26. Next to an engine-related analysis, this graph reveals the shifting activities of the driver as well as information on chassis balance.

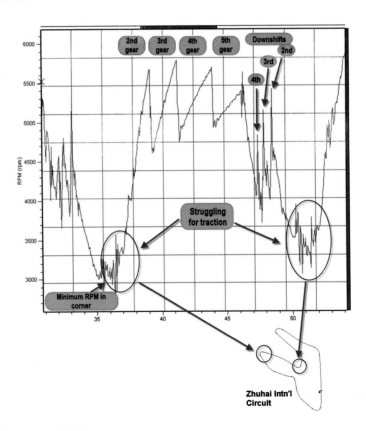

Figure 3.26 Engine RPM trace

This trace was logged on the Zhuhai International Circuit. The illustration shows the area from and between the two indicated corners. The first corner is a right-hand hairpin turn taken in second gear followed by a short straight. The second corner is a tight lefthander, again taken in second gear. The typical sawtooth pattern indicates upshifts as the driver goes through the gearbox from second to fifth gear. Shift RPM varies between 5700 and 5800 RPM and the engine reaches 5400 RPM in fifth gear before the driver applies the brakes. Downshifting is indicated by the steep up-going spikes in the graph as the driver blips the throttle to synchronize the engine and gearbox.

The minimum corner RPM is somewhat difficult to read from the graph, as the jaggedness of the trace indicates a car struggling to find traction out of the corner. The hairpin turn was exited at an engine speed of approximately 3100 RPM. A quick glance at the power curve of this car's engine indicates if a lower gear should be selected or another ratio be used. (Gearing is investigated more thoroughly in chapter 6.)

3.5.2 Logging Vehicle Speed

The speed trace is the results graph. It is the best way to conclude if a change on the car or in driving style produced any result. This is the reason why most analysis work is done with the speed graph as a reference. It is also the easiest trace to use for track navigation. Because this graph represents a typical layout of each track (indicating corners between acceleration and deceleration zones) and the signal is used so much in analysis work, an experienced data engineer looks more closely at the speed trace rather than at a track map to find a location on the track.

Figure 3.27 tracks the vehicle speed of a GT car during a lap around Zhuhai. A rising line represents acceleration, while a downward slope means the car is losing speed. Minimum cornering speed and top speed on the straights are important performance measures of this graph, and comparing these to previous outings shows where time was gained or lost. Use this graph to evaluate braking points, aerodynamic configurations, and engine tweaks.

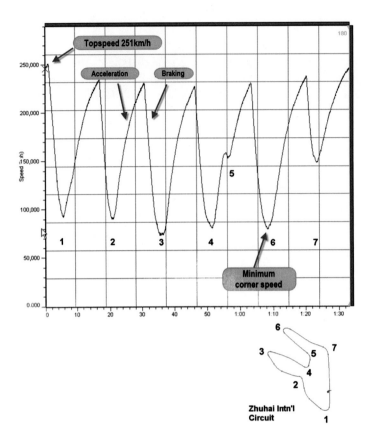

Figure 3.27 Vehicle speed trace

A general glance at the speed trace helps establish some track characteristics. Is it a high-speed track with many high *g*-force corners, or is it primarily a "Mickey Mouse" track with numerous tight corners and heavy braking zones? What kind of base setup should be used for the track in question? Another way to visualize this is to picture the speed data in a histogram. Notice the differences in achieved speeds for the same car between Zhuhai (Figure 3.28) and Monza (Figure 3.29).

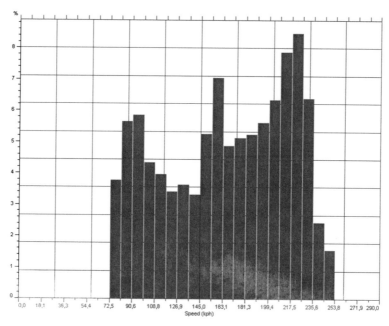

Figure 3.28 Speed histogram of Zhuhai

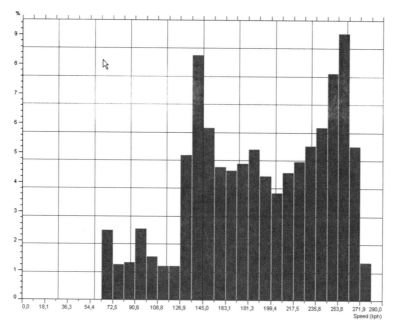

Figure 3.29 Speed histogram of Monza Autodrom

3.5.3   Logging Throttle Position

The throttle position signal measures what the driver is doing with his right foot on the accelerator pedal. Throttle position usually is expressed as a percentage, with zero percent meaning the driver is completely off the accelerator pedal and 100% equaling full throttle.

Looking at the throttle trace in isolation is not very illustrative. It is, however, one of the most important channels for diagnosing chassis or driver issues. Figure 3.30 shows an example of a throttle position trace. This channel becomes an important analysis tool when viewed with other channels, as numerous examples in the remainder of this book will show.

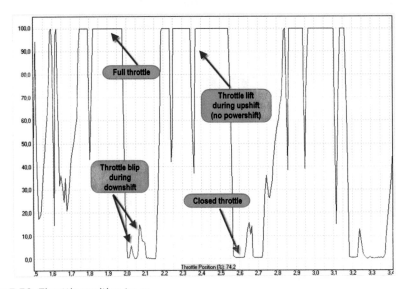

Figure 3.30 Throttle position trace

3.5.4   Logging Steering Angle

As with throttle position, steering angle is a driver activity channel. It records the angle at which the steering wheel is turned and, just like throttle position, is an invaluable diagnostic tool. Steering angle can be expressed as degrees turned by the steering wheel, spindle, or rim, as well as steering rack travel in millimeters. The shape of the graph is the same in all cases (Figure 3.31).

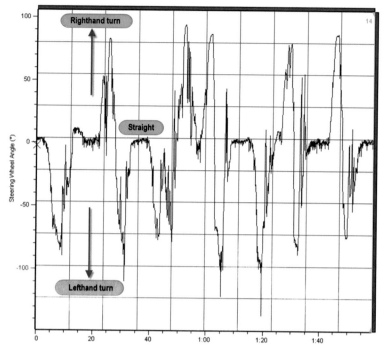

Figure 3.31 Steering angle trace (expressed as angle of the steering wheel in degrees)

If the sensor is properly calibrated, zero degrees steering angle means that the car is traveling straight. The SAE Vehicle Axis System [3-2] defines a positive steering wheel angle for right-hand turns. The way the steering angle trace is pictured in graphs depends on the way the sensor is mounted, but it usually is also user-definable in the software. Note that there are examples in this book in which this sign convention was not followed.

3.5.5 Logging Lateral Acceleration

Lateral g-force is the channel logged as the acceleration perpendicular to the car's center-line, and strictly speaking it measures cornering force. This channel usually is displayed in units of g-forces (1 G = 9.81 m/s^2).

Sign convention, according to the SAE Vehicle Axis System [3-2] for this trace, is the same as with the steering angle channel (i.e., positive for a right-hand turn). In Figure 3.32, a positive value indicates a right-hand turn, while a left-hand turn produces a negative lateral g-force value. Note that there are examples in this book in which this sign convention is not followed.

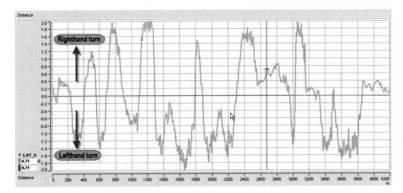

Figure 3.32 Lateral acceleration trace

The maximum values for cornering acceleration depend on the available grip (known as the friction coefficient between road and tire) and the normal load working on the tires. Physically, Equation 3.4, where V = vehicle speed and R = corner radius, applies.

$$G_{\text{lat}} = \frac{V^2}{R} \qquad \text{(Eq. 3.4)}$$

Therefore, the higher the speed at which a corner with a given radius is negotiated, the higher the lateral acceleration is. This means that a car generating a certain amount of grip and downforce at a certain speed has a theoretical maximum speed through a corner with a given radius.

The lateral g-force trace helps in analyzing handling behavior and absolute cornering power and is also a parameter in numerous mathematical channels used in this book.

3.5.6 Logging Longitudinal Acceleration

Longitudinal g-force is the acceleration logged along an axis parallel to the car's centerline (i.e., perpendicular to the lateral g-force). It is basically the acceleration created by the engine's power or the deceleration due to application of the brakes. A positive value is used for acceleration. For deceleration, the sign for the longitudinal g-force is negative [3-2].

An example of longitudinal acceleration trace is given in Figure 3.33, from which some standard features can be read. Maximum braking effort is displayed as the minimum value of the downward dips as the car decelerates. This value is higher if braking commences at a higher speed because the effect of aerodynamic drag adds to the braking effort. Maximum forward acceleration decreases as speed increases, also an effect of aerodynamic drag. On long straights, forward acceleration is close to zero when engine power output matches the aerodynamic resistance. The short downward spikes occurring during forward acceleration represent up-shifts into a higher gear (see chapter 6).

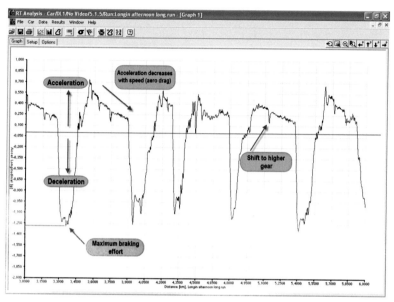

Figure 3.33 Longitudinal acceleration trace

If a longitudinal *g*-force sensor is not present, another solution is to differentiate the speed channel. Speed and longitudinal acceleration are related through Equation 3.5.

$$G_{\text{long}}(t) = \frac{dV(t)}{dt}$$

(Eq. 3.5)

Most analysis software packages allow differentiation of a channel. Express the speed channel used as input for the differentiation in meters per second (1 km/h = 0.278 m/s), so that the output is in m/s². Then convert to *g*-forces if necessary.

A calculated longitudinal acceleration trace is less accurate because differentiating is basically filtering, and it depends mainly on the differentiation time used by the software and the sampling frequency used to log the speed channel. This way, events such as gearshifts may not be visible in the data.

Longitudinal acceleration displayed with lateral *g*-forces in an *X-Y* graph forms the popular traction circle, a useful visualization technique illustrating how the potential of the tires is used. This graphical representation is covered in chapter 7.

3.5.7   Logging Suspension Travel

The six basic signals covered in the previous sections already give the engineer a significant amount of information about chassis and driver performance. Equipping the car with four suspension travel potentiometers helps in further diagnosing vehicle dynamics. Because suspension travel is used extensively in the following chapters in mathematical channels, a review of basic properties of the signal is needed.

Suspension movement typically is measured as shock absorber displacement. With this signal, a sign convention and a short explanation of nomenclature is necessary. All ingoing shock travel from static ride height is considered positive. When the wheel goes up relative to the chassis, the sensor signal has a positive sign. This motion is called bump. The opposite is true for all outgoing shock travel from static ride height. This is called droop. Shock absorber specialists use the names bump and rebound, but this actually refers to the gradient of the sensor signal. A positive gradient (ingoing shock travel, regardless of static position) is called bump travel, while a negative gradient (outgoing shock travel, regardless of static position) is referred to as rebound travel (Figure 3.34).

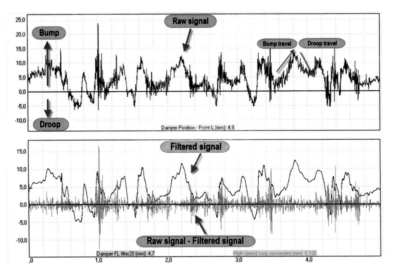

Figure 3.34 Suspension movement trace

Pictured is the signal from a damper potentiometer measuring suspension travel at the front left wheel. The upper trace is the raw, unfiltered signal. This measurement combines two different categories of suspension movement in one signal.

1. Low-speed movement
   This includes the suspension movement in response to chassis attitude changes due to weight transfer (pitch and roll) and to the varying aerodynamic loads at different

speeds. The lower portion of Figure 3.34 shows the suspension movement signal after a filter (20-sample moving average filter) is applied. This trace represents the low-speed movement of this suspension corner.

2. High-speed movement

   The suspension movement induced by road irregularities and curbs takes place at a higher frequency than the low-speed movement. In Figure 3.34, this movement is separated from the raw signal by subtracting the filtered signal from it. It is this portion of the data that was used to insert missing timing beacons in the data earlier in this chapter.

Remember that suspension travel is being measured here, not wheel travel (Figure 3.35). When the motion ratio of the suspension is known, wheel travel can be calculated from the suspension travel signal using Equation 3.6.

$$MR = \frac{x_{wheel}}{x_{suspension}}$$ (Eq. 3.6)

With MR = Motion ratio

   x_{wheel} = wheel movement

   $x_{suspension}$ = suspension movement

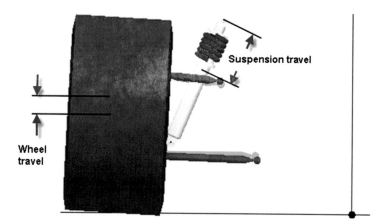

Figure 3.35 Suspension travel versus wheel travel

The motion ratio can be measured statically by jacking up the wheel to a certain distance and measuring the stroke of the shock absorber (or recording it electronically). If a good suspension geometry software package is available, this ratio can be calculated as well. To get the wheel movement, create a mathematical channel that multiplies the suspension movement channel with the motion ratio.

Ensure that the potentiometers actually measure shock absorber travel. Sometimes the sensors are mounted in such a way that there is a motion ratio between sensor travel and shock absorber movement. This should be corrected for in the sensor configuration.

3.6   A Possible Approach to the Testing of Sensor Readings

The ultimate objective in racing is minimizing the time requested by the man-machine combination to complete a lap, and this result is mainly achieved through a constant optimization of the vehicle dynamic behavior.

When it comes to analyze the dynamics of a race car, track data generally represents one of the main sources of information for engineers. Considering the aggressive environment in which race car data acquisition systems need to operate (vibrations, high temperatures, etc.), a robust check on the accuracy of acquired data is therefore the prerequisite for a correct analysis of the vehicle dynamics.

In-car data are typically measurements of physical quantities which describe various aspects of vehicle behavior ranging from global vehicle kinematics (e.g., forward speed, longitudinal and lateral acceleration at the CG) to the single component behavior observed in terms of displacement, force/torque, temperature, and so on. (e.g., suspension movements, tire vertical forces, tire temperatures).

A possible approach to the testing of track data accuracy is the one based on the comparison between the in-car measurement and the expected value for the observed quantity as obtained from mathematical calculations. Any difference between the measurement and the calculated value exceeding the desired tolerance will help the engineer to spot a possible problem in the sensor or simply to offset the reading accordingly.

It is to be noted that simple calculations in the static and/or steady-state domain of vehicle behavior can be adopted for the purpose of track data check. For example, the test of sensor readings can be greatly simplified if conducted during the straight line steady-state motion of the car going across the pit-lane.

The following pictures show graphically a possible implementation of the above-mentioned approach to the check of track data from a set of commonly used sensors in motorsport.

In Figure 3.36 the PIT_LANE green trace shows the window of steady-state motion for the car traversing the pit-lane. Within the window, forward vehicle speed (red trace) is constant leading to zero longitudinal acceleration (yellow trace); lateral acceleration at vehicle CG (cyan trace) is also zero as a result of a zero steering wheel angle input (purple trace). All readings look therefore reasonable in relation to each other, ensuring the correct identification of the desired straight line steady-state motion useful to the check of all other measurements. The PIT_LANE trace has been defined within the data acquisition software in use as a condition obtained by crossing specific ranges for above quantities and some additional information such as pit-limiter status.

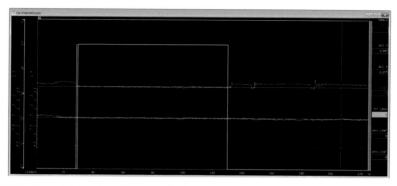

Figure 3.36 Speed, lateral and longitudinal acceleration, and steering angle of a car traversing the pit-lane (Courtesy of BHAI TECH srl.)

Next to the resized window discussed above, data from suspension movements (DAMP_XX red and yellow traces), front and rear axle ride heights (RH_X yellow and purple traces), yaw rate (GYRO orange trace), and tire vertical loads (Fz_XX red and yellow traces) are displayed in Figure 3.37.

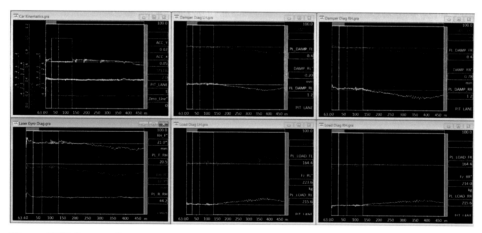

Figure 3.37 Suspension movement, ride heights, yaw rate, and tire vertical loads during pit-lane phase (Courtesy of BHAI TECH srl.)

The expected reading for the yaw rate sensor in the straight line motion under consideration is zero, and this makes the check on the reading quite straightforward.

The measurement of suspension movements and vehicle axle ride heights involves the measurement of a linear displacement. The measurement of tire vertical loads involves the measurement of a force. In order to be able to test the accuracy of these displacement and force measurements, the values expected for each quantity in the straight line steady-state motion generally need to be calculated. In particular, values for above quantities known from car setup need to be compensated for a possible change in the vehicle sprung mass occurring between the "setup" condition of the car and the actual condition of the car exiting the garage. Just as an example, a different fuel load with respect to the fuel load normally adopted when setting up the car can easily change the value expected for above-mentioned readings.

Assuming a linear relation between vehicle weight and vehicle displacements (i.e., assumption of linear stiffness properties for the vehicle acceptable in the pit-lane motion at moderate constant speed), the math involved in the compensation of the linear displacements such as damper travels or axle ride heights is simple and does not require heavy calculations but rather accurate suspension and tire data to describe vehicle stiffness properties.

The compensation on tire vertical loads due to a change in the vehicle sprung mass is obtained by the application to setup corner weights of an appropriate offset to match actual corner weights of the car.

Calculated values for observed quantities can thus be used to test sensor readings. In Figure 3.38, a white trace featuring the PL suffix shows the expected value for the acquired data during the pit-lane motion (i.e., when the PIT_LANE condition of motion is verified). Reference values calculated externally for the various data acquired are made available into the data acquisition software in the form of constants applied to the relative set of laps. Being setup dependent, the definition of the set of constants needs to be up to date at every setup change.

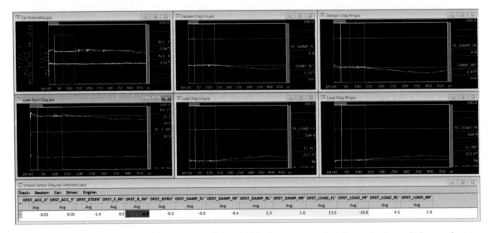

Figure 3.38 Comparison of sensor readings to their expected values during pit-lane phase (Courtesy of BHAI TECH srl.)

At the bottom of Figure 3.38, offsets between sensor readings and expected values are shown. Current offsets are calculated as the average difference between the sensor reading and the reference value over the dataset in which the PIT_LANE condition is verified. By setting alarms, it is possible to spot at first sight readings not within the desired range. For example, the rear axle ride height shows in red an offset of −6 mm which is definitely outside the tolerance range for the channel while rear suspension movements and front tire loads show in yellow offsets close to the boundaries of the tolerance range. If desired, values shown in the bottom bar can be then used to offset the readings in order to match the measurement value with the expected one.

A final consideration regards the PIT_LANE condition of motion which is verified in both the "out" and "in" lap from the garage. It is to be noted that testing sensor readings using the "in" lap generally requires the availability of tire information to describe tire stiffness properties as affected by the temperature and pressure changes occurred during the laps of the outing. How much thermal effects influence tire radial stiffness properties largely depends on the type of tire in use (higher effect on a tire for a formula car, lower effect on a tire for a GT car).

Chapter 4
Straight-Line Acceleration

Cornering is one thing, but as soon as the race car exits a turn the next challenge the driver faces is covering the following straight in the least possible time. In this chapter, analysis tools are provided to evaluate the performance of a race car in straight-line acceleration.

4.1   Torque and Horsepower

The torque and horsepower delivered to the driven wheels has been always of interest to the race engineer. Evaluation of engine changes often is performed on an engine dynamometer. However, this requires removal of the engine from the race-car, and it only shows the torque and power values measured at the flywheel.

Measuring the car's longitudinal acceleration, vehicle velocity, and engine RPM makes it possible to calculate the torque (and, therefore, the horsepower) delivered to the wheels with relatively reliable accuracy [4-1]. As mentioned in chapter 3, longitudinal acceleration can be derived from the velocity signal, so in fact the calculation can even be done only with RPM and speed available.

Torque delivered to the driven wheels must conquer primarily the external forces acting on the vehicle. These are rolling resistance and aerodynamic drag.

1. Rolling resistance is created when a tire in contact with the road surface faces a distortion in its footprint. This is called tire drag and is characterized by a nondimensional rolling resistance coefficient (R_x). A modern radial-ply tire on a passenger car typically has an R_x value of approximately 0.03. For race car tires, this value can be as little as 0.005. The rolling resistance is given in Equation 4.1, where m is the total mass of the car, and g the gravitational acceleration (9.81 m/s^2).

$$F_{\text{rolling}} = R_x \cdot m \cdot g \qquad \text{(Eq. 4.1)}$$

2. The aerodynamic drag of a vehicle depends on its frontal area, drag coefficient, and local air density and is a function of the vehicle velocity squared (Equation 4.2), where ρ is the density of air (1.187 kg/m^3 at 101325 Pa/20 °C), C_D the drag coefficient, A the frontal vehicle surface, and V the vehicle velocity.

$$D = 0.5 \cdot \rho \cdot C_D \cdot A \cdot V^2 \qquad \text{(Eq. 4.2)}$$

Equations 4.1 and 4.2 possibly imply that some coefficients need to be estimated. However, it is also possible to determine the total external resistances through a coast-down test, which is covered in chapter 13.

The torque required to overcome the total external force on the vehicle is given in Equation 4.3, with r_{rolling} the driven tires' rolling radius.

$$T_{\text{ext}} = (F_{\text{rolling}} + D) \cdot r_{\text{rolling}} \qquad \text{(Eq. 4.3)}$$

In addition to the torque required to overcome the external forces, the amount of torque available to accelerate the vehicle is given by Equation 4.4, where G_{long} is the longitudinal acceleration of the vehicle, measured by the data logging system.

$$T_{\text{mass}} = m \cdot M_f \cdot G_{\text{long}} \cdot r_{\text{rolling}} \qquad \text{(Eq. 4.4)}$$

M_f is a factor that takes into account drive-line rotational inertias and the mass factor (Equations 4.5 and 4.6).

$$M_f = \frac{M + M_r}{M} \qquad \text{(Eq. 4.5)}$$

$$M_f = 1 + 0.04 + 0.0025 \cdot i_{\text{total}}^2 \qquad \text{(Eq. 4.6)}$$

With M = translational mass = m/g

        M_r = equivalent rotational mass

        i_{total} = total gear ratio

Following this, the driven-wheel torque can be calculated with Equation 4.7.

$$T_{\text{wheel}} = \frac{T_{\text{mass}} + T_{\text{ext}}}{i_{\text{total}}} \qquad \text{(Eq. 4.7)}$$

And finally, the driven-wheel power is given by Equation 4.8 with F_{mass} defined by Equation 4.9.

$$P_{\text{engine}} = (F_{\text{rolling}} + D + F_{\text{mass}}) \cdot V \qquad \text{(Eq. 4.8)}$$

$$F_{\text{mass}} = \frac{T_{\text{mass}}}{r_{\text{rolling}}} \qquad \text{(Eq. 4.9)}$$

4.1.1 Aerodynamic Drag

At higher vehicle speeds, aerodynamic drag becomes the dominating factor and the equation for air drag force incorporates the vehicle speed squared. To calculate the power at the wheels, drag force is again multiplied by speed. Simply, the power required to overcome aerodynamic drag is closely related to the vehicle speed cubed. This means that to double the speed of a vehicle, eight times the engine power is needed. This is why engine modifications have only a small impact on top speed. An old engine that is down on power might accelerate slowly but still be able to reach close to its original top speed. For example, let's say we want to increase the top speed of a car with 10%. To do this, 33% more power ($1.10^3 = 1.33$) is required. Do not get stuck too much on top speed.

The following example is a case study on the Dodge Viper GTS-R pictured in Figure 4.1. From the distance graph pictured in Figure 4.2, the following calculation data is taken at the point indicated by the cursor:

Engine RPM = 5508 RPM
Vehicle speed V = 230.4 km/h
Longitudinal acceleration G_{long} = 0.195 G

The necessary vehicle properties to perform the calculation are the following:

Total vehicle weight m = 1323 kg
Gear ratio = 5th (i_{total} = 3.14)
Rolling radius R_{rolling} = 0.365 m
R_x = 0.025
C_D = 0.601
A = 2.3 m^2

Figure 4.1 Dodge Viper GTS-R (Courtesy of GLPK Racing)

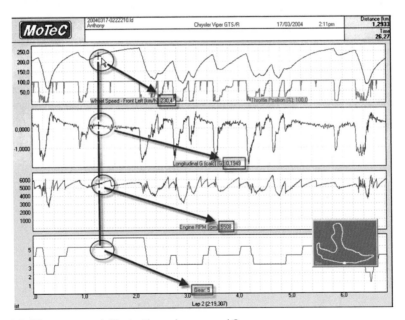

Figure 4.2 Distance graph illustrating a lap around Spa

The data was taken from a test run performed on the Circuit de Spa-Francorchamps. The top speed during that particular lap was 267 km/h. The calculation example concentrates on a random data point along the straight leading to the Les Combes chicane. At this point, the car is accelerating on a straight line. Note that at this section on the track the road runs uphill, which influences the calculation (the longitudinal acceleration here is lower than expected). If the slope of the track is known, the longitudinal force component can be calculated as an extra external resistance working on the car (see chapter 10). For simplicity, track slope is not taken into account in this calculation.

$$F_{rolling} = 0.025 \cdot 1323 \cdot 9.81 = 325 \text{ N}$$

$$D = 0.5 \cdot 1.187 \cdot 0.601 \cdot 2.3 \cdot \left(\frac{230.4}{3.6}\right)^2 = 3352 \text{ N}$$

$$T_{ext} = (325 + 3352) \cdot 0.365 = 1342 \text{ Nm}$$

$$M_f = 1 + 0.04 + 0.0025 \cdot 3.14^2 = 1.06$$

$$T_{mass} = 1323 \cdot 1.06 \cdot 1.912 \cdot 0.365 = 979 \text{ Nm}$$

$$T_{wheel} = \frac{1343 + 979}{3.14} = 739 \text{ Nm}$$

$$P_{engine} = (325 + 3352 + 2682) \cdot 64 = 406976 \text{ Nm/s}$$

With   1 Nm/s = 0.001341 HP

$$P_{engine} = 546 \text{ hp}$$

Figure 4.3 represents a dynamometer run with this engine prior to the test from which the data was taken to perform the preceding calculation. Note that below 1500 RPM the power and torque values were not measured because this engine speed is out of the measurement interval of the dynamometer. At an engine speed of 5500 RPM, the graph shows a torque measured at the flywheel of 784 Nm and a power of 614 hp. Comparing this to the result of the preceding calculation, this means that the loss of torque due to internal friction and inertia is 45 Nm, or approximately 6%.

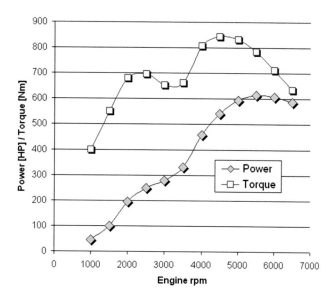

Figure 4.3 Torque and power curve of the Viper V10 engine, measured on a dynamometer

From the preceding equations, math channels can be created in the data analysis software to give the engine power or torque output over a complete lap or run. This can then be plotted against engine RPM to get an approximation of the engine power curve. An example is given in Figure 4.4. This information can be used to determine, for example, the correct gear ratios for a certain racetrack or as a benchmark to evaluate if an engine is down on power.

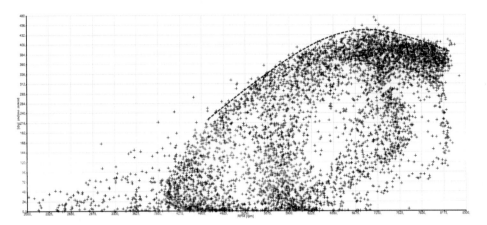

Figure 4.4 Engine power output versus engine RPM

4.1.2 Calculating Torque and Power at the Wheels

The procedure for calculating the torque and power at the wheels is time consuming (unless performed using a spreadsheet or other mathematical software package). For quick analysis purposes and to have an idea of the engine's power output, one should define a mathematical channel that calculates the power the engine is using to accelerate the car. Equation 4.4 gave the torque used to accelerate the vehicle. Converting this to horsepower gives Equation 4.10.

$$P_{mass} = G_{long} \cdot m \cdot V \cdot 0.001341 \qquad \text{(Eq. 4.10)}$$

In this equation, the units for G_{long} are m/s², m in kg and vehicle speed in m/s.

For the lap in Figure 4.2, the results of this calculation are illustrated in Figure 4.5. Interestingly, this graph also shows the power the brakes are utilizing to decelerate the vehicle, so this channel also can be used to analyze the braking effort of the car–driver combination.

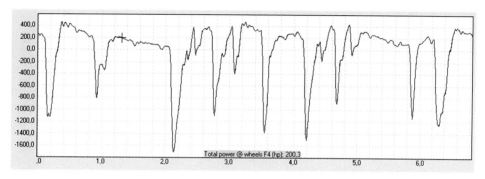

Figure 4.5 The power the engine is delivering to the wheels to accelerate the car

4.2 Traction and Longitudinal Slip

To brake or accelerate a vehicle, Newton's second law tells us that a longitudinal force needs to be developed between the ground and the tire footprint. This longitudinal force is created because of the tire mechanics, where the front of the footprint is compressed under the driving torque. The compressed part adheres to the road surface, resulting in forward stress. This stress reverses in the back part of the footprint as the tire radius recovers. In this part of the footprint, sliding occurs between the tire and the road, which is defined as slip. Slip means that the angular velocity of a driven wheel is always greater than that of a free-rolling wheel.

The longitudinal slip velocity is calculated by Equation 4.11, where V is the linear velocity measured at a driven wheel, and V_0 the linear velocity of one of the free-rolling wheels.

$$V_{slip} = V - V_0 \qquad\qquad (\text{Eq. 4.11})$$

Note that linear speeds are compared where angular velocities should be compared. However, for simplicity, the effective radius of the tire is assumed to be constant.

Further, the slip ratio (*SR*) can be defined by Equation 4.12.

$$SR = \left(\frac{V}{V_0}\right) - 1 \qquad\qquad (\text{Eq. 4.12})$$

For a free-rolling wheel $SR = 0$ and for locked braking $SR = -1$. Wheel spin generally is defined as $SR > 1$ [4-2].

Any given tire develops its maximum coefficient of friction and, therefore, its greatest longitudinal force at a given percentage of slip (Figure 4.6). When the slip ratio exceeds this value (i.e., where more torque is being applied than the tire can transmit to the road surface), the traction capacity decreases. This is true for acceleration and braking.

Tyre coefficient of friction versus slip ratio

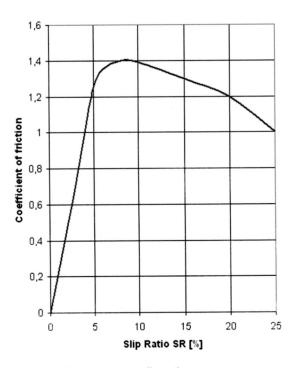

Figure 4.6 Tire coefficient of friction versus slip ratio

Multiple wheel-speed signals are required to measure slip and calculate the slip ratio for a given race car. Various configurations are possible:

- Measure one free-rolling and one driven wheel speed, preferably on the side that is loaded most of the time on the racetrack (left-hand side on a right-hand side racetrack and vice versa).

- Measure one free-rolling and two driven wheel speeds. This makes it possible to calculate separate slip values for left- and right-driven wheels and to evaluate differential work.

- Measure four wheel speeds (the best setup). Reference speed V_0 can be averaged between the two free-rolling wheels.

- Measure at least one free-rolling wheel speed and calculate the speed of the driven wheels from the engine RPM, gear ratios, and tire radius. This is the least accurate option but useful in championships where restrictions exist for the number of used wheel-speed sensors to ban traction control systems (TCSs).

Figure 4.7 illustrates data taken from a GT car around the Spa track, zoomed in on the La Source hairpin where the car decelerates from 225 km/h to approximately 55 km/h (the slowest point on the track) and follows with a hard acceleration phase.

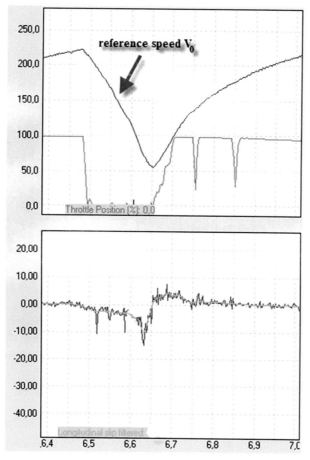

Figure 4.7 Driver Magnus Wallinder negotiating the Spa La Source hairpin corner in a GT car

The car was equipped with two Hall-effect sensors to measure the driven-wheel velocities and one to measure the undriven front-left wheel speed.

Longitudinal slip ratio is calculated as a percentage using Equation 4.13.

$$SR = 100\% \cdot \left(\frac{0.5 \cdot (WSPD_{RL} + WSPD_{RR})}{WSPD_{FL}} - 1 \right)$$ (Eq. 4.13)

Where $WSPD_{RL}$ = measured wheel speed rear left

$WSPD_{RR}$ = measured wheel speed rear right

$WSPD_{FL}$ = measured wheel speed front left

During the braking phase, the aerodynamic drag acting on the car was decreasing rapidly due to the decrease in vehicle speed, so it became more difficult for the driver to modulate the brake pedal to not lock the front wheels. During the first part of the braking phase, the slip ratio went down to approximately −3%, indicating that the tires could handle the brake torque. At a speed just below 80 km/h the slip ratio suddenly—but momentarily—drops to −15%. This means that at least one of the rear wheels is about to lock. At this point the driver, getting a warning signal from the tires that lockup is about to occur, eases off a little bit on the brake pedal, restoring the slip ratio to about −5%. From the point where the driver pushes the throttle pedal, the slip ratio becomes positive, peaking at 5%. Note that maximum slip ratio is reached when the throttle pedal is half-open. After this, the slip ratio drops off to 3%, a similar value seen during the braking phase. At higher speeds, the slip ratio becomes zero.

In general, the graph can be read per Table 4.1.

Table 4.1 Slip ratio sign convention		
Sign of slip ratio	Phase	Significance
SR positive	During braking phase	Front wheel (about to) lock
	During acceleration	Rear wheel (about to) spin
SR negative	During braking phase	Rear wheel (about to) lock
	During acceleration	Front wheel (about to) spin

Traction problems most often occur when the driver is exiting the turn, basically in a transient situation. Therefore, loss of traction or wheel spin most likely takes place first on the driven wheel that has the least load on it (i.e., the wheel at the inside of the corner). For this reason, it may be useful to calculate separate slip ratio channels for both driven wheels. These channels are pictured in Figure 4.8.

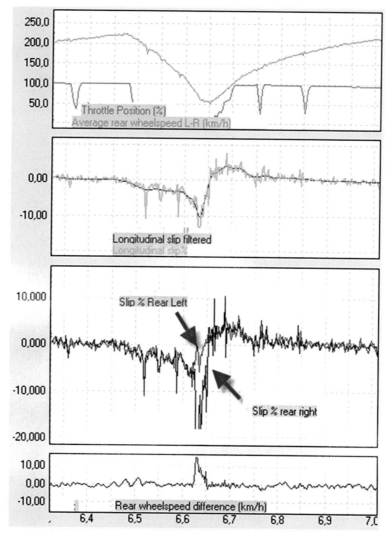

Figure 4.8 Wallinder around the Spa La Source corner

This data is taken from the same car as in Figure 4.7. This distance graph shows the separate slip ratio values for left and right rear wheels. The lower graph shows the speed difference between the two rear wheels in km/h.

The slip ratios for the two driven wheels are particularly useful for analysis. The conclusion drawn from Figure 4.8 is that the inside rear right wheel (La Source being a right-hand corner) was against the blocking limit under braking. This wheel has less load on it than the outside wheel due to the weight transfer resulting from cornering. Traction occurring out of the corner seems to be pretty good as the driver progressively applies more throttle.

The channels covered in this paragraph require the use of multiple wheel-speed sensors, using up to four digital inputs from the data logging unit. Analyzing slip ratios with driver activity and lateral/longitudinal G channels makes pinpointing handling problems much easier. It also provides the engineer good insight on the performance of the differential, ABS, and traction control systems (TCS).

Another example is given in Figure 4.9. Here we see how a driver exits a low-speed corner and accelerates onto the following straight. At the first part of the exit phase the slip ratio increases proportionally as the driver applies more throttle. At the 710 m point, the driver wants to go to full throttle. The slip ratio jumps to over 10%, which is recognized by the driver as too much (notice the difference between the speed channels of driven and rolling wheels). As a result, he performs a very small throttle lift, enough to decrease the slip ratio significantly. About 15 m later the driver applies full throttle. At this point the forward acceleration is no longer traction limited as the slip ratio drops back to zero.

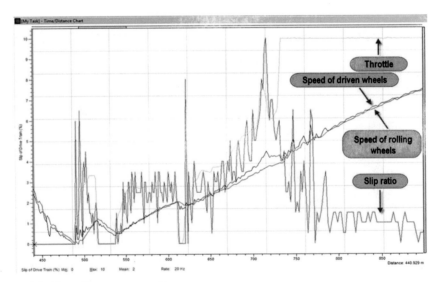

Figure 4.9 Slip ratio on corner exit

4.3   TCS and Slip Ratios

For any tire, there is a given slip ratio where the tire develops its maximum longitudinal force. The driver uses the accelerator and brake pedals to control slip ratio. ABSs and TCSs are designed to keep the tire at its maximum longitudinal force with the slip ratio as a controlled variable.

The ABS monitors the speed of the wheels and regulates the hydraulic pressure to the calipers accordingly to maximize the braking effort. By preventing the wheels from locking and keeping them at an optimal slip ratio, the system enables the driver to maintain steering control and brake the car in the shortest possible distance under most conditions. Traction control evaluates the amount of engine power transferred to the driven wheels. This can be done either by directly limiting the engine output (including cutting the fuel supply or retarding or suppressing the spark to one or more cylinders) or by applying the brake to the wheel that exceeds the optimal slip ratio.

While the ABS and brake-controlled TCS require separate actuation units, most current motor sport engine management systems can limit engine output power in case of excessive slip. In most cases, the only requirement is to wire the necessary wheel speed signals to the engine control unit (ECU) and do the programming.

Figure 4.10 shows an example of a simple engine-controlled TCS. The user can enter the desired amount of slip, in this case expressed as the difference between the linear velocity of the driven wheels and a reference speed, for different engine loads. The engine management measures the different velocities and calculates the slip. As soon as this value exceeds the aimed slip value at the given load site, the software starts progressively cutting the ignition.

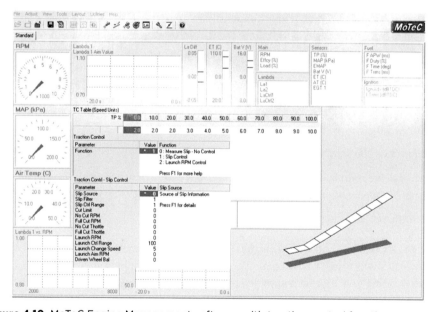

Figure 4.10 MoTeC Engine Management software with traction control function

In some series, technical regulations only allow the use of one sensor to specifically measure the vehicle's velocity. A backdoor to this rule is (when the software allows) to use a calculated channel as the driven-wheel speed for the slip ratio calculation and put a wheel-speed sensor on one of the free-rolling wheels. The speed of the driven wheels can be calculated using Equation 4.14.

$$V = \frac{2 \cdot \pi \cdot r_{\text{rolling}} \cdot n_{\text{engine}}}{i_{\text{total}}}$$

(Eq. 4.14)

This method may not be as accurate as using separate sensors on each wheel but can be useful when regulations limit speed measurements.

This description of the TCS and ABS (an ABS example can be found in chapter 5) is very limited. Keep in mind that electronically maintaining the optimum slip value of four tires is more difficult than it looks because the slip value where maximum traction occurs is not a constant and is likely to vary even during one race lap. Measuring and evaluating slip values using the method described in this paragraph provides a useful tool in TCS and ABS development.

The following example represents data taken from an endurance race car equipped with a Bosch engine-controlled TCS on the French Magny-Cours racetrack. The displayed channels are the following:

- Ignition angle during ASR (acceleration slip regulation, another commonly used name for traction control). This channel shows how much the TCS interferes with the engine ignition to decrease the slip of the driven wheels. The values for this channel are taken from a user-definable table in the engine ECU and are expressed as percentages of the original ignition angle.

- Nominal slip value represents the maximum allowable slip value for each particular instant. Channel values for this also are taken from an engine ECU table with speed, throttle position, and lateral G as variables.

- Reference speed

- Slip of drive train is the actual slip experienced by the driven wheels calculated according to Equation 4.13.

- Throttle position

Figure 4.11 shows the car during a corner exit phase. The ignition angle during the ASR trace indicates when the TCS is active. The graph shows a couple of short downward spikes indicating brief TCS activation. One spike is indicated with an arrow and occurs during a moment when the driver applies the throttle pedal. At this moment, the actual slip value shortly peaks at 6%, whereas the ECU concludes that no more than 4 % is tolerable. As soon as the actual slip ratio drops below the nominal value, the TCS deactivates.

As the driver applies more throttle, the system needs to correct more to stay within nominal slip values. Notice that at the point where the driver is applying full throttle the TC doesn't agree and limits the power output of the engine by retarding ignition with

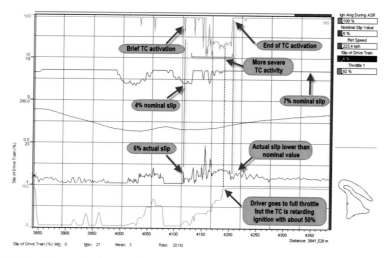

Figure 4.11 Traction control example

about 50%. The traction control activity is also very noticeable from the short upward spikes in the actual slip ratio. An example is given in Figures 4.12 and 4.13, the first with traction control and the second without.

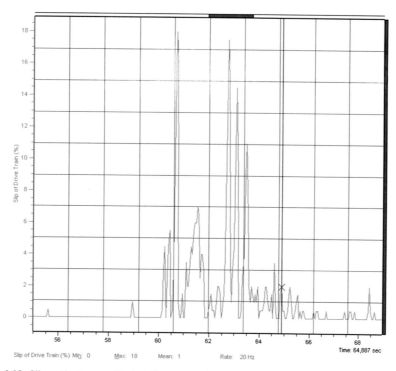

Figure 4.12 Slip ratio trace with traction control

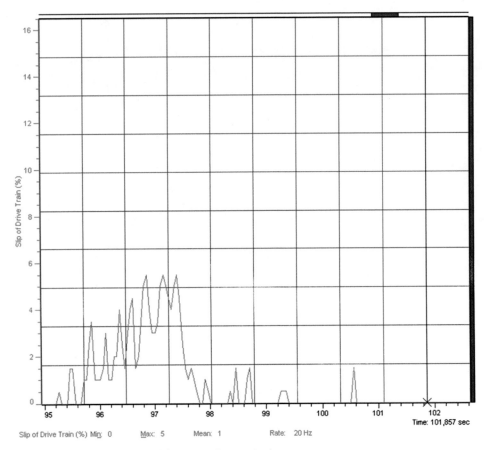

Figure 4.13 Slip ratio trace without traction control

4.4 Time versus Distance

"I catch him in the corners, but he runs away from me on the straights..." is an often-heard comment from race car drivers that could be just the illusion of a time gap versus distance. Suppose the driver is closing to within 0.4 sec to the car directly in front of him (Figure 4.14). At this point, both cars have a cornering speed of 65 km/h or 18.1 m/s. Here, 0.4 sec translates to a distance between both cars of 7 m. The cars are exactly matched in horsepower and aerodynamics, and while exiting the corner, both accelerate at exactly the same rate (as the speed trace in Figure 4.14 shows), keeping 0.4 sec between them. Halfway up the straight the cars are doing 180 km/h or 50 m/s. Now 0.4 sec translates to 20 m, a difference that reaches its maximum at the end of the straight (27 m at a speed of 265 km/h). To the driver, it seems that his opponent is running away from him, but in reality he is not. The time separation never changes; it is just an illusion.

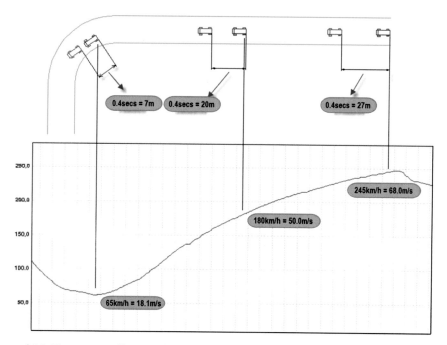

Figure 4.14 Time versus distance: both cars had a constant gap of 0.4 sec between them, but in distance the gap increases with speed

4.5   The Importance of Corner Exiting Speed

Straights on racetracks can account for 70–80% of the total track length. A race car often spends much more time on a straight at maximum acceleration than anywhere else. However, every straightaway starts with exiting the preceding corner, and maximizing the speed at which the car comes out of this corner can minimize the time until the next braking zone.

In racing literature and driving schools, corner exit speed is often a bit overrated, but the previous principle still remains true. Figure 4.15 shows two overlaid laps of the Spa track, focusing on the world-famous Raidillon curve and the following straight.

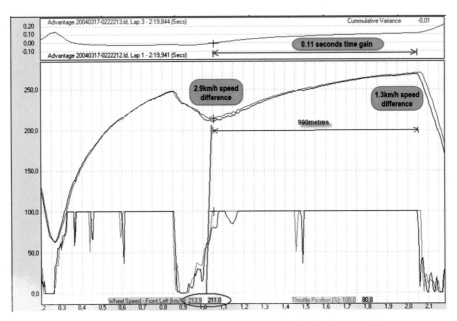

Figure 4.15 Corner exit speed and its consequences on the following straight

Both laps were run in the same car with the same driver on the same day. An aerodynamic setup change was performed on the car to cure a high-speed understeer problem, and the gray speed trace in Figure 4.15 represents the result. The driver is able to go on the throttle more fluently with the result that cornering speed increases by 2.9 km/h and the driver successfully negotiates the exit of the corner.

The straight following this corner has a length of 990 m. The lap illustrated by the black speed trace gives an average speed along this straight (calculated by the data acquisition software) of 246.41 km/h (or 68.446 m/s) and a sector time of 14.464 sec. Assuming that the car has the potential to keep the 2.9 km/h difference until the next braking point means an average speed of 249.31 km/h (or 69.252 m/s) and a sector time of 14.296 sec. By exiting this corner 2.9 km/h faster, this car gains a sector advantage of 0.17 sec. In reality, however, this was not the case.

The second lap (gray trace) has an average speed on the straightaway sector of 248.32 km/h (or 14.353 m/s) giving a sector time of 14.353 sec, a difference with the black lap of 0.11 sec. Figure 4.15 clearly shows that most of this time is gained on the first half of the straight. Aerodynamic drag increases with the square of speed. During the second lap, speed is higher; thus, there is more drag and less acceleration. In the slower lap, acceleration is higher and the difference in speed reduced. At the end of the straight, the car approaches the point where engine output is matched by drag and the car can no longer accelerate. In this case, a high-speed corner is followed by a long straight. Optimizing corner exit speed for this corner gives a net gain of just over a tenth of a second, which is a considerable advantage.

4.6   Drag Racing Specifics

A drag race is an automotive acceleration contest from a standing start between two vehicles over a predetermined distance [4-3]. The nature and rules of the game make drag racing a mathematical exercise, and data-logging can enhance effectively the success of this exercise.

The accepted standard for the distance of a drag race is a quarter mile or an eighth mile. The race begins using an electronic device commonly referred to as the Christmas tree, which displays a visual countdown to the driver through a series of lights. When competitors leave the starting line, it activates a timer that is stopped when they cross the finish line. The time between these two events is the elapsed time (ET).

A drag race is a tournament-style elimination race between two vehicles. The losing vehicle in each round is eliminated, while the winner progresses into the following round of competition.

4.6.1   ET Bracket Racing

Some classes use a handicapped form of competition called ET bracket racing [4-3]. This makes it possible for vehicles of varying performance abilities to compete with each other on an even basis. Each competitor has to predict the ET at which the vehicle will run. This is called dial-in. In a run between two cars, the slower vehicle receives a head start equal to the difference in ET.

Here's an example. Car 1 has previously covered the quarter mile in 16.68, 16.71, and 16.73 sec. The driver feels that a dial-in of 16.70 sec is appropriate. Car 2 has been timed at 13.98, 13.99, and 14.02 sec, and a dial-in of 14.00 sec is selected. This means that Car 1 receives a head start of 2.70 sec when the Christmas tree counts down to each car's start. The result of the race is determined as follows:

- If both cars run a higher ET than their dial-in, the win goes to the vehicle that crosses the finish line first.

- If both cars cover the quarter mile in their exact dial-in times, the win goes to the driver that reacted quickest to the starting signal (reaction time).

- If a car goes quicker than its dial-in, it is disqualified. This is called breakout.

- If a car reacts to the Christmas tree too quickly, it is disqualified. This is called red light.

- If both cars break out, the one that runs closest to its dial-in is the winner.

- If one car breaks out and the other car jumps the Christmas tree, the one that breaks out wins.

In sanctioned events, interval times are available to the competitors at 60, 330, 660, and 1000 ft. The 60-ft interval time is a measure of the launch from the starting line, and it often determines how quickly the rest of the run is.

Determining the appropriate dial-in consistency is of vital importance. Starting strategy, gearing, and tire pressures are some issues that need careful attention and are where a data logging system can be of assistance. Weather circumstances also play a major role in determining the vehicle's potential ET. Straight-line acceleration was covered earlier in this chapter, and the influence of the weather on engine and aerodynamics is investigated in chapter 13.

Figure 4.17 shows a run of a Top Fuel racer (figure 4.16) on the Willowbank quarter-mile drag strip. Top Fuel represents the highest class in drag racing, and the cars accelerate from 0 to 160 km/h in less than 0.8 sec. Top speeds can exceed 530 km/h. The following signals are shown: engine RPM, drive shaft RPM, throttle position, clutch fluid pressure, and speed (front wheel speed and corrected speed). These traces were created using MoTeC's i2 analysis software in which a specific drag racing template can be created.

Figure 4.16 Drag racing is a specific form of motor sport in which data acquisition also can be an advantage

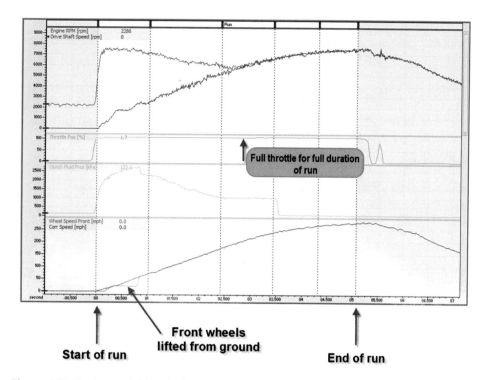

Start of run

Front wheels lifted from ground

End of run

Full throttle for full duration of run

Figure 4.17 Engine and drive shaft RPM, throttle position, clutch fluid pressure, and speed of a Top Fuel drag racer going down the quarter mile

The vertical lines indicate the different sequences of the run. The official result sheet showed the intermediate times in Table 4.2 for this particular car.

Table 4.2 Quarter mile intermediate times	
Distance	Time
60 ft	1.020 sec
330 ft	2.420 sec
660 ft	3.446 sec
1000 ft	4.315 sec
1320 ft	5.073 sec

These results can be entered manually in the analysis software, after which they are indicated in each graph.

The software calculates a corrected speed signal to determine the covered distance. In this case, the front wheel speed is corrected using the longitudinal acceleration. During the first 60 ft of the run, there is quite a difference between the measured wheel speed and the calculated corrected speed. This occurs because the front wheels of the vehicle are not in contact with the ground at this stage.

Measuring the wheel speed at the rear axle generates huge errors in the logged data because of the inherent soft spring rates of the rear tires of a Top Fuel race car. In fact, this kind of car uses the variation in tire radius due to the wheel's centrifugal forces to increase the gear ratio as drive shaft RPM increases. GPS-based speed measurement is a suitable solution for this problem.

In this example, the car reaches a maximum velocity of 283 mph, but it achieves this speed after the finish. The speed as the car crosses the finish line is 277 mph. Up to the 1000-ft point, the speed trace is nearly linear, indicating a constant longitudinal acceleration.

Another obvious fact is that the throttle pedal is on the floor for the complete duration of the run. The amount of engine power transferred to the driven wheels is determined by the clutch. The clutch and its release mechanism of a Top Fuel dragster is a complex system, and its tuning is vital for a fast ET. The clutch fluid pressure trace does not look as though it is influenced by only the driver's foot. Although electronic closed-loop systems are banned in the Top Fuel class, a mechanical system—partly hydraulic, partly pneumatic—takes care that the clutch is engaged in a controlled way over a predetermined period.

Another run of an undefined dragster is shown in Figure 4.18. This example concerns a bracket race. The driver in this case needs to lift the throttle in the last 300 ft to prevent a breakout. The driver covers the drag strip in 6.138 sec. This trace also shows the braking effect of the parachute that opens after the car crosses the finish line.

The concerned car was equipped with a three-speed gearbox with the following ratios:

1st gear	1.60
2nd gear	1.28
3rd gear	1.00

However, gear changes cannot be detected here from the engine RPM graph as is the case in a typical road racing RPM trace. Two small, rough driveshaft RPM areas hint at a gear change; in this case, use a gear position sensor to determine the used gear.

The difference in engine RPM (which remains relatively constant) and driveshaft RPM is influenced completely by the clutch. To determine the amount of slip in the clutch, use Equation 4.15.

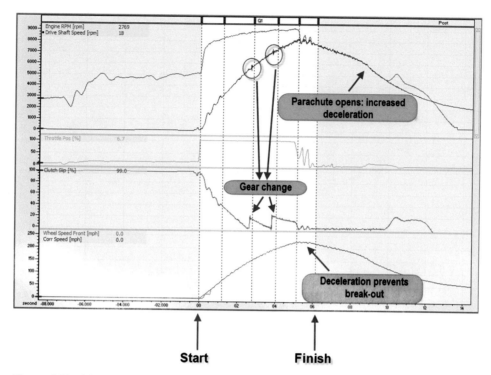

Figure 4.18 This dragster covers the quarter mile in 6.138 sec but decelerates in the last section to prevent a breakout

$$\text{Clutch Slip} = \frac{n_{\text{engine}} - (n_{\text{driveshaft}} \cdot i_{\text{total}})}{n_{\text{engine}}} \qquad \text{(Eq. 4.15)}$$

With n_{engine} = engine RPM

         $n_{\text{driveshaft}}$ = driveshaft RPM

            i_{total} = total gear ratio

The resulting mathematical channel is pictured in Figure 4.18. As in the previous example, this race is driven with the clutch instead of the throttle pedal.

Chapter 5
Braking

Acceleration is required to minimize the lap time of a given race car. Improving the acceleration capabilities of the vehicle should generally result in faster laps. Optimizing the braking action of car and driver does not directly have the same effect. However, when the time spent under deceleration can be decreased, the difference can be applied to acceleration, which results in faster lap times.

A simplified example is offered in Table 5.1, which shows the percentage of time spent under braking and acceleration during two different laps performed by the same car and driver around Circuit Zolder.

Table 5.1 Acceleration and deceleration percentages for two different laps around Circuit Zolder		
	Lap A	Lap B
Acceleration percentage	68.24%	70.78%
Deceleration percentage	31.76%	29.12%
Lap time	1'33"212	1'32"178

Between the two runs, a fresh set of tires was put on the car, which created a gain in other areas as well. However, a decrease in the total duration under braking over completion of a lap brings an advantage almost every time. This chapter demonstrates how the race car's braking system as well as the capabilities of the driver to slow the car down can be analyzed and optimized.

5.1   Braking Quickness

The act of braking begins when the driver hits the pedal. To waste as little time as possible, brake pressure must be built up as quickly as possible. An analysis of braking speed is achieved using the longitudinal acceleration channel to measure the time it takes to get to maximum braking force (Figure 5.1).

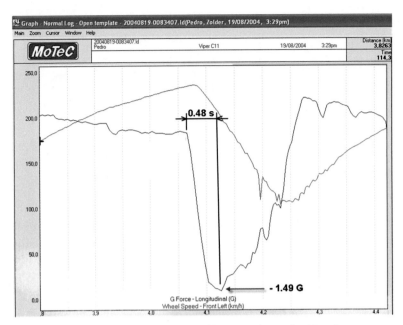

Figure 5.1 The time it takes for the driver to achieve maximum braking force

Anything under 0.5 sec is considered fast braking. This does not mean that the driver has to slam the pedal, as this probably locks up the front wheels. There needs to be a balance between a controlled buildup of braking effort and aggressiveness. Obviously, with the braking pedal the driver has a great influence on the rate of longitudinal load transfer from rear to front axle. He can control this load transfer with the speed at which pressure is applied to the pedal. (More on this will follow in chapter 14.)

The longitudinal G channel can be differentiated (by calculating the slope of the signal trace) to give a measure of braking speed. To brake the vehicle in Figure 5.1 with a maximum braking effort of 1.49 G within 0.48 sec, this differentiation shows a peak of 3.10 G/s.

5.2   Braking Effort

How does one know what the vehicle's maximum braking potential is? The simplest way to answer this question is to test it. A straight-line test indicates the highest negative longitudinal acceleration achieved under braking. The speed signals indicate when the wheels tend to lock up.

Author Buddy Fey presents a target value for the car's peak braking deceleration by comparing it with the car's cornering potential [5-1]. For cars producing up to 2 G of cornering power, maximum longitudinal Gs should be approximately 95% of the maximum lateral Gs.

This value varies slightly with the configuration of the vehicle. The following corrections should be applied where necessary:

- Front engine   −2%
- Rear engine   +2%
- Square tire contact patch   +2%
- Average tire contact patch   +0%
- Wide tire contact patch   −2%

As an example, consider the Dodge Viper GTS-R, front-engined and equipped with wide racing tires. This car is capable of cornering at 2.0 G. Therefore, the maximum braking effort for this car is the following:

$$
\begin{array}{ll}
95\% & \text{Lateral G} \\
-2\% & \text{Front engine} \\
-2\% & \text{Wide tires} \\
\hline
91\% \cdot 2.0\,G = 1.8\,G
\end{array}
$$

The maximum longitudinal deceleration that the car actually reaches can vary somewhat from corner to corner. Uphill or downhill braking increases or decreases peak longitudinal Gs, respectively. Track surface, tire temperature, wear, and compound have an influence as well.

Once the braking activity coincides with entering a corner, longitudinal Gs decrease while the tires need grip to build up cornering force. Equation 5.1 calculates combined acceleration and can be used to determine the maximum deceleration under braking while turning.

$$G_{combined} = \sqrt{G_{lat}^2 + G_{long}^2} \qquad\qquad \text{(Eq. 5.1)}$$

To find the longitudinal G, rearrange the equation as shown in Equation 5.2.

$$G_{long} = \sqrt{G_{combined}^2 - G_{lat}^2} \qquad\qquad \text{(Eq. 5.2)}$$

The Viper has a braking threshold of 1.8 G. Consider that while braking, this car is cornering at 0.5 G. Substituting these values in Equation 5.2 gives the maximum achievable braking deceleration:

$$G_{long} = \sqrt{1.8^2 - 0.5^2} = 1.73 \text{ G}$$

Figure 5.2 shows this relationship graphically. Note that this is a quarter of the traction circle (see chapter 7). From the graph, it is obvious that between 0 and 0.5 lateral G braking capabilities are not affected strongly.

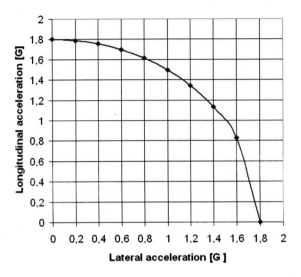

Figure 5.2 Peak longitudinal acceleration as a function of cornering acceleration

To evaluate if the driver is braking adequately, compare how closely he approaches the target set by this calculation. Not braking hard enough may not be a driver-related issue. It may be possible that the brake balance is set up improperly or that there is another problem in the vehicle configuration.

5.3   Braking Points

The discussion about braking points begins with specifying that the location of this point on the track depends on the speed at which the corner is approached. A difference in approach speed can affect significantly the braking distance (Figure 5.3). This affects the reference points the driver uses to select the braking point.

The graph shows two speed traces of the same car as it approaches a corner. The black line shows the highest top speed, 6 km/h more than the other trace. The braking point during the lap with the lower top speed has moved 17 m farther down the track. At this point, the two traces converge, indicating the braking effort was the same for the two laps.

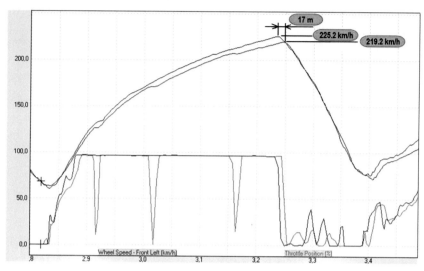

Figure 5.3 Effect of the speed at which a corner is approached on the braking point location

Effective braking is notable in the combined G graph as a smooth transition between the braking peak and the maximum lateral acceleration during cornering. Combined acceleration is effectively the instantaneous radius of the vehicle's traction circle and is either a measure of the available grip *or* the amount of grip the driver is using. In reality, the traction circle will not be circular, but for this discussion we will assume it to be. If this is the case, and the driver is always using the entire available grip, the combined acceleration will be constant and equal to the traction circle radius during the complete cornering phase, from the braking point up to the point where the driver is accelerating out of the corner again.

If this is not the case in the beginning of the braking zone, then we can conclude that the driver is braking early, as he doesn't use all available grip.

When we look at the combined acceleration channel, early braking will show up as a *valley* in the data trace during the braking phase. An example is given in Figure 5.4. In this chart, the channels lateral, longitudinal, and combined acceleration are shown. The point where the longitudinal acceleration steeply decreases is the braking point. The car develops just over 1 G deceleration at this point. As lateral acceleration is still zero at this point, the combined acceleration follows the longitudinal channel. A bit farther the driver starts to turn the car, and lateral acceleration is being built up. With longitudinal G still negative, the driver is obviously still braking. Lateral G peaks at about 1.5 G, and considering that the tires are also still slowing the car at this point, the 1 G of initial braking seems a bit low. A later braking point would have forced the driver to brake harder, resulting in a higher deceleration. The valley in the combined G trace tells us that the car could have handled this. The dotted line is an indication of what the combined G trace should have looked like.

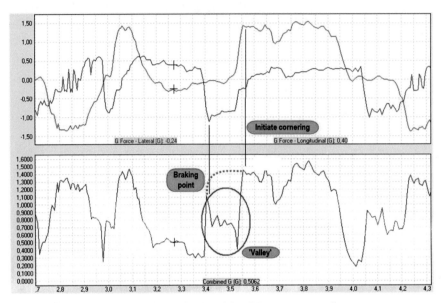

Figure 5.4 Early braking shows up in the Combined G trace as a valley

Effective braking is revealed in the traction circle graph as a near-circular transition between maximum cornering G and maximum longitudinal deceleration. It is all about using the car's tires effectively.

Another indicator for early braking can be inadequate braking effort, also known as easing on the brakes. (Determining the braking effort the driver should aim for was discussed in the previous paragraph.)

Evaluating late braking is not so easy. Begin by investigating where in the corner the lateral G peaks. A peak at mid-corner or later may indicate late braking.

5.4   Lock-up

Locking the brakes is often accompanied by big smoke tufts from the wheels. This results as often in one or more tires that are no longer round. When brake lock-up occurs, all the wheels usually do not lock. The wheel most likely to lock is the one with the least load on it (the inside of the corner), on the axle with the highest brake bias. Other factors may apply as well. This means that wheel-speed sensors on each wheel are necessary to detect lock-up during braking.

In chapter 4, the longitudinal slip ratio was defined. During the braking phase, a positive slip ratio indicates that at least one of the front wheels is about to lock, while a negative slip ratio indicates the same problem on the rear axle.

However, the easiest way to detect lock-up is the speed graphs. Figure 5.5 is an example of a car with clearly too much rear brake bias. When a wheel locks, the speed trace drops nearly vertically. When the tire regains grip (because the driver senses the wheel locking up and eases off the brake), the speed trace jumps again. Simultaneously with the downward spikes in the speed trace, the longitudinal slip percentage dives. If the front wheels are locking up, these spikes aim upward.

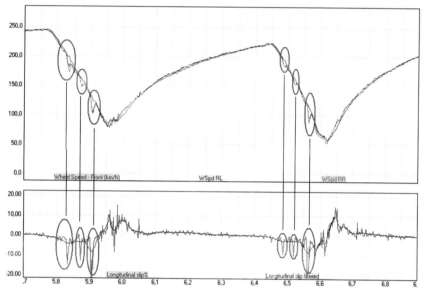

Figure 5.5 Brake lock-up shows up as a downward spike in the speed graph and in the longitudinal slip percentage

5.5   Brake Balance

Maximum braking deceleration only occurs when all tires simultaneously operate at their maximum coefficient of friction. Therefore, proper brake balance is vital. Corner-entry understeer followed by mid-corner understeer and the combination of low braking Gs can be diagnosed as too much front brake bias. Too much rear bias leads to corner-entry oversteer if not anticipated by the driver.

In extreme cases, too much brake bias on either axle leads to one or more wheels locking up. The car from which the data in Figure 5.5 was obtained clearly suffers from excessive rear brake bias.

Measuring brake line pressure makes it very easy to track the vehicle's brake balance. It is a great way to restore the proper balance when something in the brake system is changed. It reveals the brake-related activities of the driver, and the line pressures are variables in calculations for brake forces.

An example is given in Figure 5.6. At the end of the straight, the driver slams on the brakes, resulting in peak brake line pressures of 5500 kPa and 4860 kPa for the front and rear axles, respectively. After this braking peak, the driver starts to ease off the pedal pressure to avoid locking the brakes.

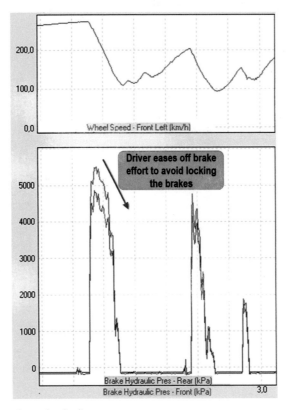

Figure 5.6 Front and rear brake line pressure

Brake balance is the distribution between front and rear brake pressure (not brake force!) and depends on the brake master cylinder diameters and the position of the brake balance bar (if applicable) relative to the position of the master cylinders. To determine the brake balance, we need to measure the pressure in the front and rear brake systems separately. With Equation 5.3 we can then define the brake balance.

$$\text{Brake Bias}_{\text{front}} = \frac{P\text{Brake}_{\text{front}}}{P\text{Brake}_{\text{front}} + P\text{Brake}_{\text{rear}}} \cdot 100\% \qquad \text{(Eq. 5.3)}$$

Where: $P\mathrm{Brake}_{front}$ = Front brake line pressure

$P\mathrm{Brake}_{rear}$ = Rear brake line pressure

The example in Figure 5.6 would show at peak brake pressure a brake balance of

$$\mathrm{Brake\ Bias}_{front} = \frac{5500}{5500 + 4860} \cdot 100\% = 53\%$$

When no brakes are applied, the value of the above channel will go to infinity. It's therefore good to gate the channel to display the brake balance value only if brake pressure is applied (e.g., front brake pressure exceeds five bars).

The brake balance channel shown in Figure 5.7 is gated to show values only when both front brake pressure exceeds 15 bars, which might be a bit high for this type of car. In the third braking zone pictured, the car brakes from 140 to 110 km/h but the brake balance calculation is not triggered. When the 15-bar condition is not met, the channel will return zero.

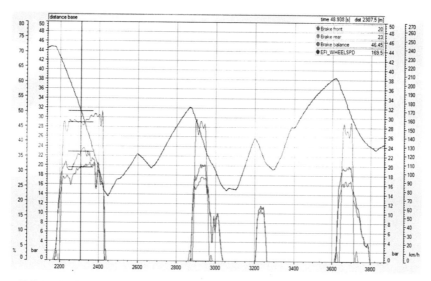

Figure 5.7 Brake balance math channel

It is useful to look at a lap-by-lap value of the brake balance in a run chart (maximum or average per lap) to quickly locate situations where the driver modifies the balance bar position. The graph in Figure 5.8 shows the lap-by-lap average brake balance during a race. The red arrow indicates a pit stop where a driver change was performed. The new driver changed the brake balance over the next couple of laps before going back to a similar value as the first driver.

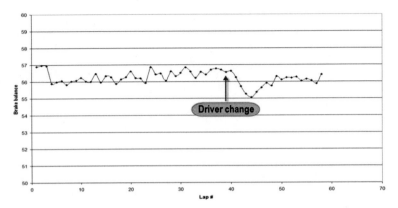

Figure 5.8 Average brake balance values over the duration of a race

Something interesting in this chart is the fact that the brake balance values of the second driver are much more consistent than those of the first one. In fact, brake balance is not only influenced by the master cylinder sizes and balance adjuster. Compliance in the system will influence the dynamic pressure distribution. A driver with a more consistent braking technique will be better able to cover up such a problem because compliance in the brake system will vary proportionally to variations in pedal pressure and therefore also brake pressure.

Figure 5.9 shows another run chart example, this time of all laps done on a test day with a GT car. In the morning the test was started on a wet track, and as the track dried out, we can see how the driver adapts the brake balance to the changing track conditions. Once the track was fully dry, the brake balance adjuster was not touched for the rest of the day.

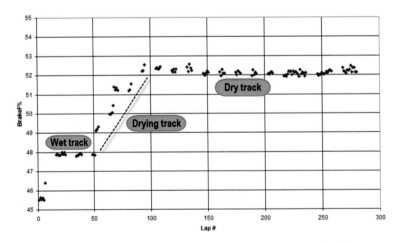

Figure 5.9 Average brake balance values over the duration of a test day that started with wet track conditions

When calculating the average value of the brake balance channel, you need to be careful that this calculation doesn't take zero values into account as we want a true average of the brake pressure distribution. When the software is not able to exclude zero values from a calculation, it's better to use the maximum value as a lap statistic. In this case you do need to check with which values you gate the math channel, as friction and compliance in the brake system might shift the brake balance to the front at the end of a braking zone.

The math channel for brake balance can be useful to identify specific problems in the brake system and/or pedal box design of the car. In theory, fluids being incompressible, when the driver hits the brakes the relationship between front and rear brake pressure should be constant. In practice this is often different. Compliance in the braking system (calipers, brake lines, master cylinders) and pedal box causes variation in the brake balance.

Figure 5.10 is an *X-Y* graph of front versus rear brake pressure. This graph shows a small amount of scatter, indicating that for a given front brake pressure there is a variation in rear brake pressure. This undesirable effect can have various causes. Caliper deformation or free-play in the pedal box assembly can lead to inconsistent brake pressure distribution.

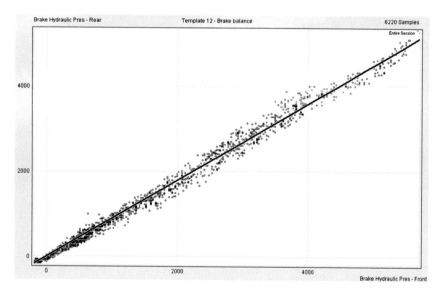

Figure 5.10 Front versus rear brake line pressure

Another way to visualize compliance in the braking system is pictured in Figure 5.11. This graph plots brake balance against front brake pressure. It illustrates the variation in pressure distribution for any given front brake pressure. For low pressures, this variation is high (free-play in the pedal box assembly), and it diminishes as brake pressure rises. Brake balance variation at higher pressures is caused by caliper or brake pad deformation or expansion of the brake hoses. A braking system with a consistent brake pressure distribution shows less than a 5% variation in brake balance from 15-bar front pressure onwards [5-2]. This is clearly not the case in Figure 5.11. The graph shows a brake balance variation of 10% at 20 bars, and the target of 5% is only reached at 40 bars. Between 40 and 60 bars, the graph shows a strange "bump." This variation in brake balance probably is caused by brake caliper deformation. This also can be seen in Figure 5.10. This data was taken from the same session. At 40 bars there is a shift in brake balance. Getting rid of this type of braking system compliance is vital to achieving optimum braking performance.

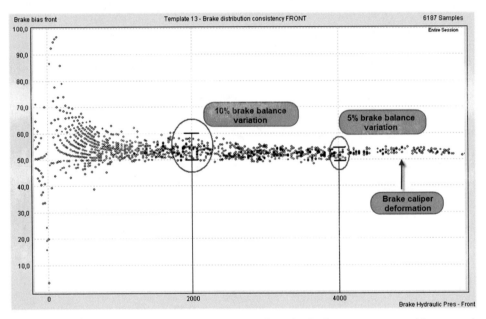

Figure 5.11 This *X-Y* plot of brake balance against front brake line pressure provides a good method to check the brake balance consistency

What kind of effect a badly designed braking system can have is illustrated by the example in Figure 5.12. In one single braking zone we can observe a variation in brake balance of 12%! As long as the pedal pressure is kept constant, the balance remains more or less consistent. But as the driver comes (smoothly) off the brakes, the brake balance increases steeply to the front axle. At the end of the braking zone there's even a moment where the front pressure exceeds the rear pressure. Such a large shift in brake balance will without a doubt have a profound effect on the mid-corner balance of this car.

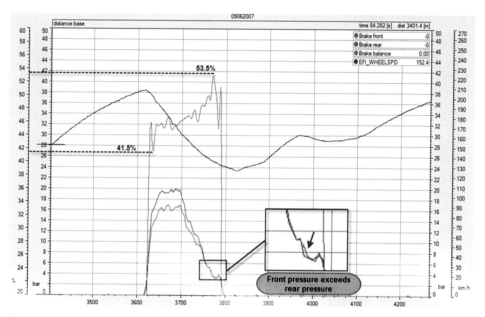

Figure 5.12 This brake balance shift will obviously have a serious effect on the vehicle's cornering balance

Figure 5.13 shows a better brake balance consistency, despite large pedal pressure variations by the driver. However, at the beginning and end of the braking zone the brake balance rises steeply. This is probably caused by static friction in the braking system (friction in pedal box mechanism, oil seals, and so on).

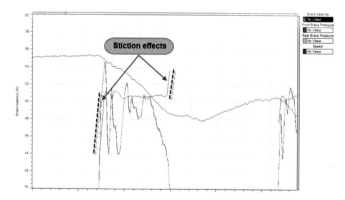

Figure 5.13 Good brake balance consistency, but at the beginning and end of the braking zone there are some friction effects in the brake system

5.6   Pedal Travel

Brake pressure sensors are valuable for checking the braking system. Additionally, measuring the travel of the brake pedal provides useful information. If brake pressure channels are not available, logging pedal travel at least provides some information that would be revealed by the pressure channels. It tells when and how the driver applies the brakes; however, it does not reveal anything about the brake balance.

Checking pedal travel and brake line pressures provides a good indication of brake pad thickness. This can be particularly useful in endurance races. As the brake pads wear, more pedal travel is required to achieve the same brake line pressures. Pedal travel also indicates braking consistency. The previous paragraph showed that pedal box free-play leads to inconsistent brake balance. Figures 5.10 and 5.11 illustrated a vehicle with poor pedal box rigidity. A plot of front brake pressure against pedal travel from the same session in this car is pictured in Figure 5.14. It shows that significant brake pressure only is being built up after ten10 mm pedal travel. After that, there is a significant degree of variation in brake pressure for any given pedal travel value.

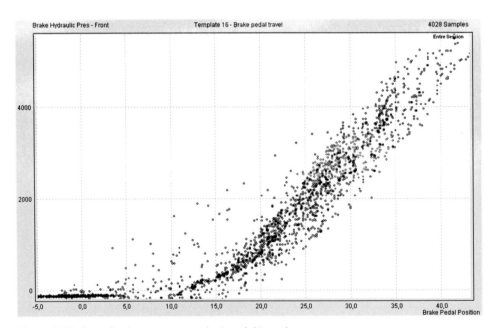

Figure 5.14 Front brake pressure against pedal travel

5.7   ABS

ABS systems constantly monitor the rotating speeds of the four wheels. We've seen already in *chapter 4* that any tire develops its maximum longitudinal force at a given slip ratio. The purpose of a motor sport grade antilock brake system (ABS) is to ensure that during braking the four wheels are kept as close as possible to this slip ratio and eventually to prevent locking one or more wheels. The ABS controller looks for decelerations from the wheel speed signals that are out of the ordinary. If a wheel is about to lock, the system will decrease the braking pressure to this specific wheel until it accelerates again. After that, pressure is reapplied until an abnormal deceleration is detected again. This process is done at a high frequency (felt by the driver through the brake pedal), before the wheel can significantly change its speed. This causes the wheel to slow down at the same rate as the car, with the tires near the point of optimum slip ratio.

ABS activity will be visible on the brake pressure signals and brake balance. The brake balance math channel will not be consistent and might look a bit as that on a car without ABS but with poor pedal box stability, although the high-frequency pressure modulations of the system are mostly recognizable. Figure 5.15 shows an example of a car decelerating into a low-speed corner. At the beginning of the braking zone, the rear brake pressure signal shows high-frequency pressure variations that do not result in big shifts in brake balance. Here the ABS is keeping the rear tires as near as possible to the point of locking. But as the driver decreases the pedal pressure toward the point of turn-in, there are some big shifts in brake balance. The car is turning now, and the lower load on the inside front tire causes it to lock. The ABS reacts to this by decreasing the pressure on this front wheel.

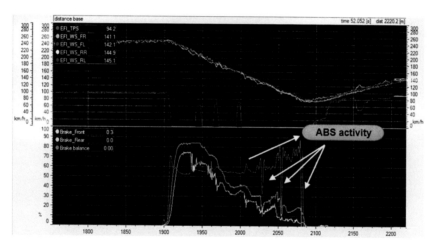

Figure 5.15 ABS activity indications on brake balance math channel

Another example is given in Figure 5.16. In this graph, two big ABS interventions can be seen, clearly as a reaction to a locking rear wheel. Notice how first rear pressure decreases, followed by a decrease of front pressure to prevent overshooting of the front wheels. Interesting here as well is the small amount of rear brake pressure visible when the car accelerates out of the corner. The right rear wheel exceeds its optimum slip ratio, and brake pressure is applied by the ABS system, which in this case works as a traction control system as well.

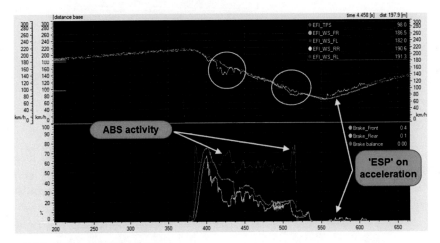

Figure 5.16 ABS and ESP activity

5.8   Brake Temperature Measurement

Brakes work by converting kinetic energy into heat through the creation of friction between the brake pads and the rotors. The continual heating and cooling of brake pads, rotors, and calipers during a race must be controlled in order to extract the optimum performance out of the braking system. Brakes are designed to operate in a certain temperature range. Operating temperatures outside this range will cause lower friction levels and more wear, or both.

Infrared temperature sensors measuring the brake disc temperature (Figure 5.17) can be very useful to help the team control brake cooling requirements, brake balance settings, or even choosing the right brake components for specific conditions.

Figure 5.17 Infrared brake temperature sensors (Courtesy of Texense)

The example in Figure 5.18 shows a lap around Monza in a high-downforce single-seater car. Front left-hand (LH) and right-hand (RH) brake temperatures are measured. This graph clearly shows in what temperature range the brakes are operating and how fast the temperature builds up as the driver hits the brakes. More important, however, are the cooling-down periods after the brake pressure is released. The shape of the downward trace can be influenced by the teams by changing the size of the brake cooling air inlets or blanking of these inlets. In this example there is a difference between LH and RH cooling, which should be investigated. This is not necessarily an aerodynamic problem. The difference is made at lower speed, just when the driver comes off the brakes, so it's probably being caused by friction in the brake system.

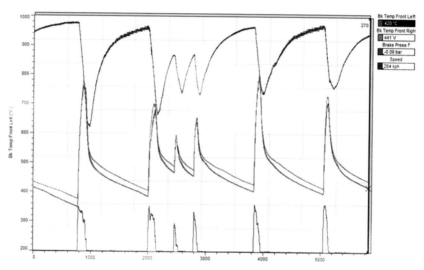

Figure 5.18 Front LH and RH brake disc temperature measurements for a lap around Monza in a high-downforce single seater car

One sensor per wheel is in most cases not necessary, but equipping one front and one rear wheel with IR sensors gives some very interesting information about the braking system.

Figure 5.19 shows brake pressure together with front and rear brake temperatures for a lap around the Brazilian Interlagos track. From the two temperature channels, a temperature brake balance is calculated with the following formula:

$$\text{Brake Temp Balance} = \frac{T\text{brake}_{front}}{T\text{brake}_{front} + T\text{brake}_{rear}} \cdot 100\%$$ (Eq. 5.4)

With $T\text{brake}_{front}$ = Front brake temperature [°C]

$T\text{brake}_{rear}$ = Rear brake temperature [°C]

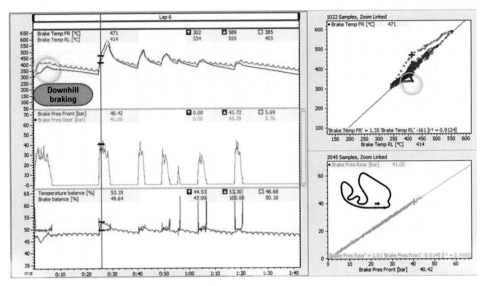

Figure 5.19 Front right and rear left brake temperature for a lap around Interlagos in a Porsche 996 GT2

Brake temperature balance is also graphically illustrated by the scatter plot of front versus rear brake temperatures. For all but the first two braking zones, the temperature balance is around 50%, dropping off a bit during the cooling-down periods (more front brake cooling). This balance goes together with a mechanical brake balance of 50%. Changing this will obviously change the temperature distribution as well.

The first two braking zones are interesting. In the first braking zone (indicated by the yellow circles in Figure 5.19) we can see the rear temperature rising faster than the front, and the temperature balance goes down to 45%. Although we have about 35 bars of front brake pressure, which is similar to the other braking points on the track, the temperatures increase a lot slower than normal. The reason for this is that this braking zone is on a part of the track which goes significantly downhill.

The second braking zone is slightly uphill, which is not a complete explanation of why the temperature balance is more to the front here than normal. This is the hardest braking point on the track with a lot of forward weight transfer. Because of the duration of the braking activity, the front brakes have more time to heat up and will eventually push the temperature balance forward. The shorter braking durations in the following corners make this not possible there.

The relationship between the mechanical brake balance and temperature balance can be illustrated by using lap statistics. Figure 5.20 shows for the duration of a race (the data is taken from the same vehicle as in Figure 5.19) the average values for these two channels lap by lap. There's a clear change in brake balance during the second part of the race, but the temperature balance doesn't follow this instantaneously.

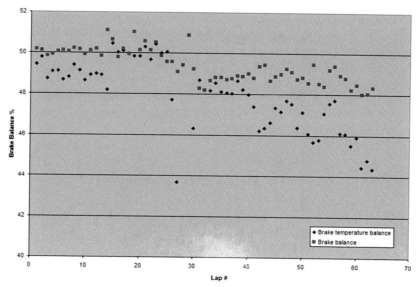

Figure 5.20 Lap-by-lap mechanical and temperature brake balance

Of course the mechanical balance is not the only influential factor on the temperature distribution. It is very probable that at the end of the race the brake wear was to such an extent that the driver had to back off with his braking. Investigating the driver's braking application will clear up what was really happening.

The derivative of the brake temperature signals (Equations 5.5 and 5.5) tells us at which speed temperature is being built up when brake pressure is applied, and how fast this temperature is dissipating in the air after the braking zone.

$$\text{Front Brake Temp Speed} = \frac{d\left(Tbrake_{front}(t)\right)}{dt} \ [\degree C/s] \tag{Eq. 5.5}$$

$$\text{Rear Brake Temp Speed} = \frac{d\left(Tbrake_{rear}(t)\right)}{dt} \ [\degree C/s] \tag{Eq. 5.6}$$

In these channels we can separate the data from when the driver applies the brakes from the data when he's not. The resulting channels (Equations 5.7–5.10) are suitable to extract statistics from that can be displayed in run charts.

$$\text{Front Brake Temp Build-up} = \frac{d\left(Tbrake_{front}(t)\right)}{dt} \cdot \left(PBrake_{FRONT} > 10 \text{ bar}\right) \tag{Eq. 5.7}$$

$$\text{Rear Brake Temp Build-up} = \frac{d\left(Tbrake_{rear}(t)\right)}{dt} \cdot \left(PBrake_{FRONT} > 10 \text{ bar}\right) \tag{Eq. 5.8}$$

$$\text{Front Brake Cooling Speed} = \frac{d\left(Tbrake_{\text{front}}(t)\right)}{dt} \cdot (PBrake_{\text{FRONT}} < 10 \text{ bar}) \qquad \text{(Eq. 5.9)}$$

$$\text{Rear Brake Cooling Speed} = \frac{d\left(Tbrake_{\text{rear}}(t)\right)}{dt} \cdot (PBrake_{\text{FRONT}} < 10 \text{ bar}) \qquad \text{(Eq. 5.10)}$$

Figure 5.21 gives an example of what these channels look like. The brake temperature build-up channels give us the speed at which temperature is created when the brakes are applied. This speed is of course very much dependent of the technique used by the driver, but with consistent driving it's possible to draw conclusions from this channel regarding brake pad compound choices, master cylinder sizes, and so forth.

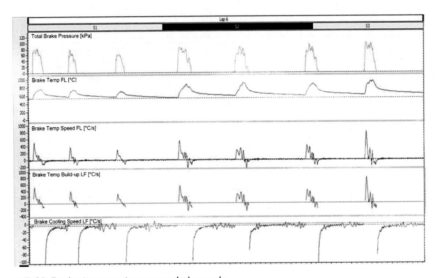

Figure 5.21 Brake temperature speed channels

The brake cooling speed channels give us a measure of how fast the heat resulting from the brakes is being dissipated in the air. When we take the average of this channel per lap, a lower average will mean more effective cooling.

The example in Figure 5.22 shows how useful brake temperature measurements can be to evaluate different brake system components. It shows a number of graphs outlining the differences between two different brake pad compounds on a 1250 kg GT3 car. The graphs were created using the signal of a single front brake temperature sensor.

The big graph on the left shows lap by lap the maximum, minimum, and average brake temperature. The dashed lines represent the data recorded with compound A, the solid lines the compound B data. The two tests were performed by the same driver, and no cooling changes were done during the test. The first apparent observation is that the

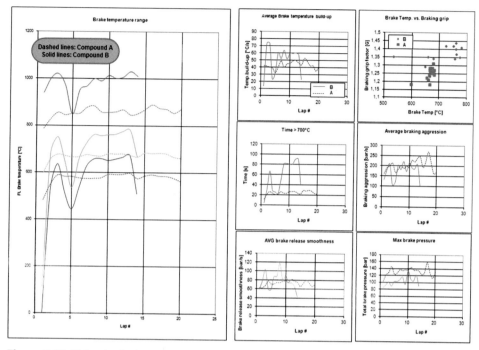

Figure 5.22 Using brake temperature measurements to evaluate the differences between different brake pad compounds

B compound pads have a much larger temperature range, primarily caused by higher maximum temperatures. The drop-off in lap five was caused by a slower lap.

The top middle graph shows the average brake temperature build-up per lap. It shows us that the temperature builds up faster with the B pads, resulting in more initial bite. The graph below gives the time per lap that the temperature is above 700 °C, which was the critical temperature for endurance purposes. Here the A compound seems much more consistent, and the lower temperature peaks are confirmed here. However, the top-right graph indicates that the B pads need a higher temperature to achieve significantly higher friction values than the A pads. The graph below shows that the braking aggression (see chapter 14 for more information on braking aggression) by the driver was more or less the same during the two tests. The lower-left graph indicates how the A pads require more brake pressure to slow down the vehicle. Finally, the lower middle graph compares brake release smoothness (see chapter 14) for the two types of pads. The release smoothness is much more consistent with the A compound, indicating better modulation characteristics for these pads.

Chapter 6
Gearing

The gearbox is a device that allows the engine to operate within its power-band (i.e., the RPM range where the engine delivers the most of its power) for a wide speed range. This is an additional responsibility for the driver, who is already trying to balance the car based on the limits of grip produced by the tires. Data-logging is very useful in evaluating the shifting techniques of the driver and can help with selecting the most efficient gear ratios for any given racetrack.

Analyzing the driver's shifting technique can be broken into two categories: up-shifting (i.e., changing to a higher gear) and down-shifting (i.e., changing to a lower gear).

6.1   Up-shifting

When analyzing logged data, there are two important items with regard to the up-shifting procedure—the shifting point and the duration of the up-shift.

6.1.1   Shifting Point

The shifting point depends on the shape of the engine power curve, more specifically the total area beneath the power curve situated within the engine's operating range.

As an example, take a Formula 3 single-seater car. Table 6.1 gives the gearbox configuration for this car. The speeds are calculated at a shift point of 7000 RPM. In Figure 6.1, the speed versus engine RPM is graphically represented. Figure 6.2 shows the power curve of the engine.

Table 6.1 Gearbox properties of an F3 car, shifting point at 7000 RPM			
	Total gear ratio i_{tot}	Speed at shift RPM [km/h]	RPM drop
1st gear	7.79	98.5	—
2nd gear	5.48	140.1	2079
3rd gear	4.72	162.5	966
4th gear	3.94	195.1	1167
5th gear	3.28	234.0	1167
6th gear	2.95	260.5	713

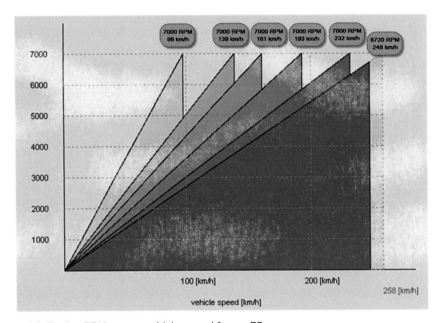

Figure 6.1 Engine RPM versus vehicle speed for an F3 car

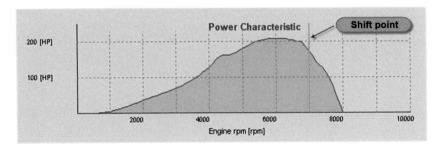

Figure 6.2 Power curve for the example F3 car

Assume one is trying to find the optimum gearshift RPM for third gear. From third to fourth gear, the engine RPM drops approximately 1200. So, with the earlier mentioned shift point of 7000 RPM, the engine picks up in fourth gear at 5800 RPM. Now the area below the power curve between 5800 and 7000 RPM can be calculated. To make this easy, engine power measurements in intervals of 200 RPM are entered in a spreadsheet. These are shown in Table 6.2. By taking the sum of these measurement points in the interval determined previously, a good approximation of the area below the power curve is obtained.

Table 6.2 Power figures for an F3 engine, taken from a dynamometer test	
Engine RPM	Engine Power (HP)
2000	36
2200	42
2400	49
2600	55
2800	63
3000	70
3200	78
3400	88
3600	100
3800	114
4000	128
4200	150
4400	162
4600	162
4800	169
5000	181
5200	191
5400	200
5600	205
5800	207
6000	209
6200	208
6400	205
6600	201
6800	197
7000	172
7200	142
7400	138

Taking the sum of these figures gives us the following:

5800 RPM	207 HP
6000 RPM	209 HP
6200 RPM	208 HP
6400 RPM	205 HP
6600 RPM	201 HP
6800 RPM	197 HP
+ 7000 RPM	172 HP
Total:	1399 HP

To find the right shift RPM for third gear, the interval must be determined that provides as much area as possible under the power curve. In the previous example, the power figure at 7000 RPM is rather low compared to the lower revs. Therefore, it is necessary to change the shift point to 6800 RPM and obtain the following results:

5600 RPM	205 HP
5800 RPM	207 HP
6000 RPM	209 HP
6200 RPM	208 HP
6400 RPM	205 HP
6600 RPM	201 HP
+ 6800 RPM	197 HP
Total:	1432 HP

Repeating this exercise finally gives an optimum shift point at 6500 RPM. In the same way, the required shift point in each gear can be calculated. To illustrate the importance of shifting at the correct engine speed, an acceleration test on a straight line of 1 km is simulated using Bosch's LapSim software package. (See chapter 15 for more information on lap time simulation.) During the first run, the driver shifts at 7000 RPM. During the second run, the shift point is decreased by 500 RPM. The results are given in Figures 6.3 and 6.4.

By decreasing the shift point for all gears by 500 RPM, the elapsed time after 1000 m of straight-line acceleration is 0.12 sec less than before, and the top speed is increased by 6 km/h. In this situation, it is necessary to decrease the shift RPM to increase the area under the engine power curve, but for different engines the opposite also can be true. In this case, ensure that increasing the shift RPM does not affect the reliability of the engine. Get the advice of the engine builder.

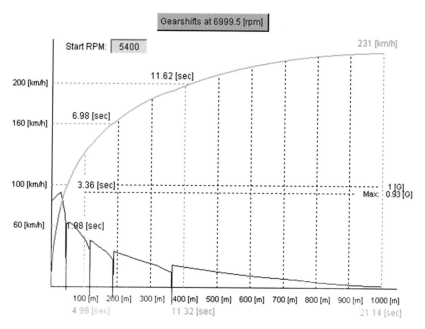

Figure 6.3 Simulation of 1000 m straight-line acceleration, shifting gears at 7000 RPM

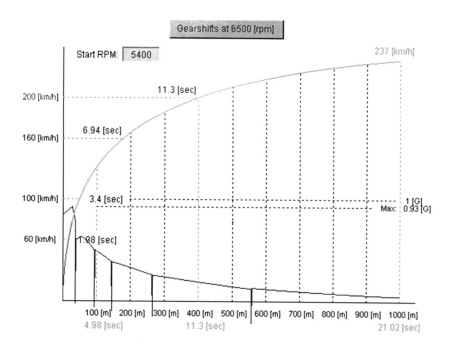

Figure 6.4 Simulation of 1000 m straight-line acceleration, shifting gears at 6500 RPM

We can also use the logged data to evaluate if a driver shifts at the optimal point. In Figure 6.5 two different drivers are shown accelerating down a straight. One of the two clearly shifts consistently higher. At the end of the straight it becomes obvious that the higher shift points are no advantage, as his top speed is 3 km/h slower. Always look at data of different laps, as wind, traffic, and other track conditions can influence the top speed at the end of a straight.

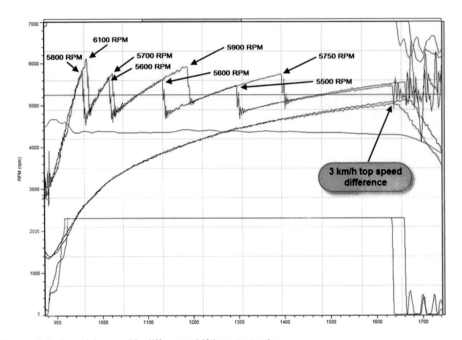

Figure 6.5 Two drivers with different shifting strategies

The longitudinal acceleration trace can confirm if the shift point is chosen properly. During straight-line acceleration the longitudinal acceleration will decrease. The rate at which it decreases depends on the available engine power and the aerodynamic drag. Up-shifts show up in the longitudinal G trace as short, vertical spikes, which we conveniently use to measure gearshift times (see the next section). The longitudinal acceleration at which this spike recovers when the up-shift is finished should be in line with the slope of the longitudinal G trace before the up-shift. If there is an offset in longitudinal G before and after the gearshift, this means that the chosen shift RPM is too low. Figure 6.6 is an example of a correct shift point, and Figure 6.7 shows the effect of a too low shift RPM.

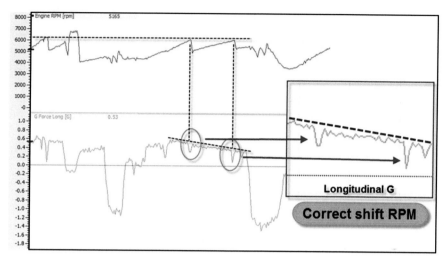

Figure 6.6 Correct shift RPM

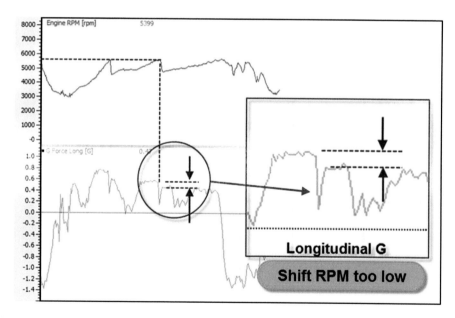

Figure 6.7 Shift RPM too low

6.1.2   Shift Duration

The other important point to note in up-shifting is the shift duration. Because time spent between gears is time when the car is not accelerating, minimizing this shifting time also reduces lap time. The up-shift begins with disengaging the clutch, followed by moving the gear lever to the next gear and engaging the clutch. The input shaft needs to slow down to synchronize with the next gear ratio, which is achieved by backing off the throttle (or cutting the ignition) and depressing the clutch. There is a trade-off between up-shift duration and reliability. Quick shifts increase the wear on dog or synchronization rings but save lap time. Sound judgment is in order here.

Shift time can be determined from the logged data when the longitudinal acceleration of the vehicle is recorded. As discussed previously, shift time is the time when the car is not accelerating. This appears in the longitudinal G graph as a downward dip as shown in Figure 6.8. The shift action begins where the longitudinal force drops off and ends when the car picks up acceleration again. To get an idea about the driver's shifting technique, calculate the shift times during a lap in different gears and calculate the average.

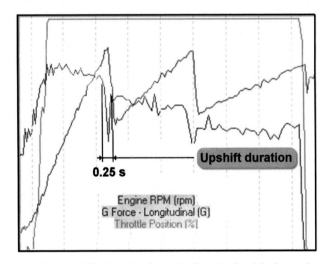

Figure 6.8 Determining up-shift duration from the longitudinal G channel

Determining shift times can help the engineer evaluate the ability of the driver to shift gears quickly, or it indicates if the gearbox is being abused. The latter is important in endurance races, particularly when there is more than one driver in the car. Table 6.3 provides some experience numbers for the up-shift duration. These depend on the driver and on the state and construction of the gearbox and clutch mechanism. Sequential gearboxes and power-shift systems (cutting the engine's ignition triggered by a signal from the gear lever) help minimize shifting time without sacrificing reliability.

To accurately measure shift time, the correct sampling frequency should be selected to log longitudinal acceleration. In Figure 6.9, two different laps by the same car are examined. From the trace logged at 10Hz, the time it takes the driver to change gears cannot be determined accurately. The reading of 10 Hz means there is a sensor reading every one-tenth of a second. Given the values in Table 6.3, this is clearly not accurate

Table 6.3 Typical shift times for various racecars	
Vehicle	Up-shift duration
F3 car	0.15 sec
Porsche 911 GT2 Turbo, synchronized H-pattern gearbox	0.35 sec
Dodge Viper GTS-R, synchronized H-pattern gearbox	0.32 sec
Dodge Viper GTS-R, sequential gearbox, no power-shift	0.23 sec
Dodge Viper GTS-R, sequential gearbox, with power-shift	0.18 sec
LMP1 Prototype, sequential gearbox, electronic paddle-shift	0.10 sec

enough. The 50-Hz line gives a reading every 0.02 sec. In this line, the downward spikes produced by up-shifts are seen clearly.

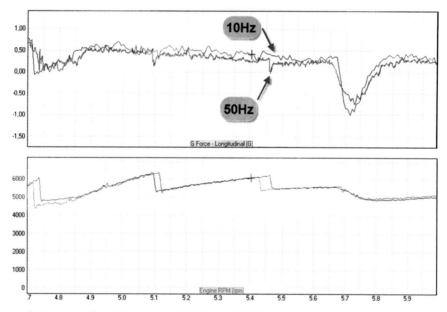

Figure 6.9 Longitudinal G sampled at 10 Hz and 50 Hz

6.2   Down-shifting

Up-shifting and down-shifting require synchronizing the engine speed with that of the transmission input speed. With up-shifting, the engine passively synchronizes RPM because it slows down as the clutch disengages. This is not the case when down-shifting because the engine needs to spin faster when it engages the lower gear. *Blipping* the throttle (Figure 6.10) as the transmission passes through neutral achieves this. When the engine is not sped up by the driver, it is by the driveline when the clutch is re-engaged, which upsets tire adhesion of a car cornering near the limit.

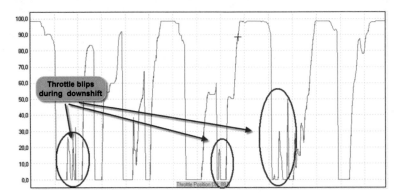

Figure 6.10 Throttle blips during down-shifting to synchronize engine and transmission input shaft RPM

Down-shifting inevitably is connected to braking, and the driver should ensure that engine and transmission RPM are synchronized properly. Failing to do so could result in snap oversteer, which is not desirable, especially when the driver is trail braking. How much blipping is necessary? Too little blipping upsets the grip at the driven wheels, while too much blipping over-revs the engine.

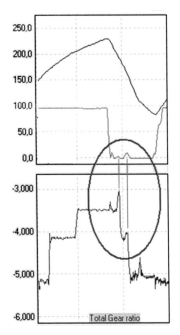

Figure 6.11 Blipping the throttle insufficiently during down-shifts shows up in the gear ratio graph as upward spikes

An example of too little throttle blipping is given in Figure 6.11. The driver actuates the throttle on down-shift to a maximum 10% throttle position. The engine RPM is raised less than necessary, which is illustrated by the upward spikes in the total gear ratio channel. How to create this channel is covered fully in the next section, but for now it is sufficient to know it defines the ratio between the speed of the driven wheels and engine RPM. Ideally, when engine and transmission input shaft revs are equal, this channel shows the actual gear ratio. If during the down-shift the engine RPM is too low when the lower gear is engaged, the transmission speeds up the engine and the gear channel momentarily increases.

Most engine over-revs occur during down-shifting and usually are due to two reasons: shifting down too quickly from a too-high engine RPM and excessive throttle blipping. The trace in Figure 6.12 illustrates a guaranteed way to destroy an engine!

6.3 The Gear Chart

The relationship between engine speed and wheel speed is linear under normal circumstances. This linearity is indicated by the total gear ratio. A common display format for gear ratios is the gear chart pictured in Figure 6.1. This chart displays the relationship between speed and engine RPM for each gear.

With the analysis software, it is possible to create an *X-Y* plot similar to the gear chart. Figure 6.13 provides an example of this. It concerns a car with a six-speed sequential gearbox. Only data points recorded during acceleration (longitudinal acceleration > 0) are plotted in the graph to determine from which minimum RPM the driver accelerated the engine.

The first conclusion apparent from this graph is that only five of six gears are used. No sections on the track require first gear to be used. Third gear is used the most, as indicated by the density of data points for this gear.

The maximum shift RPM for each gear is easily recognizable. In all gears, RPM ranges are detected that are well within the speed range for a lower gear. Here the driver

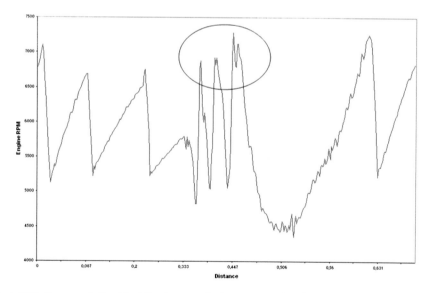

Figure 6.12 Too much throttle blipping results in over-revving the engine, as demonstrated here by an unnamed driver in a Porsche 996 around Circuit Zolder

probably is trying to use the best of the engine's torque band. Note that the engine of the car in this example has a maximum torque output of approximately 800 Nm.

Also worth noting is the scatter of data points. Theoretically, every RPM corresponds to a predetermined vehicle speed in each gear. Therefore, all the data points should fall exactly on the straight lines plotted in Figure 6.13. The deviation from the line is greatest in the lower gear, especially in the lower rev ranges. The probable cause is wheel spin upon acceleration, but the mounting location of the wheel-speed sensor also could be an influence. A sensor mounted on the left-front wheel records a speed greater than the right-front wheel in a right-hand corner, and vice versa. When both non-driven wheels have a wheel-speed signal, the average of the two can be calculated and used as the x-axis in the gear chart to remove this effect, although this probably would not provide much additional information.

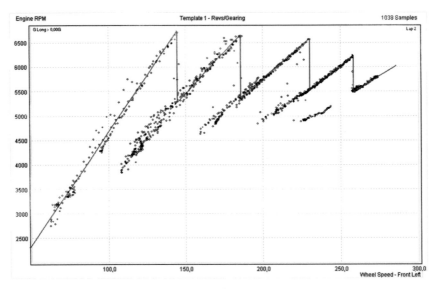

Figure 6.13 Wheel speed versus engine RPM plot

6.4   Total Gear Ratio Channel

The total gear ratio channel was used earlier in this chapter to evaluate the driver's down-shifting technique. It is a mathematical channel that expresses the relationship between engine RPM and vehicle speed. In any gear, this relationship is a constant. The graph looks like a stepped line, conveniently displaying which gear was used at any part of the track.

Vehicle speed relates to engine RPM, according to Equation 6.1.

$$V = \frac{2 \cdot \pi \cdot r_{rolling} \cdot n_{engine}}{i_{total}}$$ (Eq. 6.1)

Where V = Vehicle speed

$r_{rolling}$ = Rolling tire radius

n_{engine} = Engine RPM

i_{total} = total gear ratio

Vehicle speed and engine RPM are logged channels, so Equation 6.2 is for i_{total}.

$$i_{total} = \frac{2 \cdot \pi \cdot r_{rolling} \cdot n_{engine}}{V}$$ (Eq. 6.2)

Finally, if km/h is converted to m/s and RPM to revs/sec, the result becomes Equation 6.3.

$$i_{total} = 0.377 \cdot \frac{r_{rolling} \cdot n_{engine}}{V}$$ (Eq. 6.3)

Graphically, the mathematical channel looks like the lower trace in Figure 6.14. Note that Equation 6.3 was multiplied by –1 so that when a higher gear is used the line steps up, and vice versa. The upper trace was obtained from a gear position sensor in the sequential gearbox. To detect which gear the driver is using, this trace is obviously clearer. However, the mathematical channel also indicates anomalies such as wheel spin, wheel lockup under braking, and insufficient throttle blipping on down-shifts.

The total gear ratio channel also may be used in other mathematical channels requiring this input. To decrease the deviation from the actual gear ratio, it is also possible to use the average wheel speed of two or more wheels when multiple sensors are present.

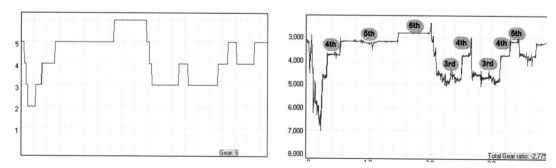

Figure 6.14 Gear position channel from sequential gearbox and calculated gear ratios from vehicle speed and engine RPM

6.5   Determining Correct Gear Ratios

Given the large amount of literature available, the subject of selecting the proper gear ratios is not covered in this book. Author Paul Van Valkenburg describes this subject excellently [6-1]. Begin by finding the optimum engine RPM in top gear and optimum shift points in the intermediate gears, as discussed in the first paragraph of this chapter. Select the top gear for the longest straight on the track and the intermediate gears for the corners and most efficient acceleration.

To select the proper gear ratio for a corner exit, first find the engine RPM in each gear where maximum longitudinal acceleration occurs, as pictured in Figure 6.15. Following that, find the RPM in the corner exit phase where the car accepts full throttle. This should be slightly below the revs for maximum acceleration. If not, correct this by selecting a different gear ratio.

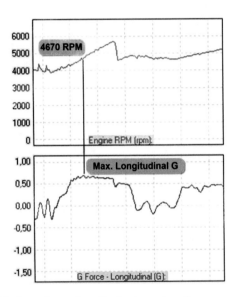

Figure 6.15 Engine RPM at maximum longitudinal acceleration

Handling problems move the point where the car accepts full throttle farther down the corner exit. Do not try to select gear ratios for a corner exit when the chassis is not balanced. Also be aware that the optimal gear for one corner may not be optimal for another. Investigate all corners leading onto a significant straight because this is where significant time can be gained.

6.6   Determining in Which Gear to Take a Corner

An often occurring discussion between driver and engineer is about in which gear it's best to take a corner. Sometimes after driving, the driver might have the question if it would have been better to take a certain corner in a higher or lower gear. If the configuration of the drive train is known, the total gear ratio channel can be modified to give us the theoretical engine RPM for a certain cornering speed in each gear. To do this, Equation 6.3 can be rearranged to Equation 6.4:

$$n_{engine} = 2.653 \cdot \frac{i_{total} \cdot V}{r_{rolling}}$$

(Eq. 6.4)

In this expression V is in km/h and $r_{rolling}$ in m.

When from this equation a math channel is created for each gear ratio, the result visualized in an X-Y plot gives us the gear chart as discussed earlier in this chapter (see Figure 6.16). The dashed lines in Figure 6.16 give us the theoretical engine RPM as a function of vehicle speed. Figure 6.17 shows the result of these channels in a distance plot for a lap around Spa-Francorchamps in a GT car.

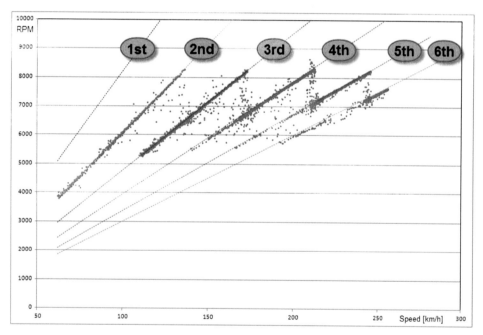

Figure 6.16 Engine RPM versus vehicle speed

To evaluate the effect of taking a corner in a different gear, these channels can now be used to have an idea about what the engine RPM will be in this different gear. Of course this method is not 100% accurate, as a different gear will produce different levels of forward acceleration which will move the locations where the driver shifts to a higher gear slightly forward or backward. But still it is an easy way to visualize and conclude quickly if it makes sense to try the specific corner in a different gear. Figure 6.18 shows a

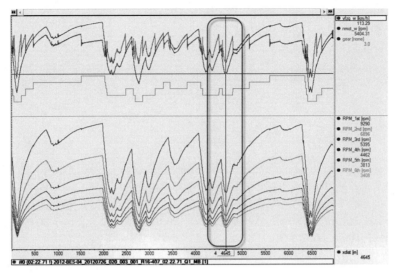

Figure 6.17 Theoretical engine RPM math channels

zoom of the area indicated by the rectangle in Figure 6.17. This specific corner is taken by the driver in third gear. The cornering speed is 113 km/h, and this corresponds in third gear with an engine speed of 5390 RPM. Assuming equal cornering speed the engine speed would be 6890 RPM in second gear or 4460 RPM in fourth. The best solution obviously depends on the shape of the engine's torque curve, but the shift of location where the driver changes to another gear also plays a role in this decision.

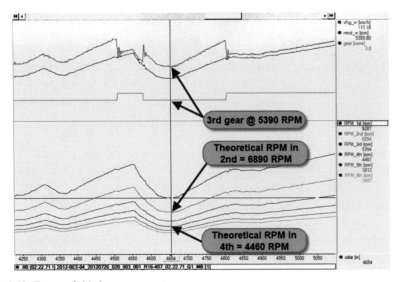

Figure 6.18 Zoom of third gear corner

Chapter 7
Cornering

Except for drag racers, all race cars negotiate corners, and the ability to do so as fast as possible minimizes lap time. This chapter covers the physics involved in cornering and how the cornering capability of a race car can be investigated using data from the logging system.

7.1   The Cornering Sequence

The car–driver combination goes through various phases when taking a corner. The cornering process basically consists of the following phases:

1. **Braking Point to Initial Turn-in Point**
   The straight-line braking phase forms an integral part of the cornering sequence because the point where the driver hits the brakes determines the location of the turn-in point and entry speed.

2. **Turn-in Point to Corner's Apex**
   The driver is usually still braking after the turn-in point (i.e., trail braking). This period is followed by a short neutral throttle period where the driver tries to carry the speed through the corner. This is not necessarily a coasting period, and it can be very short to no time at all in duration.

3. **Corner Exit**
   This phase begins when the driver goes hard on the throttle and exits the corner onto the following straight.

Figure 7.1 illustrates the different events taking place during cornering with the driver activity channels (throttle, brake pedal position, and steering wheel). These events are discussed in more detail in chapter 14 to analyze the racing line. For now, it is sufficient to show what the driver experiences when negotiating a corner.

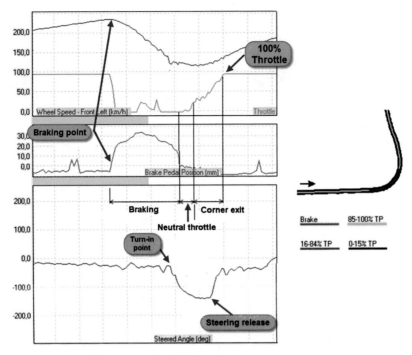

Figure 7.1 Driver activity pattern for a left-hand corner

For a car to get around a corner, a lateral force must exist to keep the car on the track. This force (or grip) comes from the car's tires and is twofold. The thread surface of the tire grips with the surface irregularities of the track, but there is also a molecular adhesion between both surfaces. For this reason, Newton's laws of friction do not apply for racing tires. Tires can develop more lateral force than the vertical load acting on them.

For a vehicle to change direction, all the tires assume a slip angle. This angle exists because of the resisting moment due to the elastic friction between the tire and road surface that develops when the tire is turned. Put simply, the slip angle is the difference between the direction the wheel is pointing and where it is heading.

From a physical point of view, this is what happens when a car develops lateral grip:

- On the straight preceding the corner that the driver wants to tackle, the steering wheel angle is fluctuating around zero, and all tires have a very small slip angle approximately equal to their toe setting. There is no lateral acceleration.

- At the turn-in point, the driver turns the steering wheel, effectively inducing a slip angle to the front tires. The front tires develop a lateral force.

- This front lateral force causes a yaw moment around the vehicle's center of gravity, which in turn induces a rear slip angle and, therefore, rear grip.

When the car develops the necessary lateral grip to get it through the corner, all four tires assume a certain degree of slip angle. The amount of slip angle for each wheel determines the lateral force that each tire develops. Figure 7.2 is a plot showing the lateral force versus the slip angle of a given tire exposed to a given vertical load. Three regions can be distinguished from this graph:

- The first is a linear, or elastic, range in which the developed lateral force is proportional to the amount of slip angle. The lateral force comes from the deformation in the thread surface (i.e., the tire's cornering stiffness).

- The second region is a transition range in which the relationship between the slip angle and lateral force is no longer linear. Here, the rear portion of the tire footprint begins to slide laterally along the ground.

- Third, after the maximum lateral force is reached, an increase in slip angle does not continue to result in a higher lateral force. This area is the frictional range because from this point the lateral force is merely a result of friction between the tire and the road surface.

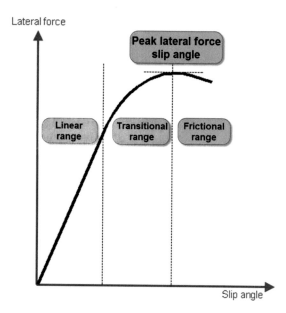

Figure 7.2 Lateral force versus slip angle

The vehicle's balance is determined by how much lateral force one end of the vehicle develops in comparison to the other end as well as which end of the vehicle reaches the tires' maximum lateral force first. An investigation using information from the vehicle's data acquisition system occurs in the following sections.

7.2   The Traction Circle

In Figure 7.3, longitudinal and lateral acceleration data is pictured of a car negotiating a series of corners. Four different points are indicated in the graph. At point 1 we can see that the longitudinal acceleration is negative while lateral G is at zero. This means that the car is braking in a straight line. At point 2 the longitudinal deceleration is still more or less the same, but the car has started to build up lateral Gs. At this point the driver is braking into the corner. Maximum lateral acceleration is reached at point 3, and here the longitudinal deceleration is reduced to almost zero Gs. Point 4 shows the car accelerating out of the corner, which is indicated with positive longitudinal acceleration and decreasing lateral Gs.

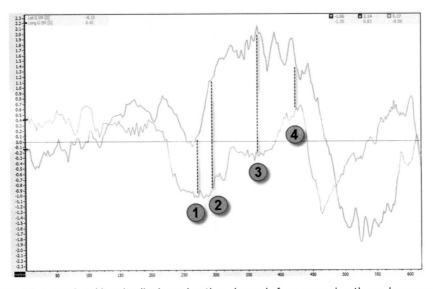

Figure 7.3 Lateral and longitudinal acceleration channels for a car going through a corner

Table 7.1 notes for all four points the respective lateral and longitudinal acceleration. When we chart these points in an *X-Y* plot, we get the result in Figure 7.4.

Table 7.1 Lateral and longitudinal acceleration figures at point 1 to 4 in Figure 7.3				
	1	2	3	4
Lateral acceleration	0.08 G	1.19 G	2.13 G	1.50 G
Longitudinal acceleration	−1.02 G	−0.79 G	−0.26 G	0.57 G

Let's go through this particular corner again using the four points in Figure 7.4. At point 1 the car was braking in a straight line. There's little to no lateral acceleration, only negative longitudinal acceleration. The arrow between the chart origin and point 1 is nearly vertical. At point 2 there's a bit less longitudinal but some amount of positive lateral acceleration. The arrow has been rotated counterclockwise around the chart

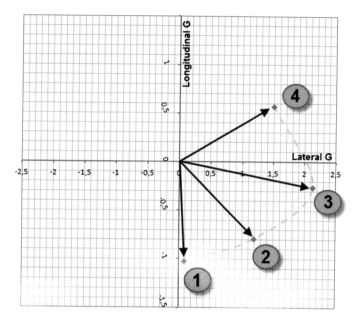

Figure 7.4 X-Y plot of acceleration data

origin. At point 3 the arrow is nearly horizontal, indicating a pure cornering phase, which is followed by an acceleration phase out of the corner.

Now, let's take every single data point for a full lap around a circuit and plot the results in an X-Y chart. An example of such a chart for a lap around the French Nogaro circuit is given in Figure 7.5 and is known as the "traction circle." A racing tire can develop approximately equal power in acceleration, braking, and cornering. Plotting the maximum forces that a tire can develop in each direction gives the traction circle of the tire. Most data acquisition packages feature an X-Y graph of lateral versus longitudinal acceleration, which is essentially the traction circle, or "g-g" diagram, for the entire vehicle. This graph represents the cornering power of the vehicle.

As we are looking here at the acceleration data of a vehicle, this graph is a representation of the total grip being developed by the four tires. The friction circle is a way of thinking about not only the grip that a vehicle can develop under given conditions but also how this grip is being utilized by the driver. The positive side of the Y-axis indicates that the vehicle is accelerating; the negative side means that it's braking. The negative X-axis means that the car is cornering to the right and vice versa. The area covered by the data points represents the acceleration envelope of the vehicle. For the traction circle to be read as illustrated in Figure 7.5, the axis system for lateral and longitudinal acceleration that was presented in chapter 3 must be adhered to.

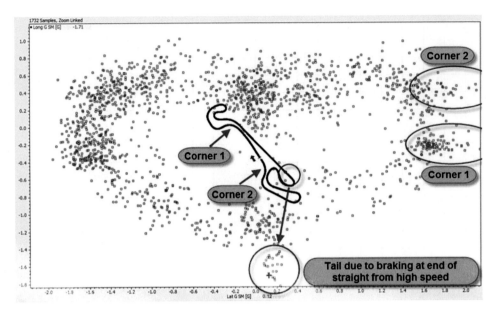

Figure 7.5 Traction circle of a lap around Nogaro

A tire's maximum grip in any direction depends on the vertical load to which it is being subjected. This implies that the size of the traction circle is not constant. In a high-down-force corner, the circle's diameter is larger than in a slow corner.

First observation from Figure 7.5 is the fact that this friction circle is not in fact circular but resembles more an ellipse. This has to do with the positive longitudinal acceleration being limited by engine power and aerodynamic drag. This last parameter (drag) helps to slow down the vehicle under braking, so therefore the longitudinal deceleration will always be larger than the acceleration.

The track map in the center of the chart has a long straight, at the end of which the top speed will be considerable, and therefore also the aerodynamic drag. When the driver brakes, the drag will help him decelerate the vehicle, which results in the small "tail" in the friction circle.

We also observe that in left-hand cornering the maximum lateral acceleration is higher than for right-hand cornering. This is because the two high-speed corners where more lateral acceleration is achieved due to aerodynamic downforce are to the left.

Friction circle diagrams are useful to evaluate if drivers are using the full grip potential of the vehicle. In the following example we look at the friction circle for two drivers going through a chicane.

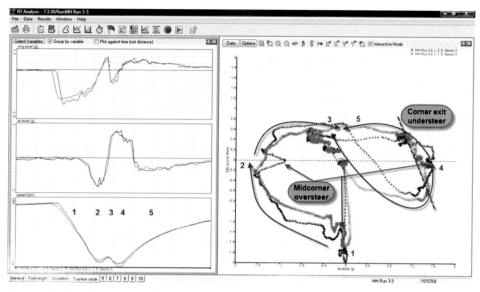

Figure 7.6 Traction circles of two drivers going through a chicane

Let's go through the diagram in Figure 7.6 and look at the differences between the two drivers. First observation is the later braking point for the driver that produced the black traces. He's also braking harder; witness the higher braking Gs (Point 1). The driver in black peaks at −2 G while the red one only reaches 1.65 G, which is a considerable difference. Before there's any cornering, both drivers shed about 0.4 G of longitudinal deceleration as speed, and therefore downforce disappears after which lateral Gs start to build up. On the transition between braking and cornering (between point 1 and 2), the friction circle radius is larger for the black trace.

At point 2 where the cars are in steady-state cornering, we see the driver in black lose about 0.4 G of lateral acceleration. This is an indication of oversteer, as we'll see later in this chapter. The red driver is cornering at about 1.6 G and keeps a higher cornering speed in the first part of the chicane.

There's a short space between the first and second part of the chicane where the drivers are shortly accelerating again (between points 2 and 3). Black is accelerating harder, and as lateral acceleration is now changing to the opposite direction, he is losing less speed. He then builds up a higher steady-state lateral acceleration (point 4), accompanied with some oversteer (although less than in the first part of the chicane). The red driver on the other hand peaks laterally only slightly less than the black driver, but he does this at a longitudinal deceleration of −0.8 G. From that point the lateral Gs decrease progressively as the car goes from deceleration to forward acceleration (indicated with the purple, dashed line). This is a typical corner exit understeer indication.

The last example (Figure 7.7) shows the friction circle for the same car on four different tracks. Every diagram contains data from the fastest lap performed during qualifying sessions on each specific track. The friction diagram is a good tool for the engineer to get an idea about the general direction of the car setup. The highest accelerations seen in the diagram give a rough idea about the importance of aerodynamic downforce. The density of the point cloud in every quadrant can give the engineer an indication about the effectiveness of asymmetric geometry settings or if either braking or accelerating out of a corner is more important. For the Adria track, for instance, setup changes that affect acceleration out of a right-hand corner (longitudinal G positive, lateral G negative) would make more sense than changes affecting the handling of the car in any of the other three quadrants. The points cloud has the highest density in quadrant one (upper left), indicating that this is where the car spends most of its time.

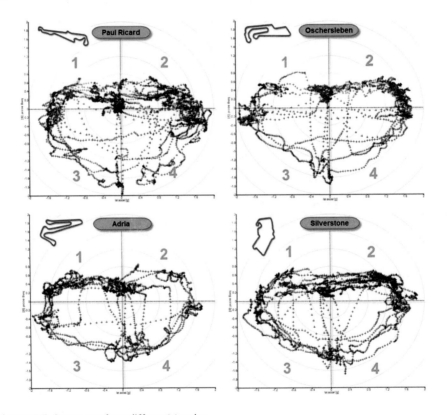

Figure 7.7 Same car, four different tracks

Consider a random point in the traction circle diagram. For this point we can calculate the length of the vector from the chart origin to the coordinate defined by the instantaneous lateral and longitudinal acceleration (see Figure 7.8). The vector sum of these two components is named combined acceleration and can be calculated using Equation 7.1.

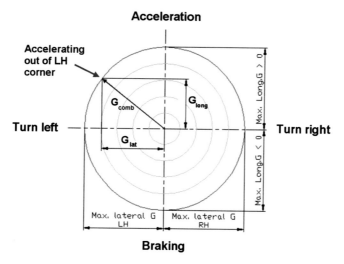

Figure 7.8 The vector sum of lateral and longitudinal acceleration gives us the combined acceleration of the vehicle

$$G_{comb} = \sqrt{G_{lat}^2 + G_{long}^2} \qquad \text{(Eq. 7.1)}$$

For a point on the friction circle with a lateral acceleration of 1.10 G and a longitudinal acceleration of 0.61 G, this means that the combined acceleration equals 1.25 G. Combined acceleration can be calculated by the software as a math channel and plotted on a time or distance graph. This graph can be particularly useful for analyzing the car's cornering potential during transient phases. It basically represents the radius of the vehicle's instantaneous traction circle. Figure 7.9 shows an example of the combined acceleration

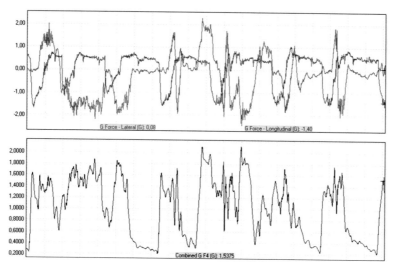

Figure 7.9 Combined acceleration

channel for a complete lap. The traction circle and combined G are good working tools for investigating the cornering potential of a race car. Because these tools illustrate the transient phases of the cornering sequence very well, they also can be applied for driver performance analysis. In chapter 8 a very simple method will be discussed, where the combined acceleration math channel is used to evaluate the grip developed by the tires.

7.3   Effects of Speed

As mentioned in the previous paragraph, the vehicle's traction circle radius is not constant. It varies with the total vertical load acting on the car's center of gravity. The most important parameter here is aerodynamic download, which is speed dependent. Therefore, a relationship exists between the vehicle's speed and its acceleration potential, both in a longitudinal and lateral sense.

Aerodynamic downforce increases proportional to the square of speed, resulting in greater cornering and braking potential. Drag has the same relationship to speed, so the more speed increases, the less power remains to accelerate the vehicle.

In the following illustrations, traction circles for different speed intervals in a single lap are pictured (Figures 7.10, 7.11, 7.12, and 7.13). Speed effects also can be illustrated by plotting longitudinal and lateral acceleration against vehicle speed. Figures 7.14 and 7.15 show this representation for the same data as in the separate friction diagrams. Figure 7.16 shows lateral acceleration versus vehicle speed for a late 1990s Formula One car.

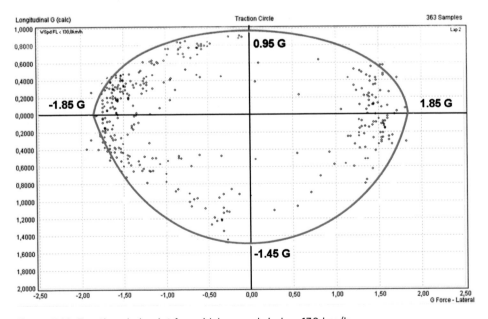

Figure 7.10 Traction circle plot for vehicle speeds below 130 km/h

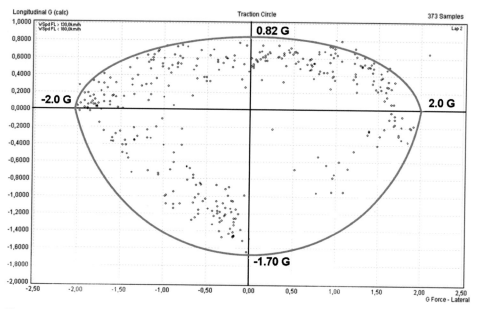

Figure 7.11 Traction circle plot for vehicle speeds between 130 and 180 km/h

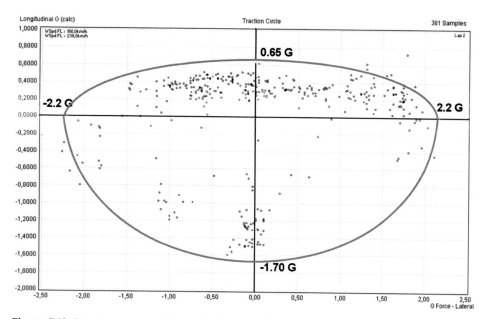

Figure 7.12 Traction circle plot for vehicle speeds between 180 and 230 km/h

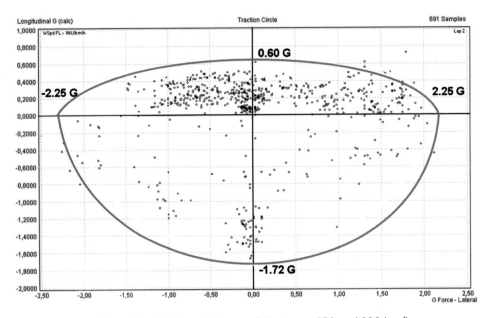

Figure 7.13 Traction circle plot for vehicle speeds between 230 and 280 km/h

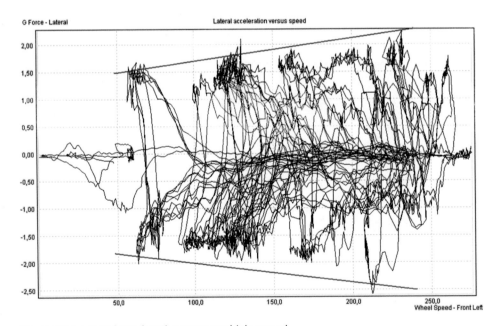

Figure 7.14 Lateral acceleration versus vehicle speed

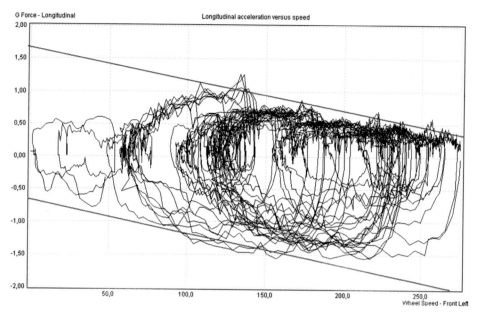

Figure 7.15 Longitudinal acceleration versus vehicle speed

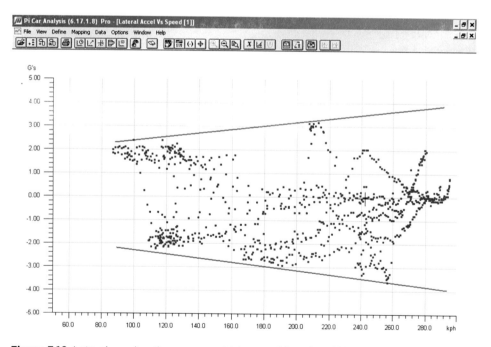

Figure 7.16 Lateral acceleration versus vehicle speed for a late 1990s F1 car during a lap around Silverstone Circuit

7.4   Driver Activities That Indicate Vehicle Balance

Vehicle balance is commonly described by the terms understeer, neutral steer, and oversteer. In a simple world, understeer causes the vehicle to "push" its front tires to the outside of the corner, whereas oversteer causes the rear axle to break out. Neutral steer is the situation where neither understeer nor oversteer are present. A more mathematical and correct definition follows later in this chapter.

The most common way to analyze cornering balance is to look at the input the vehicle acquires from the driver as a reaction to a handling problem. Steering movement and pedal activities can reveal much about the handling of the car. Steering angle, throttle position, and lateral acceleration are the channels to watch.

7.4.1   Oversteer

The driver counters oversteer by reducing the steering angle. If the oversteer is severe, this even may result in opposite lock, as demonstrated in Figure 7.17. The vehicle concerned was obviously suffering from diabolical oversteer through the complete cornering sequence. The driver desperately tries to correct the rear stepping-out by jerking

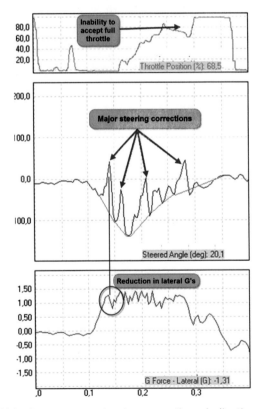

Figure 7.17 This vehicle demonstrates steering corrections, indicating severe oversteer

the steering wheel in the other direction. The gray line in the steering graph indicates approximately how the steering movement should have been addressed.

Steering corrections for oversteer very often are accompanied by little dips in the lateral G graph, parallel to the steering wheel movement. In general, lateral acceleration levels are lower than expected. Oversteer creates a rough lateral G graph as the car loses and regains grip. Variations smaller than 0.25 G and of a shorter duration than 0.3 sec are caused by irregularities in the track surface. Lateral G variations due to oversteer are confirmed in the steering angle graph.

Another oversteer indicator is when the vehicle is not willing to accept full throttle. In this example, the driver waits until the corner is completed before applying full throttle to avoid the rear stepping out.

7.4.2 Understeer

Understeer is a little more difficult to diagnose. Characteristic to understeer is the excessive steering angle. When on corner entry the steering angle gradually keeps increasing, we're dealing with understeer. In this case the steering angle will often peak before the lateral G trace. Mid-corner and corner exit understeer generally shows a gradual decrease in the lateral G trace, while steering angle increases. In this case maximum lateral acceleration will peak before the maximum steering angle. Typical of mid-corner and corner exit understeer is the reluctance of the car to accept full throttle.

Figure 7.18 shows the speed, throttle, steering angle, and lateral and longitudinal acceleration for a car traveling through a corner. Although there is a quite big steering correction at the moment that lateral acceleration starts to build up, after this the steering

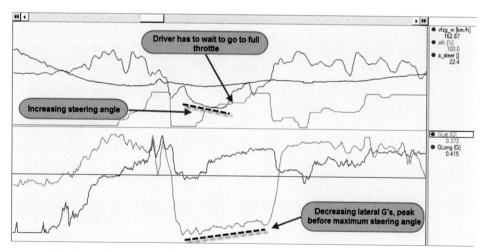

Figure 7.18 Typical understeer indicators

angle shows a gradual increase. At the same time lateral Gs decrease almost linearly. At corner exit, the driver has to wait quite long before he can go to full throttle.

Figure 7.19 shows a car going through a sharp left-hand corner. The driver turns into the corner, but the initial steering angle doesn't suffice to keep the car on its intended path. The driver has to gradually apply more steering angle. At the moment where he starts to go on the throttle again, the car regains front grip and the rear suddenly steps out. This is countered by the driver by applying opposite steering lock.

In Figure 7.20 we see speed and acceleration data of a car going through a right-hand corner. The acceleration data is also plotted in a traction circle diagram. Steering data was not available, but the traction circle gives a good idea about what's happening. The

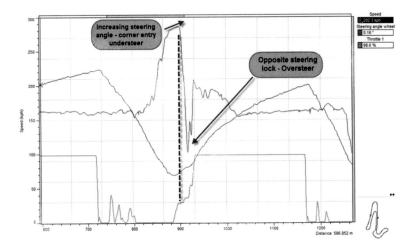

Figure 7.19 Corner entry understeer, corner exit oversteer

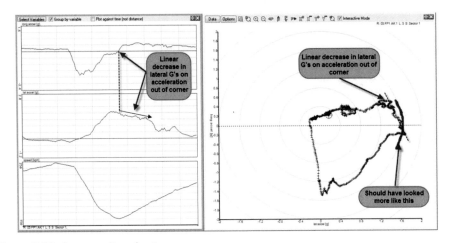

Figure 7.20 Corner exit understeer

lateral G peak is reached just before the moment where the driver releases the brakes (longitudinal Gs still negative). As the driver tries to accelerate again we can see the lateral Gs gradually decrease from this point onwards. There are no sudden losses of lateral acceleration. This tells us that this car is understeering at corner exit.

Figure 7.21 illustrates how mid-corner oversteer shows up on the traction circle diagram. On the lateral G axis we can observe some dents in the traction circle that are caused by the sudden losses in lateral acceleration typical for oversteer (see the red arrows in the distance chart) as the car looses and regains grip.

Finally, Figure 7.22 is an example of two completely different ways to get through a right-hand corner. The driver that produced the red traces obviously suffered from terrible

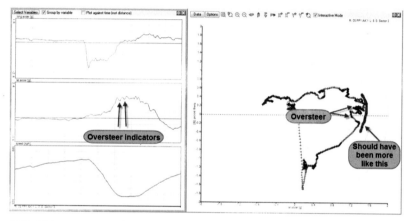

Figure 7.21 Mid-corner oversteer

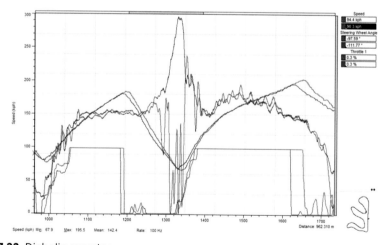

Figure 7.22 Diabolic oversteer

oversteer. Would the blue data not have been overlaid we could have thought that we were dealing with a left-hand corner.

7.5 The Understeer Angle

Figure 7.23 shows the bicycle model of a vehicle during cornering. The bicycle model is a mathematical model of the vehicle in which the track width is considered to be zero. It assumes a steady-state cornering situation where the vehicle takes a constant radius corner at very low speed. The steering angle is small, and front and rear slip angles are zero. R is the corner's turning radius and WB the wheelbase of the vehicle. When traveling at low speed and influences due to accelerations are negligible, the steering angle required to negotiate this corner δ_{Acker} is defined by Equation 7.2.

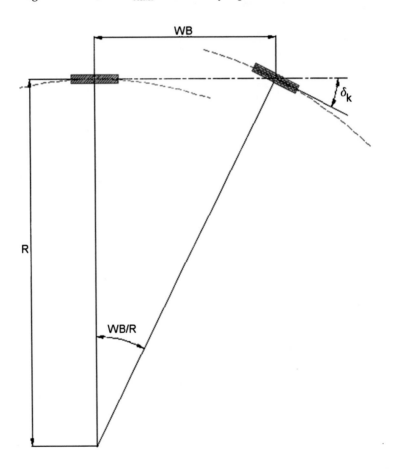

Figure 7.23 The relationship between corner radius, wheelbase, and Ackermann steering angle

$$\delta_{Acker} = \frac{WB}{R}$$

(Eq. 7.2)

This angle is called the kinematic steering angle, or Ackermann steering angle (not to be confused with Ackermann steering).

As speed increases, the tires develop a slip angle, and the difference between the front and rear slip angle determines the balance of the car. This affects the required steering angle for steady-state cornering.

SAE J670 [3-2] defines neutral steer, understeer, and oversteer as follows:

- Neutral steer: A vehicle is neutral steer at a given trim if the ratio of the steering wheel angle gradient to the overall steering ratio equals the Ackermann steering gradient.

- Understeer: A vehicle is understeer at a given trim if the ratio of the steering wheel angle gradient to the overall steering ratio is greater than the Ackermann steering gradient.

- Oversteer: A vehicle is oversteer at a given trim if the ratio of the steering wheel angle gradient to the overall steering ratio is smaller than the Ackermann steering gradient.

By this definition, the steering wheel angle gradient is the rate of change in the steering wheel angle with respect to change in steady-state lateral acceleration. The Ackermann steering gradient is the rate of change in the Ackermann steer angle with respect to change in steady-state lateral acceleration.

The overall steering ratio is the ratio between steering wheel angle and the angle of the steered wheels.

Authors Milliken and Milliken [4-2] give the following definitions for neutral steer, understeer, and oversteer:

- Neutral Steer: Steered angle = Ackermann steering angle
- Understeer: Steered angle > Ackermann steering angle
- Oversteer: Steered angle < Ackermann steering angle

An understeer angle (δ_u) can be defined as the deviation from the Ackermann steering angle needed to follow the vehicle's intended path.

$$\delta_u = \delta - \delta_{Acker}$$

(Eq. 7.3)

157

In this equation, δ is the actual steering angle of the front outside wheel. Cornering radius is determined by Equation 7.4.

$$R = \frac{V^2}{G_{lat}} \qquad \text{(Eq. 7.4)}$$

In this equation, V is the vehicle speed and G_{lat} is the car's lateral acceleration. Substituting this in the equation of Ackermann steering angle gives us Equation 7.5.

$$\delta_{Acker} = \frac{WB \cdot G_{lat}}{V^2} \qquad \text{(Eq. 7.5)}$$

Finally, this results in the formula to calculate the understeer angle (Equation 7.6).

$$\delta_u = \delta - \frac{WB \cdot G_{lat}}{V^2} \qquad \text{(Eq. 7.6)}$$

A very important point to remember here is that the definition for neutral steer, understeer, and oversteer is valid only in the linear operating range of the tires and under steady-state conditions. If the equations are applied in the nonlinear operating range of the tires, their mathematical validity is lost. However, graphically represented, they can serve quite well for comparing different vehicle configurations, as will be illustrated by some examples.

The relationship between the steering wheel angle and the front wheels of the car must be determined first to create the necessary mathematical channels in the analysis software. This is best achieved with the car on turn plates from which the wheel angle can be read. A table can be created with different steering wheel angle values and the corresponding wheel angles. Always take the reading from the wheel on the outside of the corner. This table can be entered into a spreadsheet to determine a mathematical expression of wheel angle as a function of steering wheel angle (Figure 7.24), which then can be used as a mathematical channel to define δ. Depending on the vehicle's steering geometry, this can be a complex equation.

Figure 7.24 shows a steering angle measurement performed on a Corvette C5R GT1 race car. The plotted characteristic is nearly linear and can be approximated by Equation 7.7.

$$\delta = 0.4262 \cdot \delta_{SW} \qquad \text{(Eq. 7.7)}$$

In this equation, δ_{SW} is the logged steering wheel angle in degrees. The next step is to create a math channel for the Ackermann steering angle. Considering that the wheelbase

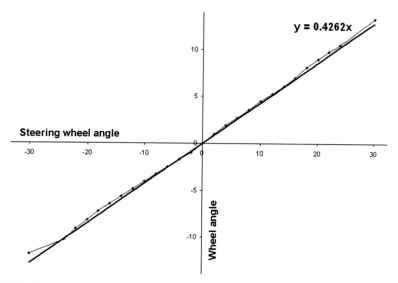

Figure 7.24 Steering wheel angle against outside corner wheel angle

of the Corvette is 2.65 m, lateral acceleration is expressed in *Gs* and vehicle speed is in km/h, the channel becomes Equation 7.8.

$$\delta_{\text{Acker}} = \left(\frac{G_{\text{lat}} \cdot 9.81}{V^2 \cdot 0.077} \cdot 2.65 \right) \cdot 57.3 \qquad \text{(Eq. 7.8)}$$

In this equation, G_{lat} is converted into m/s^2 and speed into m/s. The 57.3 factor converts radians into degrees. Now the understeer angle (δ_u) can be calculated using Equation 7.9.

$$\delta_u = |\delta| - |\delta_{\text{Acker}}| \qquad \text{(Eq. 7.9)}$$

The absolute values of wheel angle and Ackermann steering angle are taken to remove the sign convention between left- and right-hand corners. Figure 7.25 shows the Ackermann steering angle, wheel angle, and understeer angle at the indicated corner on the Dubai Motodrom, logged on the Corvette C5R.

From the definition of understeer angle, it follows that a positive value means understeer and a negative value oversteer.

In the example shown in Figure 7.25, this car has difficulty navigating to the apex of the corner. Specifically, the understeer angle channel increases on corner entry. The steering wheel movement (in this case, illustrated by the wheel angle) shows typical understeer symptoms. At mid-corner, the driver turns the steering wheel so far inward (understeer

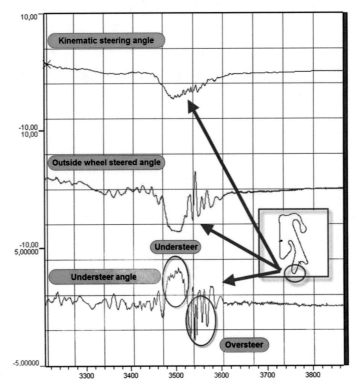

Figure 7.25 Ackermann (kinematic) steering angle, outside wheel angle, and understeer angle zoomed in at the indicated corner

angle keeps increasing) that the understeer suddenly shifts to corner exit oversteer. At this moment, the understeer angle turns negative. The graph starts fluctuating as the driver tries to keep the car in line by applying opposite steering lock.

Of course, in the preceding example, we probably would have come to the same conclusions by simply investigating steering angle, throttle, and lateral acceleration channels. Why then is it useful to go through the effort of calculating an understeer angle channel?

Projecting the understeer angle channel on top of a track map can be very illustrative. Points of interest can be located easily and quickly this way. An example for a lap with a touring car around the Hungaroring is shown in Figure 7.26.

However, the real advantage of using the understeer angle math channel lies in its potential for statistical analysis. Together with the grip factor lap statistics that will be covered

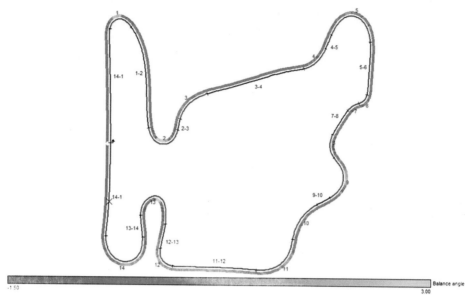

Figure 7.26 Understeer angle channel projected on a track map

in chapter 8, the average understeer angle per lap can give the engineer a very good idea about the performance of the vehicle over time. It is very useful to investigate:

- Consequences of setup changes
- Differences between different tire constructions or compounds
- Evaluate trends in vehicle balance as tires get older, fuel tank gets emptier, and so on
- Evaluate differences in driving style
- Evaluate differences in track conditions (together with grip factor statistics)

A high average understeer angle value means that the car in question will be prone to understeer. The lower the average, the more the balance will go toward oversteer. By clever gating of the understeer angle channel we can even investigate the vehicle balance during specific cornering phases (corner entry or exit). The usability of the average understeer angle as lap statistic will be illustrated with a couple of examples.

Table 7.2 presents the average understeer angle for a run of five consecutive laps in a rear-wheel drive GT1 car. There is a very clear trend toward less understeer or oversteer (decreasing average understeer angle). The fastest lap time was achieved in the lap with the highest average understeer angle.

Table 7.2 Average understeer angle for five consecutive laps		
	Lap time	Average understeer angle (°)
Lap 1	1:26.115	1.01
Lap 2	1:25.318	1.02
Lap 3	1:25.496	0.91
Lap 4	1:25.677	0.77
Lap 5	1:26.822	0.72

The lap-by-lap chart in Figure 7.27 shows the average understeer angle per lap for the duration of a 60-min race with a driver change at around half the race distance. The second driver continued on the tires used by the first driver. It's quite clear that over the distance the balance of the car goes toward more oversteer, indicated by the decreasing trend of the average understeer angle.

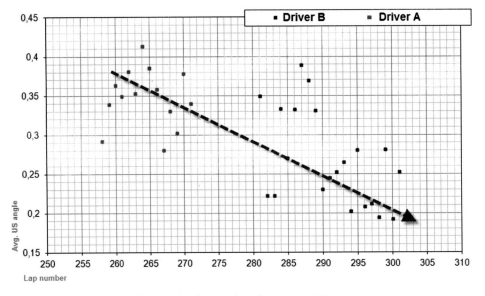

Figure 7.27 Average understeer angle run chart for a complete race

Drivers with different driving styles often require different directions in vehicle setup. A good example of this is given in Figure 7.28. This plot shows the lap time as a function of average understeer angle. The data was taken from a three-day test session in a Saleen S7R GT1 car done by two different drivers. It's clear from the graph that during this test the vehicle balance varied in a large range, with average understeer angle going from slightly negative toward a maximum of 1.2°.

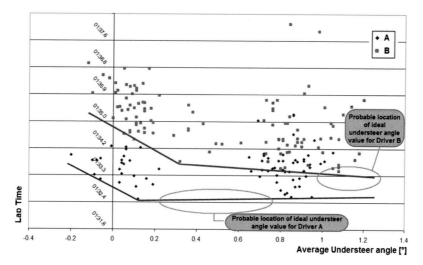

Figure 7.28 Average understeer angle versus lap time

Driver A was clearly the quicker driver, and his fastest lap times were achieved when the average understeer angle was very low. The data of Driver B shows a trend where lap times get quicker as understeer angle increases. He will be quicker with a vehicle set up for more understeer, whereas Driver A obviously likes a more twitchy rear axle. As the car is entered in endurance races and both drivers need to drive it, a compromise needs to be found where both drivers have a considerable amount of confidence in the car.

Although this definition of over- and understeer is not 100% mathematically accurate where race cars are operating mainly in the nonlinear range of the tires, the average understeer angle math channel is still a very powerful tool to analyze the balance of the vehicle and detect trends over longer periods of time.

7.6 Vehicle Balance with a Yaw Rate Sensor

The vehicle's angular rate of rotation around an axis perpendicular to the ground through the center of gravity can be measured with a gyro. This is basically the rate of change in heading or yaw angle (Figure 7.29).

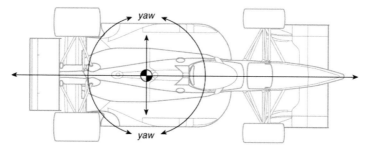

Figure 7.29 Yaw angle

In the previous section, methods for determining if a car is understeering or oversteering (i.e., to determine the balance state of the car) were reviewed. Yaw rate measurements show how this balance state is changing.

A vehicle that is beginning to oversteer experiences an increase in yaw rate, whereas understeering causes a decrease in yaw rate. A change in balance can be quantified by comparing the actual yaw rate to a theoretical value, which is a similar calculation (as explained previously) as the one to determine the understeer angle.

In a steady-state maneuver, a vehicle changes heading at a rate ω (the angular velocity) depending on its speed V and corner radius R as defined in Equation 7.10.

$$\omega = \frac{V}{R}$$ (Eq. 7.10)

Substituting Equation 7.4 for corner radius R gives Equation 7.11.

$$\omega = \frac{G_{lat}}{V}$$ (Eq. 7.11)

Attitude velocity ω_{att} now can be defined as the difference between measured yaw rate (r) and angular velocity (Equation 7.12).

$$\omega_{att} = r - \omega = r - \frac{G_{lat}}{V}$$ (Eq. 7.12)

In Figure 7.30, a graph illustrates attitude velocity for the indicated corner on the Bahrain Grand Prix track. Because lateral acceleration is logged in Gs and speed in km/h, Equation 7.11 is modified into a mathematical channel to express angular velocity in deg/sec (Equation 7.13).

$$\omega = \left(\frac{9.81 \cdot G_{lat}}{0.277 \cdot V} \right) \cdot 57.3$$ (Eq. 7.13)

The result then is subtracted from the measured yaw rate to give the attitude velocity. A positive value (yaw rate > angular velocity) means that the vehicle tends to oversteer, and a negative value (yaw rate < angular velocity) indicates a vehicle with an understeering tendency.

The example in Figure 7.31 shows a car going through a double apex left-hand corner. The pictured channels are speed, yaw rate, angular velocity, and attitude velocity. From this last channel we can see two main balance issues. On corner entry, where the car

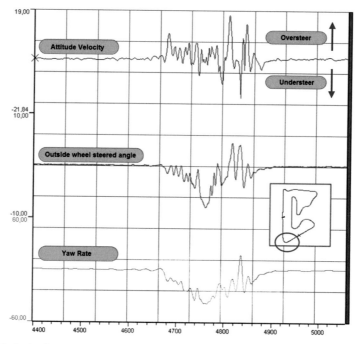

Figure 7.30 Attitude velocity

starts to yaw (develop a slip angle), attitude velocity goes negative at first, but then there is a significant positive peak, indicating that the rear wants to step out. Just before the second apex, a similar peak occurs.

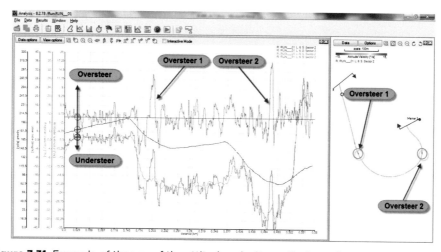

Figure 7.31 Example of the use of the attitude velocity math channel

165

As with the equation for determining the understeer angle, this mathematical channel does not take into account tire slip angles. Furthermore, to obtain an accurate result, the gyro must measure the yaw rate at the vehicle's center of gravity. Attitude velocity is again a useful channel to overlay on a track map, as illustrated on the map in Figure 7.31. The two locations in the corner where the car starts to oversteer are clearly recognizable.

7.7 Front and Rear Lateral Acceleration

If lateral acceleration on the front and rear axles can be measured separately, the assumption can be made that the axle on which the highest value is measured will develop the highest degree of grip. The following applies:

Front lateral acceleration > Rear lateral acceleration   OVERSTEER

Front lateral acceleration < Rear lateral acceleration   UNDERSTEER

In Figure 7.32, front and rear lateral acceleration traces are pictured. A mathematical channel is created in which front lateral acceleration is subtracted from rear lateral acceleration. This means that understeer shows up as a positive value, and oversteer results in a negative value.

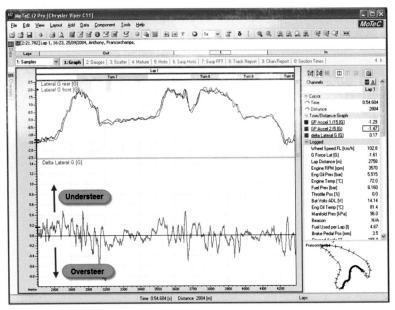

Figure 7.32 Evaluation of oversteer and understeer by comparing lateral acceleration on the front and rear axles

The sensors must be placed at the location where the vehicle centerline intersects with the front and rear axle centerline. This is not always easy. If measured correctly, the comparison of front and rear lateral acceleration can be very helpful in vehicle balance analysis.

In the absence of a gyro, yaw rate can be determined from front and rear lateral acceleration channels by first calculating the yaw acceleration (Equation 7.14).

$$a_{yaw} = \frac{G_{lat(rear)} - G_{lat(front)}}{WB} \qquad \text{(Eq. 7.14)}$$

With $G_{lat(rear)}$ = rear axle lateral acceleration

$G_{lat(front)}$ = front axle lateral acceleration

WB = wheelbase

Then integrate this to get yaw rate (Equation 7.15).

$$r = \int a_{yaw}(t) \cdot dt \qquad \text{(Eq. 7.15)}$$

During a longer time period, this integration loses much of its accuracy because of noise in the signal and accelerometer drift. For short durations, however, it can be useful.

Chapter 8
Understanding Tire Performance

Tires are by far the most important components on any race car, and understanding their behavior is probably one of the highest priorities for any engineer working in motor racing. Data acquisition systems can be used to record data that helps us to understand the tires better and tune the car in such a way that their performance is optimized. This chapter will focus on objectively determining the tire performance with some simple techniques. Tire pressure and temperature are the most important parameters for the engineer, so techniques are discussed to measure and interpret this information.

8.1   Estimating Grip Levels

In the previous chapter, the principle of the traction circle and combined acceleration as a math channel for the radius of the traction circle was discussed. In this section, the combined acceleration channel will be used to give us a statistical representation of the grip developed by the tires of the car *or* the portion of this grip being used by the driver.

It should be clear that when we plot the combined acceleration channel against distance, the larger the area beneath the resulting plot, the more grip the vehicle developed on the track or section of the track being looked at. We could integrate the combined acceleration channel in function of lap distance to obtain a lap statistic that is a measure of the amount of grip developed during a single lap. The accuracy of this calculation would be greatly dependent on the accuracy of the lap distance channel. Simply taking the average value of the combined acceleration channel per lap would be a better solution.

The problem with this approach would be that we can't compare results between different tracks as the number of high- and low-speed corners and the amount of straights would skew the average combined acceleration values. We will therefore need to gate the combined acceleration channel for certain situations in order to get a reliable lap statistic for average grip. Through clever signal gating, we can assess objective numbers to the grip the car is producing in different situations, namely:

- Overall grip
- Braking grip
- Acceleration grip
- Cornering grip
- Aerodynamic grip

We now need to set the boundaries to determine these situations. To calculate an overall grip factor, we take the combined acceleration over the course of a lap but only display situations that are grip limited. That way, we exclude straight-line acceleration where engine power and aerodynamic drag are the limiting factors in the acceleration of the car.

We could create a math channel that simply shows the original combined acceleration channel when it exceeds 1 G. The choice of this boundary value naturally depends on the type of car and its tires and aerodynamic properties. An example of how this math channel will look is shown in the second distance chart in Figure 8.1.

The same approach can be used to calculate a grip factor math channel for cornering conditions (and that way excluding grip limited straight-line braking and acceleration). Cornering conditions could be defined as lateral G exceeding 0.5 G, for example.

A braking condition could be triggered once longitudinal G drops below –1 G. Traction grip boundary conditions are a longitudinal acceleration higher than zero and at the same time lateral Gs higher than 0.5 G.

Finally, aerodynamic grip implies a speed dependency so aero grip is defined in situations where lateral acceleration exceeds 1 G and speed is higher than 120 km/h.

As said before, the values of the boundary conditions are user-definable and could vary between different cars to get good results.

Figure 8.1 shows an example of distance graphs of all the grip factor math channels. The average channel values per lap (or per sector, corner) will be a powerful statistic to evaluate grip levels over time.

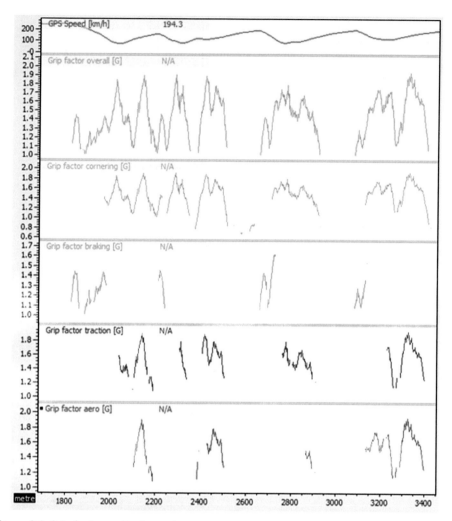

Figure 8.1 Grip factor math channels

Table 8.1 gives the average grip factor values of a certain car for a sequence of 20 laps. The car started this run on a new set of tires. When we plot the overall grip factor lap by lap (Figure 8.2) it shows very clearly how the tire performance drops off as a function of lap number.

Table 8.1 Average grip factors for a run of 20 consecutive laps						
Lap number	Lap time	Grip factor overall	Grip factor cornering	Grip factor braking	Grip factor traction	Grip factor aero
1	1'34.7	1.46	1.36	1.38	1.42	1.50
2	1'34.6	1.47	1.35	1.40	1.40	1.46
3	1'34.5	1.48	1.40	1.42	1.42	1.48
4	1'34.7	1.47	1.38	1.39	1.42	1.50
5	1'35.0	1.45	1.36	1.38	1.40	1.46
6	1'35.1	1.44	1.36	1.43	1.38	1.47
7	1'35.5	1.45	1.34	1.40	1.37	1.46
8	1'35.4	1.45	1.37	1.38	1.38	1.47
9	1'35.4	1.44	1.34	1.38	1.36	1.44
10	1'35.5	1.44	1.36	1.38	1.37	1.46
11	1'35.9	1.44	1.34	1.42	1.35	1.42
12	1'36.0	1.42	1.32	1.42	1.34	1.42
13	1'36.1	1.41	1.34	1.34	1.40	1.41
14	1'36.0	1.43	1.34	1.43	1.36	1.43
15	1'36.5	1.41	1.33	1.37	1.37	1.42
16	1'36.7	1.41	1.33	1.34	1.35	1.41
17	1'36.4	1.43	1.33	1.40	1.37	1.43
18	1'36.3	1.42	1.32	1.41	1.35	1.41
19	1'36.9	1.39	1.31	1.39	1.34	1.39
20	1'36.7	1.38	1.30	1.33	1.31	1.40
Average	**1'35.7**	**1.43**	**1.34**	**1.39**	**1.37**	**1.44**

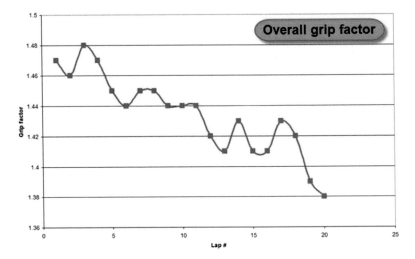

Figure 8.2 Average overall grip factor from Table 8.1 plotted lap by lap

Figure 8.3 is a nice example of how changing track conditions can influence a car's performance. This type of chart is called a radar chart. A radar chart is used to display three or more variables on a two-dimensional chart. The following example shows five axes, the five grip factors.

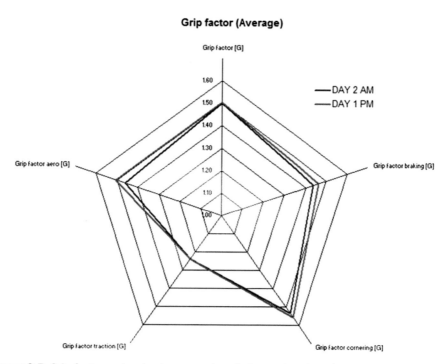

Figure 8.3 Grip factor radar chart—comparison between two test days

The data was taken from a two-day test session. The red data was recorded on the first day, the blue data the day after. Between the two recordings nothing of the car's configuration was changed and on both instances it was driven with a new, identical set of tires.

The overall grip factor is only slightly higher on day one. There's a significant difference in the braking and aerodynamic grip factor. On the first day there was more aero and braking grip than on day two. The reason for this was that the wind turned 180° the second day. At the place on the track where aerodynamic performance was vital, the car now found itself with a tailwind instead of a headwind. This decreased aerodynamic drag at that location forced the driver to brake earlier. The other consequence was that the downforce acting on the car decreases as well, causing a lower cornering speed. The influence of aero grip on lap time can be seen in Figure 8.4 for this particular car and track.

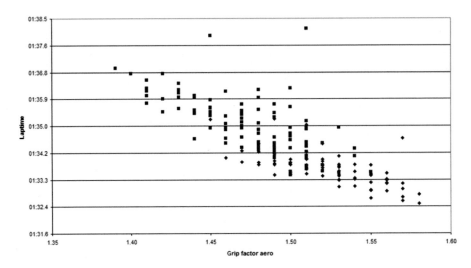

Figure 8.4 Influence of aerodynamic grip on lap time

The run chart in Figure 8.5 shows traction grip tracked during the course of a complete race weekend. Notice the sudden drop in grip factor in the second stint of the race. Here it started raining. This type of chart is called a run chart and shows in this case one statistical value of average traction grip factor per covered lap. (More on how run charts can be used follows in chapter 17.)

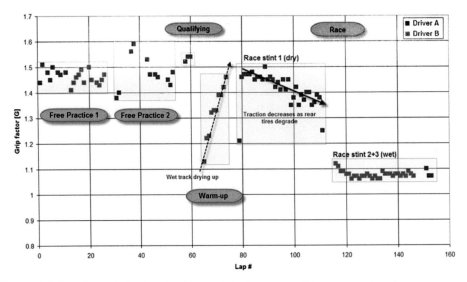

Figure 8.5 Traction grip factor development during a complete race weekend

8.2 Working with Tire Pressure Monitoring Systems

A TPMS (tire pressure monitoring system) is an electronic measurement system designed to monitor the air pressure inside pneumatic tires and mainly exists as a safety system to indicate possible tire punctures. Most motor sport systems consist of sensors which are placed inside each rim and transmit their pressure data to a receiver unit placed in the car over a radio frequency. Often the temperature of the air inside the tire is registered as well. We can define the following functions for a motor sport TPMS:

- Diagnostics function: detection of pressure loss, punctures

- Tire pressure management: to determine if the chosen cold tire pressures are correct, pressure increase during tire preheating

- Determination of the tire's optimum working range

- The tire pressure signals can be used in advanced math channels in the data analysis software (e.g., pressure dependent tire spring rate)

The example in Figure 8.6 shows TPMS data for a run of 12 laps with a GT car. The upper graph shows the tire pressure for the four wheels, and the lower graph shows the corresponding temperature of the air inside the tire. The tire pressures between the four tires vary between 1.5 and 1.8 bars, the lower ones being the front tire pressures. The trend in the tire temperature follows this. Although the data from the out lap tells us that these tires where already on the car during the previous outing, it seems to take about four to five laps for the pressures and temperatures to stabilize. Any setup changes done in the pit lane before this outing can only be objectively evaluated after the pressures have stabilized.

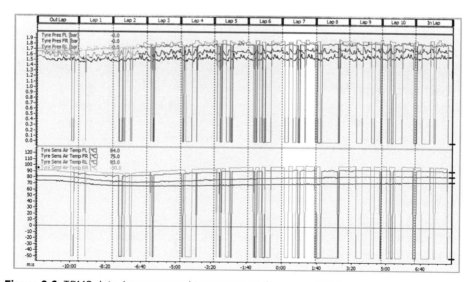

Figure 8.6 TPMS data (pressure and temperature) for a run of 12 laps

Both pressure and temperature charts show a number of downward spikes where the channel values drop to zero. This is because of a bad radio frequency reception between sensor and TPMS receiver module. The rear signals show the most interference, and indeed they are at the largest distance from the receiver module. When the tire pressures would be displayed on the dashboard and maybe linked to an alarm when a pressure drops below a certain alarm value, the drops in radio reception would give the driver the wrong information. This problem can be solved by creating an alarm with a Boolean operation that evaluates if, together with a tire pressure value of zero, there is still a normal tire temperature signal. If this also is at zero, it is safe to say that either the sensor has failed or there is a momentary loss of reception.

By taking some basic statistics such as the average or maximum tire pressure per lap and putting the results in a run chart, you can investigate how long it takes for a tire to reach a stable operating condition. An example of this is shown in Figure 8.7. This chart shows lap-by-lap average tire pressure for two different cars but with the same type of tires. The tires are preheated before the car leaves the pit lane. However, also in this example it's apparent that it takes quite a while for the pressures to stabilize. The shown run covers a period of 20 consecutive laps.

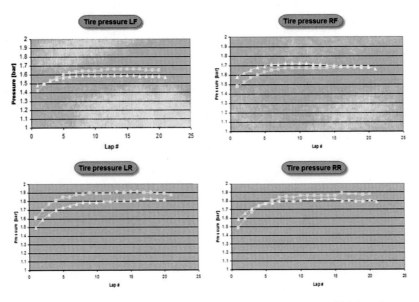

Figure 8.7 Run chart with average tire pressure per lap during a run of 20 laps for two different cars

When we look at the yellow data points in the chart, we can safely say that after seven laps the pressures are at stable operating conditions. At this time the pressures are the following:

$$
\begin{array}{c|c}
1.58 & 1.70 \\
\hline
1.80 & 1.80
\end{array}
$$

Let's consider the case when the driver would have come in after three laps to do a setup change. At this time the pressures would have been

$$
\begin{array}{c|c}
1.52 & 1.65 \\
\hline
1.65 & 1.68
\end{array}
$$

To give us an idea about the effect these different pressures would have on the balance of the car, we calculate the ratio between front and rear tire pressure. After seven laps this would be

$$
\frac{1.58 + 1.70}{1.58 + 1.70 + 1.80 + 1.80} = 47.67\%
$$

And after three laps:

$$
\frac{1.52 + 1.65}{1.52 + 1.65 + 1.65 + 1.68} = 48.77\%
$$

It's safe to say that any conclusions about vehicle balance after three laps are invalid when the car is being set up for longer runs. It may well lead the engineer in the wrong direction with the setup, and the behavior of the car during a longer run can be completely different.

Figure 8.8 shows the corresponding (maximum) tire air temperatures for these two cars. From this chart as well it's clear that it takes seven laps before the tires have reached a stable operating condition. After these seven laps the respective temperatures are:

$$
\begin{array}{c|c}
85 & 88 \\
\hline
105 & 99
\end{array}
$$

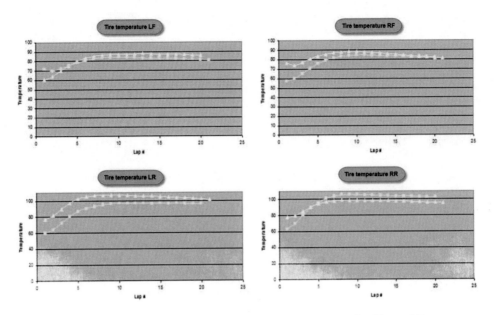

Figure 8.8 Run chart with the corresponding tire air temperatures for Figure 8.7

Again, when the car would come in after three laps it would give a different picture:

$$
\begin{array}{c|c}
70 & 75 \\
\hline
90 & 85
\end{array}
$$

When we calculate the front/rear temperature balance, we get the following results:

7 Laps:
$$\frac{85+88}{85+88+105+99} = 45.89\%$$

3 Laps:
$$\frac{70+75}{70+75+90+85} = 45.31\%$$

If we consider that the air (or nitrogen) that we put into our tires is an ideal gas (a gas conforming to a fixed relation between pressure, volume, and temperature), we can use the Ideal Gas Law (Equation 8.1) to calculate the tires' cold tire pressure at a standardized temperature from the pressure and temperature data of the TPMS.

$$\frac{P_1}{T_1} = \frac{P_2}{T_2} \Rightarrow P_1 = P_2 \cdot \frac{T_1}{T_2} \qquad \text{(Eq. 8.1)}$$

Where P_1 = Cold tire pressure in bar

T_1 = Temperature at which the cold tire pressure has been set in Kelvin

P_2 = Hot tire pressure in bar

T_2 = Hot tire temperature corresponding to P_2 in Kelvin

Let's consider the following example:

Hot tire pressure measured by TPMS: $P_2 = 1.85$ bars

Tire air temperature measured by TPMS: $T_2 = 75\ °C$

Please note that the pressure measured by the TPMS is relative to atmospheric pressure (when the pressure sensor reads zero bar it means ambient pressure). This means that we have to add one bar to P_2 to get absolute air pressure. Tire air temperature is measured in degrees Celsius. To get the cold tire pressure in the correct units we have to modify Equation 8.1 as follows:

$$P_1 = \left((P_2 + 1) \cdot \frac{T_1 + 273.15}{T_2 + 273.15} \right) - 1 \qquad \text{(Eq. 8.2)}$$

We would like to calculate the cold tire pressure P_1 at a tire air temperature of 15 °C (288.15 K). Entering these numbers into Equation 8.2 gives us:

$$P_1 = \left((P_2 + 1) \cdot \frac{T_1 + 273.15}{T_2 + 273.15} \right) - 1 = \left((1.85\ \text{bar} + 1) \cdot \frac{15\,°C + 273.15}{75\,°C + 273.15} \right) - 1 = 1.36\ \text{bar}$$

Figure 8.9 shows TPMS data for a seven-lap run. The lower chart shows the corresponding cold tire pressures at a temperature of 20 °C based on Equation 8.2.

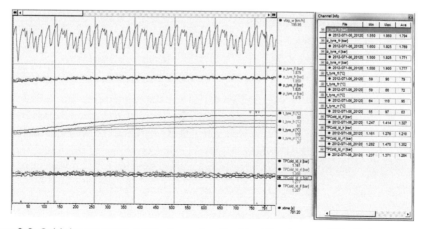

Figure 8.9 Cold tire pressure estimation using the Ideal Gas Law and TPMS data

8.3   Working with Infrared Tire Temperature Sensors

As noted before, most racing TPMSs will also give you a signal per wheel for the temperature of the air inside the tire. However, we are more interested in what's happening with that part of the tire which is in direct contact with the asphalt. This can be done using infrared (IR) temperature sensors aimed at the thread of the tire. Mounting this kind of sensor on the car can be sometimes difficult, especially at the front where, ideally, the sensor moves together with steering angle in order to measure a fixed point on the tire. Figure 8.10 shows an example of three IR sensors mounted toward a front wheel on a Corvette C6R GT1 car. A typical IR sensor calibration curve will look like the one pictured in Figure 8.11. One of the important items to keep in mind during installation is the mounting distance between the sensor and the tire thread surface (see Figure 8.12). This distance, together with the type of lens used in the sensor, determines the area of which the sensor signal will present the average temperature. This area will increase proportionately to the sensor mounting distance. When the sensor is aimed vertically at the tire thread, the mounting distance will change when the wheel goes into bump or droop travel, which induces an error in the measurement. This situation is to be avoided.

Infrared tire temperature measurement will produce information about

- The ideal working range of the tires
- The time needed to get the tire up to correct conditions
- Balance of the car
- Lateral load transfer
- Tire compound and construction
- Tire wear
- Camber
- Tire pressures
- Steering and suspension geometry
- Driving style
- And other issues

Ideally, three sensors per tire will enable us to observe the tire temperature distribution across the tire thread surface, but one sensor per wheel will also give much information. We will start with some examples that will make clear what kind of information can be extracted from one sensor per wheel. After that, some examples of three sensors per wheel will show what extra benefits this configuration can bring.

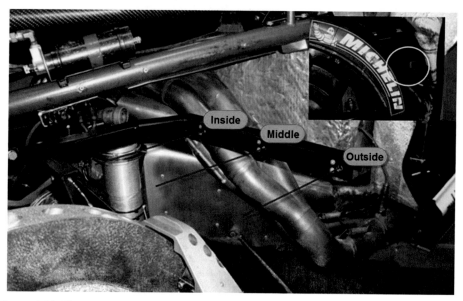

Figure 8.10 Three IR temperature sensors mounted with a bracket on the left-front brake caliper of a GT1 car

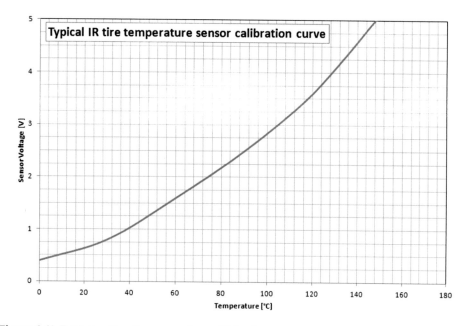

Figure 8.11 Typical calibration curve for an IR tire temperature sensor

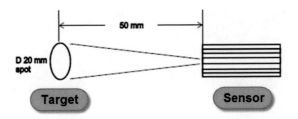

Figure 8.12 Mounting distance between sensor and tire thread determines the surface of which the average temperature is measured

8.4   Where Does Tire Temperature Come From?

To get an idea of how temperature is built up at the tire thread surface, we take a closer look at Equation 8.3. This formula is based on a thermal tire model developed by Danny Nowlan [8-1] and used to predict the average tire thread temperature in the Chassissim lap time simulation software.

$$\frac{C_p \cdot \rho_T}{HF} \cdot \frac{\partial T}{\partial t} = \sqrt{(F_y \cdot \alpha \cdot V)^2 + (F_x \cdot SR \cdot V)^2} - \kappa \cdot (T_T - T_{\text{amb}}) - \kappa_{\text{track}} \cdot (T_T - T_{\text{track}}) \qquad \text{(Eq. 8.3)}$$

Equation 8.3 gives the rate of temperature change in the tire thread surface ($\partial T/\partial t$) depending on a large amount of parameters:

F_y	Lateral tire force
F_x	Longitudinal tire force
α	Tire slip angle
SR	Tire slip ratio
V	Speed
κ	Thermal conductivity between tire and air
κ_{track}	Thermal conductivity between tire and track surface
T_{tire}	Average tire thread surface temperature
T_{track}	Track temperature

The multiplier $\dfrac{C_p \cdot \rho_T}{HF}$ represents the thermal properties of the tire in which C_p is the heat capacity of the tire and ρ_T the density of the tire compound. HF is a scale factor. The equation shows us that the increase or decrease in temperature of a rotating tire is governed by three terms (see Figure 8.13):

1. Loss of temperature between the tire thread surface and the surrounding air

2. Loss of temperature between the tire thread surface and the track

3. Generation of temperature because of lateral and longitudinal force in the tire contact patch

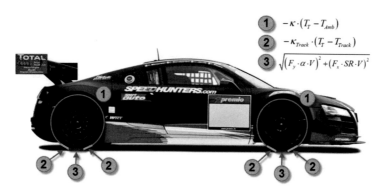

Figure 8.13 Schematic illustration of the three terms governing the speed of tire temperature variation

An example of the temperature evolution of the left rear tire on a car going through a right-hand corner is given in Figure 8.14. This graph shows vehicle speed, lateral and longitudinal acceleration, and the middle tire surface temperature of the left rear tire. During the straight before the corner (area 1 in Figure 8.14) we can see the temperature decreasing over time. There is no lateral force acting on the tires, and the longitudinal acceleration decreases to almost zero with increasing speed. This means that the term $\sqrt{(F_y \cdot \alpha \cdot V)^2 + (F_x \cdot SR \cdot V)^2}$ is almost zero and $\frac{\partial T}{\partial t}$ is nearly completely determined by the thermal conductivity between tire thread and air/track surface.

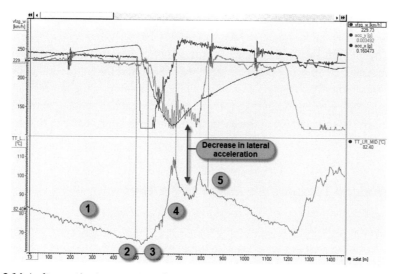

Figure 8.14 Left rear tire temperature for a car going through a right-hand corner

Point 2 in Figure 8.14 indicates where the driver starts braking. At this point, longitudinal acceleration goes from zero to a local (negative) maximum but at the same time speed decreases. We can also safely assume that this wheel will have a negative slip ratio at the time of braking. We do not see any significant change in the tire temperature. When we look at the $\sqrt{(F_y \cdot \alpha \cdot V)^2 + (F_x \cdot SR \cdot V)^2}$ term again, it's clear that F_y is still zero. F_x and SR increase, but the speed is decreasing (the driver is braking) and at a rapid speed (longitudinal deceleration goes to a maximum). F_x will not be that high because at this time it has probably little vertical load on it. This means that in this example the increase of temperature because of forces in the tire contact patch is more or less balanced out by the cooling effect of air and track surface.

It all changes the moment lateral acceleration starts to build up (point 3 in Figure 8.14). From this point we can see a rapid increase in tire temperature which peaks at about the same place as the lateral acceleration (at point 4). The car is still braking, so everything said so far is still valid at point 3. Now, however, F_y and α will increase while the decrease in speed will get smaller. This effect will overrule the cooling effects and $\frac{\partial T}{\partial t}$ will increase.

Because this corner has a double apex, we can see a short decrease in lateral acceleration. Although the driver is accelerating again after point 4 and speed is increasing, the drop in F_y and α still causes the tire temperature of this wheel to drop. It picks up again at the second lateral acceleration peak.

At point 5 the car is accelerating in a straight line again where the tire will be cooled down by air and asphalt.

In conclusion, we can state that in order to create tire temperature we need to maximize lateral or longitudinal force, slip angle, or slip ratio and speed. A combination of all these points will create the highest temperature increases. Obviously, the driver has a lot of control of these parameters, so different driving styles (e.g., V-style corner entry/exit versus corner entry with a lot of trail braking) will result in different tire temperatures. We can influence these parameters as well by altering the setup of the car. Indeed, a big part of setting up a car comes down to thermal management and making sure the tires spend as much time as possible in the optimal temperature range. Later in this chapter this will be discussed in more detail.

8.5   Working Temperature Range of the Tires

Infrared tire temperature sensors are ideal to investigate at which temperature a tire works most efficiently. We can relate tire temperature and cornering force through the lateral acceleration signal in a graph as illustrated in Figure 8.15. This graph shows the absolute value of lateral acceleration as a function of tire temperature (average of left-hand and right-hand wheel) for a front and a rear axle. The upper extremities of the two charts (indicated with the green line) depict how maximum lateral acceleration corresponds to a certain temperature. What is interesting is that for a lateral acceleration of 1.8 G for example is achieved within a temperature range between 53 and 73 °C for the front tire and between 61 and 93 °C for the rear tire. The car reaches its maximum lateral acceleration values within this temperature range.

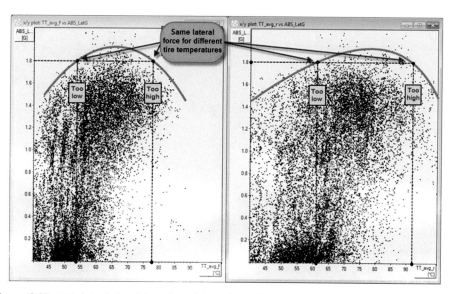

Figure 8.15 *X-Y* plot of absolute value of lateral acceleration versus front and rear tire temperature

It speaks for itself that the more data points are within this ideal temperature range, the better the tires on this axle will work and the more cornering force will be available. In Figure 8.16 a complete lap is shown of the same car with speed and lateral acceleration in the upper chart and left-hand, right-hand, and average tire temperature for front and rear axle, respectively, in the lower two charts. The low and high tire temperature boundaries derived from Figure 8.15 are indicated as horizontal lines.

A good example of how tire temperature readings can help in diagnosing setup problems is shown in the circled area in Figure 8.16. This is a right-hand corner at significant speed where the shape of the lateral acceleration trace shows us that the car is understeering. In the temperature graphs we can see in this area that the average rear tire temperature is exactly where we want it, with the left rear temperature on the high limit of the range and the right rear on the lower limit. On the front axle the average axle temperature is already on the high limit of the ideal temperature interval. The left front tire rises to a temperature that's significantly outside the ideal range. This is the wheel that is taking all the load transfer so it will also see the largest tire temperature increase. To cure the understeer in this case the setup of the car needs to be modified so that the temperature gradient $\frac{\partial T}{\partial t}$ of the left front wheel decreases. This way, more time will be

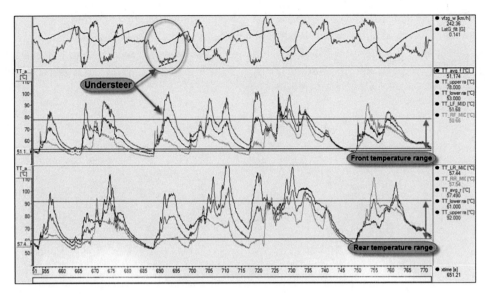

Figure 8.16 Tire temperature range during a complete lap

spent in the ideal tire temperature range. How this can be done is discussed in the next section of this chapter.

Once we know the ideal temperature range of the tires, math channels can be created that calculate for each tire the time per lap (as percentage of lap time) that the tire temperature was within this ideal range. The higher this value for a specific tire on the car, the more efficient the tire performance will be. Figure 8.17 shows an example of some

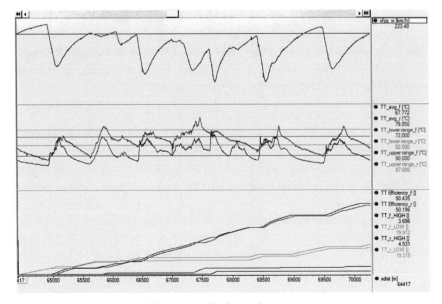

Figure 8.17 Tire temperature efficiency math channels

tire temperature efficiency math channels for a complete lap. Speed and front and rear average tire temperature are shown in the upper two charts. The ideal temperature range is defined as

Front: 72 °C to 90 °C

Rear: 82 °C to 97 °C

The math channels in the lower chart give the following information:

- Tire temp. Efficiency Front: Time counts up when the front tire temperature is above 72 °C and below 90 °C

- Tire temp. Efficiency Rear: Time counts up when the rear tire temperature is above 82 °C and below 97 °C

- Tire temp. Front LOW: Time counts up when the front tire temperature is below 72 °C

- Tire temp. Rear LOW: Time counts up when the rear tire temperature is below 82 °C

- Tire temp. Front HIGH: Time counts up when the front tire temperature exceeds 90 °C

- Tire temp. Rear HIGH: Time counts up when the rear tire temperature exceeds 97 °C

The results of these channels are expressed in seconds. To have a value that is comparable from lap to lap the channel needs to be expressed as a percentage of the total lap time. Figure 8.18 shows a run chart containing the maximum value per lap for a race of

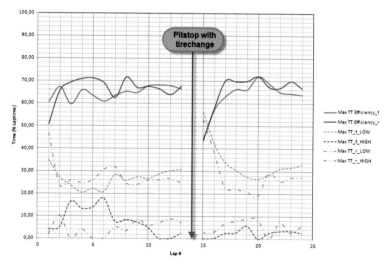

Figure 8.18 Tire temperature efficiency math channels—the maximum lap values displayed in a run chart

25 laps with a pit stop (including tire change) in lap 14. This run chart shows a well-balanced car where both axles have a quite high tire temperature efficiency. At the start of the race and just after the pit stop the tire temperature is low because the tires were not preheated. The starting driver did a good job in heating up the front tires compared to the rears as tire temperature stabilizes already after one lap. After the pit stop the picture is slightly different as the rear tires are at temperature after two laps while the front tires take a bit longer to get into the efficient temperature range.

8.6   Lateral Load Transfer and Tire Temperature

Now that we can determine the tire's optimum temperature range, the question remaining is obviously how we can make sure that we get the tire in this operating range. Referring back to Equation 8.3, we determined that in cornering phases the lateral component $(F_y \cdot \alpha \cdot V)^2$ had the biggest influence on tire temperature build-up. If we consider an axle of the car in a cornering situation, we can state that the slip angle α of the inside wheel is more or less equal to that of the outside wheel. At the same time the longitudinal velocity of both wheels is more or less the same. However, there is a significant difference in F_y between inside and outside wheels. F_y will normally be significantly bigger on the outside wheel than on the inside. This causes the temperature of the outside wheel to increase much faster than that of the inside (see Figure 8.19).

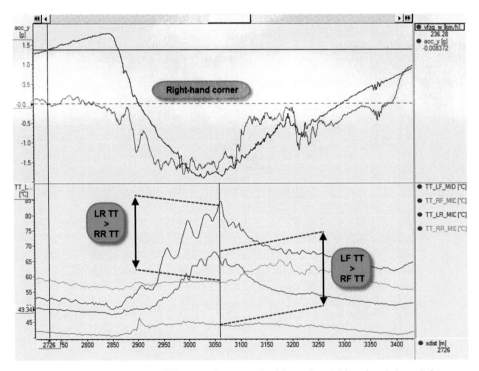

Figure 8.19 Tire temperature difference between inside and outside wheels in a right-hand corner

The magnitude of the lateral tire forces of inside (F_{yi}) and outside (F_{yo}) wheel are directly dependent on the amount of lateral load transfer during cornering. At a given lateral acceleration the static vertical load on the outside wheel will be increased with ΔF_z, while the static load on the inside wheel will be decreased with the same amount. This will result in an increase in lateral force on the outside wheel and a (larger) loss of lateral force on the inside wheel (see Figure 8.20). Slip angle and longitudinal velocity of these two wheels being assumed equal, it is this load transfer that causes the difference in outside and inside tire temperature, and we can therefore say that more load transfer will result in a higher difference between inside and outside tire temperature and vice versa.

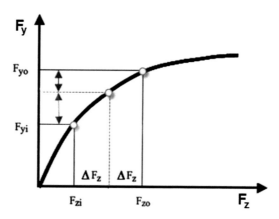

Figure 8.20 The effect of lateral load transfer on the inside and outside tire lateral force

We can use the effects of lateral load transfer to try to get our tire temperatures in the range where the tires work most efficiently. This will of course always remain a balancing act because decreasing lateral load transfer on the front axle will increase it on the rear axle and vice versa.

On the other side, the measured difference between inside and outside tire temperature of the front and rear axle can tell us something about the relative lateral load transfer on these two axles. We can create two simple math channels expressing the difference between left-hand and right-hand tire temperature:

$$\Delta T_{tire_{FRONT}} = T_{tire_{LF}} - T_{tire_{RF}} \qquad \text{(Eq. 8.4)}$$

$$\Delta T_{tire_{REAR}} = T_{tire_{LR}} - T_{tire_{RR}} \qquad \text{(Eq. 8.5)}$$

If we plot these channels against front and rear lateral load transfer (calculating lateral load transfer will be discussed in chapter 10) for a single lap we get the chart in Figure 8.21. The shape of this chart will change when setup changes influencing the lateral load transfer (spring rates, antiroll bars, damping, suspension geometry, tire pressure) are done to the car.

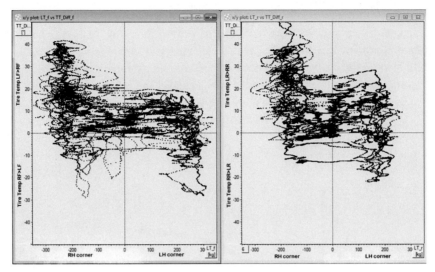

Figure 8.21 Front and rear inside to outside tire temperature difference versus lateral load transfer

The way the shape of this type of graph will change with different setup changes is illustrated in two examples (Figures 8.22 and 8.23). The first example shows the effect of a change in the front antiroll bar rate. The colored data represents a lap done with a soft front antiroll bar setting, and the black data was recorded when the roll bar was in a hard position. Larger temperature differences are seen between inside and outside wheels with the harder antiroll bar.

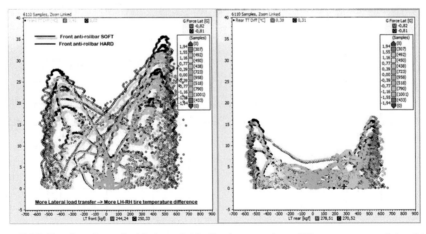

Figure 8.22 Front and rear inside to outside tire temperature difference versus lateral load transfer—comparison between a front antiroll bar in soft and hard position

The second example shows a comparison between different tire pressures. The inside/ outside tire temperature difference on the front axle is significantly higher with the

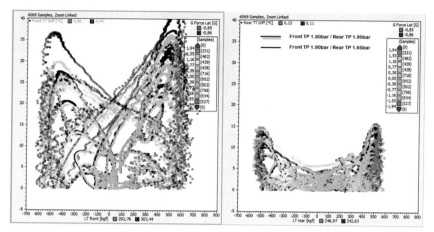

Figure 8.23 Front and rear inside to outside tire temperature difference versus lateral load transfer—comparison between different tire pressures

1.90/1.65 bar pressure combination compared to 1.80/1.90 bar. Here we have to take into account that besides the change in lateral load transfer we are also changing the slip angle of the tire where maximum lateral force is achieved.

In conclusion, in order to investigate the balance of the vehicle we need to look at two things:

- On which axle is the tire temperature outside the optimum range?
- What is the difference between the tire temperature of the inside and outside tires, and on which axle is this difference the most significant?

Figure 8.24 shows a zoomed view of a car going through Stowes Corner at Silverstone. Speed, lateral acceleration, and steering angle are pictured together with the inside/outside tire temperature difference for front and rear axles. From the steering angle and

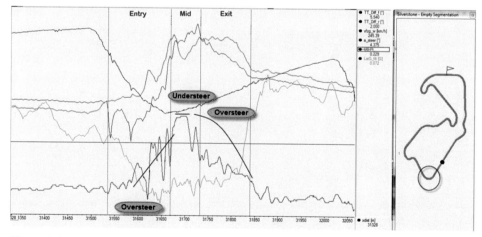

Figure 8.24 Front and rear inside to outside tire temperature difference and vehicle balance

lateral acceleration trace we can diagnose that this car has oversteer on corner entry, understeer at mid–corner, and (controllable) oversteer on corner exit. Let's look now at the differences between the outside and inside tire temperature. We can see at corner entry that the difference between left-hand and right-hand tire temperature at the rear axle starts to increase significantly earlier than on the front axle. The front difference shows two downward spikes that seem to coincide precisely with a wheel which is about to lock, as can be deduced from the speed trace. The front tire temperature difference only starts to increase once maximum lateral acceleration is reached. At the location in the corner where the minimum speed is reached, the front tire temperature difference takes an almost vertical jump upward, and we see that at this moment the car starts to understeer. While understeering, the front difference keeps increasing gradually, while the rear temperature difference decreases. As the driver goes back on the throttle, the front difference decreases in a more or less linear way while the rear difference increases shortly and then stays constant for the duration of the corner exit phase. In this example, the car seems to exhibit understeer when the front tire temperature difference exceeds the rear difference and oversteer when the rear exceeds the front. This is not necessarily always the case as the increase in tire temperature due to slip angle, speed, lateral force, slip ratio, and longitudinal force depends on the construction and compound of the tire, tire pressure, suspension geometry, and other setup parameters, and these might be significantly different between front and rear axle. Figure 8.25 shows for the same corner the temperature range for the front and rear tires. At corner entry it seems that the front tires are immediately in a better temperature range. The fronts are the tires that take more vertical load during braking, so Equation 8.3 tells us that temperature build-up will be easier on this axle. Here we also see that the difference between the rear inside and outside tire builds up quicker at the rear than at the front. Just before the mid-corner phase, the left front tire temperature spikes up rapidly and jumps far outside the optimum temperature range. The right front tire doesn't build up any tire temperature at

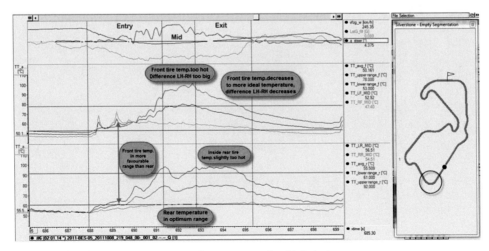

Figure 8.25 Tire temperature operating range and vehicle balance

all, so the average temperature of the two front wheels remains on the upper edge of the optimum range. Here it's the difference between the front wheels that is making the car understeer, and it's an indication of too much lateral load transfer. A softer antiroll bar or softer springs on the front axle would be possible solutions here to cure the problem. At corner exit the left front temperature gradually drops off toward a more favorable range, but at the same time the left rear tire temperature remains constant on corner exit and remains slightly out of range. This causes the slight oversteer on corner exit.

8.7   Tire Workload Distribution

Tire temperature can be seen as a measure for the energy stored in the tire contact patch. By comparing the temperature of each wheel to the sum of the temperatures of all four wheels, we can determine which tire is doing the biggest amount of work. For this, the following math channel can be created for each wheel:

$$\text{TT\%}_i = \frac{T_{\text{tire}_i}}{T_{\text{tire}_{\text{LF}}} + T_{\text{tire}_{\text{RF}}} + T_{\text{tire}_{\text{LR}}} + T_{\text{tire}_{\text{RR}}}} \cdot 100\% \qquad \text{(Eq. 8.6)}$$

With: $\text{TT\%}_i$ = Percentage of tire temperature compared to sum of all four tire temperatures

   i = LF, RF, LR, RR

   $T_{\text{tire}i}$ = Tire temperature (i = LF, RF, LR, RR)

In the example in Figure 8.26, the left rear tire is obviously doing most of the work.

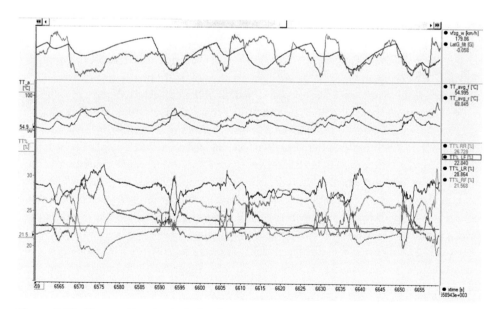

Figure 8.26 Tire workload calculation from tire temperatures

8.8   Camber Evaluation with Tire Temperature Sensors

One of the most basic and useful measurements when a car stops in the pit lane is taking tire pressures and temperatures at three locations across each tire. The temperature data is used to evaluate the amount of camber run on each wheel by looking at the spread between inside and outside shoulder and taking into account the track layout. Figure 8.27 is an example of such a measurement. The right-hand average temperatures are significantly higher than on the left hand, meaning that the track has probably more corners to the left. On the right-hand side of the car the temperature spread between the inside and outside shoulder of front and rear tires indicates that some more camber could be used.

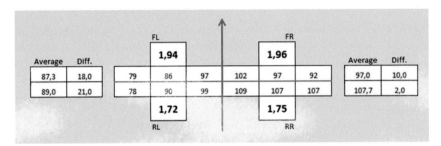

Figure 8.27 Pit lane tire pressure and temperature measurement

This kind of measurement is very useful but still has some important limitations. It gives an average picture of what happened when the car was out on the track. The temperature measurements also greatly depend on the shape of the last corner before the pit lane entry, the length of the pit lane, and how long it takes for the team to take the measurements.

Equipping all wheels with three infrared tire temperature sensors will enable us to constantly monitor the temperature spread across each tire and to evaluate camber separately for each corner. In Figure 8.28, temperature data of the front wheels is displayed for a complete lap. The lateral acceleration signal is calibrated such that positive values correspond to a left-hand turn and negative values to a right-hand turn. We evaluate the tire temperature spread for the seven corners indicated in the graph in Table 8.2. The gray-colored cells indicate the wheel with the biggest cornering potential, which is therefore the most important in each specific corner. Except for corners 1 and 2 the static camber on the left front wheel of this car seems to be correct. Because of the track layout the right front wheel is most of the time at the inside of the corner, and the temperature spread shows us that the wheel could use less static camber. However, in left-hand corners where this wheel is at the outside, the static camber seems to be good or even not enough. The suspension geometry of this car could probably use a bit more dynamic camber change in combination with less static camber to get the temperature spread on the inside wheel controlled better.

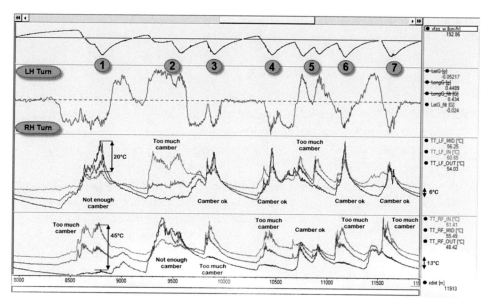

Figure 8.28 Corner-by-corner camber evaluation with tire temperature sensors

		Left Front Wheel		Right Front Wheel	
1	Right-hand corner	Outside temperature 20 °C higher than inside	Not enough camber	Inside shoulder increasing too much in temperature	Too much camber
2	Left-hand corner	Inside shoulder increasing too much in temperature	Too much camber	Inside temperature too low compared to outside and middle temperature	Not enough camber
3	Right-hand corner	Spread OK	Camber OK	Inside shoulder increasing too much in temperature	Too much camber
4	Right-hand corner	Spread OK	Camber OK	Inside shoulder increasing too much in temperature	Too much camber
5	Left-hand corner	Too much spread inside/outside	Too much camber	Spread OK	Camber OK
6	Right-hand corner	Spread OK	Camber OK	Inside shoulder increasing too much in temperature	Too much camber
7	Right-hand corner	Spread OK	Camber OK	Inside shoulder and middle increasing too much in temperature	Too much camber

Table 8.2 Corner by corner camber evaluation

A math channel describing the spread between inside and outside shoulder tire tempera-ture can be created to give a more visual indication on the amount of camber:

$$\Delta T_{\text{tire}_i}(\text{In}/\text{Out}) = T_{\text{tire}_i}(\text{In}) - T_{\text{tire}_i}(\text{Out}) \qquad \text{(Eq. 8.7)}$$

With $\qquad i = LF, RF, LR, RR$

$T_{\text{tire}_i}(\text{In})$ = Inside shoulder tire temperature

$T_{\text{tire}_i}(\text{Out})$ = Outside shoulder tire temperature

For the same lap as in Figure 8.28, the results of these math channels are given in Figure 8.29. The average value per lap of this channel is a useful statistic to evaluate wheel camber over larger datasets. For the lap displayed in Figure 8.28, the average temperature spread was 7.15 °C for the left front tire which could be acceptable and 14.73 °C on the rear axle, indicating as we concluded before that this tire has too much camber.

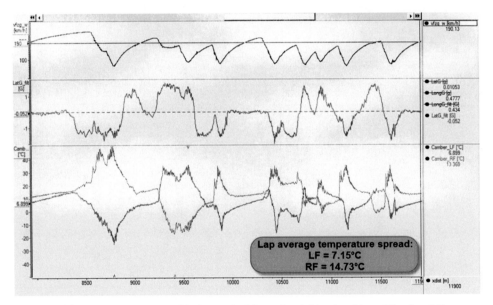

Figure 8.29 Temperature spread between inside and outside shoulder of the front tires

8.9   Tire Pressure Evaluation with Tire Temperature Sensors

We can also use the tire temperature channels to give us an indication if the tire pressure that we are running is correct or not. To do this, we compare the temperature of the inside and outside shoulder to that of the center section of the tire (see Figure 8.30 for a somewhat exaggerated illustration). A tire with a pressure that's too low will have shoulder temperatures that are higher compared to the center section of the tire. A too high pressure will result in the opposite situation. We can calculate a math channel that gives us the difference between the center tire temperature and the average of the inner and outer temperature (to take into account camber effects).

$$PTemp_i = T_{tire_i}(\text{Center}) - \frac{T_{tire_i}(\text{In}) + T_{tire_i}(\text{Out})}{2}$$ (Eq. 8.8)

With $\quad i$ = LF, RF, LR, RR

$T_{tire_i}(\text{Center})$ = Center tire temperature

$T_{tire_i}(\text{In})$ = Inside shoulder tire temperature

$T_{tire_i}(\text{Out})$ = Outside shoulder tire temperature

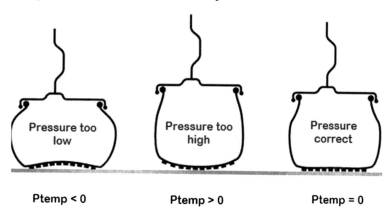

Figure 8.30 Tire pressure evaluation with tire temperature sensors

When the result of this channel is positive, it means that the tire pressure is too high; when it's negative the tire pressure is too low. In the example in Figure 8.31, the right front and left rear tire pressures are fine, as the values fluctuate without large variation around zero. The right rear tire pressure is a bit too high, but the left front is definitely too low. The average values of these channels make excellent lap statistics that show how tire pressure develops over a number of laps (see Figure 8.32). Here as well right front and left rear tire pressures are fine over the displayed 11-lap run while the left front tire is still marginally too low in pressure in the last lap and the right rear tire pressure is slightly too high during the complete run.

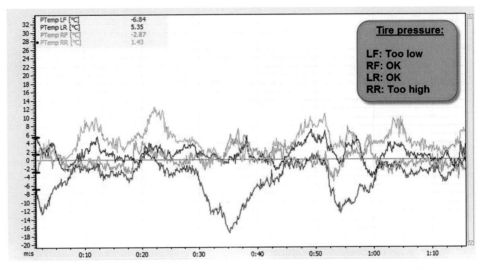

Figure 8.31 Evaluating tire pressure by comparing the shoulder temperatures with the center temperature

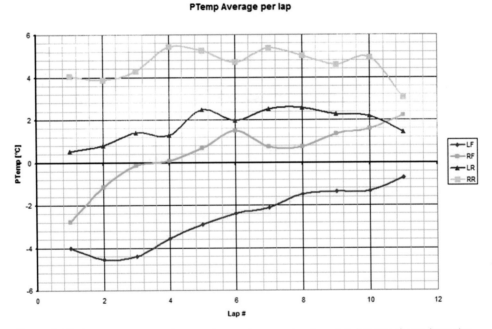

Figure 8.32 Average pressure temperature values per lap for an 11-lap run shows how tire pressure builds up and stabilizes

Chapter 9
Quantifying Roll Stiffness Distribution

The car's oversteer/understeer balance during cornering is determined by the load distribution between the front and rear axles. Suspension tuning is all about influencing this balance by adjusting the vehicle's roll stiffness distribution by altering spring rates, rollbar rates, damping, tire pressures, and so on, until the desired understeer/oversteer balance is achieved. This chapter shows how the data acquisition system can assist in determining references for the suspension setup and how the effects of setup changes can be analyzed quickly.

Some setup reference numbers are discussed that can be easily calculated with the mathematical options in the data analysis software or, if possible, by exporting the required channels into a spreadsheet. They help characterize the suspension and serve as a future reference for setting up the car.

9.1   Measuring Suspension Roll Angle

To calculate the roll stiffness from the logged data we first need to determine the roll angle of the chassis. For this, suspension travel needs to be measured by suspension potentiometers.

During cornering, the total roll angle of the vehicle will be made up of three components:

- Roll angle due to lateral weight transfer of the unsprung mass: This is proportional to the unsprung mass, the dynamic tire radius, track width, and tire spring rate.

- Roll angle due to geometric weight transfer: This is the roll angle due to the roll center height.

- Roll angle due to lateral weight transfer of sprung mass: This is proportional to the sprung mass, sprung mass center of gravity height, and track width. The distribution between front and rear axles depends on the roll stiffness of these axles.

The first two angles in the list added together make the tire roll angle. It should be clear that from suspension travel measurement we can only calculate the roll angle due to lateral weight transfer of the sprung mass or suspension roll angle. The other two angles can be determined if suspension travel measurement is combined with ride height measurement (laser sensors) or calculated when all necessary parameters are known. Math channels for front and rear suspension roll angle (in degrees) can be created using the following equations:

$$\alpha_{\text{RollSuspF}} = \text{ArcTan}\left[\frac{(x_{\text{SuspensionLF}} - x_{\text{SuspensionRF}}) \cdot MR_{\text{F}}}{T_{\text{F}}}\right] \cdot 57.3 \qquad \text{(Eq. 9.1)}$$

$$\alpha_{\text{RollSuspR}} = \text{ArcTan}\left[\frac{(x_{\text{SuspensionLR}} - x_{\text{SuspensionRR}}) \cdot MR_{\text{R}}}{T_{\text{R}}}\right] \cdot 57.3 \qquad \text{(Eq. 9.2)}$$

With
$x_{\text{SuspensionLF}}$ = Front left suspension movement [mm]

$x_{\text{SuspensionRF}}$ = Front right suspension movement [mm]

$x_{\text{SuspensionLR}}$ = Rear left suspension movement [mm]

$x_{\text{SuspensionRR}}$ = Rear right suspension movement [mm]

MR_{F} = Front suspension motion ratio [–]

MR_{R} = Rear suspension motion ratio [–]

T_{F} = Front track width [mm]

T_{R} = Rear track width [mm]

Figure 9.1 shows the result of these math channels for data taken from a Formula One car in Hockenheim. Vehicle speed, lateral acceleration, and front and rear suspension roll angle are pictured. The roll angle traces follow the shape of the lateral acceleration trace, which is logical because lateral acceleration is indeed what causes lateral load transfer and thus makes the suspension roll. Another observation is that the rear suspension roll angle is larger than the one at the front. A more detailed explanation of this follows later in this chapter.

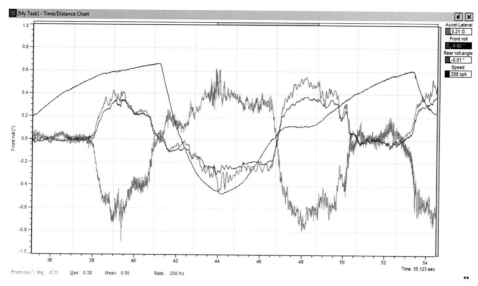

Figure 9.1 Front and rear suspension roll angle of a Formula One car

9.2 The Roll Gradient

In vehicle dynamics, it is common to characterize the roll stiffness of a vehicle in normalized form as degrees of body roll per unit of lateral acceleration. This parameter is called the roll gradient. Here is a practical example of how the roll gradient is related to the car's roll stiffness. Table 9.1 provides an overview of the dynamic parameters of a GT-type racecar. This data was calculated by SusProg3D, a software package used for suspension geometry analysis.

Equation 9.3 is the basic definition of roll gradient with α_{roll} being the overall vehicle roll angle and G_{lat} the lateral acceleration acting on the center of gravity.

$$RG = \frac{\alpha_{\text{roll}}}{G_{\text{lat}}}$$ (Eq. 9.3)

From the data in Table 9.1, the roll moment (M_{roll}) at a lateral acceleration of 1 G is calculated. M_{roll} is defined by Equation 9.4.

$$M_{\text{roll}} = h_{\text{roll}} \cdot (W_{\text{sF}} + W_{\text{sR}})$$ (Eq. 9.4)

With h_{roll} = Distance between the car's center of gravity and the roll axis (the imaginary line connecting front and rear roll centers)

201

W_{sF} = Static sprung weight of the front axle

W_{sR} = Static sprung weight of the rear axle

Table 9.1 SusProg3D calculation of vehicle parameters from a GT racecar		
Parameter	Front	Rear
Roll center height	46.49 mm	51.03 mm
Track width	1649.54 mm	1684.19 mm
Wheelbase	2402.87 mm	
Vehicle weight	636.00 kg	739.50 kg
Unsprung weight	61.00 kg	98.00 kg
Lateral acceleration	1 G	
Vehicle center of gravity		
From ground	369 mm	
From front axle centerline	1291.84 mm	
Sprung center of gravity		
From ground	372.50 mm	
From front axle centerline	1267.11 mm	
Above roll axis	323.61 mm	
Antiroll stiffness—Axle		
Tires	97368.66 kgcm/°	112147.73 kgcm/°
Springs	40752.86kgcm/°	23765.06 kgcm/°
Antiroll bar	64312.73kgcm/°	22255.07 kgcm/°
Total	50535.40kgcm/°	32630.23 kgcm/°
Antiroll stiffness—Car		
Tires	209516.38 kgcm/°	
Springs	64517.92 kgcm/°	
Antiroll bar	86567.80 kgcm/°	
Total	83165.62 kgcm/°	
Roll angle		
Tires	0.28 °	0.19 °
Suspension	0.22 °	0.31 °
Total	0.50 °	0.50 °

Figure 9.2 illustrates the mentioned parameters.

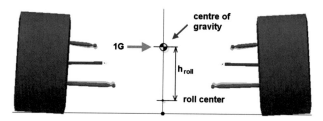

Figure 9.2 Distance between center of gravity and roll center

In Table 9.1, the following information is provided:

$W_{sF} = 636 - 61 = 575$ kg

$W_{sR} = 739.5 - 98 = 641.5$ kg

h_{roll} = Sprung CoG height above roll axis = 323.61 mm

Entering this information into Equation 9.4 gives us:

$$M_{roll} = 32.361 \text{ cm} \cdot 1216 \text{ kg} = 39351 \text{ kgcm}$$

The roll angle then can be expressed as a function of roll moment (Equation 9.5).

$$\alpha_{roll} = \frac{M_{roll}}{K_{rolltot}} \qquad\qquad \text{(Eq. 9.5)}$$

$K_{rolltot}$ is the total roll stiffness of the car, which is 83166 kgcm/deg (Table 9.1). Because the roll moment is calculated at a lateral acceleration of 1 G, Equation 9.4 equals the roll gradient (*RG*):

$$RG = \frac{39351 \text{ kgcm}}{83166 \text{ kgcm}/^\circ} = 0.473 \text{ }^\circ/G$$

The data in Table 9.1 is calculated for a lateral acceleration of 1 G. The total roll angle of the vehicle in this table is 0.5 degrees, which equals the roll gradient calculated above.

Note that this calculation uses the total roll stiffness, including the stiffness of the tires. The method explained later in this section calculates roll gradients using the data from the suspension displacement channels, which do not measure deflection of the tires. If the elasticity of the tires is not taken into account in the calculation, RG becomes as shown below with $K_{rolltot} = 64518 + 86568 = 151086$ kgcm/deg (because antiroll bar and suspension springs are parallel springs, these can be added together).

$$RG = \frac{39351 \text{ kgcm}}{151086 \text{ kgcm}/^\circ} = 0.260 \; ^\circ/G$$

Tables 9.2 and 9.3 state some typical numbers for roll gradient from different literature sources.

Table 9.2 Typical roll gradients [4-2]	
Very soft–Economy and basic family transportation, pre-1975	8.5 °/G
Soft–Basic family transportation, after 1975	7.5 °/G
Semi-soft–Contemporary middle market sedans	7.0 °/C
Semi-firm–Sport sedans	6.0 °/C
Firm–Sport sedans	5.0 °/G
Very firm–High performance (e.g., Camaro Z28, Firebird TransAm)	4.2 °/G
Extremely firm–Contemporary very high-performance sports (e.g., Corvette), street cars extensively modified to increase roll stiffness	3.0 °/G
Hard–Racing cars only	1.5 °/G
Active suspension, servo-controlled roll stiffness, roll-in, zero roll, and roll out all possible	—

Table 9.3 Typical roll gradients [9-1]	
Stiff high-downforce race cars	0.2–0.7 °/G
Low downforce sedans	1.0–1.8 °/G

Both references state that race cars with any amount of downforce have a roll gradient lower than 1.5 deg/G. Table 9.4 shows some measured examples of various race cars. These numbers were derived from suspension potentiometer data, and tire spring rates were not taken into account. When the roll angle of the tires is added to the measured suspension roll angle, the roll gradients in Table 9.4 are greater.

Table 9.4 Typical roll gradients for various types of race cars	
2002 Formula One car	0.03–0.10 °/G
2001 IndyCar	0.10–0.20 °/G
2010 Superleague Formula single-seater	0.08–0.15 °/G
2004 Dodge Viper GTS-R race car	0.44–0.55 °/G
2004 Corvette C5R GT1 race car	0.20–0.40 °/G
2006 Corvette C6R GT1 race car	0.25–0.35 °/G
2011 Audi LMS GT3 race car	0.30–0.50 °/G

By measuring the lateral acceleration and the movement of the suspension, a math channel can be created to calculate the car's roll gradient. From the suspension data, the overall roll angle of the car can be calculated by creating the mathematical channel in Equation 9.6. This equation results in a positive roll angle when the chassis rolls clockwise and vice versa, facing forward along the vehicle's longitudinal centerline. This is in accordance with SAE's Vehicle Axis System [3-2].

$$\alpha_{roll} = \arctan\left(\frac{(x_{suspensionLF} - x_{suspensionRF})\cdot MR_F + (x_{suspensionLR} - x_{suspensionRR})\cdot MR_R}{T_F + T_R}\right)\cdot 57.3 \quad \text{(Eq. 9.6)}$$

With
α_{roll} = Total suspension roll angle [°]
$x_{suspensionLF}$ = Front left suspension movement [mm]
$x_{suspensionRF}$ = Front right suspension movement [mm]
$x_{suspensionLR}$ = Rear left suspension movement [mm]
$x_{suspensionRR}$ = Rear right suspension movement [mm]
MR_F = Front suspension motion ratio [–]
MR_R = Rear suspension motion ratio [–]
T_F = Front track width [mm]
T_R = Rear track width [mm]

If the analysis software package allows the use of X-Y graphs, a chart can be created illustrating the roll angle versus lateral acceleration as shown in Figure 9.3. The advantage of putting this information in a graph is that in one view it shows the vehicle's maximum

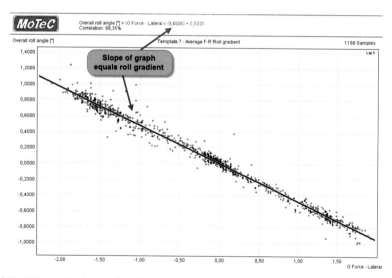

Figure 9.3 X-Y graph of overall roll angle versus lateral G, taken from a lap around Nürburgring in a Dodge Viper GTS-R

roll angle and the acceleration at which this angle is reached. It shows this for left- and right-hand cornering. The relationship between roll angle and lateral acceleration is linear in most cases (although not in the case where progressive suspension elements are used), and the slope of the graph equals the roll gradient. In the illustration, the equation for a linear trend line is calculated. The roll gradient, or the slope of the trend line, is 0.48 °/G in this case.

Note further that this calculation is made taking the roll angle of the suspension springs and antiroll bars into account. This does not include the roll angle resulting from tire deflection.

The *X-Y* plot in Figure 9.3 shows a certain degree of scatter in the data points, which can be explained by the following:

- Accuracy of the suspension position measurements
- The damping of the system momentarily changing the roll stiffness distribution of the car
- Chassis torsion, especially when driving over big bumps or curbs
- Friction in suspension components

Each axle also can be viewed separately and roll gradients calculated for the front and rear suspension. For this, the overall roll angle in the *X-Y* graph is replaced by the roll angle of the front and rear suspension, respectively. From the same session covered by Figure 9.3, the front and rear roll gradients are shown in Figures 9.4 and 9.5.

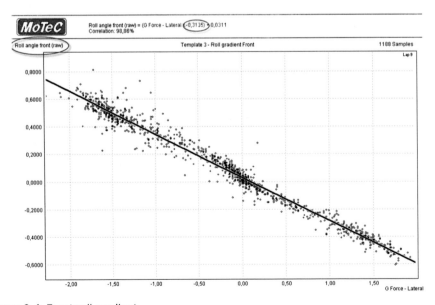

Figure 9.4 Front roll gradient

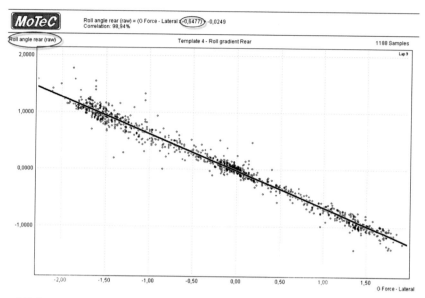

Figure 9.5 Rear roll gradient

In Equation 9.6, the overall roll gradient is calculated from the average roll angle between the front and rear suspension, and the lateral force remains the same. This means that the overall roll gradient is the average between the front and rear roll gradient.

The advantage of calculating front and rear roll gradients separately is the information obtained about the roll stiffness distribution of the vehicle. The lower the roll gradient is on one side of the vehicle, the higher the resistance is to roll movement on that side, and vice versa.

From these roll gradients, the actual roll stiffness of the front and rear suspension can be calculated. However, for analysis purposes, merely observing roll gradients provides the engineer with a good idea about the roll stiffness distribution and the effects of setup changes on this distribution.

If the driver is pleased with the car's handling during a track session, the roll gradients can be recorded as a future reference for that particular racetrack. If in a following test or race on this track the handling is not as good as before, the engineer can try to restore the same roll gradients with the proper setup changes to obtain a known starting point.

9.3   Using Roll Gradients as a Setup Tool

How useful roll gradients can be is illustrated with an example. In Figures 9.4 and 9.5, the analysis software calculated these numbers:

$$RG_F = 0.3135\ \%/G$$
$$RG_R = 0.6477\ \%/G$$

This means that the overall roll gradient (RG) is 0.4806 %/G. The car in question has the properties given in Table 9.5:

Table 9.5 Vehicle properties	
Front axle weight	636 kg
Rear axle weight	739 kg
Front axle unsprung weight	61 kg
Rear axle unsprung weight	98 kg
Front roll center height (h_{RCf})	46.5 mm
Rear roll center height (h_{RCr})	51 mm
Front spring rate (per wheel) (SR_f)	260 kg/cm
Rear spring rate (per wheel) (SR_r)	180 kg/cm
Front suspension motion ratio (MR_F)	1.373
Rear suspension motion ratio (MR_R)	1.725
Front antiroll bar motion ratio (MR_{rollF})	1.495
Rear antiroll bar motion ratio (MR_{rollR})	1.550
Front track width (T_F)	1650 mm
Rear track width (T_R)	1685 mm
Wheelbase (WB)	2403 mm
Height sprung center of gravity from ground (h_{CoG})	372 mm

First h_{roll} is calculated:

Front sprung weight: $W_{sF} = 636 - 61 = 575$ kg

Rear sprung weight: $W_{sR} = 739 - 98 = 641$ kg

Using basic statics and trigonometry, the equation for h_{roll} becomes Equation 9.7.

$$h_{roll} = h_{CoG} - \left(h_{RCf} + \frac{(h_{RCr} - h_{RCf}) \cdot W_{sR}}{W_{sF} + W_{sR}} \right) \qquad \text{(Eq. 9.7)}$$

So the result for h_{roll} in this example becomes

$$h_{roll} = 372 - \left(46.5 + \frac{(51-46.5)\cdot 641}{575+641}\right) = 323 \text{ mm}$$

Entering this into Equation 9.4 gives the roll moment at a lateral acceleration of 1 G:

$$M_{roll} = 32.3 \text{ cm} \cdot 1216 \text{ kg} = 39277 \text{ kgcm}$$

The total roll stiffness is given by Equation 9.8.

$$K_{rolltot} = \frac{M_{roll}}{RG} \quad \text{(Eq. 9.8)}$$

So,

$$K_{rolltot} = \frac{39277}{0.4806} = 81725 \text{ kgcm}/°$$

With the front and rear roll gradient, it can be determined how this total roll stiffness is distributed between the front and rear axle (Equations 9.9 and 9.10).

$$K_{rollf} = K_{rolltot} \cdot \frac{RG_R}{RG_F + RG_R} \quad \text{(Eq. 9.9)}$$

$$K_{rollr} = K_{rolltot} - K_{rollf} \quad \text{(Eq. 9.10)}$$

With K_{rollf} = Roll stiffness of front axle

K_{rollr} = Roll stiffness of rear axle

So, K_{rollf} = 55083 kgcm/° and K_{rollr} = 26642 kgcm/°. The roll stiffness distribution is biased 67.4% to the front.

Because suspension springs and antiroll bars are parallel springs, Equations 9.11 and 9.12 apply.

$$K_{rollf} = K_{rollfSPRINGS} + K_{rollfARB} \quad \text{(Eq. 9.11)}$$

$$K_{rollr} = K_{rollrSPRINGS} + K_{rollrARB} \quad \text{(Eq. 9.12)}$$

With $K_{\text{rollfSPRINGS}}$ = Roll stiffness of front axle due to suspension springs

         K_{rollfARB} = Roll stiffness of front axle due to antiroll bar

       $K_{\text{rollrSPRINGS}}$ = Roll stiffness of rear axle due to suspension springs

         K_{rollrARB} = Roll stiffness of rear axle due to antiroll bar

The springs now on the car result in the following wheel rates (Equation 9.13):

$$WR = \frac{SR}{MR^2}$$

(Eq. 9.13)

With WR = Wheel rate

      SR = Spring rate

      MR = Suspension motion ratio

$$WR_f = \frac{260}{1.373^2} = 138 \text{ kg/cm}$$

$$WR_r = \frac{180}{1.725^2} = 60 \text{ kg/cm}$$

The roll stiffness produced by these wheel rates can be determined using Equations 9.14 and 9.15.

$$K_{\text{rollfSPRING}} = \frac{T_F^2 \cdot WR_f}{2} \cdot \frac{\pi}{180}$$

(Eq. 9.14)

$$K_{\text{rollrSPRING}} = \frac{T_R^2 \cdot WR_r}{2} \cdot \frac{\pi}{180}$$

(Eq. 9.15)

This gives

$$K_{\text{rollfSPRING}} = \frac{\pi \cdot 165^2 \cdot 138}{360} = 32785 \text{ kgcm/}°$$

$$K_{\text{rollrSPRING}} = \frac{\pi \cdot 168.5^2 \cdot 60}{360} = 14866 \text{ kgcm/}°$$

Using Equations 9.11 and 9.12, the roll stiffness (measured at the wheel) produced by the antiroll bars becomes

$$K_{\text{rollfARB}} = K_{\text{rollf}} - K_{\text{rollfSPRINGS}} = 55083 - 32785 = 22298 \text{ kgcm/}°$$

$$K_{\text{rollrARB}} = K_{\text{rollr}} - K_{\text{rollrSPRINGS}} = 26642 - 14866 = 11776 \text{ kgcm/}°$$

The actual antiroll bar rates are

$$SR_{rollf} = MR_{rollf}^2 \cdot K_{rollfARB} = 1.495^2 \cdot 22298 = 49837 \text{ kgcm}/°$$
$$SR_{rollr} = MR_{rollr}^2 \cdot K_{rollrARB} = 1.550^2 \cdot 11776 = 28292 \text{ kgcm}/°$$

As an example, an attempt assumedly is made to resolve a steady-state understeer problem with this car, but the overall roll gradient needs to remain the same. To do this, the front axle weight transfer could be decreased (i.e., the front roll stiffness decreased). This requires a higher front roll gradient. The problem is solved by mounting different springs with which the engineer would like to obtain a roll stiffness bias of 65% on the front axle. To maintain the same overall roll gradient, the front and rear springs must be changed. What spring rates must be put on the car?

First, the required roll gradients are determined:

$$RG_{F(required)} = 0.35 \cdot 2 \cdot 0.4806 = 0.336 \text{ °/G}$$
$$RG_{R(required)} = 0.65 \cdot 2 \cdot 0.4806 = 0.625 \text{ °/G}$$

The total roll stiffness remains the same. From this the required front and rear roll rate can be calculated:

$$K_{rollf(required)} = 81725 \cdot \frac{0.625}{0.9612} = 53140 \text{ kgcm}/°$$
$$K_{rollr(required)} = 81725 - 53140 = 28585 \text{ kgcm}/°$$

As the suspension springs and antiroll bar are parallel spring rates, the required roll rates for the new springs become

$$K_{rollfSPRING(req.)} = 53140 - 22298 = 30842 \text{ kgcm}/°$$
$$K_{rollrSPRING(req.)} = 28585 - 11776 = 16809 \text{ kgcm}/°$$

With Equations 9.14 and 9.15 the corresponding wheel rates can be determined:

$$WR_{f(req.)} = \frac{360 \cdot K_{rollfSPRING(req.)}}{\pi \cdot T_F^2} = \frac{360 \cdot 30842}{\pi \cdot 165^2} = 130 \text{ kg/cm}$$
$$WR_{r(req.)} = \frac{360 \cdot K_{rollrSPRING(req.)}}{\pi \cdot T_F^2} = \frac{360 \cdot 16809}{\pi \cdot 168.5^2} = 68 \text{ kg/cm}$$

And finally, with the suspension motion ratios, this can be translated to the required spring rates:

$$SR_{f(req.)} = 130.0 \cdot 1.373^2 = 245 \text{ kg/cm}$$
$$SR_{r(req.)} = 68 \cdot 1.725^2 = 202 \text{ kg/cm}$$

In this example, the roll stiffness distribution is shifted rearward by changing the front and rear spring rates, which is required to achieve the desired roll gradients. In addition, the stiffness of the antiroll bars is measured. Different setup changes require small variations in the previous calculations.

9.4   Front to Rear Roll Angle Ratio

Another reference number that tells something about the roll stiffness distribution is the ratio (ς) between the rear and front roll angle, the roll ratio (Equation 9.16):

$$\varsigma = \frac{\alpha_{RollSuspR}}{\alpha_{RollSuspF}}$$ (Eq. 9.16)

With $\alpha_{RollSuspR}$ = Rear suspension roll angle [°]

$\alpha_{RollSuspF}$ = Front suspension roll angle [°]

This ratio also can be calculated from the front and rear roll gradients using Equation 9.17.

$$\varsigma = \frac{RG_R}{RG_F}$$ (Eq. 9.17)

If the software allows, the relationship between the front and rear roll angle also can be illustrated in an X-Y graph as shown in Figure 9.6. Note that this is usually a linear relationship (as the roll ratio is constant), except for progressive suspension systems. The graph shows the same pattern of scatter as the roll gradient X-Y graphs for the same reasons.

In Figure 9.6, the ratio between the rear and front roll angle is 2.02. This means that in this particular situation the front roll angle is about half the rear roll angle. Remember that suspension roll angle is being addressed. The total vehicle roll angle is the sum of the suspension roll angle and the roll angle induced by the tire spring rates.

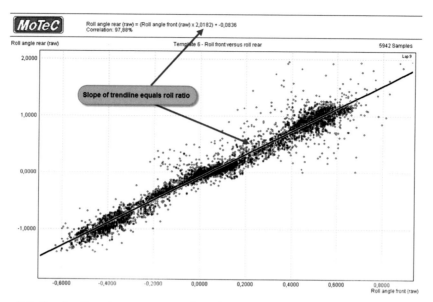

Figure 9.6 Front roll angle versus rear roll angle

Assuming an infinitely stiff chassis, Equation 9.18 is true, with $\alpha_{\text{RollSuspF}}$ and $\alpha_{\text{RollSuspR}}$ being the front and rear suspension roll angle, respectively, and $\alpha_{\text{RollTiresF}}$ and $\alpha_{\text{RollTiresR}}$ the roll angles induced by the front and rear pairs of tires, respectively.

$$\alpha_{\text{RollSuspF}} + \alpha_{\text{RollTiresF}} = \alpha_{\text{RollSuspR}} + \alpha_{\text{RollTiresR}} \qquad \text{(Eq. 9.18)}$$

Expressing the rear suspension roll angle as a function of the front suspension roll angle gives us Equation 9.19.

$$\alpha_{\text{RollSuspF}} + \alpha_{\text{RollTiresF}} = \varsigma \cdot \alpha_{\text{RollSuspF}} + \alpha_{\text{RollTiresR}} \qquad \text{(Eq. 9.19)}$$

From this another expression for ζ follows (Equation 9.20):

$$\varsigma = \left(\frac{\alpha_{\text{RollTiresF}} - \alpha_{\text{RollTiresR}}}{\alpha_{\text{RollSuspF}}} \right) + 1 \qquad \text{(Eq. 9.20)}$$

With this expression, the effect of roll stiffness variations on one axle on ζ can be investigated. The possibilities are summarized in Table 9.6.

213

Table 9.6 Changing the roll stiffness on one vehicle axle, either on the suspension or the tires, and its effects on ζ		
	INCREASE	DECREASE
Front Roll Stiffness		
Suspension	ζ increases	ζ decreases
Tires	ζ decreases	ζ increases
Rear Rolls Stiffness		
Suspension	ζ decreases	ζ increases
Tires	ζ increases	ζ decreases

From Equations 9.17 and 9.20, it can be concluded that when the tire spring rates change (due to a different construction or running a different tire pressure), the suspension roll gradients change also.

For example, the example in Table 9.1 had the following roll angles at a lateral acceleration of 1 G:

Front	Suspension	0.22 °
	Tires	0.28 °
	Total	0.50 °
Rear	Suspension	0.32 °
	Tires	0.19 °
	Total	0.50 °

So ζ = 0.32/0.22 = 1.45.

Now, let's assume that the rear tire spring rate is increased by 10% so instead of 453 kg/cm, this result becomes 498 kg/cm. Running the calculation again using a suspension kinematics software package offers the following results:

Front	Suspension	0.21 °
	Tires	0.28 °
	Total	0.49 °
Rear	Suspension	0.32 °
	Tires	0.17 °
	Total	0.49 °

ζ becomes 0.32/0.21 = 1.52 and has increased by 4.8%.

To correct this back to the old roll ratio by modifying the spring rate, the rear wheel rate needs to be increased by 25% (to 120 kg/cm) to approach the old roll ratio.

Front	Suspension	0.21 °
	Tires	0.28 °
	Total	0.49 °
Rear	Suspension	0.30 °
	Tires	0.20 °
	Total	0.49 °

ζ becomes 0.30/0.21 = 1.43.

In this particular example, a 10% change to the tire spring rates equals a 25% change to the car's spring rate!

9.5   Using the Roll Ratio as a Setup Tool

The practical application of the roll angle ratio is illustrated using a real-world example. Figures 9.7 and 9.8 give the roll ratio (ζ) before and after a change to the front antiroll bar setting. The first graph shows a lap done by Bert Longin in a Dodge Viper on the Circuit Zolder racetrack. In this situation, the front antiroll bar was in full soft position. In the second graph, this antiroll bar was adjusted to full hard, changing the vehicle roll stiffness distribution by quite a margin.

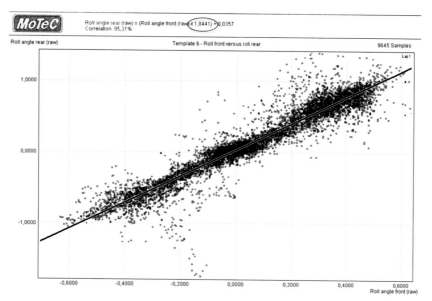

Figure 9.7 Front versus rear roll angle during a lap around Zolder in a Dodge Viper GTS-R, driven by Bert Longin; front antiroll bar in softest position

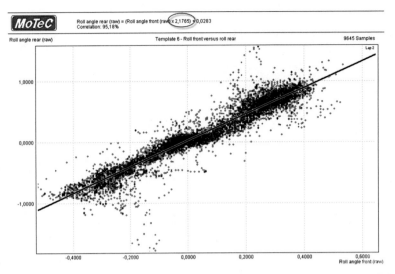

Figure 9.8 Same car, same driver, and same set of tires, now with the front antiroll bar in its hardest position

The roll gradients are not illustrated in a graph, but Table 9.7 summarizes the three calculated roll stiffness characteristics. Both front and rear roll gradient have decreased in magnitude (the total roll stiffness of the car is increased by the harder front antiroll bar), the biggest step being made at the front. An increased roll ratio indicates the amount with which the roll stiffness distribution was moved toward the front axle.

Table 9.7 Measured roll gradients and roll ratio before and after the setup change		
	Soft front antiroll bar	Hard front antiroll bar
Front roll gradient (RG$_F$)	0.2754 °/G	0.2253 °/G
Rear roll gradient (RG$_R$)	0.5386 °/G	0.5137 °/G
Roll ratio (ζ)	1.8441	2.1765

The charts in Figures 9.7 and 9.8 also show that by changing the front antiroll bar stiffness from its minimum to maximum the front maximum roll angle decreases approximately 0.1 deg, whereas the rear maximum roll angle remains the same.

The roll ratio together with front and rear roll gradients are excellent lap metrics to evaluate the mechanical balance of the car over a longer period of time. Figure 9.9 shows an example of this (note that the roll gradients are expressed in mm suspension roll per unit of lateral acceleration). This kind of graph reveals what influence different trends in front and rear tire pressures have on the roll stiffness distribution of the car.

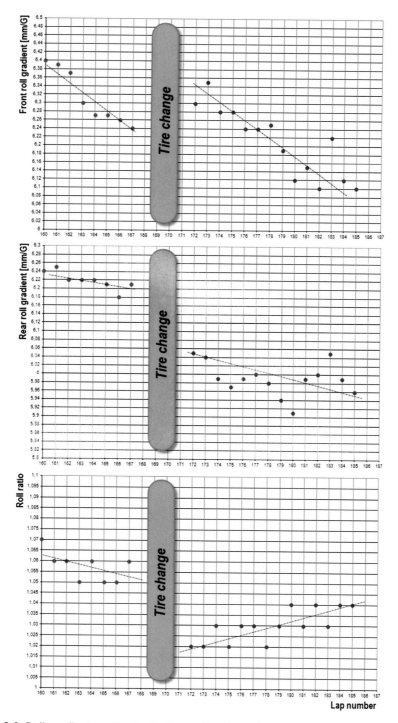

Figure 9.9 Roll gradients and roll ratio for multiple laps visualized in run charts

All the equations in the previous paragraphs are valid when chassis torsion rates are not taken into consideration. In practice, the chassis spring rate may not be high enough to be of no importance in these calculations. Chassis torsion spring rates influence the roll stiffness distribution of the vehicle and therefore the roll gradients change as well. However, when comparing setups within one vehicle, the chassis spring rate can be ignored because normally it is a parameter in the vehicle configuration that does not change.

9.6   Suspension Troubleshooting

In the previous sections, linear functions were created from some suspension parameters. In the case where a progressive suspension is applied, these functions are not linear. Where linear suspension components are applied and roll gradients or roll angle ratio are not constants, something is wrong. Figure 9.10 shows an example of this situation.

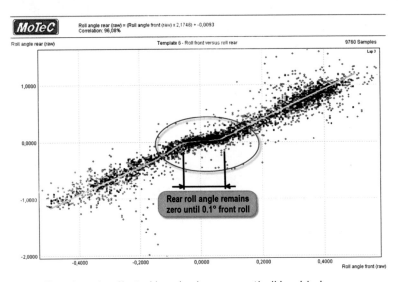

Figure 9.10 Roll angle ratio affected by a broken rear antiroll bar blade

In this example, there is obviously a problem with the suspension. The rear roll angle remains zero until the front angle reaches 0.1 deg. In this particular example, the rear antiroll bar blade was broken.

Another example of a possible problem is shown in Figure 9.11. A run chart of the suspension roll ratio is given for a 12-lap run by an LMP2 prototype. In the first 6 laps the roll ration varies slightly between 1.2 and 1.3, but thereafter it starts to increase at a higher rate. At the end of lap 12 the car entered the pit lane, with the driver reporting a tire puncture. Can we determine from the data in Figure 9.11 if it was a front or rear tire that was losing pressure? Referring to Table 9.6 and knowing that on one axle the roll stiffness is being decreased by reduced tire pressure, we can conclude that an increasing roll ratio means that a front tire is losing pressure.

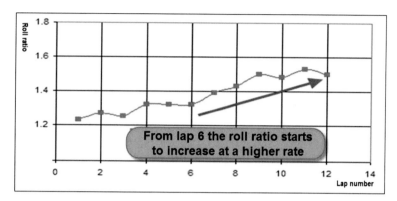

Figure 9.11 Roll angle ratio lap statistics indication a tire puncture

LMP2 prototypes such as the one that produced the data in the preceding example are often equipped with telemetry systems. As it is often impractical to send the complete damper position signals over the limited telemetry bandwidth, it is useful to calculate lap statistics for roll gradient and roll ratios not only to provide simple objective data about the balance of the car, but also to detect potential tire punctures. In conjunction with tire pressure sensors, roll gradient and roll ratio statistics can be a useful sanity check to determine if there's really a puncture or if there's a sensor problem. The advantage of sending simple lap statistics instead of complete data channels is that it takes up virtually no memory in the telemetry data stream.

9.7   Pitch Gradient

Similar to the roll gradient, it is possible to calculate a gradient for the vehicle's pitch movement. The pitch angle can be calculated from the suspension position channels and expressed as a function of longitudinal g-force with β_{pitch} being the vehicle's pitch angle measured at the chassis centerline and G_{long} being the longitudinal acceleration acting on the car's center of gravity (Equation 9.21).

$$PG = \frac{\beta_{pitch}}{G_{long}}$$

(Eq. 9.21)

Unlike the roll gradient, the pitch gradient is not dependent on chassis torsion (the pitch angle being determined at the vehicle's longitudinal centerline). Pitch gradient also is not commonly a linear function when anti-squat and anti-dive suspension geometry is applied. It is, however, a good way to visualize different setups graphically and

characterize a suspension. Figure 9.12 shows an *X-Y* plot of the pitch angle against longitudinal acceleration that clearly illustrates this.

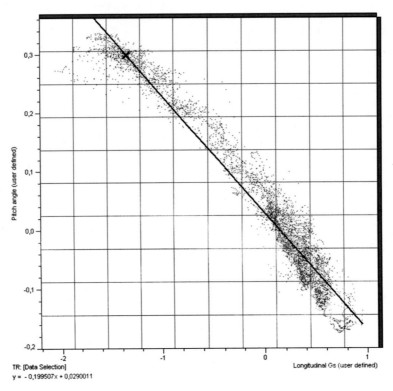

Figure 9.12 Pitch gradient

Chapter 10
Wheel Loads and Weight Transfer

The principal task of the race engineer is to balance the vertical loads acting on the tires as well as possible in order to maximize the cornering, braking, and acceleration capability of the vehicle. It is therefore very useful to actually know what these vertical loads are. There are different ways to determine the static load distribution, the dynamic lateral and longitudinal weight transfers, and the effect of aerodynamics, track slope, banking and track surface bumps on the vertical tire loads. Some of the effects can be measured by using suspension load cells; others need to be calculated from suspension potentiometer data and technical specifications of the vehicle.

To be able to determine the dynamic wheel loads, we need to measure or calculate the following items:

- Static corner weights
- Lateral weight transfer
- Longitudinal weight transfer
- Track banking and slope effects
- Aerodynamic forces
- Effects of bumps and road surface irregularities

In this chapter, we'll derive the math channels that give us the four dynamic vertical loads for a given race car in every possible situation.

10.1   Lateral Weight Transfer

A car in a turn will experience a centrifugal force acting on its center of gravity that tends to throw the car out at a tangent to its intended path. This force is resisted by the lateral force developed by the tires. Because of the fact that the center of gravity is above the ground, load is transferred from the wheels at the inner side of the corner to those at the outside. This situation is illustrated in Figure 10.1 for a right-hand turn, where the cornering forces (F_L and F_R) result in a lateral acceleration (G_{Lat}). The reacting inertial force is calculated as Equation 10.1.

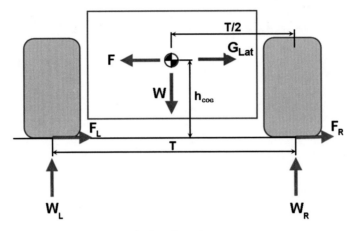

Figure 10.1 Lateral weight transfer (right-hand turn)

$$F = W \cdot G_{lat} \qquad \text{(Eq. 10.1)}$$

By taking the moments about one of the wheel centers, the weight transfer due to cornering is found (Equation 10.2).

$$\Delta W_{Lat} = \frac{W \cdot G_{lat} \cdot h_{COG}}{T} \qquad \text{(Eq. 10.2)}$$

Where W = vehicle weight [kg]

ΔW_{Lat} = Total lateral weight transfer; increase in left side load and decrease in right side load [kg]

h_{COG} = Center of gravity height from ground [m]

T = Track width [m]

G_{lat} = Lateral acceleration at center of gravity [G]

Equation 10.2 indicates that the total lateral weight transfer is proportional to the lateral acceleration and the center of gravity height and inversely proportional to the track width. This means that weight transfer increases with the weight of the car and the height of the center of gravity and decreases with a greater track width. Let's assume a single-seater with the following properties:

Left-hand side car weight $W_L = 254$ kg

Right-hand side car weight $W_R = 254$ kg

$$G_{lat} = 1.0 \text{ G}$$

$$h_{COG} = 381 \text{ mm}$$

$$T = 1435 \text{ mm}$$

In these conditions $\Delta W_{Lat} = \dfrac{(254 \text{kg} + 254 \text{kg}) \cdot 1G \cdot 0.381 \text{m}}{1.435 \text{m}} = 134.88 \text{kg}$

The total load on the left-hand wheels will be 254 + 134.88 = 388.88 kg, and on the right-hand wheels 254 −134.88 = 119.12 kg.

The center of gravity height can be determined by first weighing the car on a level surface and then raising its rear end and weighing the front end again (Figure 10.2).

Figure 10.2 Determining the center of gravity height requires the rear end of the car to be raised by a substantial amount

The following procedure should be observed:

- Each shock absorber should be replaced by a solid link to eliminate any suspension travel. The length of these links should be dimensioned carefully to put the car at its exact static ride height. Inaccuracy here can influence greatly the scale readings.
- The tires should be overinflated as much as possible to limit sidewall flexing.
- All fluids should be at the right level.

- A driver should be in the car (or at least an object that is equivalent to the driver's weight).

- The total weight on the front axle should be measured while the car is on a level surface.

- The rear end of the car should be raised as much as possible. The calculation is based on the change in weight on the front wheels in relation to the angle to which the car is raised. The higher the distance the car can be raised, the bigger the shift in front wheel weight and the more accurate the height calculation.

- The height of the center of gravity above the axle centerlines now can be calculated using Equation 10.3 (see Figure 10.3).

$$h = \frac{WB \cdot \Delta W}{W \cdot \tan \alpha} \qquad \text{(Eq. 10.3)}$$

With WB = Wheelbase

W = Total vehicle weight

$\Delta W = W_{f2} - W_{f1}$

W_{f1} = Front weight measured on level surface

W_{f2} = Front weight measured with raised rear axle

Tan $\alpha = B/A$

$A = \sqrt{WB^2 - B^2}$

- To obtain the height of the center of gravity above the ground plane, the tire radius should be added to the calculated height above axle centerlines (h).

- Often the center of gravity is close to the wheel center height, and the change in front weight as the car is jacked up is small. To get the best results, measure at different jacking heights and average the results.

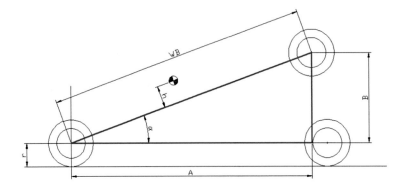

Figure 10.3 Center of gravity height calculation

Equation 10.2 defines the total amount of lateral weight transfer of a car during cornering. However, what we now would like to know is how this total amount of lateral weight transferred is distributed between the front and rear axle. There are three mechanisms that govern this distribution:

- Lateral weight transfer of the unsprung mass (ΔW_{uF} and ΔW_{uR})
- Lateral geometric weight transfer (ΔW_{gF} and ΔW_{gR})
- Lateral weight transfer of the sprung mass (ΔW_{sF} and ΔW_{sR})

The suspension splits the total weight of the vehicle into sprung weight (chassis, bodywork, and driveline) and unsprung weight (tires, wheels, brakes, and about half of the suspension links and drive shafts). Because the weight transfer of the unsprung mass is not influenced by the roll stiffness of the suspension, it is calculated separately.

Understand that this portion of the total lateral weight transfer is *not* measured by any suspension load cells, nor can it be calculated from the suspension potentiometer readings. It is, however, calculable using Equations 10.4 and 10.5.

$$\Delta W_{uF} = \frac{W_{uF} \cdot G_{lat} \cdot h_F}{T_F} \quad \text{(Eq. 10.4)}$$

$$\Delta W_{uR} = \frac{W_{uR} \cdot G_{lat} \cdot h_R}{T_R} \quad \text{(Eq. 10.5)}$$

With W_{uF}/W_{uR} = Front/rear unsprung weight

G_{lat} = Lateral acceleration

h_F/h_R = Front/rear unsprung center of gravity height

T_F/T_R = Front/rear track width

The unsprung center of gravity height is often estimated as the tire's dynamic radius, although with modern three-dimensional CAD packages a more accurate estimation can be done.

Geometric weight transfer results from a direct application of the tire forces to the chassis through the front and rear roll centers. In addition, this part of the lateral weight transfer cannot be measured with the suspension load cells or potentiometers. However, it can be calculated if the front and rear roll center locations are known (Equations 10.6 and 10.7).

$$\Delta W_{gF} = \frac{W_{sF} \cdot G_{lat} \cdot \left[\dfrac{a}{WB}\right] \cdot h_{RCf}}{T_F} \quad \text{(Eq. 10.6)}$$

$$\Delta W_{gR} = \frac{W_{sR} \cdot G_{lat} \cdot \left[\dfrac{WB - a}{WB} \right] \cdot h_{RCr}}{T_R}$$

(Eq. 10.7)

With W_{sF}/W_{sR} = Front/rear sprung weight

G_{lat} = Lateral acceleration

h_{RCf}/h_{RCr} = Front/rear roll center height from ground

T_F/T_R = Front/rear track width

WB = Wheelbase

a = Distance between rear axle centerline and sprung mass center of gravity

The sprung weight transfer makes the chassis roll during cornering. It is resisted by the suspension springs, shock absorbers, and antiroll bars. Sprung weight transfer can be measured with suspension load cells or calculated from the suspension potentiometer signals.

The total sprung weight transfer can be determined with Equation 10.8.

$$\Delta W_s = \frac{W_s \cdot G_{lat} \cdot h_{roll}}{T}$$

(Eq. 10.8)

ΔW_s is the total lateral weight transfer of the sprung mass. The equation is very similar to the one for the total vehicle lateral weight transfer, but only the sprung mass is taken into account, and instead of the height between ground and the vehicle's center of gravity, the distance between the roll axis and sprung center of gravity is observed (h_{roll}). The roll axis is the imaginary line connecting the front and rear roll center, as pictured in Figure 10.4.

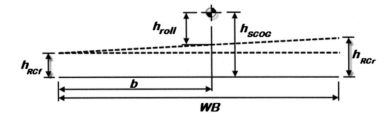

Figure 10.4 Calculation of h_{roll}

Assuming the overall vehicle center of gravity is known, the sprung mass center of gravity can be estimated with the following equation:

$$h_{\text{SCoG}} = 2 \cdot h_{\text{CoG}} - \left(\frac{h_{\text{F}} + h_{\text{R}}}{2} \right) \qquad \text{(Eq. 10.9)}$$

From Figure 10.4 we can now derive h_{roll}:

$$h_{\text{roll}} = h_{\text{SCoG}} - h_{\text{RCf}} - \frac{b}{WB} \cdot (h_{\text{RCr}} - h_{\text{RCf}}) \qquad \text{(Eq. 10.10)}$$

The distribution of the total lateral sprung weight transfer on front and rear axle depends on the distribution between front and rear suspension roll stiffness:

$$\Delta W_{\text{sF}} = \frac{W_{\text{s}} \cdot G_{\text{lat}} \cdot h_{\text{roll}}}{T_{\text{F}}} \cdot q \qquad \text{(Eq. 10.11)}$$

$$\Delta W_{\text{sR}} = \frac{W_{\text{s}} \cdot G_{\text{lat}} \cdot h_{\text{roll}}}{T_{\text{R}}} \cdot (1 - q) \qquad \text{(Eq. 10.12)}$$

with

$$q = \frac{K_{\text{rollf}}}{K_{\text{rollf}} + K_{\text{rollr}}} = \frac{RG_{\text{R}}}{RG_{\text{F}} + RG_{\text{R}}} \qquad \text{(Eq. 10.13)}$$

K_{rollf} = Roll stiffness of front axle (at the wheels)

K_{rollr} = Roll stiffness of rear axle (at the wheels)

RG_{F} = Front roll gradient

RG_{R} = Rear roll gradient

Notice that q can be calculated by using the front and rear roll gradients, which—as we've seen in chapter 9—are a measure for the suspension roll stiffness. By measuring suspension roll angles, it's quite easy to determine the roll gradients.

Finally, the total lateral weight transfer is determined by adding all the portions together (Equation 10.14).

$$\Delta W_{\text{Lat}} = \Delta W_{\text{uF}} + \Delta W_{\text{uR}} + \Delta W_{\text{gF}} + \Delta W_{\text{gR}} + \Delta W_{\text{sF}} + \Delta W_{\text{sR}} \qquad \text{(Eq. 10.14)}$$

All the preceding equations can be modeled into the analysis software through math channels. An example of the results is given in Figure 10.5. Except for calculating the suspension roll gradients, no suspension deflection or force measurement was used in these channels. The only real input channel is the lateral acceleration. The lateral weight transfer calculation is basically a simulation for the conditions seen by the vehicle around the track. This may be a coarse method, but in any case it's a good starting point to get a feel of the dynamic vertical loads a tire will experience during cornering and the factors influencing this.

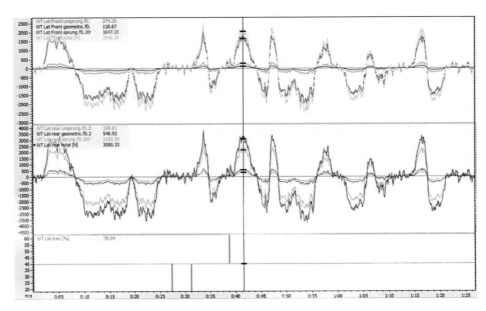

Figure 10.5 Lateral weight transfer math channels

As an example, we consider a car with the following properties:

Total weight W = 1284 kg

Front axle weight W_F = 599 kg

Rear axle weight W_R = 685 kg

Front total unsprung weight W_{uF} = 40 kg

Rear total unsprung weight W_{uR} = 45 kg

Center of gravity height above ground h_{COG} = 366 mm

Front roll center height above ground h_{RCf} = −20.6 mm

Rear roll center height above ground h_{RCr} = 29.2 mm

Wheelbase WB = 2685 mm

Front track width T_F = 1651 mm

Rear track width T_R = 1645 mm

Front unsprung center of gravity height from ground (= front dynamic tire radius) h_F = 325 mm

Rear unsprung center of gravity height from ground (= rear dynamic tire radius) h_R = 345 mm

Front roll stiffness distribution $q = 55.21\%$

The car is cornering with a lateral acceleration of 1.5 G.

To determine the weight transfer distribution between front and rear axles we need to first calculate separately the geometric weight transfer and the weight transfer of the unsprung and sprung masses.

Lateral weight transfer of the unsprung mass:

$$\Delta W_{uF} = \frac{W_{uF} \cdot G_{lat} \cdot h_F}{T_F} = \frac{40 \cdot 1.5 \cdot 0.325}{1.651} = 11.8\,\text{kg}$$

$$\Delta W_{uR} = \frac{W_{uR} \cdot G_{lat} \cdot h_R}{T_R} = \frac{45 \cdot 1.5 \cdot 0.345}{1.645} = 14.2\,\text{kg}$$

The distance a between the rear axle center line and the sprung mass center of gravity:

$$a = 2.685 \cdot \frac{599 - 40}{599 + 685 - 40 - 45} = 1.252\,\text{m}$$

Geometric lateral weight transfer:

$$\Delta W_{gF} = \frac{W_{sF} \cdot G_{lat} \cdot \left[\dfrac{a}{WB}\right] \cdot h_{RCf}}{T_F} = \frac{(599 - 40) \cdot 1.5 \cdot \left[\dfrac{1.252}{2.685}\right] \cdot -0.0206}{1.651} = -4.9\,\text{kg}$$

$$\Delta W_{gR} = \frac{W_{sR} \cdot G_{lat} \cdot \left[\dfrac{WB - a}{WB}\right] \cdot h_{RCr}}{T_R} = \frac{(685 - 45) \cdot 1.5 \cdot \left[\dfrac{1.4325}{2.685}\right] \cdot 0.0292}{1.645} = 9.1\,\text{kg}$$

The height of the sprung center of gravity:

$$h_{SCOG} = 2 \cdot h_{COG} - \left(\frac{h_F + h_R}{2}\right) = 2 \cdot 0.366 - \left(\frac{0.325 + 0.345}{2}\right) = 0.397\,\text{m}$$

Roll axis height:

$$h_{roll} = h_{SCOG} - h_{RCf} - \frac{WB - a}{WB} \cdot (h_{RCr} - h_{RCf}) = 0.397 + 0.0206 - \frac{1.4325}{2.685} \cdot (0.0292 + 0.0206) = 0.391\,\text{m}$$

Lateral weight transfer of the sprung mass:

$$\Delta W_{sF} = \frac{W_s \cdot G_{lat} \cdot h_{roll}}{T_F} \cdot q = \frac{1199 \cdot 1.5 \cdot 0.391}{1.651} \cdot 0.5521 = 235.2\,\text{kg}$$

$$\Delta W_{sR} = \frac{W_s \cdot G_{lat} \cdot h_{roll}}{T_R} \cdot (1-q) = \frac{1199 \cdot 1.5 \cdot 0.391}{1.645} \cdot (1-0.5521) = 191.5\,\text{kg}$$

Total front lateral weight transfer:

$$\Delta W_F = 11.8 + (-4.9) + 235.2 = 242.1\,\text{kg}$$

Total rear lateral weight transfer:

$$\Delta W_R = 14.2 + 9.1 + 191.5 = 214.8\,\text{kg}$$

10.2 Longitudinal Weight Transfer

A car that is accelerating or braking in a straight line will be exposed to an inertial reaction force at its center of gravity, similar to the centrifugal force while cornering. The principle is illustrated in Figure 10.6.

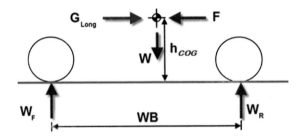

Figure 10.6 Longitudinal weight transfer

The following equation gives us the total amount of longitudinal weight transfer:

$$\Delta W_{Long} = \frac{W \cdot G_{long} \cdot h_{COG}}{WB} \qquad \text{(Eq. 10.15)}$$

Note the similarity with Equation 10.2 for the total amount of lateral weight transfer. In this equation, lateral acceleration has been replaced by longitudinal acceleration. As positive longitudinal acceleration values correspond to a vehicle that is accelerating, and negative acceleration to braking, the result of Equation 10.15 is the amount of weight that is added to the rear axle under acceleration and subtracted from the front. We can create a math channel in the analysis software from Equation 10.15 to get an idea of the amount of longitudinal weight transfer during a lap around a circuit.

10.3 Banking and Grade Effects

As discussed earlier in this chapter, the effects of lateral weight transfer were investigated on a flat track surface. The picture changes somewhat when the car negotiates a banked corner, as illustrated in Figure 10.7. The gravitational force (W) can be resolved into a force parallel to the road surface ($W \cdot \sin \alpha$) and perpendicular to it ($W \cdot \cos \alpha$). The centrifugal force (here named $G_{\text{Lat}\alpha}$ to indicate the banking angle) that exists during cornering on a banked corner is no different than what occurs when the car is on a horizontal surface. However, this is not the lateral acceleration measured by the accelerometer in the vehicle. There is also a component of the centrifugal force along an axis perpendicular to the road surface (Equations 10.16 and 10.17).

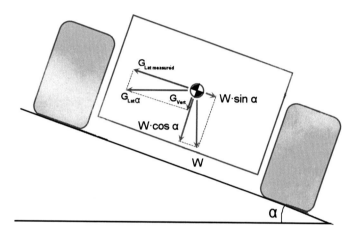

Figure 10.7 The effects of banking

$$G_{\text{latMeasured}} = G_{\text{lat}\alpha} \cdot \cos \alpha \qquad \text{(Eq. 10.16)}$$

$$G_{\text{vertMeasured}} = G_{\text{lat}\alpha} \cdot \sin \alpha \qquad \text{(Eq. 10.17)}$$

Where $G_{\text{latMeasured}}$ = Lateral acceleration measured by vehicle accelerometer

$G_{\text{vertMeasured}}$ = Vertical acceleration measured by vehicle accelerometer

α = Banking angle

This means that the wheel loads are influenced in two ways. First, the weight force perpendicular to the road is $W \cdot (G_{\text{lat}\alpha} \cdot \sin \alpha + \cos \alpha)$. Second, the inertial force creating the lateral weight transfer is $W \cdot (G_{\text{lat}\alpha} \cdot \cos \alpha + \sin \alpha)$.

The banking angle can be determined by Equation 10.18.

$$\alpha = \arctan\left(\frac{G_{\text{vert}} - 1}{G_{\text{lat}}}\right)$$ (Eq. 10.18)

Figure 10.8 shows an example of a 2001 Indycar taking a lap around Phoenix International Raceway. The following channels are given:

- Speed

- Banking: This block-shaped trace defines the banking of the track as a function of distance. The banking figures were taken from Figure 10.9.

- Accel Lateral: This is the measured lateral acceleration of the vehicle.

- LatG Corrected: This is a mathematical channel that defines the real lateral acceleration experienced by the vehicle by dividing the measured acceleration by the cosine of the banking angle.

- Difference: This mathematical channel calculates the difference between actual and measured lateral acceleration.

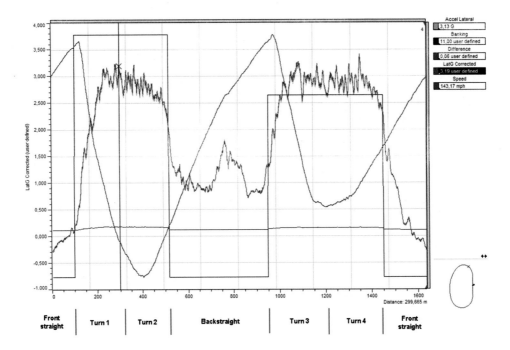

Figure 10.8 A lap around Phoenix International Raceway (PIN) by a 2001 Indycar (Courtesy of Cosworth Electronics, England)

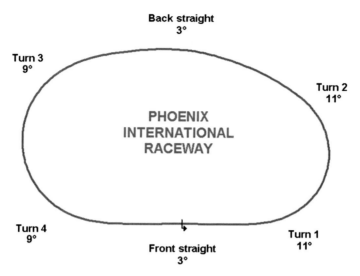

Figure 10.9 PIN turn nomenclature and banking angles

At the cursor point in Figure 10.8, the measured lateral acceleration is 3.13 G. At this point on the track, the banking angle is 11 deg. The real lateral acceleration experienced by the vehicle is:

$$G_{lat\alpha} = \frac{G_{latMeasured}}{\cos(\alpha)} = \frac{3.13}{\cos(11°)} = 3.19 \text{ G}$$

A similar effect takes place when the vehicle runs up or down a sloped road, as pictured in Figure 10.10. Depending on the size of the slope angle θ, the total normal force is reduced to $W \cdot \cos \theta$. In addition, because of a weight component parallel to the road surface, the slope angle creates a longitudinal weight transfer. The front and rear axle weights (W_F and W_R) are as given in Equations 10.19 and 10.20.

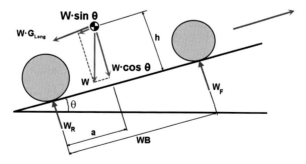

Figure 10.10 The effects of track slope

$$W_{\mathrm{F}} = W \cdot \frac{a}{WB} \cdot \cos\theta - W \cdot \frac{h}{WB} \cdot \left(G_{\mathrm{long}} + \sin\theta \right) \qquad \text{(Eq. 10.19)}$$

$$W_{\mathrm{R}} = W \cdot \frac{WB - b}{WB} \cdot \cos\theta + W \cdot \frac{h}{WB} \cdot \left(G_{\mathrm{long}} + \sin\theta \right) \qquad \text{(Eq. 10.20)}$$

With a = Distance between rear axle centerline and center of gravity

       WB = Wheelbase

       G_{long} = Longitudinal acceleration

To calculate the slope angle, Equation 10.21 applies.

$$\theta = \arctan\left(\frac{G_{\mathrm{vert}} - 1}{G_{\mathrm{long}}} \right) \qquad \text{(Eq. 10.21)}$$

10.4   Total Wheel Loads

In the previous sections, a method to calculate the lateral and longitudinal load transfers was proposed. If the aerodynamic forces acting on the front and rear axle can be estimated, we are now armed to at least have a good idea about the four dynamic wheel loads.

To calculate the individual loads on each wheel, the effect of each of the following mechanisms must be determined:

- Static weight distribution[*]
- Lateral weight transfer
  - Unsprung lateral weight transfer
  - Geometric lateral weight transfer
  - Sprung lateral weight transfer[*]
- Longitudinal weight transfer
  - Unsprung longitudinal weight transfer
  - Geometrical longitudinal weight transfer
  - Sprung longitudinal weight transfer[*]
- Banking effects[*]
- Track slope effects[*]
- Aerodynamic forces
  - produced by body[*]
  - produced by wheels
- Bumps and road surface irregularities[*]

The items in the list above marked with an asterisk are measurable with suspension load cells. The rest is not. The total load on each wheel is the sum of all the listed effects.

The static weight distribution can be determined through the suspension load cells or, alternatively, simply defined as constants taken from the vehicle setup sheet. Of course, measuring them directly is better, as it takes variations in fuel level into account.

The methods to calculate the portions of lateral weight transfer that are not possible to measure with load cells were covered previously. The same methods would apply for the longitudinal weight transfer. However, often it suffices to simply calculate the total longitudinal weight transfer.

If track banking and slope data is available, the resulting effects can be calculated by correction of lateral and longitudinal acceleration channels. They are also "seen" by the suspension load cells.

Aerodynamic forces produced by the body can be measured with the suspension load cells. Those forces produced by the wheels (which can be significant for open-wheeled cars) are not seen by these transducers.

Finally, bumps and road surface irregularities form the high-speed content present in the suspension force signals. The forces involved can also be calculated from suspension potentiometer readings.

We can calculate the suspension forces at the wheel using the suspension potentiometer signals. Figure 10.11 shows the parameters involved to calculate the total vertical load on each wheel. As mentioned previously, the unsprung mass and geometric lateral/

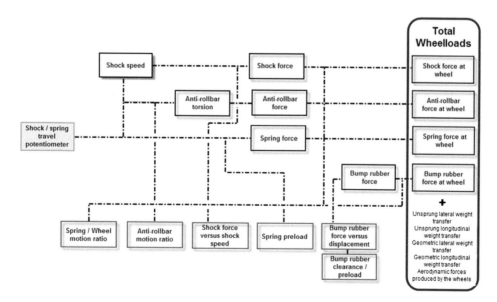

Figure 10.11 Wheel load calculation procedure using the suspension potentiometer signals

longitudinal weight transfer should be calculated separately. From the shock travel potentiometers we can calculate the forces produced at the wheel by the spring, antiroll bar, bump rubber, and shock absorber.

The force produced at the wheel by the suspension springs can be calculated using the following equation:

$$F_{Spring@wheel} = \frac{SR}{MR} \cdot x_{suspension}$$ (Eq. 10.22)

In this equation SR is the respective spring rate, MR is the suspension motion ratio (wheel travel/suspension travel) and $x_{suspension}$ is the travel of the spring. To this force, the effect of any spring preload should be added. This equation also assumes that the potentiometers are zeroed with the car at static ride height.

Bump rubbers are normally engaged only when the shock absorber is compressed some distance from static ride height. Bump rubbers are used not only to prevent the shock absorbers from bottoming out but also to control the ride height, especially in cars where aerodynamics are of vital importance. In this case the bump rubber is an integral part of the suspension and will have a significant effect on the wheel loads. The equation for the bump rubber force at the wheel is very similar to Equation 10.22. However, where suspension springs are often linear, bump rubbers typically are not. Figure 10.12 shows an example of a typical relationship between bump rubber force and compression. The first step creating the necessary math channels to calculate bump rubber forces is to establish the equation of bump rubber force versus compression.

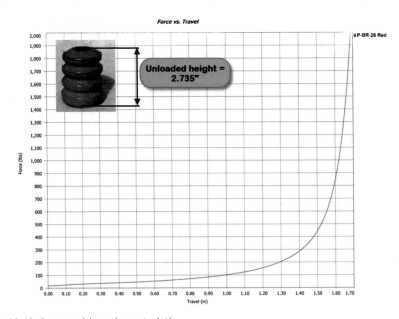

Figure 10.12 Bump rubber characteristic

The distance that the shock absorber needs to travel before the bump rubber is engaged (bump rubber gap) needs to be measured statically with the car on the setup scales (see Figure 10.13). The values for the four suspension corners should be stored as constants in the analysis software.

When the suspension potentiometers are zeroed at static ride height, the following equation for bump rubber force at the wheel can be defined:

$$x_{\text{suspension}} \leq x_0 \Rightarrow F_{\text{BR@wheel}} = 0$$

$$x_{\text{suspension}} > x_0 \Rightarrow F_{\text{BR@wheel}} = \frac{BRSR(x_{\text{suspension}} - x_0)}{MR} \cdot (x_{\text{suspension}} - x_0) \qquad \text{(Eq. 10.23)}$$

In this equation x_0 is the suspension position at static ride height and $BRSR(x_{\text{suspension}} - x_0)$ is the momentary spring rate of the bump rubber as a function of its compression $(x_{\text{suspension}} - x_0)$.

The force produced by the antiroll bars is logically dependent on the difference between left-hand and right-hand suspension movement. The force produced by the roll bar at the wheel can be calculated as follows:

$$F_{\text{ARB@Wheel}} = \frac{x_{\text{SuspensionLeft}} - x_{\text{SuspensionRight}}}{MR_{\text{ARB}}} \cdot K_{\text{ARB}} \qquad \text{(Eq. 10.24)}$$

where K_{ARB} is the antiroll bar rate, and MR_{ARB} is the bar's motion ratio (wheel travel/roll bar movement). When $F_{\text{ARB@wheel}}$ is the force at the left-hand wheel, then $-F_{\text{ARB@wheel}}$ is the antiroll bar force at the right-hand wheel.

Finally, the force produced at the wheel by the shock absorber is proportional to the speed at which the shaft moves. The damping rate of the shock absorber will generally

Figure 10.13 Bump rubber gap

not be constant over the complete velocity range. As with the bump rubber equation, it's necessary to define the characteristic of the shock mathematically. Consider the example in Figure 10.14. In this shock absorber characteristic, two linear rates can be determined, respectively, for bump and rebound movement. When these rates are calculated, the following equation applies for the shock absorber force at the wheel:

$$F_{\text{shock@wheel}} = \frac{a \cdot v_{\text{shock}}}{MR} + b \qquad \text{(Eq. 10.25)}$$

In this equation, v_{shock} is the speed of the shock absorber shaft (derivative of the suspension movement).

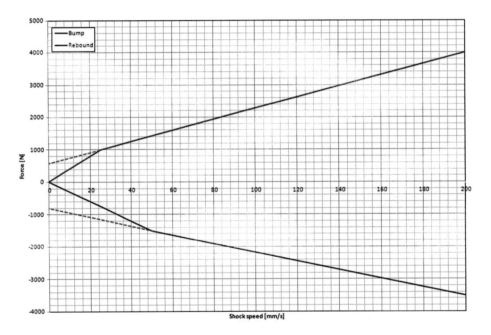

Figure 10.14 Shock absorber characteristic

For the example in Figure 10.14, the values of a/MR and b are given in Table 10.1.

Table 10.1 Values for a/MR and b for low and high speed			
	Speed interval	a/MR	b
Bump	0 to 25 mm/s	40	0
	Above 25 mm/s	17.14	571.43
Rebound	0 to 50 mm/s	−30	0
	Above 50 mm/s	−13.33	−833.33

When all force components are known, they can be added together to give us the total vertical load on each wheel corner. The results look as shown in Figures 10.15 and 10.16.

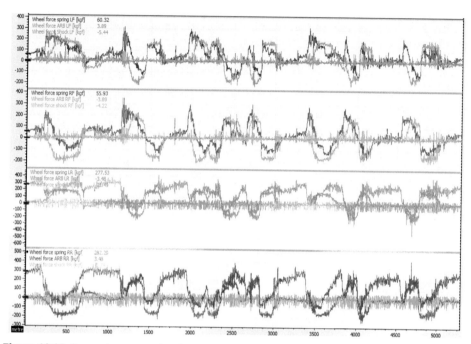

Figure 10.15 Separate suspension force components per wheel

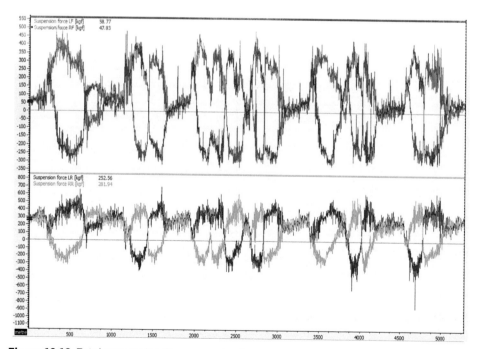

Figure 10.16 Total suspension force per wheel

10.5   Determining Wheel Loads with Modal Analysis

Without considering camber change, toe change, and other wheel movements, an individual suspension corner basically lets the wheel go up and down. A four-wheel suspension system can have combinations of compression and extension at either wheel corner. Any position of or motion in this system can be described in millimeters of one or more of four fundamental modes—heave, roll, pitch, and warp [10-1]. Although closely related, the suspension system modes do not describe the motions of the suspended mass, which has six degrees of freedom (heave, pitch, roll, yaw, sideslip, and forward and rearward motion). If the chassis is not considered infinitely stiff, warp is the seventh degree of freedom (chassis torsion). This can be envisioned as the tire contact patches moving in heave, roll, pitch, and warp as the vehicle moves over the track. The chassis also moves in these four modes, while suspension motions make up the difference.

Each mode has a spring rate and a damping rate, depending on the suspension system's components. The car springs provide the basic wheel rates for the four modes. Roll bars, third springs, and the chassis add to the wheel rate in some modes while leaving others unaffected. These rates are not necessarily linear, but for simplification they are considered to be so in the rest of this chapter. The shock absorbers provide the damping rates for all four modes. In the case of a conventional suspension with four shock absorbers, the damping rate for all four modes is equal.

Heave is the synchronous motion of all four wheels, all in the same direction (Figure 10.17). The total force developed by heave motion is the sum of the vertical forces acting on each wheel as a result of the sum of each wheel displacement. For this motion, an elasticity constant (K_H) can be defined that relates the heave force to the wheel displacements (Equation 10.26).

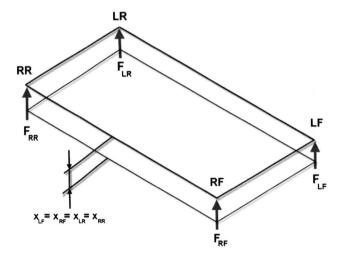

Figure 10.17 Heave

$$F_{LF} + F_{RF} + F_{LR} + F_{RR} = K_H \cdot (x_{LF} + x_{RF} + x_{LR} + x_{RR}) \qquad \text{(Eq. 10.26)}$$

Pitch is a synchronous motion where front and rear wheel pairs move in opposite direction (Figure 10.18). In this case, the elasticity constant (K_p) relates the total pitch force to the pitch displacement (Equation 10.27).

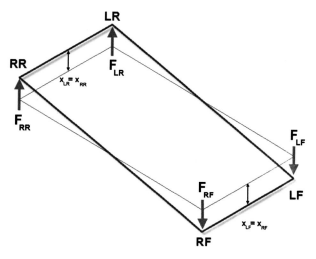

Figure 10.18 Pitch

$$F_{LF} + F_{RF} - F_{LR} - F_{RR} = K_H \cdot (x_{LF} + x_{RF} - x_{LR} - x_{RR}) \qquad \text{(Eq. 10.27)}$$

Roll is also a synchronous oppositional motion but between the left and right wheel pairs (Figure 10.19). The roll rate (K_R) is the ratio between the total roll force and the roll displacement (Equation 10.28).

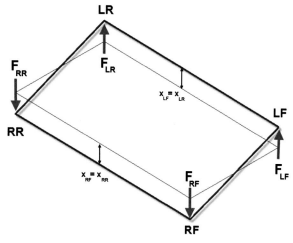

Figure 10.19 Roll

$$F_{LF} - F_{RF} + F_{LR} - F_{RR} = K_H \cdot (x_{LF} - x_{RF} + x_{LR} - x_{RR}) \qquad \text{(Eq. 10.28)}$$

Finally, warp is the synchronous motion of diagonal wheel pairs in opposite directions (Figure 10.20). The warp rate (K_w) establishes the relationship as shown in Equation 10.29.

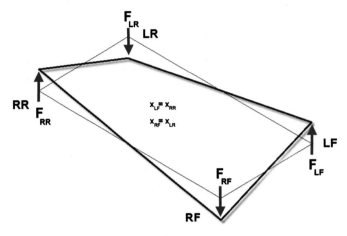

Figure 10.20 Warp

$$F_{LF} - F_{RF} - F_{LR} + F_{RR} = K_H \cdot (x_{LF} - x_{RF} - x_{LR} + x_{RR}) \qquad \text{(Eq. 10.29)}$$

Illustrating how the four modes can be composed from the individual wheel movements, Figure 10.21 features four recorded wheel-travel signals of a vehicle going through a right-hand corner. In this case, compression is indicated with a positive sign, while extension is negative. The cursor is pointed at one particular point where the driver is starting to accelerate out of a corner. The car is simultaneously running off a curb with the left-rear wheel. The wheel positions are as follows:

Left front x_{LF} = 9.12 mm (compression)

Right front x_{RF} = 3.49 mm (extension)

Left rear x_{LR} = 37.29 mm (compression)

Right rear x_{RR} = 6.46 mm (compression)

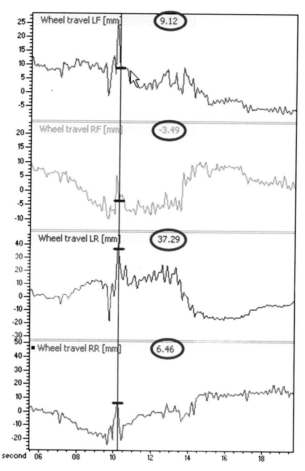

Figure 10.21 Wheel travel signals of a vehicle in steady-state cornering and running over a curb

These are graphically indicated in Figure 10.22. The four-mode displacements are calculated as follows:

Heave:	9.12 + (−3.49) + 37.29 + 6.46 = 49.38 mm
Pitch:	9.12 + (−3.49) − 37.29 − 6.46 = −38.12mm
Roll:	9.12 − (−3.49) + 37.29 − 6.46 = 43.44 mm
Warp:	9.12 − (−3.49) − 37.29 + 6.46 = −18.12 mm

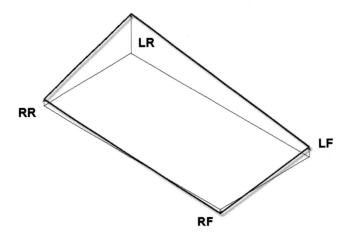

Figure 10.22 Wheel positions at the indicated cursor point in Figure 10.21

The negative sign in front of the amount of pitch indicates that the body is moving rearward (i.e., suspension compression is greater on the rear axle). The warp is also negative, which indicates that the cumulative wheel travel on the right front/left rear diagonal is higher than that on the left front/right rear.

The plane formed in Figure 10.22 by the four suspension corners does not indicate the chassis attitude. If the track surface is completely flat (which in this example it clearly is not), the sprung mass experiences 12.3 mm of heave (total suspension heave divided over four corners). It pitches 19.1 mm downward on the rear axle and the same amount upward on the front axle. The sprung mass rolls 21.7 mm, and the chassis twists 9.1 mm.

Figure 10.23 shows the four suspension system modes, calculated from the wheel-travel signals. At the point indicated by the cursor, the following values are given:

Heave = 9.52 mm

Pitch = –7.33 mm

Roll = 36.21 mm
Warp = –13.75 mm

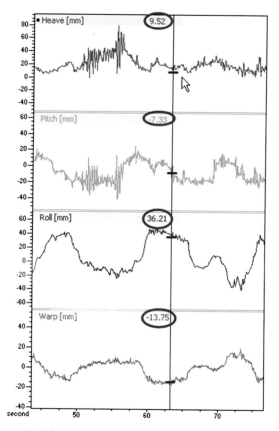

Figure 10.23 Mathematical channels of the four suspension system modes

The corresponding wheel positions can be calculated as follows:

$$x_{LF} = \frac{Heave + Pitch + Roll + Warp}{4} = 6.16\,mm$$

$$x_{RF} = \frac{Heave + Pitch - Roll - Warp}{4} = -5.06\,mm$$

$$x_{LR} = \frac{Heave - Pitch + Roll - Warp}{4} = 16.70\,mm$$

$$x_{RR} = \frac{Heave - Pitch - Roll + Warp}{4} = -8.27\,mm$$

The values of the four modes can be used to estimate how loads are being transferred between the four wheel corners. Therefore, the wheel rate of each mode must be determined. For a conventional suspension system with four springs and two antiroll bars, the wheel rates for heave and pitch are equal (Equation 10.30).

$$K_H = K_P = \frac{1}{2} \cdot (WR_f + WR_r) \qquad \text{(Eq. 10.30)}$$

With WR_f = Wheel rate of front suspension springs

WR_r = Wheel rate of rear suspension springs

Similarly, if a chassis of infinite stiffness is assumed, the wheel rates for roll and warp are equal as well. In Equation 10.31, WR_{Rollf} is the wheel rate of the front antiroll bar and WR_{Rollr} the wheel rate of the rear antiroll bar.

$$K_R = K_W = \frac{1}{2} \cdot (WR_f + 2 \cdot WR_{Rollf}) + \frac{1}{2} \cdot (WR_r + 2 \cdot WR_{Rollr}) \qquad \text{(Eq. 10.31)}$$

Often the suspension setup features different spring rates and antiroll bar rates on the front and rear axles, and the motion ratio for these components can vary from one axle to another. To calculate the dynamic load distribution over the four suspension corners, the asymmetries between axles must be considered because there is a difference in load transfer between them when roll and warp wheel rates at the front and rear axles are not equal. This effect is one of the most important ways to influence the vehicle's understeer/oversteer balance (Equation 10.32).

$$a = b = \frac{1}{2} \cdot (WR_f + 2 \cdot WR_{Rollf}) - \frac{1}{2} \cdot (WR_f + 2 \cdot WR_{Rollf}) \qquad \text{(Eq. 10.32)}$$

With a = Front-to-rear asymmetry between front and rear axle for roll

b = Front-to-rear asymmetry between front and rear axle for pitch

Using either Equations 10.33 and 10.34 or the suspension roll gradients mentioned earlier in this chapter (Equation 10.13), the weight transfer bias for roll and warp between the front and rear axles now can be determined.

$$q = \frac{K_R + a}{K_R - a} - 1 = \frac{WR_f + 2 \cdot WR_{Rollf}}{WR_r + 2 \cdot WR_{Rollr}} - 1 \qquad \text{(Eq. 10.33)}$$

$$w = \frac{K_W + b}{K_W - b} - 1 \qquad \text{(Eq. 10.34)}$$

As previously indicated, on a conventional suspension system, q always equals w as long as the chassis stiffness is considered infinite. There are, however, suspension systems providing warp rates that are softer than the roll rate.

For example, the four modal rates are calculated for the data in Table 10.2.

Table 10.2 Example suspension parameters	
Front spring rate SR_f = 28 kg/mm	Rear spring rate SR_r = 32 kg/mm
Front antiroll bar rate SR_{Rollf} = 60 kg/mm	Rear antiroll bar rate SR_{Rollr} = 40 kg/mm
Front spring motion ratio MR_f = 1.373	Rear spring motion ratio MR_r = 1.725
Front antiroll bar motion ratio MR_{Rollf} = 1.495	Rear antiroll bar motion ratio MR_{Rollr} = 1.566
Left-front corner weight W_{LF} = 318 kg	Left-rear corner weight W_{LR} = 369 kg
Right-front corner weight W_{RF} = 318 kg	Right-rear corner weight W_{RR} = 369 kg

$$WR_f = \frac{SR_f}{MR_f^2} = 14.9 \text{ kg/mm}$$

$$WR_r = \frac{SR_r}{MR_r^2} = 10.8 \text{ kg/mm}$$

$$WR_{Rollf} = \frac{SR_{Rollf}}{MR_{Rollf}^2} = 26.8 \text{ kg/mm}$$

$$WR_{Rollr} = \frac{SR_{Rollr}}{MR_{Rollr}^2} = 16.3 \text{ kg/mm}$$

$$K_H = K_P = \frac{1}{2} \cdot (WR_f + WR_r) = 12.85 \text{ kg/mm}$$

$$K_R = K_W = \frac{1}{2} \cdot (WR_f + 2 \cdot WR_{Rollf}) + \frac{1}{2} \cdot (WR_r + 2 \cdot WR_{Rollr}) = 55.96 \text{ kg/mm}$$

$$a = b = \frac{1}{2} \cdot (WR_f + 2 \cdot WR_{Rollf}) - \frac{1}{2} \cdot (WR_r + 2 \cdot WR_{Rollr}) = 12.58 \text{ kg/mm}$$

$$q = w = \frac{K_R + a}{K_R - a} - 1 = 0.58$$

From Equations 10.26, 10.27, 10.28, 10.29, the definition of the wheel load on each suspension corner can be derived as

$$F_{LF} + F_{RF} + F_{LR} + F_{RR} = K_H \cdot (x_{LF} + x_{RF} + x_{LR} + x_{RR}) = X$$

$$F_{LF} + F_{RF} - F_{LR} - F_{RR} = K_P \cdot (x_{LF} + x_{RF} - x_{LR} - x_{RR}) = Y$$

$$F_{LF} - F_{RF} + F_{LR} - F_{RR} = K_R \cdot (x_{LF} - x_{RF} + x_{LR} - x_{RR}) = Z$$

$$F_{LF} - F_{RF} - F_{LR} + F_{RR} = K_W \cdot (x_{LF} - x_{RF} - x_{LR} + x_{RR}) = T$$

The right-hand side of these equations can be considered as a constant. The modal displacements can be measured and the wheel rate of each mode calculated following the method covered previously. From this follows

$$F_{LF} + F_{RF} = \frac{X+Y}{2}$$

$$F_{LR} + F_{RR} = \frac{X-Y}{2}$$

$$F_{LF} - F_{RF} = \frac{Z+T}{2}$$

$$F_{LR} - F_{RR} = \frac{Z-T}{2}$$

Solving these equations for F_{LF}, F_{RF}, F_{LR}, and F_{RR} gives

$$F_{LF} = \frac{1}{4} \cdot (Z+T) + \frac{1}{4} \cdot (X+Y)$$

$$F_{RF} = \frac{1}{4} \cdot (X+Y) + \frac{1}{4} \cdot (Z+T)$$

$$F_{LR} = \frac{1}{4} \cdot (Z-T) + \frac{1}{4} \cdot (X-Y)$$

$$F_{RR} = \frac{1}{4} \cdot (X-Y) - \frac{1}{4} \cdot (Z-T)$$

So

$$F_{LF} = \frac{1}{4} \cdot \left(\begin{array}{l} K_H \cdot (x_{LF} + x_{RF} + x_{LR} + x_{RR}) + K_P \cdot (x_{LF} + x_{RF} - x_{LR} - x_{RR}) + \\ K_R \cdot (x_{LF} - x_{RF} + x_{LR} - x_{RR}) + K_W \cdot (x_{LF} - x_{RF} - x_{LR} + x_{RR}) \end{array} \right)$$

$$F_{RF} = \frac{1}{4} \cdot \left(\begin{array}{l} K_H \cdot (x_{LF} + x_{RF} + x_{LR} + x_{RR}) + K_P \cdot (x_{LF} + x_{RF} - x_{LR} - x_{RR}) - \\ K_R \cdot (x_{LF} - x_{RF} + x_{LR} - x_{RR}) - K_W \cdot (x_{LF} - x_{RF} - x_{LR} + x_{RR}) \end{array} \right)$$

$$F_{LR} = \frac{1}{4} \cdot \left(\begin{array}{l} K_H \cdot (x_{LF} + x_{RF} + x_{LR} + x_{RR}) - K_P \cdot (x_{LF} + x_{RF} - x_{LR} - x_{RR}) + \\ K_R \cdot (x_{LF} - x_{RF} + x_{LR} - x_{RR}) - K_W \cdot (x_{LF} - x_{RF} - x_{LR} + x_{RR}) \end{array} \right)$$

$$F_{RR} = \frac{1}{4} \cdot \left(\begin{array}{l} K_H \cdot \left(x_{LF} + x_{RF} + x_{LR} + x_{RR} \right) - K_P \cdot \left(x_{LF} + x_{RF} - x_{LR} - x_{RR} \right) - \\ K_R \cdot \left(x_{LF} - x_{RF} + x_{LR} - x_{RR} \right) + K_W \cdot \left(x_{LF} - x_{RF} - x_{LR} + x_{RR} \right) \end{array} \right)$$

Finally, the asymmetries between the front and rear axles for roll and warp must be taken into account and the modal spring forces added to the static wheel load:

$$F_{LF} = W_{LF} + \frac{1}{4} \cdot \left(\begin{array}{l} K_H \cdot \left(x_{LF} + x_{RF} + x_{LR} + x_{RR} \right) + K_P \cdot \left(x_{LF} + x_{RF} - x_{LR} - x_{RR} \right) + \\ K_R \cdot \left(x_{LF} - x_{RF} + x_{LR} - x_{RR} \right) \cdot q + K_W \cdot \left(x_{LF} - x_{RF} - x_{LR} + x_{RR} \right) \cdot \left(1 - w \right) \end{array} \right)$$

$$F_{RF} = W_{RF} + \frac{1}{4} \cdot \left(\begin{array}{l} K_H \cdot \left(x_{LF} + x_{RF} + x_{LR} + x_{RR} \right) + K_P \cdot \left(x_{LF} + x_{RF} - x_{LR} - x_{RR} \right) - \\ K_R \cdot \left(x_{LF} - x_{RF} + x_{LR} - x_{RR} \right) \cdot q - K_W \cdot \left(x_{LF} - x_{RF} - x_{LR} + x_{RR} \right) \cdot \left(1 - w \right) \end{array} \right)$$

$$F_{LR} = W_{LR} + \frac{1}{4} \cdot \left(\begin{array}{l} K_H \cdot \left(x_{LF} + x_{RF} + x_{LR} + x_{RR} \right) - K_P \cdot \left(x_{LF} + x_{RF} - x_{LR} - x_{RR} \right) + \\ K_R \cdot \left(x_{LF} - x_{RF} + x_{LR} - x_{RR} \right) \cdot \left(1 - q \right) - K_W \cdot \left(x_{LF} - x_{RF} - x_{LR} + x_{RR} \right) \cdot w \end{array} \right)$$

$$F_{RR} = W_{RR} + \frac{1}{4} \cdot \left(\begin{array}{l} K_H \cdot \left(x_{LF} + x_{RF} + x_{LR} + x_{RR} \right) - K_P \cdot \left(x_{LF} + x_{RF} - x_{LR} - x_{RR} \right) - \\ K_R \cdot \left(x_{LF} - x_{RF} + x_{LR} - x_{RR} \right) \cdot \left(1 - q \right) + K_W \cdot \left(x_{LF} - x_{RF} - x_{LR} + x_{RR} \right) \cdot w \end{array} \right)$$

These equations can be entered as mathematical channels into the data analysis software. The result of this is given in Figure 10.24, where a lap around Nurburgring is illustrated. For ease, use an interactive setup sheet in a spreadsheet that is linked to the data analysis software (chapter 2). In this spreadsheet, the modal wheel rates can be calculated and used by the analysis software as session constants. This software option is provided in most popular data acquisition packages. Because setup changes can be stored in the setup sheet, the analysis software can link the right constants to each data file. Keep in mind that the wheel loads calculated in Figure 10.24 represent only portions of the load the wheel actually experiences. Only the forces acting on the wheels that are distributed to the chassis through the springs are determined with the previous equations. Geometric and unsprung weight transfer are not taken into account by this calculation, but they can be calculated and added to the total wheel loads separately using the methods outlined earlier in this chapter.

Another way to figure out the individual wheel loads using the suspension potentiometer signals is to calculate the forces developed by the suspension springs and antiroll bars and then resolve them with their respective motion ratios to forces at the wheels. The advantage of analyzing the vehicle's modal responses is that the four suspension corners are seen as one system and the effect of each suspension parameter on the complete system can be investigated.

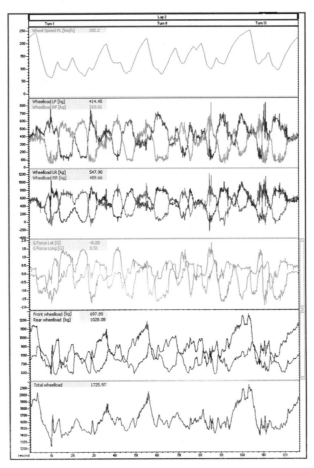

Figure 10.24 Calculated wheel loads from modal displacements and wheel rates

10.6   Measuring Wheel Loads with Suspension Load Cells

The accuracy of the wheel load calculations can be improved greatly by measuring the strain in the suspension members with load cells and calibrating these so that they output the vertical loads acting on the wheels. The greatest accuracy improvement is the sensor resolution. By measuring the load directly, the wheel loads do not need calculation through spring and wheel rates; those variables do not come into play. Remember again that suspension load cells do not measure unsprung or geometric weight transfer.

Figure 10.25 shows the four dynamic (i.e., static weight not included) wheel loads measured on an early 1990s Formula One car during a lap around Hockenheim Ring. These four traces clearly show the change in load at each wheel as the car accelerates, brakes, and negotiates corners. The increase in downforce as speed increases is also apparent. By manipulating these signals and using them in mathematical channels, the different components making up the total wheel loads can be investigated.

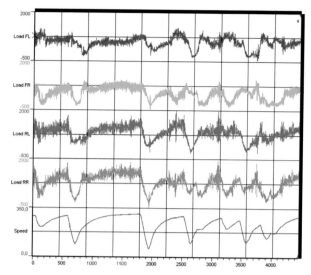

Figure 10.25 Wheel loads determined with strain gage measurement (Courtesy of Pi Research, England)

Adding the four wheel loads creates a channel that gives the total download on the car. Illustrated in Figure 10.26, this channel clearly shows the amount of downforce that develops—the trace is almost identical to the speed trace. This is not the case with a low-downforce car. This channel also can be used to investigate the effect of banked corners and track slopes. These track properties change the measured vertical load.

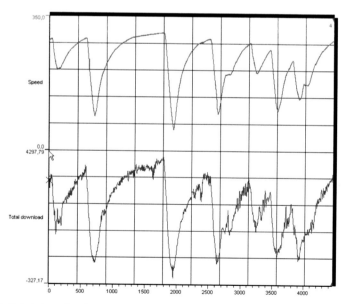

Figure 10.26 Total download (Courtesy of Pi Research, England)

Lateral sprung weight transfer can be determined by creating the following math channels:

Front weight transfer = $F_{LF} - F_{RF}$

Rear weight transfer = $F_{LR} - F_{RR}$

The bias between front and rear axles is as given in Equation 10.35. These channels are shown in Figure 10.27.

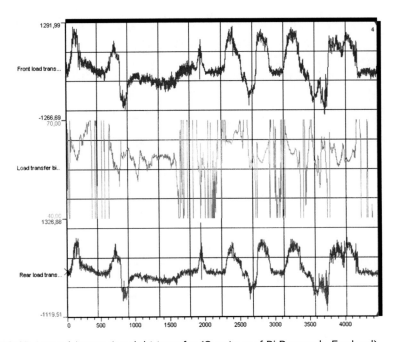

Figure 10.27 Lateral (sprung) weight transfer (Courtesy of Pi Research, England)

The channel showing the lateral weight transfer bias between the front and rear axles is particularly useful to investigate transient effects at corner entry and exit. The shock absorbers temporarily change the lateral weight transfer distribution to a value different than that of steady-state cornering.

$$\text{Weight transfer bias} = \frac{\text{Front weight transfer}}{\text{Front weight transfer} + \text{Rear weight transfer}} \cdot 100\% \quad \text{(Eq. 10.35)}$$

For a quick analysis of steady-state weight transfer (e.g., after a spring or antiroll bar change), the X-Y chart in Figure 10.28 is helpful. The slope of this graph gives the ratio between rear and front lateral weight transfer.

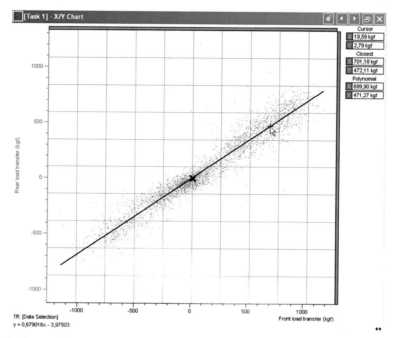

Figure 10.28 *X-Y* chart of rear versus front lateral weight transfer (Courtesy of Pi Research, England)

Similarly, the longitudinal weight transfer can be determined using Equation 10.36 as a math channel (Figure 10.29). In addition, the percentage of load on the front axle is given in Equation 10.37.

$$\text{Longitudinal weight transfer} = F_{LR} + F_{RR} - F_{LF} - F_{RF} \qquad \text{(Eq. 10.36)}$$

$$\text{Longitudinal weight bias} = \frac{F_{LF} + F_{RF}}{F_{LF} + F_{RF} + F_{LR} + F_{RR}} \cdot 100\% \qquad \text{(Eq. 10.37)}$$

The longitudinal weight bias graph clearly shows how weight is shifted forward during braking and rearward during acceleration. On the straights, it is possible to determine the shift in aerodynamic center of pressure with increasing speed.

10.7   Tire Spring Rates

Until now, the suspension system was considered as having four springs and two antiroll bars, but the tires represent four more spring rates that also influence the lateral weight transfer distribution. The proposed method for calculating the wheel loads from the suspension modes did not take the tire spring rates into account. However, when the wheel

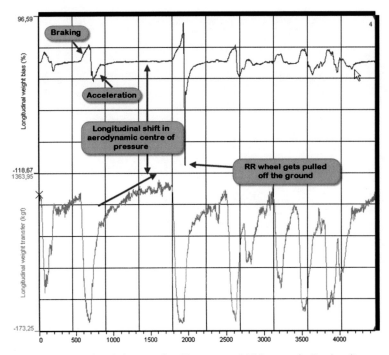

Figure 10.29 Longitudinal weight transfer (Courtesy of Pi Research, England)

loads are measured directly by suspension load cells, the measured load distribution incorporates the lateral weight transfer bias through the tire spring rates.

Each tire spring works in series with the corresponding suspension spring and parallel to the antiroll bar on that axle. Therefore, the roll rate bias (q) (Equation 10.33) can be rewritten to take into account the tire spring rates SR_{Tiref} and SR_{Tirer} (Equation 10.38).

$$q = \frac{\left(\dfrac{WR_f \cdot SR_{Tiref}}{WR_f + SR_{Tiref}}\right) + 2 \cdot WR_{Rollf}}{\left(\dfrac{WR_r \cdot SR_{Tirer}}{WR_r + SR_{Tirer}}\right) + 2 \cdot WR_{Rollr}} - 1 \qquad \text{(Eq. 10.38)}$$

This equation can be used only if the tire spring rates are known, which often is not the case. The best way to assess the lateral weight transfer bias is to measure the wheel loads directly.

10.8   Chassis Torsion

When calculating lateral weight transfer distribution on the front and rear axles, it has been always assumed that the chassis stiffness is of such magnitude that it can be ignored. This may not be necessarily the case. A flexible chassis could be considered as an extra (torsion) spring in the suspension system. Calculated weight transfers may not represent the real situation when ignoring the chassis stiffness.

Chassis stiffness not only implies the rigidness of the frame but also the compliance in the suspension pick-up points, bodywork attachments to the chassis, and engine and driveline support points on the chassis.

The nonlinear behavior of the race car tire provides the means of tuning the vehicle's handling balance by changing the amount of weight transfer on one axle. For an under-steering car, the engineer normally tries to decrease the weight transfer on the front axle or increase it at the rear, and vice versa for an oversteering car. However, the car handling can be influenced only in this way if the chassis serves as a platform to feed the involved torques through.

In the following discussion, distinguish between the different components that make up the overall vehicle roll angle—suspension roll, tire roll, and chassis torsion. As an example, the following suspension roll angles were measured on a race car:

Front suspension roll angle = 16.61 mm
Rear suspension roll angle = 30.71 mm

This vehicle's respective front and rear roll (wheel) rates are 78.54 kg/mm and 23.38 kg/mm. The tire spring rates are 50 kg/mm (front) and 55 kg/mm (rear).

If a chassis with a finite torsion stiffness is considered, Equation 10.39 applies with $\alpha_{\text{RollSuspF}}$ = front suspension roll angle, $\alpha_{\text{RollTiresF}}$ = front tires roll angle, $\alpha_{\text{RollSuspR}}$ = rear suspension roll angle, $\alpha_{\text{RollTiresR}}$ = rear tires roll angle, and α_{torsion} = chassis torsion angle.

$$\alpha_{\text{RollSuspF}} + \alpha_{\text{RollTiresF}} = \alpha_{\text{RollSuspR}} + \alpha_{\text{RollTiresR}} + \alpha_{\text{torsion}} \qquad \text{(Eq. 10.39)}$$

This equation differs from the definition given in the previous chapter by the addition of a torsion component (α_{torsion}).

Multiplying front and rear roll angles with the corresponding roll rates gives the lateral weight transfer on each axle:

$$\Delta W_{\text{sF}} = 16.61 \cdot 78.54 = 1304.5 \, \text{kg}$$
$$\Delta W_{\text{sR}} = 30.71 \cdot 23.38 = 718.0 \, \text{kg}$$

The tire roll angles ($\alpha_{\text{RollTiresF}}$ and $\alpha_{\text{RollTiresR}}$) are

$$\alpha_{\text{RollTiresF}} = \frac{1304.5}{2 \cdot 50} = 13.0\,\text{mm}$$

$$\alpha_{\text{RollTiresR}} = \frac{718.0}{2 \cdot 55} = 6.5\,\text{mm}$$

Entering these values in Equation 10.39 finally gives the chassis torsion angle $\alpha_{\text{torsion}} = 7.6$ mm. When this is related to the overall lateral weight transfer, the torsional stiffness of the chassis (SR_{Chassis}) is known:

$$SR_{\text{Chassis}} = \frac{\frac{1}{2} \cdot (\Delta W_{\text{sF}} + \Delta W_{\text{sR}})}{\alpha_{\text{torsion}}} = 133.4\,\text{kg/mm}$$

Compared with the front roll stiffness, the magnitude of chassis torsion in this example certainly affects the lateral weight transfer distribution between the front and rear axles. In this case, do not ignore the torsion stiffness of the chassis.

Chapter 11
Shock Absorbers

Cars are equipped with shock absorbers to minimize variation in contact between tires' contact patches and the track surface and to control transient chassis movements due to lateral, longitudinal, and vertical acceleration. The influence of shock absorbers on race car dynamics is investigated in this chapter.

11.1   Shock Absorber Velocity Analysis

The force developed by a spring is proportional to its compression (Equation 11.1).

$$F_{spring} = SR \cdot s_{spring}$$

(Eq. 11.1)

With F_{spring} = Spring force (N)

SR = Spring rate (N/mm)

s_{spring} = Spring compression (mm)

Shock absorbers are speed-sensitive. They develop a force proportional to the speed at which they compress or extend (Equation 11.2).

$$F_{shock} = C \cdot v_{shock}$$

(Eq. 11.2)

Where v_{shock} is the velocity of the damper shaft in mm/s, which is normally positive when the shock absorber is in compression (bump) and negative when it's extended (rebound). C is the damping rate, expressed in Ns/mm.

Basically, this means that a spring develops its highest force at maximum deflection, whereas a shock absorber reaches maximum force at maximum shaft velocity. Shock absorber speed is an important parameter to measure to understand shock absorber performance. Modern race car shock absorbers are often adjustable, and adjustments apply

257

to different velocity ranges. By identifying the speed of the shock absorber in problem areas, setup adjustments may be better assessed.

Damper shaft velocity math channels can be created by taking the derivative of the damper position signals (Equation 11.3). Please note that Equation 11.3 uses the notation s_{shock} for the shock absorber movement instead of s_{spring} as these may not necessarily be the same. For a complete lap, the resulting signal will look as pictured in Figure 11.1.

$$v_{shock}(t) = s_{shock}(t) \cdot \frac{d}{dt}$$
(Eq. 11.3)

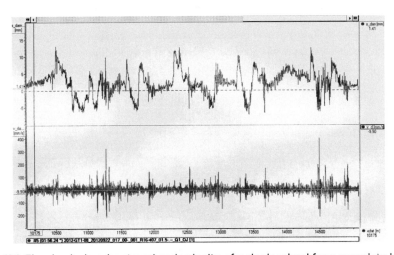

Figure 11.1 The shock absorber travel and velocity of a single wheel for a complete lap

A quick look at this trace shows us a small amount of peaks in the region of ±200 mm/s (including two big ones over 300 mm/s), while the bulk of the shock speed is located between ±30 mm/s. Except for maximum and minimum values (where did a driver go over the curbs?) this graph doesn't suit itself for any meaningful conclusions. As said, the shock absorber has a twofold objective. Let's first have a look at the shock absorber travel and speed as it handles a single bump in the track surface (see Figure 11.2). Local maxima in the damper position trace indicate a change in direction from bump to rebound or vice versa. At these points the spring force will always show a local maximum as well. However, at the same time the shock speed will be zero, and while shock force is proportional to speed, this will be zero also. Shock force will reach a local maximum there where the derivative of shock absorber position shows a local maximum.

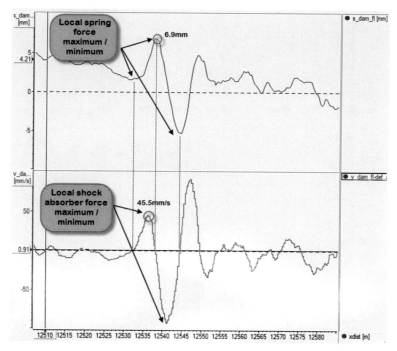

Figure 11.2 The shock absorber travel and velocity of a single wheel going over a bump

To get an idea of the magnitude of the forces, let's consider the trace in Figure 11.2. The damper position trace increases to a local maximum of 6.9 mm in bump (compression). A 200 N/mm spring would produce a force of 1380 N. Just before the local maximum in spring travel, the damper shaft reaches a maximum speed of 45.5 mm/s. Assuming a damping rate of 15 Ns/mm we have a local damping force at this point of 683 N.

The second objective of the shock absorber is to control the transient movement of the chassis due to lateral, longitudinal, and vertical accelerations. Figure 11.3 shows the suspension roll angle of a car going through a corner. The derivative of this channel gives us the roll speed. These roll speed channels indicate that the shock absorbers add force to the wheels somewhere between the moment the roll movement is initiated and the maximum roll angle (at corner entry) and between the point that the roll angle starts to decrease and where it returns to zero again (at corner exit). The area in between shows a roll speed of nearly zero. This area is called steady-state cornering, during which the vehicle balance is influenced mainly by the lateral weight transfer distribution due to the suspension springs and antiroll bars.

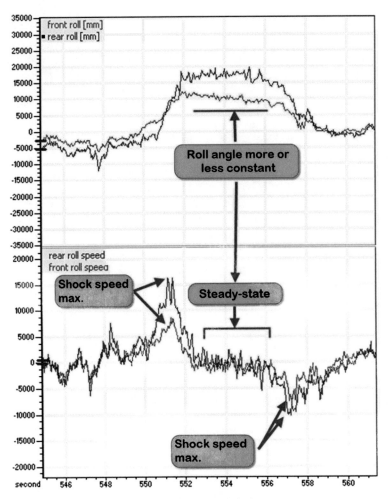

Figure 11.3 The roll angle and roll speed of a car negotiating a corner

So, similar to a single bump event, the maximum suspension force will occur where the roll angle reaches a local maximum. At such a location, the roll speed will inevitably be zero, and therefore the shock absorbers will not develop any force. The maximum shock absorber forces will be developed between the start of the roll movement and the maximum roll angle, where the roll speed reaches a local maximum.

11.2   Determining in Which Range to Tune the Shock Absorbers

Adjustable shock absorbers are very often used to tune the corner entry or exit balance of the race car. These shocks typically have variable settings for bump and rebound (see example in Figure 11.4). Changes to shock absorber settings with the aim of changing the transient balance of the car generally are done in the low speed area (< 25 mm/s). In this range the damping rate will influence how quickly weight is transferred to/from each suspension corner during chassis movements in roll and pitch and therefore how fast each tire is being (un)loaded.

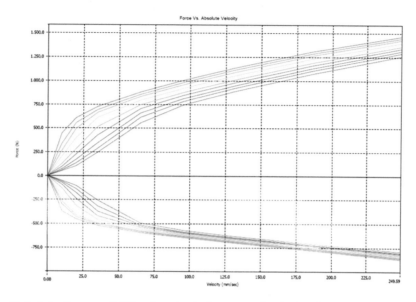

Figure 11.4 Adjusting possibilities for a typical race car shock absorber

To tune this balance with shock settings, first the phase of the corner in which the handling problem occurs needs to be determined. Next, we need to identify which wheel is in bump or rebound motion. Figure 11.5 shows wheel speed, lateral acceleration, and the four shock displacement and velocity channels for a car negotiating the first lefthander after the start/finish line on the Zolder Circuit. The corner is divided into four separate sections:

- Section 1: Straight-line Braking

  The speed trace shows where braking begins. Both front wheels suddenly go into bump and remain relatively constant until cornering commences. Both rear wheels extend more gradually into rebound.

- Section 2: Initial Cornering While Continuing to Brake

  Here the left-front (on the inside of the corner) shock absorber extends again (rebound), while on the right-front wheel it continues to fluctuate around a stable average. The left-rear wheel goes even more into rebound as the right rear decreases its compression (or goes into rebound movement).

- Section 3: Steady-state Cornering Phase, Followed by Throttle Application (While Still Cornering)

During this phase, the front wheels remain in constant compression, while the rear wheels go into bump upon throttle application. Note that despite the two rear wheels being in bump movement, the left-rear shock absorber is still in extension (i.e., longer than its static length). The right-rear shock absorber already was compressed and now compresses even further.

- Section 4: Corner Exit, Steering Wheel Unwinds

As the vehicle's roll angle decreases, the right-hand wheels go into rebound, and the left-hand wheels into bump.

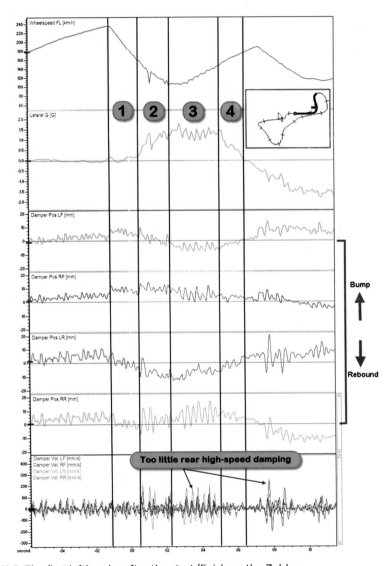

Figure 11.5 The first lefthander after the start/finish on the Zolder

These observations are summarized in Table 11.1 and can be used to suggest changes in shock absorber settings. For instance, in the case of understeer during initial cornering, front rebound could be decreased to improve the compliance between the left-front tire and the track surface. Furthermore, a low-speed damping change on the front axle would have no influence on handling during a steady-state cornering phase. Apart from the high-speed movement caused by track irregularities, there is no substantial movement in the low-speed region of the front shock absorbers in this corner section. Tables like this tend to suggest asymmetric shock absorber settings, because often during cornering the wheels on the opposite side on an axle experience an opposite movement. Asymmetry, however, creates different handling characteristics in left- and right-hand corners. Although in some cases asymmetric damping settings can improve the car's balance, concentrate on the wheel creating the least amount of grip (which is usually the wheel on the inside of the corner) and keep the changes in damping the same on the left- and right-hand sides.

Table 11.1 Shock movement and wheel position summary for traces in Figure 11.5

	Section 1 Straight-line braking		Section 2 Initial cornering + braking		Section 3 Steady-state cornering		Section 4 Corner exit – acceleration	
	Wheel position	Shock movement	Wheel position	Shock movement	Wheel position	Shock movement	Wheel position	Shock movement
LF	Compression	Bump	Compression	Rebound	Extension	—	Extension	Bump
RF	Compression	Bump	Compression	—	Compression	—	Compression	Rebound
LR	Extension	Rebound	Extension	Rebound	Extension	Bump	Compression	Bump
RR	Extension	Rebound	Compression	Bump	Compression	Bump	Compression	Rebound

The shock absorber speed traces in Figure 11.5 provide a good indication of the high-speed damping characteristics of this vehicle. One conclusion drawn from this data is that the rear axle has too little high-speed damping in bump and rebound. During the steady-state cornering phase in this left-hand corner, the right-rear shock absorber experiences speeds far greater than those of the other three wheels. This is confirmed in the next (right-hand) corner where the same occurs on the left-rear shock absorber. The rear axle does not handle road irregularities as well as the front axle, thereby increasing the rear tires' contact patch load variation and therefore decreasing the maximum grip level in the tires.

We can visualize the direction in which a shock absorber moves within the low-speed range with a math channel that takes the respective suspension travel channel, filters out the high-speed content, and differentiates the result against time. The example in Figure 11.6 shows the original shock absorber movement trace in the lower chart in blue. The red trace overlaid on this is the filtered version of the shock absorber movement. The middle chart shows the derivative of the filtered position math channel and indicates whether the shock absorber is traveling in bump (channel values > 0) or in rebound (channel values < 0). We can now project this channel for each suspension corner on a track map, as shown in Figure 11.7. The track map shows red when the shock absorber direction math channel is above zero and blue when it's lower than zero. This kind of visualization makes it very clear at each location around the track which shock absorber is in bump or in rebound and makes it easier to decide for which range to adjust the shock absorber.

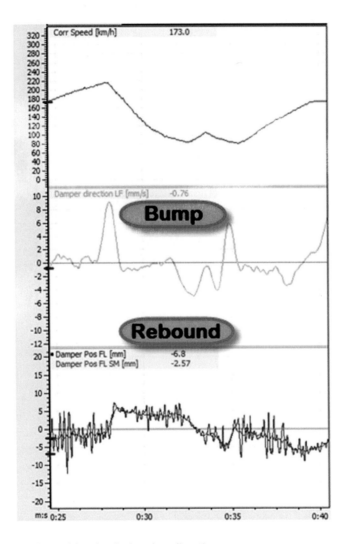

Figure 11.6 Math channel for shock absorber direction

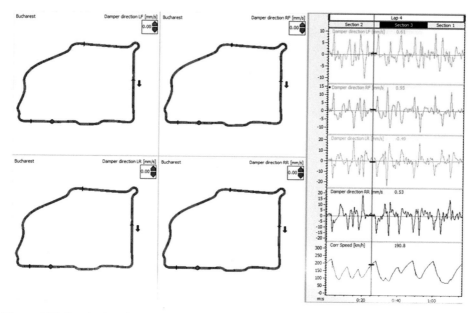

Figure 11.7 Shock absorber direction projected on track maps

11.3 Shock Speed Ranges

As mentioned earlier in this chapter, damping adjustments in the low-speed range influence the transient handling of the car, whereas the high-speed range takes care of road input. To put some figures with it, the shock absorber speed range is divided into the sections in Table 11.2.

Table 11.2 Shock absorber speed range	
Speed range	Influence
Below 5 mm/s	Friction (damper shaft and seals, suspension joints)
5–25 mm/s	Inertial chassis motion (roll, pitch, and heave)
25–200 mm/s	Road input (bumps)
Plus 200 mm/s	Curbs

The first speed interval (below 5 mm/s) is dominated primarily by friction in the suspension system. Most race cars have a considerable amount of sliding contact pivots (spherical bearings), but also the contact surface between the shock absorber shaft and the seals in its housing can account for a significant portion of the total suspension friction. Other than mechanically trying to minimize friction, not much damping tuning occurs in this speed range. However, this does not mean that suspension friction should be ignored.

Generally called the low-speed area, the second speed interval (5–25 mm/s) is where the shock absorber responds to chassis motions resulting from braking, accelerating, and cornering. This is also the area with the greatest influence on how the driver feels the car.

Road input results in shock absorber speeds above 25 mm/s. Damping in this area should be optimized to minimize tire contact patch load variation. The ability of a suspension to cope with road input is rarely assessed reliably by a driver. However, some techniques are available to analyze this using a data acquisition system. (This topic is discussed in the next chapter.) Finally, curbs typically result in shock absorber speeds greater than 200 mm/s.

To visualize how much time a shock absorber is spending in each time interval, one can prepare a histogram of the shock speed math channel (Figure 11.8). Depending on the calibration of the linear potentiometers measuring shock travel, the negative values in the histogram represent rebound travel and positive bump, or vice versa. The shock speed histogram of the vehicle's shock absorbers can be used as a tuning tool, a method pioneered by Claude Rouelle in his data acquisition seminars [9-1].

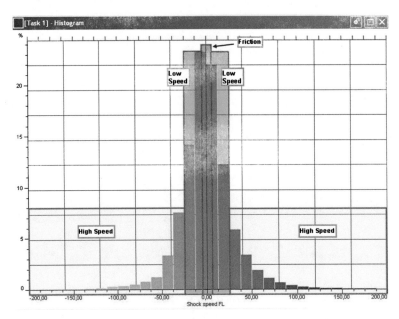

Figure 11.8 Shock absorber speed ranges illustrated in a shock speed histogram

11.4   The Shock Speed Histogram

The shock speed histogram is essentially a characterization of the shock absorber while it is on the car. Much more than a time-based graph, the shock speed histogram shows us how much time the shock absorber is spending in each speed interval. It tells us something about the behavior of the shock integrated into the vehicle's suspension system. This makes the shock speed histogram a very useful tool for suspension tuning.

11.4.1 Shock Speed Histogram Shape—A Mathematical Approach

To investigate what kind of effect different suspension parameters will have on the shape of the shock speed histogram we mathematically model a wheel corner as a very basic mass spring damper system as illustrated in Figure 11.9. To keep it simple, we do not take into account any unsprung mass or tire spring rate.

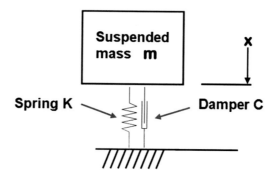

Figure 11.9 Mass spring damper system

In this system, m represents the suspended mass of the wheel corner; K is the suspension spring rate, and C the shock absorber's damping coefficient. This system can be described by the following equation:

$$m \cdot x'' + C \cdot x' + K \cdot x = 0 \qquad \text{(Eq. 11.4)}$$

This definition states that the sum of suspended mass (m) times its acceleration (x''), the speed of the mass (x') multiplied by a damping constant (C), and the mass displacement (x) times a spring rate (K) equals zero. Equation 11.4 can be rearranged to the following differential equation:

$$x'' + \frac{C}{m} \cdot x' + \frac{K}{m} \cdot x = 0 \qquad \text{(Eq. 11.5)}$$

Next, we define the following parameters:

$$\omega_0 = \sqrt{\frac{K}{m}} \qquad \text{(Eq. 11.6)}$$

$$\zeta = \frac{C}{2 \cdot \sqrt{m \cdot K}} \qquad \text{(Eq. 11.7)}$$

267

ω_0 is called the natural frequency of the system, and ζ is the damping ratio. With these two parameters, we can rearrange Equation 11.5 again:

$$x'' + 2\zeta\omega_0 \cdot x' + \omega_0^2 \cdot x = 0 \qquad \text{(Eq. 11.8)}$$

To solve this differential equation, we assume that $x = e^{\gamma t}$, so $x' = \gamma e^{\gamma t}$ and $x'' = \gamma^2 e^{\gamma t}$. When we substitute this in Equation 11.8 we get:

$$\gamma^2 + 2\zeta\omega_0 \cdot \gamma + \omega_0^2 = 0 \qquad \text{(Eq. 11.9)}$$

The solution of this second order differential equation is:

$$\gamma = -\zeta\omega \pm \sqrt{(\zeta\omega)^2 - (\omega_0^2)^2} \qquad \text{(Eq. 11.10)}$$

To make it a bit easier we substitute $a = \omega_0^2$ and $b = \zeta\omega$:

$$\gamma = -b \pm \sqrt{b^2 - a^2} \qquad \text{(Eq. 11.11)}$$

Now we need to consider three cases:

- $b^2 - a^2 > 0$

  In this case, the damping force is significantly larger than the spring force and the system is considered to be *over-damped*. We can calculate γ as two real numbers. The general solution of the system will be

  $$x(t) = Ae^{\gamma_1 t} + Be^{\gamma_2 t} \qquad \text{(Eq. 11.12)}$$

  A and B are constants that depend on the initial conditions of x and x'.

- $b^2 - a^2 = 0$

  Here the damping force balances the spring force, which is called *critical damping*. In this case, $\gamma_1 = \gamma_2 = -b = -a$, resulting in the following solution for the system:

  $$x(t) = Ae^{-at} + Be^{-at} \qquad \text{(Eq. 11.13)}$$

- $b^2 - a^2 < 0$

  Now the damping force is less than the force of the spring (under-damped system), and the solutions from Equation 11.11 will be the complex numbers $-b \pm i\sqrt{a^2 - b^2}$. With $\alpha = \sqrt{a^2 - b^2}$ the general solution for the system becomes:

  $$x(t) = e^{-bt} \cdot (A \cdot \sin\alpha t + B \cdot \cos\alpha t) \qquad \text{(Eq. 11.14)}$$

Using Matlab and Equations 11.12 to 11.14, we can now simulate a basic suspension corner that is excited by a single bump and investigate the shape of the resulting shock speed histogram. For example, consider the cases in Table 11.3. For each case, the shock absorber speed is evaluated for the 20 sec following an excitation of the suspension by a 10 mm bump.

Table 11.3 Example quarter corner parameters			
Configuration	Mass m	Spring rate K	Damping constant C
Case 1	300 kg	280 N/mm	100 Ns/mm
Case 2	300 kg	280 N/mm	150 Ns/mm
Case 3	300 kg	150 N/mm	150 Ns/mm
Case 4	400 kg	150 N/mm	150 Ns/mm

Figure 11.10 shows the simulation results of the initial suspension configuration. The histogram shows an individual peak at –7.5 mm/s, corresponding to the speed at which the shock absorber extends directly after the wheel passes over the bump. Then the wheel goes into bump again with a local maximum of 4.5 mm/s. This also shows up as a local concentration in the shock speed histogram. It takes another two oscillations of the suspension to completely process the bump, and these make up the peak around zero in the histogram.

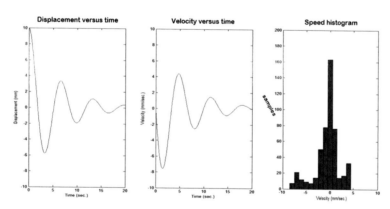

Figure 11.10 Mass m = 300 kg; spring rate K = 280 N/mm; damping constant C = 100 Ns/mm

In Figure 11.11 the damping rate of the suspension corner was increased. The velocity versus time graph shows a slightly lower initial rebound speed (–6.8 mm/s). The following compression results in a significantly lower maximum speed (3 mm/s). This means that the corresponding local concentration in the histogram moves closer to zero. The time period over which the shock speed is evaluated remains a constant 20 sec, and this suspension configuration processes the bump quicker than the soft damping setup. This means that the histogram has a much higher peak around a shock speed of zero.

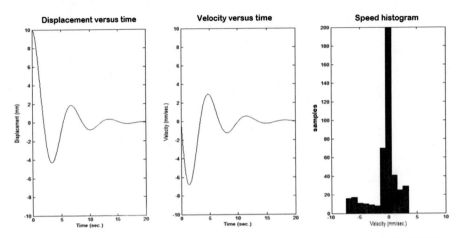

Figure 11.11 Mass m = 300 kg; spring rate K = 280 N/mm; damping constant C = 150 Ns/mm

Next, the damping constant remains the same as in the previous configuration, but the spring rate is decreased to 150 N/mm. The results in Figure 11.12 show that the local maximum shock speeds are lower now. With the softer spring rate, the damping rate now has a bigger influence. The suspension oscillations take longer in time, confirmed by the higher local concentrations around –5 mm/s (rebound) and 2.5 mm/s (bump).

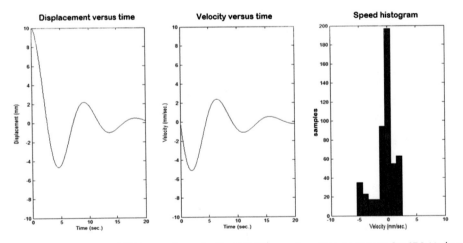

Figure 11.12 Mass m = 300 kg; spring rate K = 150 N/mm; damping constant C = 150 Ns/mm

Finally, with the other parameters unchanged, the sprung mass is increased, resulting in the graphs in Figure 11.13. Despite the higher damping constant, the soft spring rate in combination with the higher mass increases the local maxima in the shock speed versus time graph. This results in a histogram with a wider base with a lower peak around zero.

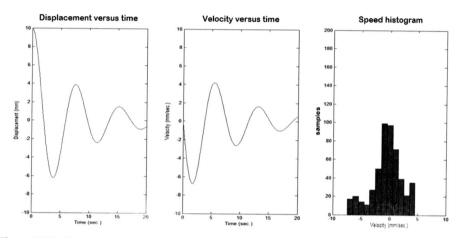

Figure 11.13 Mass *m* = 400 kg; spring rate *K* = 150 N/mm; damping constant *C* = 150 Ns/mm

Of course the preceding histograms will never result in a perfect Gauss distribution, as we're looking at only one single event, but the illustrations do give us an idea of the influence of different suspension parameters on the shape of the histogram. Some general conclusions from the graphs follow:

- Increasing the damping constant will make the histogram peak around zero higher and make the foot of the histogram less wide (the histogram becomes sharper).

- Softening the spring rate has a similar effect. The suspension will in this case be more compliant, and as the damping constant remains the same, there's more damping force to slow down the movement of the sprung mass.

- Increasing the sprung mass lowers the peak of the histogram and makes the foot wider. The increased mass makes it more difficult for the spring and damper to slow down the movement, so there is more speed variation.

11.4.2 Shock Speed Histogram Shape—What Do We Want?

The first thing that needs to be emphasized here is that the shock speed histogram is a tool and should be used as such. It will not show you the ideal setup of the car! It is a statistical snapshot in time of the car's suspension behavior, and this is not limited to what the shock absorbers are doing. Its shape will vary with changes in damping settings, springs, antiroll bars, mass, tire construction, tire pressure, and so on.

Theoretically, to optimize mechanical grip, setup adjustments should be implemented to make the shock speed histogram as symmetrical as possible. Ideally, the histogram resembles a Gaussian distribution (also known as normal distribution or bell curve). The goal here is to maintain a tire contact patch load that is as constant as possible.

When looking at a wheel passing over a single bump, initially there is a positive shock speed when the bump is hit and then a negative speed as the wheel passes over it. To maintain the balance of the chassis, positive and negative velocities should be as close as possible to each other in magnitude and duration. Now, extrapolate this picture to a complete lap around the track, where each shock movement applies to this condition and the result is a perfectly symmetrical shock speed histogram. In other words, an ideal suspension setup dissipates equal amounts of energy into the shock absorber in bump and rebound movements.

Figure 11.14 shows histograms of the four corners of a race car. The data was taken from the same lap as in Figure 11.5. Lighter color bars indicate how much time is spent in the high-speed range (shock speed > 25 mm/s). The total percentage of time spent in each of these ranges is indicated in each histogram for bump and rebound travel. Additionally, the average speed in bump and rebound is indicated in the graphs.

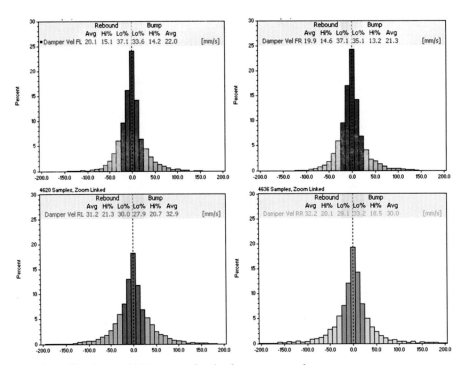

Figure 11.14 Shock speed histograms for the four corners of a race car

Table 11.4 summarizes the percentage of time spent in each speed range. The third column illustrates the difference between the bump and rebound durations. The fourth column shows the average between bump and rebound to offer an indication of how much time is spent at low and high speed, regardless of the direction of damper travel. In this example we can conclude that in the high-speed range there is not a great deal of asymmetry between bump and rebound, the maximum difference being 1.6% for the right-rear corner. The low-speed range can use some tweaking. The left-front shock absorber spends 3.5% more time in rebound, while the right rear is 5.1% more in bump. Therefore, the left-front shock absorber could use a bit less rebound damping (or more bump) and the right rear less bump damping (or more rebound).

Table 11.4 Shock speed asymmetries between bump and rebound		Bump	Rebound	Difference	Average
LEFT FRONT	Lo%	33.6	37.1	3.5	35.4
	Hi%	14.2	15.1	0.9	14.7
RIGHT FRONT	Lo%	35.1	37.1	2.0	36.1
	Hi%	13.2	14.6	1.4	13.9
LEFT REAR	Lo%	27.9	30.0	2.1	28.9
	Hi%	20.7	21.3	0.6	21.0
RIGHT REAR	Lo%	33.2	28.1	−5.1	30.7
	Hi%	18.5	20.1	1.6	19.3

Although there is reasonable symmetry in the high-speed range, Figure 11.5 showed us already that there is not enough rear high-speed damping. This is confirmed in the shock speed histograms. There is a difference of approximately 6% between the front and rear high-speed ranges. To obtain a more even distribution between the front and rear, the rear high-speed damping should be increased in bump and rebound.

The shock speed histograms in Figure 11.14 were created from data covering an entire lap. Particular corners can be magnified. However, in this case, attention should be paid to the beginning and ending point of the magnified area. These points should have approximately the same shock potentiometer value. If this is not the case, one shock absorber spent more time in the bump or rebound phase, which creates an offset in the shock speed histograms.

So we know that for mechanical grip we would like all our histograms to look like perfect Gauss curves with minimal differences between left- and right-hand sides of the car. The picture changes, however, once aerodynamics come into play. Often, shock absorbers are not used only to handle the transient characteristics of the vehicle and the irregularities in the track surface. In many cases, they are also used to control the attitude of the chassis. An example of this is a race car possessing considerable aerodynamic downforce with excessive front rebound damping applied to jack the car's nose down to improve the airflow under the car. In this case, the front downforce pushes the front of the car down, creating a greater rake angle (the longitudinal angle of inclination of the vehicle floor). A high rebound damping helps keep it there. This kind of setup will not result in symmetrical shock speed histograms, and the ideal shape of the histogram will probably be considerably different to a Gauss curve.

Concerning the ideal shape of the shock speed histogram, more questions need to be asked. How high do we want the histogram peak, or how wide does the base of the histogram need to be? There is no easy answer to this, and it all depends on experience with a specific type of car. With time, this experience will indicate which shape of the speed histogram is ideal for a specific application and what type and magnitude of setup modification will change the shape to what extent. It needs to be stressed again that the shock speed histogram is an analytical tool that should be used to describe what is going on with the vehicle suspension. In the next section, some additional parameters will be discussed to mathematically describe the histogram shape.

11.4.3 Statistical Analysis

Some software packages offer the possibility to create the shock speed histograms automatically. If this is not possible, the user will have to create the graphs. In both cases it is important to pay attention to the following in order to be able to compare histograms:

- Make sure that the number of bins is sufficient

- Make sure that the width of the bins is always the same

- Make sure that the vertical axis scaling is the same for all histograms

- Make sure that the horizontal axis is the same for all histograms and that you choose the same maximum damper velocity for both bump and rebound

Except for the average shock speed percentages in bump and rebound in the high- or low-speed ranges as calculated in the previous example, other statistical parameters can be employed to provide more information about the histogram shape. These parameters also make it easier to compare different histograms. Often the following statistical functions are not available in the data acquisition analysis software. Therefore, the data in the next example is imported into a spreadsheet. This spreadsheet, including the sample data, can be downloaded from *http://jorge.segers.googlepages.com/technical*. Figure 11.15 shows the output of this spreadsheet. As indicated previously, for mechanical grip, the ideal shock speed histogram resembles a normal distribution curve. Therefore, a measured histogram is parameterized by determining how much it deviates from a normal distribution.

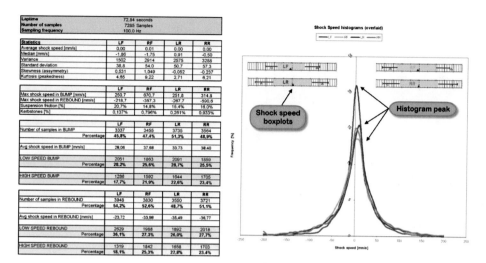

Figure 11.15 Shock speed histogram statistics

11.4.3.1 Histogram Peak or Height of the Zero Bin

The first thing to check in a shock speed histogram is the height of the "zero" bin. This is the boundary between bump and rebound velocities, and the height of this bin will tell us something about the relative suspension stiffness of the four suspension corners. In Figure 11.15, there's a reasonable difference in zero bin height between the left-front corner and the rest. Left front goes up to 21% while the other three corners are around 14–15%. Assuming a symmetrical setup of the car in this example, before making any drastic changes, the engineer should check if the tire pressures being used are correct. If the problem remains, asymmetric damping settings might equalize the zero bin heights on the front axle.

The zero bin height is an important setup reference number. If a race car is performing well on a certain track with a given zero bin height for each histogram, it will probably not perform well when these heights vary away from these numbers.

In the preceding example the zero bin includes data where the shock speed was between −0.5 and +0.5 mm/s, so it includes some bump and some rebound speeds. Some software packages create histograms without a zero bin, such as the example in Figure 11.16. In this case, the zero bin should be calculated by taking the sum of the bin content directly left and directly right of zero.

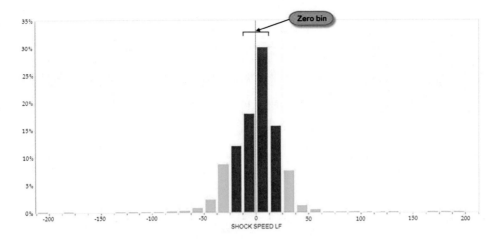

Figure 11.16 When there is no zero bin, the zero bin height is the sum of the bin height directly left and right from the zero axis

In the preceding example, the height of the zero bin would be 30.16 + 18.02 = 48.18%, and this bin would include shock speed values between –12.5 and +12.5 mm/s. In this example it would also probably be better to choose a smaller bin width, as the zero bin contains about half of all the measured samples.

11.4.3.2 Average Shock Speed

The average shock speed should always be close to zero. If this is not the case, there is probably something wrong with the suspension travel sensors, its configuration, or the math channel that calculates the shock speed.

11.4.3.3 Median

One property of a normal distribution is that the median value $\mu_{1/2}$ (the middle value of an array) equals the average value of that distribution. For instance, in the array 5, 7, 8, 10, 15, the average is 9 and the median 8. In the case of the shock speed histogram, in order to obtain a symmetrical histogram the median should be as close to zero as possible.

A median greater than zero indicates that there are more measured samples in the bump range, and a negative median signifies a greater number of samples in the rebound range. In other words, $\mu_{1/2}$ is a first measure of the asymmetry of the shock speed histogram between bump and rebound.

11.4.3.4 Variance and Standard Deviation

Variance and standard deviation are two statistical measures with the same meaning; they measure dispersion (i.e., the scattering of measured values around their average). Variance σ^2 is the average distance of each data point from the average value of all the samples. For a discrete collection of samples, it can be expressed mathematically as Equation 11.15.

$$\sigma^2 = \frac{1}{N} \cdot \sum_{i=1}^{N}(x_i - \mu)^2$$

(Eq. 11.15)

Where N = Total number of samples

μ = Average value of all samples

Standard deviation σ is simply the square root of the variance (Equation 11.16).

$$\sigma = \sqrt{\frac{1}{N} \cdot \sum_{i=1}^{N}(x_i - \mu)^2}$$

(Eq. 11.16)

Standard deviation is expressed in the same units as the measurement; in the case of this example, it is in mm/s. A small σ indicates that the data points are clustered closely to the histogram's average (which indicates a stiff suspension). Meanwhile, a large σ indicates that they are distributed a significant distance from the average. Essentially this is a measure of the width of the shock speed histogram. A large standard distribution indicates that the shock absorber sees more high-speed movement and vice versa. The left-front shock absorber in Figure 11.15 has a lower standard deviation than the other three corners, so by comparison it experiences less high-speed movement. The graph clearly shows that the base of the left-front shock speed histogram is considerably less wide than the other three.

Pay attention to the fact that the standard deviation does not tell us anything about the possible asymmetry between the bump and rebound side of the histogram.

11.4.3.5 Skewness
Skewness is a measure of the asymmetry of the shock speed histogram. A histogram biased to the bump side has negative skew. A positive skew means the histogram is biased to the rebound side (Figure 11.17).

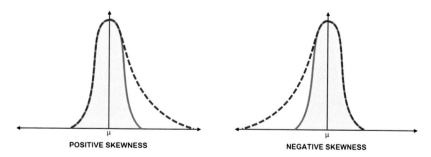

Figure 11.17 Skewness

Mathematically, skewness A can be expressed as Equation 11.17. A normal distribution has a skewness equal to zero. If the shock speed average and median are not equal, skewness is not zero.

$$A = \frac{N}{(N-1)\cdot(N-2)} \cdot \sum_{i=1}^{N}\left(\frac{x_i-\mu}{\sigma}\right)^3 \qquad \text{(Eq. 11.17)}$$

Where N = Total number of samples

       μ = Average value of all samples

       σ = Standard deviation of all samples

11.4.3.6 Kurtosis

Kurtosis is the degree of peakedness of a distribution. A higher kurtosis histogram has a sharper peak and fatter tails, and a lower kurtosis histogram has a more rounded peak with wider shoulders (Figure 11.18).

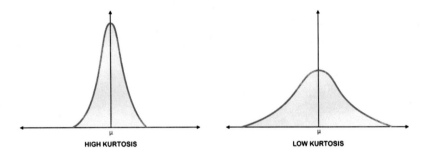

Figure 11.18 Kurtosis

Equation 11.18 determines the kurtosis of a distribution. Kurtosis indicates that the collection of samples is spread in a wider fashion than the normal distribution entails. A normal distribution has a kurtosis of zero (mesokurtic). A distribution with positive kurtosis is called leptokurtic and one with a negative kurtosis is platykurtic. In the example that was covered in Figure 11.15, all histograms are leptokurtic, but the front shock absorbers have a higher kurtosis than the rear ones. This means that more movement on the front shock absorbers is concentrated in the low-speed range.

$$G_2 = \left[\frac{N\cdot(N+1)}{(N-1)\cdot(N-2)\cdot(N-3)} \cdot \sum_{i=1}^{N}\left(\frac{x_i-\mu}{\sigma}\right)^4\right] - \frac{3\cdot(N-1)^2}{(N-2)\cdot(N-3)} \qquad \text{(Eq. 11.18)}$$

If a histogram has a higher kurtosis, this does not mean necessarily that it has a lower standard deviation. The distributions pictured in Figure 11.18 may well have the same standard deviation.

11.5　The Shock Speed Box Plot

Above the overlaid shock speed histograms in Figure 11.15, four box plots corresponding to each suspension corner are shown. A box plot is an alternative way to visualize the distribution of a data series. It represents five descriptive statistics of the data set:

- Minimum value of the data set

- 25th percentile

- Median

- 75th percentile

- Maximum value of the data set

However, for the application of the box plot with shock speed data, it is better to use the 15th and 85th percentiles instead of the minimum and maximum values of the data set. Additionally, the average shock speed in both bump and rebound can be integrated in the graph. The result is shown in Figure 11.19.

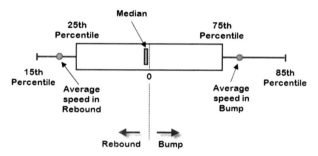

Figure 11.19　Box plot configuration

A percentile is the value of a variable below which a certain percent of samples fall. For example, the 15th percentile is the value below which 15% of the samples fall. If for a certain shock speed signal we have a 15th percentile of −35 mm/s, this means that 15% of the data set has a speed less than this value. Practically, this tells us that we have 15% of the data with a rebound velocity higher than 35 mm/s. An 85th percentile of 30 mm/s means that 15% of the data has a value higher than this. The 50th percentile equals the median of the data set.

The required percentiles to construct the shock speed box plot can be calculated by sorting the data set from the smallest value to the highest. The index of the percentile can be determined with Equation 11.19.

$$i = \frac{n \cdot p_i}{100} + 0.5$$

(Eq. 11.19)

Where i = Percentile index

n = Number of samples in the data series

p_i = Percentile

As an example, let's say we want to calculate the 25th percentile of the following data series (already sorted ascending):

5   9   12   18   21   22   26   29   30   38   46   59

The percentile index becomes:

$$i = \frac{12 \cdot 25}{100} + 0.5 = 3.5$$

This means that the requested percentile is located between the third and fourth data sample. When the percentile index is not an integer number, the exact value for the percentile can be found by linear interpolation between the two respective data samples. The 25th percentile for the preceding example would therefore be 16.

The box plot is merely an alternative way to display shock speed data. The advantages of the box plot are the possibility to quickly compare different data sets (or the four suspension corners) and the ease of construction that does not involve subjective judgments. Two individuals will construct the same box plot for a given data set, which is not necessarily true for a histogram (choice of number of bins, bin width, and so on). On the other hand, the box plot will hide some details that the histogram provides, and it's less intuitive to distinguish between low-speed and high-speed damping. Figure 11.20 shows an example of the four shock speed box plots for a vehicle containing data of a complete lap. Because the boundaries of the box are defined by the 25th and 75th percentiles, it contains exactly half of the amount of samples in the data series. This means that a bigger box corresponds to a flatter histogram. The right-rear box plot has a 25th percentile of –27 mm/s and a 75th percentile of 27 mm/s. The median is exactly at 0 mm/s and also the 15th and 85th percentiles correspond. Except for the minus sign, the average shock speed in bump and

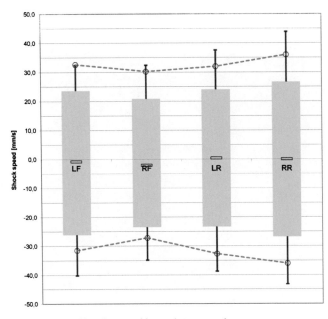

Figure 11.20 Shock speed box plot example

rebound are equal. This means that the corresponding shock speed histogram will be very close to symmetrical.

The right-front box plot shows a slightly negative median. The 25th percentile is –23 mm/s and the 75th is 21 mm/s. The same difference is seen between the 15th and 85th percentiles, and there is 3 mm/s difference between the average shock speed in bump and rebound. This suspension corner has more damping in rebound compared to bump.

In another example, two different configurations of one suspension corner are compared. Figure 11.21 shows the box plots and the shock speed histograms for both configurations. In addition to these graphs, Table 11.5 gives the corresponding statistics for the two configurations.

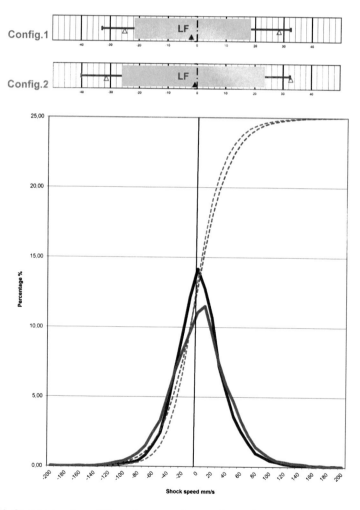

Figure 11.21 Comparing two different suspension configurations using shock speed histograms and box plots

Table 11.5 Shock speed statistics for the example in Figure 11.21		
Shock speed statistic	Configuration 1	Configuration 2
Zero bin height	14.17%	11.51%
Percentage low-speed bump	27.0%	25.0%
Percentage low-speed rebound	31.6%	25.0%
Percentage high-speed bump	19.9%	24.1%
Percentage high-speed rebound	21.5%	25.9%
Average shock speed in bump	28.32 mm/s	32.64 mm/s
Average shock speed in rebound	−25.05 mm/s	−31.48 mm/s
Median	−2.03 mm/s	−0.79 mm/s
Standard deviation	36.5 mm/s	43.3 mm/s
Skewness	0.845	0.814
Kurtosis	5.69	8.85

The main observation, both from the histograms as from the box plots, is that the first configuration has more of the data concentrated in the low-speed range, and the second configuration has a flatter but wider histogram shape. Although Table 11.5 indicates that the percentages spent in low speed and high speed are divided equally over bump and rebound ranges, the histogram, but even more the box plot (looking at the percentile locations), shows clearly that there is nevertheless some amount of asymmetry in the distribution. Another interesting point to make in this example is that configuration 1 has a lower kurtosis value but a higher zero bin width compared with configuration 2. Remember that kurtosis is a parameter that tells us something about the histogram shape, not about the absolute value of the histogram peak.

The dashed lines in Figure 11.21 are the cumulative totals of the shock speed histogram bins and are effectively the integral of the shock speed histogram. They are another convenient way of clarifying the distribution of the shock speed data.

It should be clear that to analyze shock speed data in the most efficient manner, it is beneficial to use a combination of the tools covered in this chapter: graphically with shock speed histograms and box plots and mathematically using statistics.

11.6   Shock Speed Run Charts

In the previous sections, a number of techniques were discussed for the visualization of shock speed data. These techniques concentrated always on data from a single complete lap. Run charts (which are covered in more detail in chapter 17) provide a way to detect trends in lap-by-lap statistics and can also be applied on shock speed data. The most

...

important statistics necessary to draw any conclusion about suspension behavior from shock speed data are the times spent in bump and rebound and in high and low speed. For this, some math channels can be created in the analysis software that keep track of the time spent by each shock absorber in a specific range, an example of which is shown in Figure 11.22. The math channel evaluates if the shock speed is in a predefined range, and if this is the case it integrates a channel with a constant value of one. This results in the time that the shock speed was within the specified range. If the shock speed is outside the defined range, the channel remains constant. At the end of the lap the integrated time needs to be reset to zero. The maximum value for each lap can then be plotted in run charts such as in Figure 11.23, where the following statistics were included:

- Time per lap spent in low-speed bump (0 to 25 mm/s)
- Time per lap spent in low-speed rebound (0 to –25 mm/s)
- Time per lap spent in high-speed bump (above 25mm/s)
- Time per lap spent in high-speed rebound (below –25 mm/s)

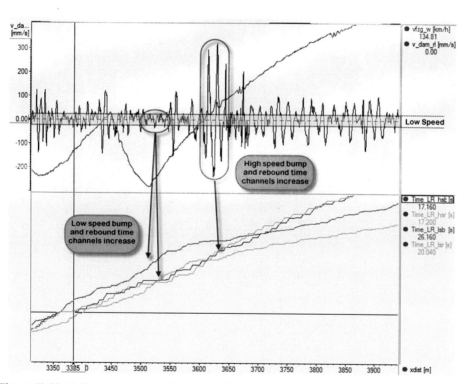

Figure 11.22 Math channels to calculate the time a shock absorber (in this case, the left rear) spends in low- and high-speed bump and rebound

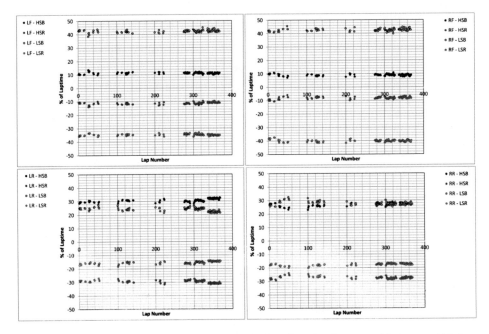

Figure 11.23 Run charts showing for each shock absorber the time spent in low and high speed for bump and rebound movement during a complete race event

These graphs give a very quick overview of the complete race weekend from the first practice session until the end of the race. The effect of setup changes can be efficiently evaluated and referenced to all other laps done during the weekend. It also makes spotting problems a lot less complicated.

In Figure 11.24 only the graph of the left-rear corner from the example in Figure 11.23 is given. The different sessions are clearly recognizable, and trends in these four shock speed statistics can be easily tracked. Other statistics that could easily be calculated in and exported from the analysis software are the following:

- Average shock speed in bump
- Average shock speed in rebound
- Shock speed standard deviation
- Shock speed histogram zero bin height (e.g., by calculating the time per lap that shock speed is between −5 and 5 mm/s)

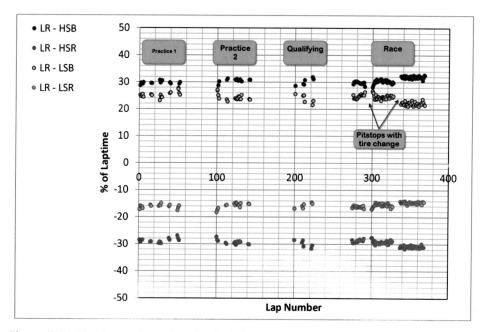

Figure 11.24 Shock speed run chart for the left-rear shock absorber

Chapter 12
Suspension Analysis in the Frequency Domain

This chapter introduces frequency analysis, a method that can be used to optimize the interface between the vehicle and the road surface. This chapter is written by Josep Fontdecaba I. Buj, engineering director at Creuat S.L., a Spanish company specializing in interconnected suspension systems. Given his expertise in suspension optimization, it is more appropriate that he write this part of the book.

12.1   Introducing Frequency Analysis

Analyzing vehicle suspension is undertaken to understand and optimize the interface between the vehicle and the road. In this section, some analysis tools and concepts are proposed that may be useful for this purpose. These methods imply some complex calculations that possibly are not within the scope of a user's data acquisition analysis software. Therefore, this type of analysis is conducted primarily by exporting the logged data into a mathematical package (e.g., Matlab, MathCAD, or a spreadsheet) or into customized software packages.

The suspension of a four-wheeled vehicle can be defined as a combination of rigid and elastic components that link each wheel to the vehicle body. In effect, the suspension is designed to behave as rigidly as possible in response to lateral and longitudinal forces while allowing a softer response to vertical movements to cope with road irregularities.

Although springs and dampers define the main properties of the vehicle suspension, one must consider the suspension's geometrical properties, the distribution of the vehicle's mass, and the tire properties to prepare a useful model.

In addition to the model complexity, the suspension analysis must take into account the random nature of the input, which is a combination of road irregularities and dynamic loads induced by the driving conditions.

The nature of this problem is very complex. This text focuses on the effect of springs and dampers because they are responsible for the vertical movements of the wheels (i.e., the vertical movements of the vehicle body with respect to the road).

The frequency analysis is one of the best analysis tools because it can handle efficiently the road input, cover the entire range of body movements, and characterize suspension behavior.

In terms of functionality, the purpose of the suspension is twofold. First, one needs it to isolate the vehicle body movements from the dynamic forces generated by the vehicle driving conditions and the irregularities of the road. Second, one needs it to help the tires follow the terrain to maximize their grip capacity.

From this, it follows that the suspension must minimize the following:

- The body movements induced by driving and the road input
- The tire load fluctuations induced by driving and the road input

The first requirement represents a contradiction. Body movements generated by driving dynamics are minimized with stiff suspension components, and road input is isolated better with soft settings.

The second requirement is easier to fulfill with soft settings. Nevertheless, the suspension needs to distribute tire loads in a particular way to keep the desired car balance, so in this case there are other considerations.

Given these requirements, it is not easy to optimize the suspension. Any configuration is partially optimal, making a compromise necessary. This creates the need for powerful analysis tools that make it easier to select the correct compromises.

Those trying to improve the response to vertical road input could easily achieve this with soft springs and dampers. Soft settings also guarantee minimum tire load fluctuations as the tires follow the road with smaller changes in suspension forces.

However, soft settings cannot handle the dynamic forces induced by driving. The suspension influences other vehicle properties such as steering response time, balance, transient lateral stability, driver feel, traction, and (in some cases) aerodynamic issues. The pitch movement at braking and the roll movement in cornering should be controlled because these negatively influence the suspension geometry and the optimal tire contact patch. These movements can be reduced with the appropriate geometry adjustments, but this approach has many side effects. Most race cars make very limited use of them.

Basically, the suspension needs to be as soft as possible for the vertical movement (and the warp movement as well) but stiffer for pitch and roll movements.

Pitch and roll movements are influenced greatly by the driving conditions, meaning the input frequencies indicate a different spectrum than the road input. This issue alone justifies performing the frequency analysis.

Grip is a concept related to how the tire adheres to the road. Such adherence can be increased with the appropriate material (i.e., rubber compounds) and with the load on the tire. Once the tires are selected, the suspension must maintain the load on the tire and keep it as high as possible. Intuitively, the tire should follow the terrain, so the irregularities do not translate into tire deflections. This intuitive reasoning is called *minimizing tire load fluctuations*.

In addition, the nonlinear behavior of grip forces versus tire loads (Figure 12.1) is ultimately responsible for the car's balance. The suspension is designed usually to take advantage of balance by transferring weight differently on the front and rear axles during roll. This normally is achieved using different settings for roll stiffness on the front and rear, so the suspension settings can make the car oversteer or understeer, depending on the nonlinear characteristics of the tires.

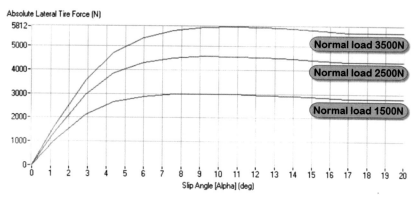

Figure 12.1 Nonlinear tire characteristics

For race cars, tires play a significant role in the suspension analysis and optimization. Compound characteristics are important when combined with the vehicle's suspension because of the low-damping capabilities of the tires. There is also the need to work the tires so they quickly reach operating temperatures. It is fundamental to consider the tire parameters carefully to analyze their influence on grip.

Weight transfers are induced in the suspension because of lateral and longitudinal acceleration. Although the total magnitude of these weight transfers cannot be altered by the suspension, they can be influenced by it in the following ways:

- The suspension can distribute the total amount of weight transfer over four wheels.

- The suspension can minimize weight transfer fluctuations to avoid the lower tire load values that cause the start of breakaway under limited maneuver conditions.

Therefore, if load fluctuations are the key issue to consider when optimizing the suspension, frequency analysis is the tool of choice.

One can attempt to measure suspension movements and loads with the aim of characterizing vehicle response to road input. Ultimately, judgments must be made based on the results obtained. Many race cars install position and load sensors in some key suspension elements. In some cases, accelerometers are installed not only on the car body but also in the wheel hubs.

Measurements are required because not all data is known. Normally appropriate laboratory measuring devices can characterize spring rates and damper rates quite accurately. However, the entire suspension system includes many unknown parameters and nonlinear elements, sometimes becoming too complex. Therefore, measurements must be taken under operating conditions.

Nevertheless, there are important limitations to measuring data on track. Competition vehicles have nonconstant and nonlinear characteristics that are very difficult to model. A real circuit is the only place to record data for optimizing the suspension settings, but crucial data items such as tire contact patch load are impossible to measure because there is no sensor for a rolling tire. Other inputs, such as road actual position, are also difficult to measure accurately. In general, the following are limitations for an appropriate analysis:

- Logged data is limited to the available (and possible) sensors.
- Logged data is limited to the logging capabilities (i.e., resolution and frequency).
- Logged data is lap-, circuit-, and weather-dependent.
- On-circuit tests are expensive, particularly when considering the previously mentioned limitations.

The four-post rig is an alternative to some limitations of on-track logged data. This approach offers a more structured test bed that can address the specific measurements and test conditions, therefore providing more concise answers to the characterization of the suspension system.

The four-post rig positions the vehicle on four posts under each wheel, with each post acting as an actuator that simulates the road input. Each actuator is controlled ultimately by a computer that dictates the generated road input and records the measurements to later correlate the two sets of data. These tests normally are conducted by generating movements within a range of frequencies, so it becomes relatively easy to determine the response based on a frequency.

The four-post rig can provide information that avoids some limitations of circuit-logged data from sensors. This poses several advantages:

- It provides sensors for tire contact patch load (not possible to record on track).

- It provides sensors for tire deflection (input road known and wheel position measurable).

- There is no lap/circuit dependency.

- It is cost-effective.

Nevertheless, the four-post rig also has limitations:

- Static tire behavior is quite different from a rolling tire.

- Car balance assessment is unreliable.

- Aerodynamic load simulation requires additional actuators and cannot generate the interaction of aerodynamic forces with the suspension.

In general, the information recorded during a rig test is useful for comparing the performance of different suspension configurations quantitatively and for detecting anomalies or major deviations from the expected behavior. This information is used normally to provide the best damper settings for the spring configurations chosen after tests on the circuit track.

The test rig data analysis relies heavily on frequency analysis. The road input is generated by sweeping a known range of relatively pure frequencies. This makes the analysis simpler and more reliable.

Test rig engineers use rig test data in the form of the following:

- Main frequency transfer functions
  - Body movement amplitude versus road input amplitude
  - Contact patch load fluctuations versus road input amplitude
- Scale parameters (extracted from frequency analysis)
  - Suspension elasticity rates versus frequency
  - Suspension damping rates versus frequency
- Modal components

Measured parameters of a suspension, taken on the circuit or at the four-post rig, generally are used to find the optimal configuration and make decisions about changes to be made.

To set up a suspension, the engineer ideally seeks to do the following:

- Minimize the energy absorbed by the vehicle
- Minimize the energy absorbed by the suspension components (dissipated in the dampers)
- Maintain the body movement response within acceptable limits for race driving parameters (constraints related to camber and castor angle changes)
- Maintain the vehicle height within acceptable limits (under aerodynamic conditions)
- Avoid tire load fluctuation to prevent tire contact breakaway

Such decisions are easier to make with a proper understanding of the vehicle dynamics' dependency upon the suspension.

12.2   Frequency Analysis versus Time-Space Analysis

An analysis of the actual movement as a function of time is often difficult to use because it is linked too often to the event under analysis. Time-space analysis is used for simulations that attempt to predict the exact response of the system to a very specific event. This can only be useful in the context of an extremely powerful simulation effort, which otherwise can be very expensive and not useful for understanding the basics of the problem to generalize conclusions.

Although not the most intuitive method, frequency analysis is used effectively to understand the behavior and identity of a suspension configuration.

A study of discrete inputs offers a large amount of information about a suspension system. The two graphs in Figure 12.2 illustrate the one-dimensional movement of suspended body (*mxy*) as a time response to the input movement (*xy*). This could be the oversimplification of the vehicle movement induced by road input, a step in height (first graph), or a bump (the second graph).

These two graphs reveal much about the suspension behavior but are too specific to the selected input. The graphs may change significantly if the amplitude or the steepness of the input ramps is changed. Therefore, they are not very useful for understanding if the suspension response will be adequate under other input conditions.

Nevertheless, these tests make it easy to obtain an intuitive sense of damper effectiveness. Figures 12.3 and 12.4 show an over-damped and an under-damped configuration, respectively, that are obvious from the graph, but a good measure of damper effectiveness is complex to achieve. A much more refined method is required that provides the measurable effectiveness of the suspension and characterizes the response to any input.

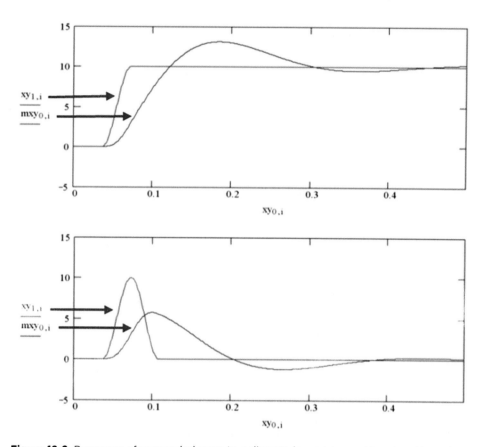

Figure 12.2 Response of suspended mass to a discrete input (stepped input and bump)

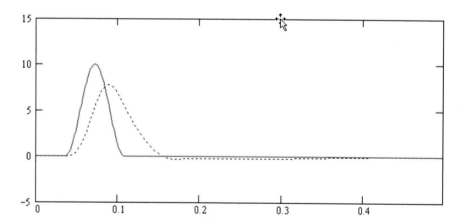

Figure 12.3 Over-damped configuration

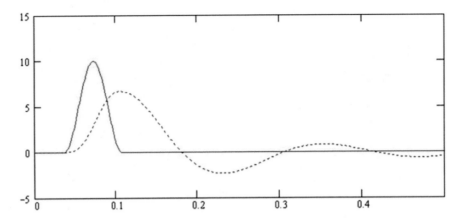

Figure 12.4 Under-damped configuration

The frequency analysis generates the spectrum of frequencies that a signal contains. Road input is basically a noise signal and is understood as a combination of many different pure frequencies. The transformation from the input signal to the frequency spectrum is known as the Fourier transform.

Named after Joseph Fourier, the Fourier transform is one of many mathematical ways used to understand the world better through complex tricks. Fourier transforms have many scientific applications in signal processing, acoustics, optics, physics, and many other areas. In signal processing, it is used systematically to deconstruct a signal into its component frequencies and amplitudes.

The Fourier transform acts as a filter. It combines the input signal with each harmonic function for every frequency to determine how that signal matches with that frequency. Given the input signal [x(t)], the Fourier transformation is calculated with the square integral of Equation 12.1.

$$X(\omega) = \frac{1}{\sqrt{2 \cdot \pi}} \int_{-\infty}^{\infty} x(t) \cdot e^{-i\omega t} dt \qquad \text{(Eq. 12.1)}$$

The result is another function [X(ω)] that contains the amplitude and phase of each frequency component. In other words, this transformation shows the content of each pure frequency in the input signal [x(t)].

As an example, Figure 12.5 shows the four Fourier transforms of the suspension movement channels, measured by suspension potentiometers. These sensors actually measure the difference between the wheel and body movement. It can be argued that minimizing the peaks in these graphs optimizes the suspension settings.

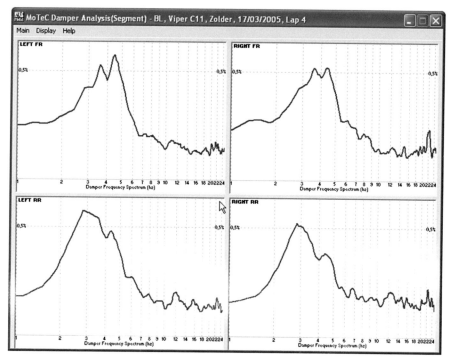

Figure 12.5 The Fourier transforms of suspension potentiometer signals provide detailed information about vehicle suspension characteristics

12.3   Theoretical Analysis

In any theoretical analysis, one begins with a model of what needs to be analyzed. Four-wheel vehicles and race cars are quite complex systems, so choose an adequate model that characterizes the system with the acceptable degree of detail.

Most suspension analyses begin with a simple model of a suspended mass (Figure 12.6) that is held by an elastic and damped link. This model is adequate for the first approach but soon is found to be oversimplified.

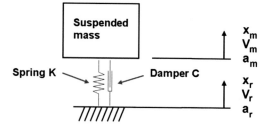

Figure 12.6 A simple suspended mass system with one spring and one damper

In a vehicle, there are two important issues that require extra elements:

- The vehicle actually is suspended over four wheels (four suspension links). These links provide three degrees of freedom that may require separate analysis. In addition, the hyper-static configuration (one more link than degrees of freedom) introduces a fourth component related to weight distribution.

- Because suspension links are far more complex, they require consideration of additional masses (e.g., the wheel hub) and an additional spring and damping to account for tire deflection.

The first issue requires a modal analysis that separates each wheel movement combination:

- Vertical movement (all wheels moving in the same direction)
- Pitch movement (front and rear wheels moving in opposite directions)
- Roll movement (right and left wheels moving in opposite directions)
- Warp (unrelated to body movements but responsible for weight distribution changes when the vehicle is over a non-planar surface)

The modal analysis is discussed later in this chapter. Discussion continues here about the frequency analysis of a single suspended mass that subsequently can be translated to each modal movement.

The second issue concerning the complexity is covered in most quarter-vehicle models and at a minimum must address the fact that the wheel mass cannot be neglected and the tire deflects under load. This model (Figure 12.7) takes into account that the wheel mass is a secondary suspended mass with a link to the ground, the tire, and the suspension link to the vehicle body.

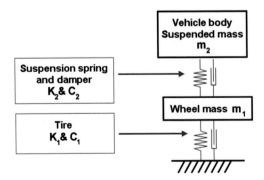

Figure 12.7 Mass-spring system taking into account the nonsuspended wheel mass and tire spring and damping rate

Normally, the wheel mass is much smaller than the body mass. Therefore, it is associated with higher frequencies and the actual contact patch load fluctuations.

The single suspended mass system (Figure 12.6) is easy to characterize mathematically. In this system, consider the position, velocity, and acceleration of the suspended mass and the road surface (the input signal). Position (Equation 12.2), velocity (Equation 12.3), and acceleration (Equation 12.4) are derived as time functions.

$$x = x(t) \qquad \text{(Eq. 12.2)}$$

$$V = \frac{d}{dt} x(t) \qquad \text{(Eq. 12.3)}$$

$$a = \frac{d}{dt} V(t) = \frac{d^2}{dt^2} x(t) \qquad \text{(Eq. 12.4)}$$

To solve this system, find how the suspended mass reacts when the road input is excited with a pure harmonic signal.

In this system, the physics of the spring and damper verify Equations 12.5 and 12.6.

$$F_m = K \cdot (x_r - x_m) + C \cdot (V_r - V_m) \qquad \text{(Eq. 12.5)}$$

$$F_m = m \cdot a_m \qquad \text{(Eq. 12.6)}$$

F_m is the force applied to the suspended mass resulting from the spring's compression and the damper's reaction. The constant weight of the mass is ignored for the dynamic analysis. If this system is linear (not true in reality but a useful approximation), a pure harmonic signal in the road induces a pure harmonic movement in the mass. Equations 12.7 and 12.8 describe the pure harmonic movements.

$$x_r = Xa_r \cdot \sin(\omega \cdot t) + Xb_r \cdot \cos(\omega \cdot t) \qquad \text{(Eq. 12.7)}$$

$$x_m = Xa_m \cdot \sin(\omega \cdot t) + Xb_m \cdot \cos(\omega \cdot t) \qquad \text{(Eq. 12.8)}$$

If the previous differential equations are solved assuming the time functions, one can find a solution that calculates the mass movement parameters (Xa_m and Xb_m) from the road input movement parameters (Xa_r and Xb_r) as Equation 12.9.

$$\begin{pmatrix} Xa_m \\ Xb_m \end{pmatrix} = \frac{M_{KC}}{M_{KC} + M_M} \cdot \begin{pmatrix} Xa_r \\ Xb_r \end{pmatrix} \qquad \text{(Eq. 12.9)}$$

with

$$M_M = \begin{pmatrix} -m \cdot \omega^2 & 0 \\ 0 & -m \cdot \omega^2 \end{pmatrix}$$

$$M_{KC} = \begin{pmatrix} K & -C \cdot \omega \\ -C \cdot \omega & K \end{pmatrix}$$

This solution is very interesting because it produces a quick way to calculate the reaction of the system to a particular input frequency. Later in this chapter, how this translates into a system frequency analysis is covered.

This method applies to more complex systems to obtain not only the suspended mass induced movement but also the movements of other components of the suspension (wheel) and the fluctuations of the forces involved.

Once the solution to the previous equation is determined, one can represent the suspended mass response to different frequencies. Figure 12.8 illustrates the amplitude ratio between input and induced movement, and Figure 12.9 gives the phase angle between input and induced movement.

These graphs are logarithmic-scaled representations of the suspended mass oscillation amplitude and phase angle given a unitary input signal amplitude. The graph in Figure 12.8 is called the transfer function. This graph is particularly comprehensive as it covers an important range of frequencies. For very low frequencies, the suspended mass copies the input signal (transfer function value near 1). For very high frequencies, the suspended mass remains isolated from the input signal; the transfer function value is near zero. There is, however, a particular frequency in which the transfer function value is at a maximum. This is the resonant frequency, and if there is no damping, the function tends toward the infinite.

This graph shows the ratio between the input signal magnitude and the suspended mass movement amplitude. The transfer function (Equation 12.10) is calculated from Equation 12.9.

$$\left| \frac{M_{KC}}{M_{KC} + M_M} \right| \tag{Eq. 12.10}$$

This function in the frequency domain permits identifying the critical points of the vehicle suspension relative to human perceptions:

- Resonant frequency
- Resonant amplitude
- Noise level

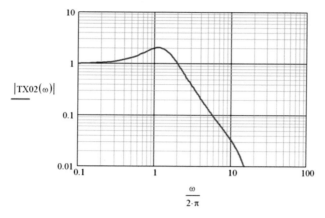

Figure 12.8 Suspended mass response to different frequencies

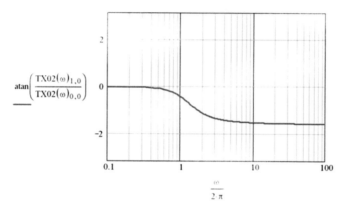

Figure 12.9 Phase difference between input signal and induced suspended mass movement for different frequencies

Normally, the simplified model is a first approximation that is only valid when the wheel mass is small (relative to the body mass) and the tire stiffness high (relative to the suspension stiffness). The main problem is the tire has too little damping, and most of the suspension damping relays only in the suspension damper itself. This, in addition to other considerations, requires that the model include the wheel and tire.

The effect of the wheel is multiple. Because the tire has little damping, it must be supplied with slightly stiffer damping in the suspension. The wheel mass helps isolate the vehicle body from the noise of the road input at the expense of more contact patch load fluctuations. All in all, it is important, beyond comfort issues, to reduce the wheel weight primarily to avoid the undesired effects of the lack of a damping component for the tire.

In the transfer function, the presence of the wheel creates some modifications in the range of frequencies associated with the wheel mass and the added spring rates that link it to the system.

In this model, the three useful transfer functions are as indicated in Figure 12.10.

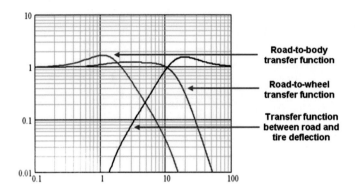

Figure 12.10 Suspension system transfer functions

- The road-to-body transfer function shows the effect of road input on the vehicle body movement.

- The road-to-wheel transfer function helps to show how the wheel movement follows the road.

- The road-to-wheel deflection transfer function indicates the suspension's capability to maintain the contact patch load and therefore guarantee grip on irregular surfaces.

As an example, a quarter-vehicle with the following configuration is considered:

Suspended mass = 300 kg

Spring rate = 20 N/mm

Tire spring rate = 300kN/mm

Damping rate = 3800 N/ms^{-1}
Tire damping rate = 300 N/ms^{-1}

The effect of the wheel mass is observed in Figure 12.11. The plots illustrate two clear effects of the wheel mass increase:

- The transfer function increases near the wheel natural resonant frequency to approximately 10 Hz, although it quickly decreases at higher frequencies (noise).

- Road-tire deflection increases significantly near the wheel natural resonant frequency of approximately 10 Hz.

The plots illustrate two clear effects of the increase in wheel mass, therefore justifying the pursuit of light wheel hubs, resulting in tighter regulations in many race car competitions.

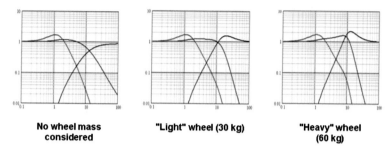

No wheel mass considered   **"Light" wheel (30 kg)**   **"Heavy" wheel (60 kg)**

Figure 12.11 The effect on the transfer functions of nonsuspended mass

When the wheel and tire effects are taken into account, identifying the problems associated with inadequate damping rates is easier. The plots in Figure 12.12 show the effect not only on body control but also on tire contact patch load fluctuations when the damper rate deviates from normal.

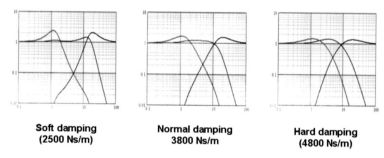

Soft damping (2500 Ns/m)   **Normal damping 3800 Ns/m**   **Hard damping (4800 Ns/m)**

Figure 12.12 Effect of different damping rates on the transfer functions

The effects of under-damped configurations are obvious, and the body frequency response function (FRF) peak is considerably higher. Nevertheless, over-damped configurations produce larger FRF values in the range of frequencies between 1 and 10 Hz, which have a negative impact on grip and comfort. Similar considerations should be taken into account when increasing the suspension stiffness or using softer tire spring rates.

In reality, the suspension link between the road and the vehicle body incorporates many more elements that contribute to the response to the road input. In general, parasitical springs such as nonrigid links or under-damped bushes generate problems at certain frequencies. These problems can be identified with rigorous study of all suspension components. A complete suspension model can include all these elements plus the aerodynamic damping in the scheme in Figure 12.13, which produces transfer functions illustrated in Figure 12.14.

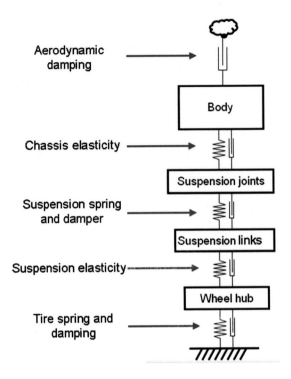

Figure 12.13 Detailed suspension model

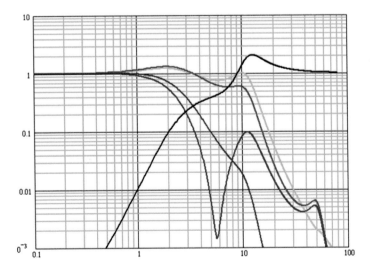

Figure 12.14 Transfer functions of a detailed suspension model as pictured in Figure 12.13

12.4 Suspension Optimization Using Frequency Analysis

To optimize suspension performance, the parameters that best reduce the body movements and tire load fluctuations must be found. These two goals may not respond to the same suspension parameters, so finding the ideal solution requires a compromise.

The transfer function provides a useful tool for characterizing and eventually evaluating the suspension performance. The transfer functions provide two ratios important for evaluating the movement isolation (stability) of the vehicle body and the tire load fluctuations (grip) separately. These ratios are the following:

- Transfer function between the road input and body movements
- Transfer function between the road input and tire deflection

Figure 12.15 illustrates these two transfer functions. Stability is associated inversely to either the maximum value body movement transfer function or the area between the curve and the unitary value (in other words, a function with a constant value of one). Grip can be associated inversely to either the maximum value of the tire deflection transfer function or the area between the curve and the unitary value.

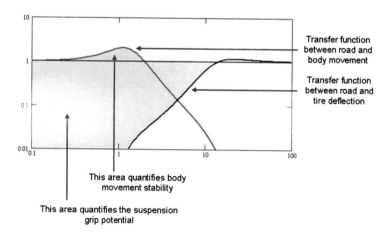

Figure 12.15 Grip and stability quantification using the transfer functions

The criteria based on the previously mentioned areas can be more precise. Nevertheless, this can be quite dependent on the input signal (road) spectrum. Therefore, the simpler criteria based on maximum values of the curves is used normally. Using the maximum value of each curve, the optimal values of dampers that minimize these values can be calculated. Figure 12.16 shows the optimization curves for both criteria in the same plot.

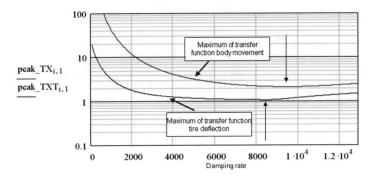

Figure 12.16 Optimization curves for body movement and tire deflection transfer functions

This graph illustrates that the optimal damper values employed to optimize stability and grip are different. In fact, this situation coincides with the popular idea that a soft suspension provides better grip, although the optimal values are for relatively stiff settings.

12.5   Modal Analysis

The quarter-vehicle model utilized thus far is a very useful model for analyzing the vertical movement of the car and, to a certain extent, the pitch movement. These two movements have more to do with the inertia of the vehicle and involve the greatest dynamic loads on the suspension. However, roll movement involves initially a much smaller inertia and then a much stiffer elasticity when the antiroll bars are added to the suspension springs. With this in mind, a different analysis must be performed for each body movement.

Modal analysis [10-1] combines the four independent wheel movements into something that corresponds more precisely to the body movements known as heave, roll, and pitch. Since these three movements imply combinations of wheel movements, it makes sense that these combinations are used.

The four wheel movements define a system with four degrees of freedom. When transforming the movements into modal combinations, the four modal movements are obtained: three that correspond to the body movements and a fourth associated with additional movement among the wheels (Figure 12.17).

Considering each wheel movement (Equations 12.11, 12.12, 12.13, 12.14), modal movements can be calculated as the average of the appropriate wheel movement combinations (Figure 12.18).

$$x_{H} = \frac{1}{4} \cdot (x_{LF} + x_{RF} + x_{LR} + x_{RR})$$ (Eq. 12.11)

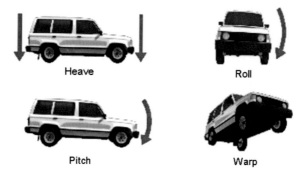

Figure 12.17 The four suspension modes (Courtesy of Creuat S.L.)

$$x_P = \frac{1}{4} \cdot (x_{LF} + x_{RF} - x_{LR} - x_{RR})$$ (Eq. 12.12)

$$x_R = \frac{1}{4} \cdot (x_{LF} - x_{RF} + x_{LR} - x_{RR})$$ (Eq. 12.13)

$$x_X = \frac{1}{4} \cdot (x_{LF} - x_{RF} - x_{LR} + x_{RR})$$ (Eq. 12.14)

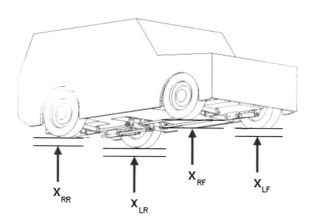

Figure 12.18 Individual wheel movements (Courtesy of Creuat S.L.)

The movement combinations are expressed easily with a linear transformation represented by a matrix shown in Equation 12.15.

$$\begin{bmatrix} x_H \\ x_P \\ x_R \\ x_X \end{bmatrix} = \begin{bmatrix} 1 & 1 & 1 & 1 \\ 1 & 1 & -1 & -1 \\ 1 & -1 & 1 & -1 \\ 1 & -1 & -1 & 1 \end{bmatrix} \cdot \begin{bmatrix} x_{LF} \\ x_{RF} \\ x_{LR} \\ x_{RR} \end{bmatrix}$$ (Eq. 12.15)

With this notation, the four modal movements are defined in the simplest way (Equation 12.16).

$$M = \begin{bmatrix} 1 & 1 & 1 & 1 \\ 1 & 1 & -1 & -1 \\ 1 & -1 & 1 & -1 \\ 1 & -1 & -1 & 1 \end{bmatrix}$$

(Eq. 12.16)

It is possible to use different coefficients that define off-centered pivot points for each movement, but this adds unnecessary complexity at this point.

This modal analysis is extended easily not only to movements but also to velocities, accelerations, and forces that are combined in a modal fashion as Equations 12.17, 12.18, 12.18 clearly show.

$$X_M = M \cdot X_W$$

(Eq. 12.17)

$$V_M = M \cdot V_W$$

(Eq. 12.18)

$$F_M = M \cdot F_W$$

(Eq. 12.19)

When forces and movements are combined, defining modal elasticities and modal damping ratios becomes possible. For heave movement, the modal elasticity can be defined as Equation 12.20.

$$F_{LF} + F_{RF} + F_{LR} + F_{RR} = K_H \cdot (x_{LF} + x_{RF} + x_{LR} + x_{RR})$$

(Eq. 12.20)

The vertical spring rate (K_V) relates the modal vertical movement to the modal vertical force. This is generalized to all movements as Equation 12.21.

$$F = K \cdot X$$

(Eq. 12.21)

where

$$F = \begin{bmatrix} F_H \\ F_P \\ F_R \\ F_X \end{bmatrix} = \begin{bmatrix} 1 & 1 & 1 & 1 \\ 1 & 1 & -1 & -1 \\ 1 & -1 & 1 & -1 \\ 1 & -1 & -1 & 1 \end{bmatrix} \cdot \begin{bmatrix} F_{LF} \\ F_{RF} \\ F_{LR} \\ F_{RR} \end{bmatrix}$$

and

$$X = \begin{bmatrix} x_H \\ x_P \\ x_R \\ x_X \end{bmatrix} = \begin{bmatrix} 1 & 1 & 1 & 1 \\ 1 & 1 & -1 & -1 \\ 1 & -1 & 1 & -1 \\ 1 & -1 & -1 & 1 \end{bmatrix} \cdot \begin{bmatrix} x_{LF} \\ x_{RF} \\ x_{LR} \\ x_{RR} \end{bmatrix}$$

The elasticities matrix (K) in the modal space and the elasticities on the wheel movement space are related with Equations 12.22 and 12.23.

$$K = M^{-1} \cdot R \cdot M \qquad \text{(Eq. 12.22)}$$

$$K = \begin{bmatrix} K_H & a & 0 & 0 \\ b & K_P & 0 & 0 \\ 0 & 0 & K_R & c \\ 0 & 0 & d & K_X \end{bmatrix} \qquad \text{(Eq. 12.23)}$$

The matrix K offers the advantage that it shows more intuitive values when addressing the vehicle movement analysis. The main modal elasticities are in the matrix diagonal:

- K_H Vertical elasticity
- K_P Pitch elasticity
- K_R Roll elasticity
- K_X Warp elasticity

In addition, the off-diagonal coefficients a, b, c, and d represent the differences in elasticities between the front and rear wheel springs. In a conventional suspension, a and b relate to the front/rear differences in spring rates and c and d to the differences of a and b plus the front/rear antiroll bar stiffness. These parameters are quite important because they define the car's balance. Specifically, d is related to the oversteer or understeer tendency of the car.

The same transformation can be applied to damper rates (Equation 12.24).

$$C = \begin{bmatrix} C_H & a & 0 & 0 \\ b & C_P & 0 & 0 \\ 0 & 0 & C_R & c \\ 0 & 0 & d & C_X \end{bmatrix} \qquad \text{(Eq. 12.24)}$$

This matrix tool is useful for nonconventional suspension systems as well as for easy integration of the different chassis components that interact with the suspension (e.g., tires or chassis rigidity).

In a conventional suspension, the elasticities are defined primarily by the springs, antiroll bars, tires, and chassis. These components are combined either in series or parallel. The following text shows how to portray them together easily with the matrix notation.

When two elements are in parallel, the net result is the addition of elasticities. In other words, the springs and antiroll bars are added to provide the antiroll elasticity (Equation 12.25).

$$K_{roll} = K_{rollSPRINGS} + K_{rollARB} \qquad \text{(Eq. 12.25)}$$

As an example, consider the configuration in Table 12.1.

Table 12.1 Elasticity parameters	
Spring rate front	240 N/mm
Spring rate rear	180 N/mm
Antiroll bar rate front	220 N/mm
Antiroll bar rate rear	100 N/mm
Tire spring rate front	350 N/mm
Tire spring rate rear	300 N/mm

With these spring and roll bar rates, the following elasticities matrix is obtained:

$$K_H = K_P = \frac{1}{2} \cdot (240+180) = 210 \text{ N/mm}$$

$$K_{rollSPRINGS} = K_{XSPRINGS} = \frac{1}{2} \cdot (240+180) = 210 \text{ N/mm}$$

$$K_{rollARB} = K_{XARB} = \frac{1}{2} \cdot (220+100) = 160 \text{ N/mm}$$

$$a = b = \frac{1}{2} \cdot (240-180) = 30 \text{ N/mm}$$

$$c = d = a + \frac{1}{2} \cdot (220-100) = 30+60 = 90 \text{ N/mm}$$

$$\begin{bmatrix} 210 & 30 & 0 & 0 \\ 30 & 210 & 0 & 0 \\ 0 & 0 & 210 & 30 \\ 0 & 0 & 30 & 210 \end{bmatrix} + \begin{bmatrix} 0 & 0 & 0 & 0 \\ 0 & 0 & 0 & 0 \\ 0 & 0 & 160 & 60 \\ 0 & 0 & 60 & 160 \end{bmatrix} = \begin{bmatrix} 210 & 30 & 0 & 0 \\ 30 & 210 & 0 & 0 \\ 0 & 0 & 370 & 90 \\ 0 & 0 & 90 & 370 \end{bmatrix}$$

When two elements are in series, such as the suspension spring and the tire spring, the total spring rate can be calculated as Equation 12.26. In fact, if this is done with matrices, the expression is slightly different (Equation 12.27).

$$K_{Total} = K_{SPRING} \cdot K_{TIRE} \cdot (K_{SPRING} + K_{TIRE})^{-1} \qquad \text{(Eq. 12.26)}$$

$$K_{Total} = K_{SPRING} \cdot (K_{SPRING} + K_{TIRE})^{-1} \cdot K_{TIRE} \qquad \text{(Eq. 12.27)}$$

For the previous example, the following final elasticities matrix is given. This calculation method is very useful for understanding the influence of tires and chassis rigidity on the car balance.

$$\begin{bmatrix} 210 & 30 & 0 & 0 \\ 30 & 210 & 0 & 0 \\ 0 & 0 & 370 & 90 \\ 0 & 0 & 90 & 370 \end{bmatrix} \cdot \left(\begin{bmatrix} 210 & 30 & 0 & 0 \\ 30 & 210 & 0 & 0 \\ 0 & 0 & 370 & 90 \\ 0 & 0 & 90 & 370 \end{bmatrix} + \begin{bmatrix} 325 & 25 & 0 & 0 \\ 25 & 325 & 0 & 0 \\ 0 & 0 & 325 & 25 \\ 0 & 0 & 25 & 325 \end{bmatrix} \right)^{-1}$$

$$\cdot \begin{bmatrix} 325 & 25 & 0 & 0 \\ 25 & 325 & 0 & 0 \\ 0 & 0 & 325 & 25 \\ 0 & 0 & 25 & 325 \end{bmatrix} = \begin{bmatrix} 127.44 & 14.94 & 0 & 0 \\ 14.94 & 127.44 & 0 & 0 \\ 0 & 0 & 171.80 & 26.97 \\ 0 & 0 & 26.97 & 171.80 \end{bmatrix}$$

12.6   Modal Frequency Issues

When following the quarter-vehicle model, some assumptions are made that are partially valid. However, as stated previously, the dynamics of vertical movement cannot always be applied to the other body movements such as pitch and roll.

The differences of inertias and spring rates (the stiffer roll spring rate resulting from the antiroll bars) must be taken into account to analyze the dynamics of such movements.

Additionally, the warp movement requires a different analysis because it does not involve any vehicle body movements. In this case, the dynamic analysis takes into account the only moving elements, which are the wheels.

The vehicle body normally is considered to be a rigid solid and is analyzed as such. This is a good assumption for all dynamic considerations except for car balance, which is analyzed later. The vehicle body, as with any solid, has six degrees of freedom, but the suspension has only three: heave, pitch, and roll. For this analysis, the other degrees of freedom are considered solid.

The vertical inertia is the vehicle mass and its distribution. There can be different front/rear weights, and this has other implications. However, for roll and pitch, the mass distribution is important. These movements do not direct the same mass on each wheel because normally the mass is concentrated in the center of the vehicle, thereby reducing the inertia to roll and pitch.

When calculating the effect of the mass concentration, it is useful to identify the distance where the central mass should be separated to obtain the vehicle inertia, as indicated in Figure 12.19.

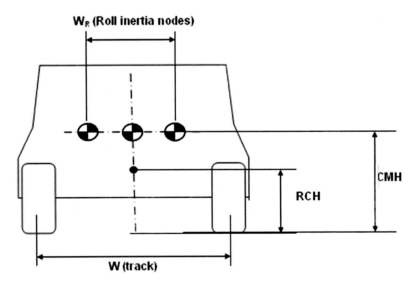

Figure 12.19 Roll inertia calculation (Courtesy of Creuat S.L.)

Normally, this distance (W_r) is smaller than the wheel track (W) distance. In this situation, when considering the roll movement, the movement of the two analogous masses is less than if they are acting on the vertical of the wheels. Therefore, they effectively behave as if the wheel equivalent mass is a fraction of the quarter-vehicle mass used for the vertical movement calculation.

The pitch movement indicates a similar problem. Due to the small overhanging masses in a car, distance L_p is less than the wheel base (L) distance (Figure 12.20). The results from the previous paragraph also apply here.

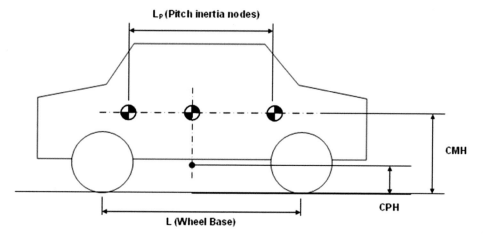

Figure 12.20 Pitch inertia calculation (Courtesy of Creuat S.L.)

Given the previous considerations, it is necessary to calculate the wheel equivalent mass for roll and pitch movements. Considering that these two movements have an instantaneous center of rotation above the ground and not factoring in other considerations, a first approximation of the mass reduction is Equations 12.28 and 12.29.

$$M_R = \frac{M \cdot \left(W_R^2 + 4 \cdot (CMH - CMR)\right)}{W^2}$$ (Eq. 12.28)

$$M_P = \frac{M \cdot \left(L_R^2 + 4 \cdot (CMH - CMP)\right)}{L^2}$$ (Eq. 12.29)

With M_R = Wheel equivalent mass for roll

M_P = Wheel equivalent mass for pitch

M = Total vehicle mass

On many street cars, the mass reduction for roll is less than 70% of the vehicle mass, with much lower values for race cars (e.g., between 40% and 20%). The mass reduction for pitch can be occasionally more than 100% of the vehicle mass but is normally close to 90%; with lower values for race cars, it can be between 60% and 80%.

The fact that the wheel equivalent mass is less than the quarter-vehicle mass has important implications for calculating the dynamics of every specific movement. Taking into account the effect of mass reduction and different spring rates (Figure 12.21), the analysis of the modal movements yields quite interesting results.

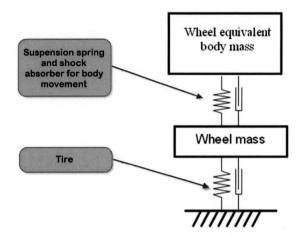

Figure 12.21 Mass spring system with wheel equivalent body mass

The graphs in Figure 12.22 are from a street car. The transfer functions for roll indicate a relatively important increase in body movements because the damper settings cannot cope with the antiroll bar stiffness added to that movement.

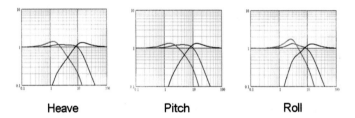

Figure 12.22 Transfer functions for heave, pitch, and roll for a street car

Race cars behave in a much more radical manner to roll. Roll inertia is reduced by design and roll stiffness increased because of race-specific requirements. In these circumstances, the wheel mass relative to the wheel equivalent body mass is much more important, the tire spring compared to the roll stiffness is comparable, and the system gets trapped with the low damping rate from the tire (Figure 12.23).

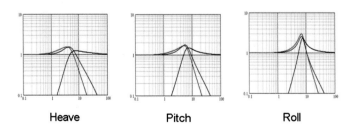

Figure 12.23 Transfer functions for heave, pitch, and roll for a race car

The fourth movement associated with wheels usually is referred to as warp or axle crossing. This is not associated to any body movement and is only responsible for the distribution of load among the wheels.

This movement is usually ignored. Conventional suspensions cannot modify the warp resistance, which involves all suspension components. Four-post rig tests use the warp movement to perform measurements for the roll stiffness, as the two are relatively similar if the body rigidity is great enough.

Wheel load distribution is important for two reasons:

- It influences grip as the fluctuations of loads reduce grip.

- Lateral load transfers define the car balance and are therefore fundamental in the car setup. The difference of weight transfers front/rear is the direct result of converting the roll movement into warp forces.

The car balance can be calculated with the modal matrix in the following way. Given the suspension modal matrix K (Equation 12.28), the car balance (weight transfer distribution) is directly proportional to Equation 12.30.

$$\frac{K_R + d}{K_R - d} - 1$$

(Eq. 12.30)

If the suspension modal matrix for the suspension, tires, and chassis is known, the system matrix can be calculated and the car balance found.

As an example, consider the following suspension elasticities matrix:

$$M_{\text{Suspension}} = \begin{bmatrix} 75 & 15 & 0 & 0 \\ 15 & 75 & 0 & 0 \\ 0 & 0 & 300 & 135 \\ 0 & 0 & 135 & 300 \end{bmatrix}$$

The apparent balance ratio is:

$$\frac{300 + 135}{300 - 135} - 1 = 163.6\%$$

Then we factor in the following tires and chassis stiffness:

$$M_{\text{Tire}} = \begin{bmatrix} 360 & 20 & 0 & 0 \\ 20 & 360 & 0 & 0 \\ 0 & 0 & 360 & 20 \\ 0 & 0 & 20 & 360 \end{bmatrix}$$

$$M_{\text{Chassis}} = \begin{bmatrix} \infty & 0 & 0 & 0 \\ 0 & \infty & 0 & 0 \\ 0 & 0 & \infty & 0 \\ 0 & 0 & 0 & 3000 \end{bmatrix}$$

Then the total suspension matrix is calculated as Equation 12.31.

$$M_{\text{Total}} = M_{\text{Chassis}} \cdot \left(M_{\text{Chassis}} + M_{\text{Tire}} \cdot (M_{\text{Tire}} + M_{\text{Suspension}})^{-1} \cdot M_{\text{Suspension}} \right)^{-1}$$
$$\cdot \left(M_{\text{Tire}} \cdot (M_{\text{Tire}} + M_{\text{Suspension}})^{-1} \cdot M_{\text{Suspension}} \right) \qquad \text{(Eq. 12.31)}$$

Therefore, the total elasticities matrix for the preceding example becomes

$$M_{\text{Total}} = \begin{bmatrix} 62 & 11 & 0 & 0 \\ 11 & 62 & 0 & 0 \\ 0 & 0 & 156 & 44 \\ 0 & 0 & 44 & 149 \end{bmatrix}$$

This matrix yields a much lower weight transfer factor:

$$\frac{156+44}{156-44} - 1 = 78.6\%$$

The matrix demonstrates that the finite chassis stiffness softens the warp mode.

The dynamic analysis of the warp movement must consider that a pure warp movement involves no body movement, so the transfer function is only between the road input and wheel movement. Tire deflection is calculated easily from the difference between the wheel movement and road input itself.

The first graph in Figure 12.24 illustrates the transfer functions of the wheel movement and tire deflection of a street car. The comfort considerations in a street car explain the insufficient damping rates that cause some loss of grip at certain wheel-tire resonant frequencies. The peak in the black curve indicates a high load fluctuation linked to the tire deflections.

In a race car (bottom graph in Figure 12.24), the lower wheel relative mass and the much higher damping rates reduce the grip problems at the wheel resonant frequency. Nevertheless, the higher warp stiffness indicates a fixed transfer function value for lower frequencies that can become important if the road input contains a low-frequency spectrum such as undulations of the road surface.

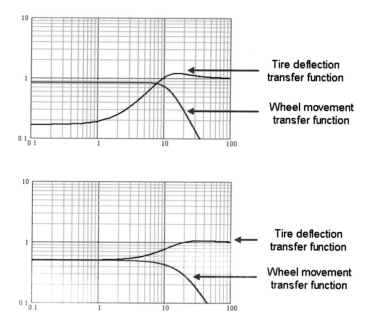

Figure 12.24 Transfer functions for warp mode (upper graph taken from a street car, lower graph from a race car)

12.7   Nonlinear Considerations

Bearing in mind that linear models are useful as a simple approximation of reality, suspension nonlinearities that limit suspension travel affect any analysis. Shock absorbers normally are neither linear nor symmetric. Nonlinearity implies that the system reacts differently depending on the amplitude of the signal. Different high- and low-speed damping also affects the way the vehicle jacks in response to road inputs.

In general, more linear damper characteristics imply that a vehicle responds in a more consistent way to road inputs. Linear dampers can make the vehicle faster, but the driver typically has a more difficult time taking advantage of the increased speed. Spring progressivity affects vehicle roll and pitch angles during maneuvers and can change the lateral balance of the vehicle along the corner.

Assuming linear components generally is acceptable as long as the measured circumstances are valid within a predetermined window. This can still be useful for analyzing the entire system in operation.

12.8 Frequency Analysis from Sensor Data

Currently, various post-rig layouts perform a frequency analysis by inducing movements through the suspension and analyzing the outcome. These tests are relatively simple and are routine for many teams.

Because post-rig tests do not test the actual car on the track, there are a few issues not easily resolved such as aerodynamics or wheel behavior. In addition, chances are that the car on the track is not necessarily identical to the car tested months ago on the rig.

The alternative is using the sensors on the car to perform the rig test on the track. Many cars have load and position sensors for each wheel. Unfortunately, chassis accelerometers primarily are limited to one 3-axial accelerometer, which for this purpose results in useful data for only the vertical modal movements.

Using on-vehicle sensors, measurements of the wheel position and wheel load (not the tire load) are obtained easily. For vertical movement, the suspension input is the average of the wheel position and load. In addition, there is the body vertical acceleration measured by the accelerometer. Figure 12.25 shows the following signals as a function of time:

- Average vertical load

- Average ride height

- Body vertical acceleration (G_{vert})

- Reference speed

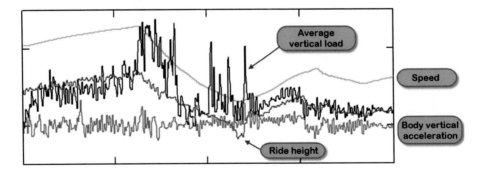

Figure 12.25 Test data illustrated in the time domain

The sample in Figure 12.25 was obtained from an actual race car at a 100-Hz sampling rate. The graph indicates 20 sec from a lap. This data is included to demonstrate that raw data does not provide much meaningful information regarding actual car behavior.

The frequency analysis works with the second derivatives of the load and the position of the wheels. To perform this analysis, the values in Table 12.2 are taken into account.

Table 12.2 Example suspension parameters	
Quarter body mass ($M_{1/4}$)	220 kg
Wheel mass (m_{wheel})	35 kg
Tire spring rate (K_{tire})	480 N/mm

These values are necessary to relate the measurements of wheel movement and force with the body movement to infer the actual tire load. These are considered with the equations of dynamics (Equations 12.32, 12.33, 12.34).

$$F_{CP} - F_{Suspension} = m_{wheel} \cdot a_{hub} \qquad \text{(Eq. 12.32)}$$

$$F_{Suspension} = M_{1/4} \cdot G_{vert} \qquad \text{(Eq. 12.33)}$$

$$a_{hub} = G_{vert} + a_{suspension} \qquad \text{(Eq. 12.34)}$$

With
F_{CP} = Tire contact patch force
$F_{Suspension}$ = Suspension force
a_{hub} = Hub vertical acceleration
G_{vert} = Body vertical acceleration
$a_{suspension}$ = Suspension acceleration

These dynamic equations relate forces and accelerations with the relevant masses of the car body and the wheel hub.

Hub acceleration (a_{hub}) also can be obtained directly with a specific sensor mounted on the wheel upright. In this example, it is calculated from the sum of body acceleration and the suspension movement acceleration derived from the position sensors. This process impairs high-frequency data because of the low sampling rates in time and space (sensor resolution) of the position sensors. Figure 12.26 shows a_{hub} and G_{vert} in the time domain, a graph that does not provide indication of vehicle behavior. To draw any significant conclusions, these measurements must be illustrated in the frequency domain.

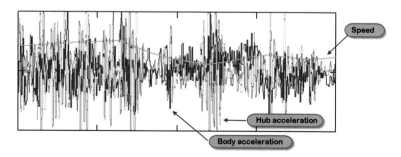

Figure 12.26 Hub and body vertical acceleration in the time domain

The contact patch load can be calculated from the wheel hub dynamics. Once the tire load is known, assuming the tire behaves as a spring, it is possible to determine the contact patch position (Equations 12.35 and 12.36).

$$F_{CP} = F_{suspension} + m_{wheel} \cdot (G_{vert} + a_{suspension})$$ (Eq. 12.35)

$$F_{CP} = K_{tire} \cdot (x_{CP} - x_{hub})$$ (Eq. 12.36)

With x_{CP} = Contact patch movement

        x_{hub} = Hub movement

From the last equation follows Equation 12.37.

$$\frac{d^2}{dt^2} F_{CP} = K_{tire} \cdot (a_{CP} - a_{hub})$$ (Eq. 12.37)

That provides the tire's contact patch acceleration (Equation 12.38).

$$a_{CP} = \frac{\frac{d^2}{dt^2} F_{CP}}{K_{tire}} + a_{hub}$$ (Eq. 12.38)

Armed with the contact patch acceleration (a_{CP}), the hub acceleration (a_{hub}), and the body acceleration (a_{body}), the FRF now can be calculated.

It is interesting to see the frequency domain of these three accelerations, as indicated in Figure 12.27: a_{hub} and G_{vert} are the data obtained from sensors; a_{CP} is the calculated acceleration of the contact patch, assuming that the tire behaves as a pure spring.

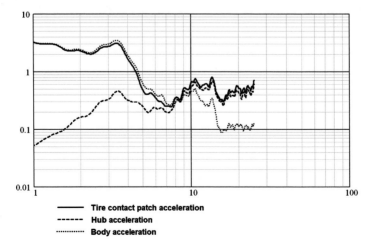

Figure 12.27 Frequency domain graph of body, hub, and tire contact patch acceleration

The actual shape of these graphs is track- and speed-specific and depends on the track surface profile. It is the relationship between these graphs that characterizes the vehicle's response through its suspension.

The graphs are coherent; the low frequencies indicate the suspension is not absorbing the movement, allowing the body to follow the track profile. At higher frequencies, the body has much less response, and the suspension absorbs most of the movements induced by road irregularities.

With these frequency response functions, the FRF diagrams can be calculated as in the earlier theoretical cases. From the frequency domain data, one can calculate Equations 12.39 and 12.40.

$$FRF_{\text{CP-body}} = \frac{Ft(G_{\text{vert}})}{Ft(a_{\text{CP}})}$$
(Eq. 12.39)

$$FRF_{\text{CP-hub}} = \frac{Ft(a_{\text{hub}})}{Ft(a_{\text{CP}})}$$
(Eq. 12.40)

With $FRF_{\text{CP-body}}$ = Frequency response function tire contact patch (body)

$FRF_{\text{CP-hub}}$ = Frequency response function tire contact patch (hub)

Figure 12.28 shows the two FRFs for the body transfer ($FRF_{\text{CP-body}}$) and the FRF for the tire ($FRF_{\text{CP-tire}}$). The thin graphs are the theoretically calculated FRFs based on the known values of masses and spring rates of the vehicle suspension.

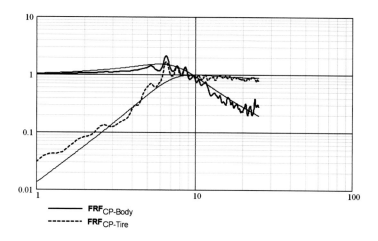

Figure 12.28 Body transfer and tire frequency response functions

What is interesting about this is that relatively accurate measurements can be obtained resulting in a suspension FRF that is reasonably consistent with those of a vehicle on the track. These calculations include some data filtering, windowing techniques, and data segmentation based on vehicle speed. Further refinements can be done, taking into account suspension geometry details such as the anti-dive that in this vehicle accounts for some suspension-added loads during braking.

This analysis was performed only for vertical movement. It is feasible to produce the same analysis for other body movements such as pitch and roll, provided one has accelerometers in the vehicle that can measure the accelerations of these movements. A sensible configuration requires one vertical acceleration sensor on each corner of the car body so that it is possible to calculate the acceleration of the extension of the body over the vertical of the wheel contact patch.

Chapter 13
Aerodynamics

Aerodynamics is a key factor in the overall performance of a race car. Aerodynamic downforce increases the tires' capability to develop cornering force, while drag reduces the engine power available for accelerating the vehicle. This chapter offers techniques for measuring aerodynamic forces with the data acquisition system.

13.1   Aerodynamic Measurements

Every object moving through the atmosphere experiences an aerodynamic force proportional to its shape, size, and speed as well as the density of the air surrounding it. The direction of the aerodynamic force generally varies from the direction of travel. It has a vertical and horizontal directional component. This also applies to a race car moving through the air, which experiences an aerodynamic force that can be divided into a horizontal (drag) and vertical component (downforce). These are the two most common aerodynamic measurements in race car engineering.

Drag is the resisting force acting on the vehicle, which is parallel and in the opposite direction to the direction of travel, primarily influencing the vehicle's top speed on the straights. Downforce is the vertical component of the aerodynamic force experienced by the vehicle. A rise in downforce increases the cornering potential of the tires and potential cornering speeds (Figure 13.1).

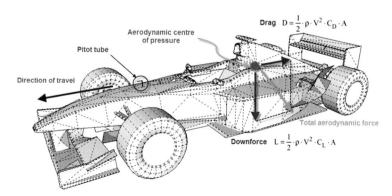

Figure 13.1 Aerodynamic forces acting on a moving vehicle

Analogous to the center of gravity in mechanical calculations, a point is defined as the area where the aerodynamic forces act on the body. This point is the center of pressure, and at its location there is no aerodynamic moment. The longitudinal location of the center of pressure represents the downforce distribution between the front and rear axles (i.e., the aerodynamic balance). This balance can be very sensitive to changes in ride eight.

The two aerodynamic force components can be calculated using Equations 13.1 and 13.2.

$$D = \frac{1}{2} \cdot \rho \cdot V^2 \cdot C_D \cdot A \qquad \text{(Eq. 13.1)}$$

$$L = \frac{1}{2} \cdot \rho \cdot V^2 \cdot C_L \cdot A \qquad \text{(Eq. 13.2)}$$

With D = Aerodynamic drag force

L = aerodynamic downforce (L = Lift)

V = Vehicle speed

ρ = Air density

C_D = Drag coefficient

C_L = Downforce coefficient (or lift coefficient)

A = Vehicle frontal area

In these equations, the term $\frac{1}{2} \cdot \rho \cdot V^2$ is the dynamic pressure, which is proportional to the difference between the static pressure away from the car and local air pressure at the point where a measurement is taken. (The measurement and consequences of dynamic pressure are covered later in this chapter.) Frontal area can be estimated as illustrated in Figure 13.2.

If the dimensionless aerodynamic coefficients (C_D and C_L) are known (e.g., from a wind tunnel test), the aerodynamic forces can be calculated by measuring the dynamic pressure. Conversely, if these coefficients are unknown or the wind tunnel tests require verification, they can be determined by directly measuring the aerodynamic forces. It gets complicated because C_D and C_L are dependent on the vehicle's front and rear ride heights. This is why measuring ride height accurately is an inherent part of aerodynamic analysis.

The effects of a change to the vehicle's aerodynamic configuration are analyzed easily by looking at cornering speeds and segment times. A change resulting in more downforce should show an increase in cornering speed in the faster corners, and the induced drag due to this change is manifested in a slower straight-line segment time and a lower top speed. The effect on lap time should be easily assessable.

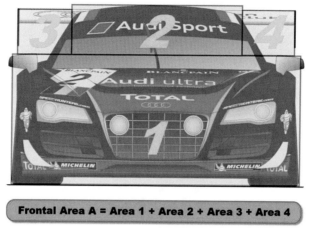

Figure 13.2 Estimation of a car's frontal area

13.2   Air Density

One determining factor in Equations 13.1 and 13.2 is the density of air (ρ), which refers to the weight of a cubic meter. A variation in air density due to changing atmospheric conditions also alters the aerodynamic forces acting on the car. A thorough understanding of these variations is necessary. Atmospheric conditions can vary significantly between test sessions. As a result, race car engineers place a high priority on understanding the impact of changing weather conditions on the performance of race cars.

Air is composed of 75.54% nitrogen, 1.3% argon, and 23.1% oxygen. The amount of air per unit of volume (air density) depends on air temperature, pressure, and humidity. This affects various vehicle performance parameters:

- Cold, dense air means a greater mass of oxygen. If the air-fuel mixture is calibrated properly for the conditions, the engine's power output is greater.

- A higher air density increases the aerodynamic forces acting on the car. Higher density means more downforce and more drag.

By carefully measuring atmospheric conditions, the density of the ambient air can be tracked to gain an understanding of the effects these changing conditions have on race car performance.

With a simple digital weather station similar to that shown in Figure 13.3, atmospheric conditions can be monitored accurately during race weekends or test sessions.

Figure 13.3 A digital weather station used to measure ambient temperature, pressure, and humidity

For racing, it is important to measure the following parameters:

- Ambient air temperature
- Ambient absolute air pressure
- Relative air humidity

The ideal gas law is considered using Equation 13.3.

$$P \cdot V = n \cdot R \cdot T$$ (Eq. 13.3)

With P = Pressure

        V = Volume

        n = Number of moles

        R = Gas constant

        T = Temperature

Air density can be expressed with the following equation:

$$\rho = \frac{P}{R \cdot T}$$ (Eq. 13.4)

With: P = Air pressure [Pa]

          R = Gas constant (287.05 J/kg°K for dry air)

          T = Air temperature (°K = °C + 273.15)

Equation 13.4 assumes that we're dealing with dry air. In reality, the effect of moisture in the air to its density needs to be taken into account. The following equation represents the density of a mixture of dry air with some amount of water molecules.

$$\rho = \frac{P_a}{R_a \cdot T} + \frac{P_w}{R_w \cdot T}$$

(Eq. 13.5)

With: P_a = Pressure of dry air [Pa]

R_a = Gas constant of dry air (287.05 J/kg°K)

P_w = Pressure of water vapor [Pa]

R_w = Gas constant of water vapor (461.495 J/kg°K)

T = Temperature

The actual water vapor pressure can be calculated using the relative humidity reading from the weather station. Relative humidity is the ratio between actual water vapor pressure and the saturation vapor pressure at a given temperature. This saturation vapor pressure can be calculated using Equation 13.6 (with T = Temperature in °C) or read from the graph in Figure 13.4.

$$P_s = 610.78 \cdot e^{\left(\frac{T}{T+238.3} \cdot 17.2694\right)}$$

(Eq. 13.6)

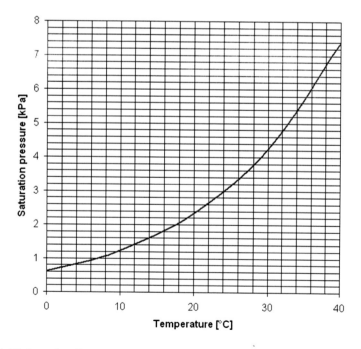

Figure 13.4 Water saturation vapor pressure versus temperature

Consider the following example:

Weather station data: Air pressure = 101639 Pa

Temperature = 23 °C = 293.15 °K

Relative humidity = 61%

Saturation vapor pressure @ 23°C = 2800 Pa

Actual vapor pressure = 2800 Pa · 0.61 = 1708 Pa

$$\rho = \frac{101639}{287.05 \cdot 293.15} + \frac{1708}{461.495 \cdot 293.15} = 1.208 + 0.013 = 1.221 \text{ kg/m}^3$$

Enter this quantity into the equations for calculating aerodynamic forces and engine output power. This may explain why a race car is not reaching the top speed it did the last time it was on a specific track or why downforce numbers are lower than expected. Being aware of the weather situation can prevent a lot of tail-chasing in situations like these.

Finally, air temperature, pressure, and humidity are not the only weather parameters affecting the race car's performance. Asphalt temperature influences the rolling resistance of the tires, and wind speed and direction alter the drag and downforce of the race car. Air temperature affects the cooling of the engine and transmission fluids, which modifies the friction in the driveline.

13.3   Dynamic Pressure

The scientific definition of dynamic pressure is the pressure of a fluid due to its motion. It is the difference between total pressure and static pressure. In race car aerodynamics, dynamic pressure is the pressure acting on the car as it travels through the air. It typically is measured with a pitot tube, as on the Ferrari Formula One car shown in Figure 13.5. The operating principle of a pitot tube is covered in more detail in chapter 18.

As indicated earlier in this chapter, dynamic pressure (Equation 13.7) is half of the air density multiplied by the vehicle speed squared.

$$q = \frac{1}{2} \cdot \rho \cdot V^2 \qquad \text{(Eq. 13.7)}$$

Dynamic pressure can also be estimated from the wheel-speed channel or a GPS-based speed signal using the Equation 13.7.

The dynamic pressure trace measured with a pitot tube resembles the calculated dynamic pressure. However, the traces deviate from one another when headwinds or

Figure 13.5 Pitot tube mounted on a Ferrari F1 car to measure dynamic pressure (Courtesy of Jaqueline Perreira do Nascimento Gramke)

tailwinds come into play or when the car is slipstreaming another car. In the case of a headwind, the actual dynamic pressure is higher than estimated. This increases drag, something that can be physically felt when riding a bicycle against the wind. Downforce levels are higher as well for the same reason. The opposite is true for a tailwind, which increases the vehicle's top speed but results in less downforce. An example is shown in Figure 13.6.

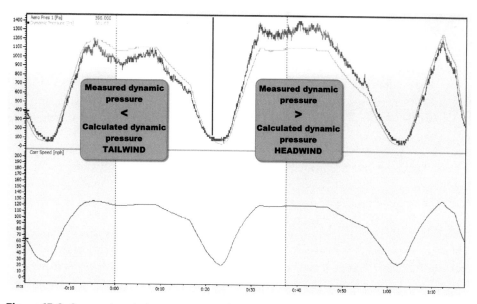

Figure 13.6 Comparison between measured and estimated dynamic pressure to evaluate wind effects

By entering the obtained results for the dynamic pressure (either by measurement or calculation) into Equations 13.1 and 13.2, the aerodynamic forces can be estimated. To do this, the drag and downforce coefficients must be known. If not available, they can be determined by directly measuring drag and downforce. The procedures to do this are covered in the following sections.

13.4 Ride Height Measurement

The aerodynamic performance of most modern race cars is highly dependent on the dynamic ride height of the front and rear axles. Ride height is defined as the distance between the ground and the underside of the vehicle (at a determined reference point) on the centerline of the front and rear axles, respectively. It can be measured directly using laser ride height sensors, or an estimation can be done using the signals of the suspension potentiometers.

13.4.1 Ride Height Calculation from Suspension Movement

By measuring suspension travel we can create a math channel that gives us an indication of the ground clearance between the chassis and track surface. To determine the ride height, we need to convert suspension travel to wheel travel and subtract this from the ride height in static condition. Mathematically, we can express this as follows:

$$RH_{SuspFRONT} = RH_{StaticFRONT} - \frac{x_{suspensionLF} + x_{suspensionRF}}{2} \cdot MR_f \qquad \text{(Eq. 13.8)}$$

$$RH_{SuspREAR} = RH_{StaticREAR} - \frac{x_{suspensionLR} + x_{suspensionRR}}{2} \cdot MR_r \qquad \text{(Eq. 13.9)}$$

These equations result in one ride height channel for front and rear, respectively. That is why the average value of the left-hand and right-hand suspension positions is used. MR_f and MR_r are the respective motion ratios of front and rear suspension, which are the ratios of wheel travel and suspension travel. Please note that for this calculation to be correct, the suspension potentiometers need to be zeroed in static position.

The results of these ride height channels only take the suspension travel into account. The effects of tire deformation on the ride height are not considered by these equations. When, for example, a stiffly sprung single-seater race car is considered, most of the variation in ride height will probably be caused by tire deformation.

When good tire data is available and the tire radius variation as a function of the vertical load on the tire and the rotational speed of the wheel is known, it is possible to include these relationships into the ride height math channels. Some analysis software packages allow letting the user define look-up tables with which math channels can be created for tire radius against load and speed. An example of such a table made with MoTeC i2 is shown in Figure 13.7.

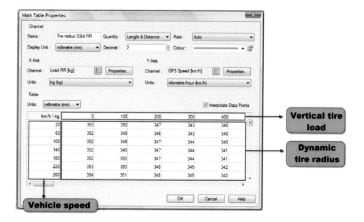

Figure 13.7 3-D Look-up table of tire radius versus vertical tire load and vehicle speed

Taking the dynamic tire radius into account, we now get the following equations for the front and rear ride heights:

$$RH_{\text{DynFRONT}} = RH_{\text{SuspFRONT}} + \frac{r_{\text{rollingLF}} + r_{\text{rollingRF}}}{2} - r_{\text{StaticFRONT}} \qquad \text{(Eq. 13.10)}$$

$$RH_{\text{DynREAR}} = RH_{\text{SuspREAR}} + \frac{r_{\text{rollingLR}} + r_{\text{rollingRR}}}{2} - r_{\text{StaticREAR}} \qquad \text{(Eq. 13.11)}$$

That taking the tire deformation into account for the calculation of ride heights can be significant is shown in Figure 13.8, where ride height math channels with and without tire radius variation are shown for a lap around the Spa-Francorchamps circuit. Of course, math channels based on Equation 13.10 and 13.11 rely primarily on the accuracy of the available tire data.

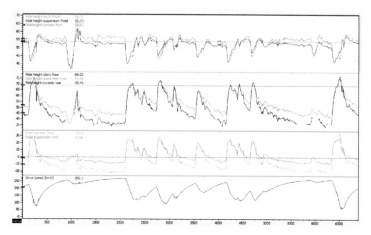

Figure 13.8 Ride height math channels with and without taking into account tire radius variation

13.4.2 Ride Height Measurement with Laser Sensors

A better option to determine the ride height is to directly measure it using laser distance sensors. For the operating principles of this kind of sensors, please refer to chapter 19 of this book. Practically, the number of sensors that is mounted on the car most of the time is three (single-seaters with two at the rear and one at the front) or four (GTs, touring cars, or prototypes with one sensor for each wheel).

Consider the example in Figure 13.9 showing the side view of a GT car equipped with two ride height sensors, one front and one rear (indicated with the yellow rectangles). We want to know the height of the chassis at the front and rear axle centerline locations.

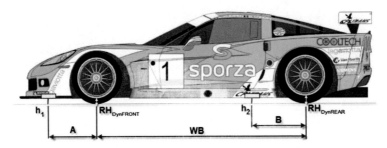

Figure 13.9 Ride height sensor longitudinal locations on a GT car

The front and rear laser signals are h_1 and h_2, and A and B are the distances between the sensors and the axle centerlines directly behind it. The front and rear ride heights at the axle centerlines can now be determined by the following equations:

$$RH_{\text{DynFRONT}} = \frac{A \cdot (h_2 - h_1)}{WB + A - B} + h_1 \qquad \text{(Eq. 13.12)}$$

$$RH_{\text{DynREAR}} = \frac{(WB + A) \cdot (h_2 - h_1)}{WB + A - B} + h_1 \qquad \text{(Eq. 13.13)}$$

In Figure 13.10, two laser sensors are placed collinearly in lateral direction at a certain distance from the vehicle centreline. In this case, the ride height at the wheel centerline is determined by Equation 13.14.

$$RH_{\text{DynFRONT}} = \frac{\left(\frac{T}{2} \cdot h_1\right)}{D} \qquad \text{(Eq. 13.14)}$$

In the case where four laser sensors are used, the preceding equations can be combined to give the four ride heights at the four tire contact patches. Subtracting the suspension

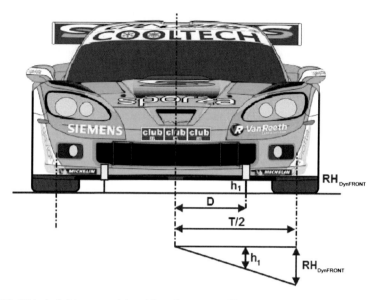

Figure 13.10 Ride height sensor lateral locations on a GT car

ride height from the laser ride height at the tire contact patch will give you the deflection of the tire.

13.5   Estimating Drag and Downforce from Logged Data

To determine the exact magnitudes of aerodynamic forces acting on the car, we need an advanced configuration of the data logging system where dynamic pressure, suspension load, and ride height are recorded together with the basic signals such as speed, engine RPM, longitudinal acceleration, suspension travel, and so on. Nevertheless, a more standard setup where the latter four signals are available gives a quite good estimation of drag and downforce levels of the car in question, and from there the aerodynamic coefficients can be estimated.

By rearranging Equations 13.1 and 13.2 we get an expression for the aerodynamic coefficients:

$$C_D \cdot A = \frac{D}{\frac{1}{2} \cdot \rho \cdot V^2} \qquad \text{(Eq. 13.15)}$$

$$C_L \cdot A = \frac{L}{\frac{1}{2} \cdot \rho \cdot V^2} = \frac{L_F + L_R}{\frac{1}{2} \cdot \rho \cdot V^2} \qquad \text{(Eq. 13.16)}$$

In Equation 13.16, L_F and L_R represent the downforce on the front and rear axles, respectively. Please note that in order to have a uniform method of comparison between different cars, the drag and lift coefficient are multiplied by the vehicle's frontal area. This also makes it unnecessary for this calculation to determine this parameter of the car.

To determine D, L_F, and L_R, we need to take into account, among other parameters, the vehicle acceleration due to engine torque and the longitudinal load transfer between front and rear axles. Equation 13.15 can be rewritten as follows:

$$C_D \cdot A = \frac{T(n_{engine}) \cdot \dfrac{i_{total}}{r_{rolling}} - M \cdot G_{long} \cdot 9.81}{\dfrac{1}{2} \cdot \rho \cdot V^2} \qquad \text{(Eq. 13.17)}$$

Where: $T(n_{engine})$ = Engine torque as function of engine RPM

i_{total} = Total gear ratio

$r_{rolling}$ = Tire rolling radius (of the driven wheels)

M = Total vehicle weight

G_{long} = Longitudinal acceleration

ρ = Air density

V = Vehicle speed

L_F and L_R can be determined by calculating the suspension forces at the front and rear wheels, respectively, and adding the total longitudinal weight transfer to the front load and subtracting it from the rear:

$$L_F = MR_f \cdot SR_f \cdot (x_{suspensionLF} + x_{suspensionRF}) + \frac{M \cdot G_{long} \cdot 9.81 \cdot h_{CoG}}{WB} \qquad \text{(Eq. 13.18)}$$

$$L_R = MR_r \cdot SR_r \cdot (x_{suspensionLR} + x_{suspensionRR}) - \frac{M \cdot G_{long} \cdot 9.81 \cdot h_{CoG}}{WB} \qquad \text{(Eq. 13.19)}$$

With MR_f = Front suspension motion ratio

MR_r = Rear suspension motion ratio

SR_f = Front suspension spring rate

SR_r = Rear suspension spring rate

$x_{suspensionLF,RF,LR,RR}$ = Suspension travel LF, RF, LR, RR (zeroed in static position)

h_{CoG} = Height of center of gravity from ground

An example of a typical GT3 car is considered in the configuration given in Table 13.1, and we calculate the aerodynamic coefficients for the point indicated by the cursor in Figure 13.11.

Table 13.1 GT3 car configuration	
Front spring rate *SRf*	350 N/mm
Rear spring rate *SRr*	200 N/mm
Front suspension motion ratio *MRf*	0.55
Rear suspension motion ratio *MRr*	0.75
Dynamic tire radius $r_{rolling}$	345 mm
Total gear ratio i_{total} (5th gear)	4.45
Engine torque *T* (at 8193 RPM)	350 Nm
Vehicle weight *M*	1380 kg
Center of gravity height h_{CoG}	360 mm
Wheelbase *WB*	2700 mm
Air density *ρ*	1.225 kg/m³

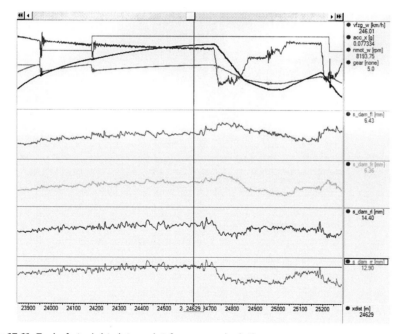

Figure 13.11 End of straight data point for aero calculations

This results in:

$$C_D \cdot A = \frac{350 \cdot \dfrac{4.45}{0.345} - 1380 \cdot 0.077 \cdot 9.81}{\dfrac{1}{2} \cdot 1.225 \cdot 68.34^2} = 1.214$$

$$L_F = 0.55 \cdot 350 \cdot (6.43 + 6.36) + \frac{1380 \cdot 0.077 \cdot 9.81 \cdot 360}{2700} = 2601 \text{ N}$$

$$L_R = 0.75 \cdot 200 \cdot (14.40 + 12.90) + \frac{1380 \cdot 0.077 \cdot 9.81 \cdot 360}{2700} = 4234 \text{ N}$$

$$C_L \cdot A = \frac{2601 + 4234}{\dfrac{1}{2} \cdot 1.225 \cdot 68.34^2} = 2.389$$

Finally, the aerodynamic balance can be determined with Equation 13.20:

$$\text{Aero\%} = \frac{L_F}{L_F + L_R} \cdot 100\% \qquad \text{(Eq. 13.20)}$$

For the preceding example, this results in the following "aerobalance":

$$\text{Aero\%} = \frac{2601}{2601 + 4234} \cdot 100\% = 38.05\%$$

13.6   The Coast-down Test

The procedure for calculating external resistances on the car was explained in chapter 4. The most significant component of these forces is aerodynamic drag. In the Dodge Viper example, an aerodynamic drag coefficient (C_D) was assumed. The ideal way to determine the C_D of a vehicle is to test it in a wind tunnel. Because this is not a financially viable option for most motor racing teams, the coast-down test presents an affordable alternative. This test involves driving the car on a straight asphalt road, preferably as smooth as possible. The car is accelerated to a certain speed and then shifted into neutral and simply allowed to coast down to a lower predetermined speed with minimum steering fluctuations. The data logging system provides the data necessary for calculating the total external forces (and also the driveline friction and inertia). Only a speed signal is required for the calculation, but a measurement of dynamic pressure is preferable.

Instead of determining the absolute drag force (or downforce), aerodynamic performance is primarily expressed by C_D (or C_L in the case of downforce). Dimensionless coefficients are used because they are independent of speed or ambient conditions. For instance, if the atmospheric pressure changes between two runs, it becomes difficult to correlate setup modifications with changes in downforce or drag because the ambient conditions influence the result. Another possibility is to include the frontal vehicle surface in the coefficient and express it as $C_D A$ as done in the example in the previous section.

When the car is coasting, there is no transfer of power to the wheels by the engine. The forces slowing the car are aerodynamic. Also contributing to the loss of speed are the rolling resistance of the wheels, the inertia and friction in the driveline, and the slope of the track on which the car is traveling.

As discussed in the previous section, aerodynamic forces relate to the vehicle speed squared. To measure the $C_D A$ of the car and have a minimal influence on the result from the rolling resistance and friction, begin coasting at a speed that is as high as possible. Influences resulting from track slope can be determined and subtracted from the result by measuring vertical acceleration.

Figure 13.12 is a graph obtained from a 2001 coast-down test in Zandvoort with a Dodge Viper GTS-R. On the start/finish straight, the driver accelerates until the next reference point on the track is reached (in this case, a bridge crossing the racetrack). Here, the driver lifts the throttle, shifts into neutral, and lets the resisting vehicle forces slow the vehicle down until it is necessary to brake for the next corner. The x-axis represents the elapsed time in seconds, and the vehicle speed is indicated on the y-axis.

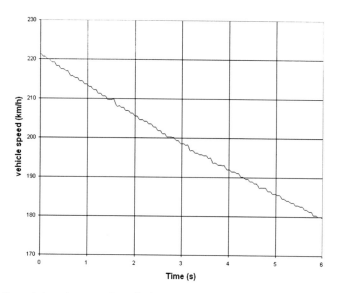

Figure 13.12 Speed signal versus time during a coast-down test performed at Circuit Zandvoort in 2001 with a Dodge Viper GTS-R

After 2 sec, the car decelerates to a speed of 205.5 km/h. At this point, Newton's law ensures that the resisting force acting on the car may be calculated using Equation 13.21 by multiplying the total vehicle mass with the longitudinal acceleration G_{long} which is obtained directly from an accelerometer signal or calculated from the speed signal.

$$F_{res} = M \cdot G_{long} \cdot 9.81 \qquad \text{(Eq. 13.21)}$$

The average deceleration in Figure 13.12 between 1 and 3 sec is

$$\frac{213 \text{ km/h} - 198.5 \text{ km/h}}{3.6 \cdot (3 \text{ s} - 1 \text{ s})} = 2.01 \text{ m/s}^2 (= 0.205 \text{ G})$$

At the time this test was conducted, the total weight of the car (including the driver) was 1260 kg, so the resisting force on the car equals

$$F_{res} = 1260 \cdot 2.01 = 2532 \text{ N}$$

For simplicity, the rolling resistance and inertias are ignored for the moment, and there is no engine torque on the driven wheels during the coast-down. This means that $F_{res} = F_{aero}$, which gives Equation 13.22 for $C_D A$.

$$C_D \cdot A = \frac{M \cdot G_{long} \cdot 9.81}{\frac{1}{2} \cdot \rho \cdot V^2} \qquad \text{(Eq. 13.22)}$$

Continuing on the example with an air density ρ of 1.187 kg/m³, we get the following result for $C_D A$:

$$C_D \cdot A = \frac{2532}{\frac{1}{2} \cdot 1.187 \cdot 57.15^2} = 1.306$$

with

$$V = \frac{1}{2} \cdot (213 + 198.5) = 205.75 \text{ km/h} = 57.15 \text{ m/s}$$

For the Dodge Viper in chapter 4, a rolling resistance of 325 N and a 6% driveline loss totaling approximately 123 N were calculated. When these are subtracted from the 2532 N measured in the coast-down test and $C_D A$ is calculated again, the result is 1.075.

This test was conducted with the rear wing at its minimum angle. To illustrate the usability of this method, $C_D A$ is calculated again with the rear wing at its maximum angle. The speed signal is shown in Figure 13.13. The signal for the minimum wing also is pictured.

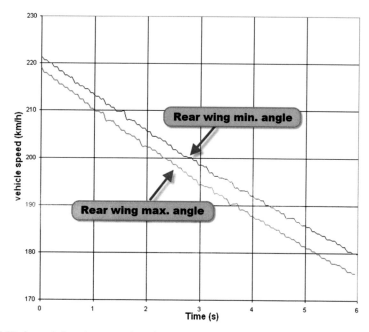

Figure 13.13 Speed signal versus time for maximum and minimum rear wing angle during a coast-down test performed at Zandvoort in 2001 with a Dodge Viper GTS-R

Look again at the speed after 2 sec, which is 202.2 km/h. A second before and after this moment, the speeds are 210.4 and 194.3 km/h, respectively, meaning longitudinal deceleration is 2.24 m/s². F_{res} becomes 2822 N (or 2374 N when the rolling resistance and inertia forces are subtracted).

This results in the following value for $C_D A$:

$$C_D \cdot A = \frac{2822}{\frac{1}{2} \cdot 1.187 \cdot 56.17^2} = 1.507$$

Or 1.268 when rolling resistance and friction are taken into account. This means that between the minimum and maximum rear wing angle, the total vehicle drag increases by 18%.

Drag measurement using coast-down testing is valuable for determining this race car parameter. However, some factors should be considered:

- Drag (and downforce) varies with air density. Preferably, comparisons should be made for coast-down tests performed on the same day, or differences in air density should be corrected for.

- Between runs, ensure that the car configuration (specifically, tire pressures and temperatures as well as engine and driveline temperatures) remains as constant as possible so that it does not influence the measurements.

- Always perform the coast-down test in two directions to take into account the influence of the wind and track gradient.

Coast-down tests are standardized SAE J1263 [13-1]. This standard states the following initial conditions and prerequisites that must be met:

- Tests should be conducted at temperatures between –1 °C and 32 °C. Data obtained at temperatures outside this range cannot be reliably adjusted to standard conditions.

- Tests shall not be run during foggy conditions.

- Tests shall not be run when wind speeds average more than 16 km/h or when peak wind speeds are more than 20 km/h. The average of the component of the wind velocity perpendicular to the test road may not exceed 8 km/h.

- Roads shall be dry, clean, and smooth and must not exceed 0.5% grade. In addition, the grade should be constant and the road should be straight since variations in grade or straightness can significantly affect results.

- Tires shall have accumulated a minimum of 160 km prior to coast-down testing.

- The tires should have at least 75% of the original tread depth remaining.

- Vehicle tires should be inflated to the manufacturer's recommended cold inflation pressure corrected for the difference between ambient temperature and tire temperature.

Coast-down testing is a testing method that inherently has some inaccuracies and assumptions, but if performed correctly it is a suitable tool to compare different configurations.

A final note on tire pressures: Increasing the tire pressure during a coast-down test decreases the vehicle's rolling resistance. However, it also increases the tires' spring rate. A greater aerodynamic downforce at higher speeds results in more tire compression, and this also affects the aerodynamic properties of the vehicle. Maintaining a higher-than-normal tire pressure therefore introduces an inconsistent variable into the test.

13.7   The Constant Velocity Test

When wind tunnel downforce data is unavailable or when evaluating wind tunnel data on the track is desired, downforce numbers can be extracted from wheel load measurements. As with drag measurements, the dimensionless force coefficient (C_L) is the main focus. Also important is how the total downforce is distributed between the front and rear axles (i.e., the location of the center of pressure).

Aerodynamic forces depend on the vehicle's ride height. To evaluate the downforce a vehicle develops, the wheel loads on the front and rear axles through the car's ride height range must be measured.

The wheel loads can be measured with strain gauges in the suspension or, alternatively, by calculating the suspension loads from suspension deflection measurements. Downforce measurements are conducted preferably as steady-state tests at a constant speed in order to minimize the influence of inertial forces [13-2]. When the aerodynamic downforce is known, $C_L A$ can be calculated with Equation 13.16.

To solve for $C_L A$ at a determined front and rear ride height, the total vertical load and dynamic pressure at those ride heights should be measured at a constant vehicle speed. The run pictured in Figure 13.14 was obtained from a test performed on an airstrip. It

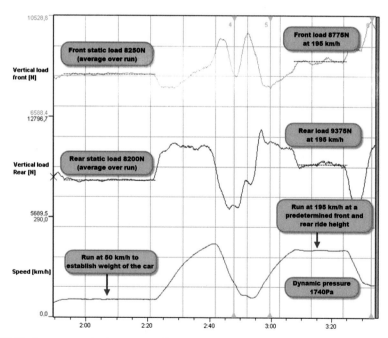

Figure 13.14 Constant velocity test performed on an airstrip to measure vehicle downforce (Data courtesy of Pi Research)

shows the front and rear vertical load and vehicle speed for two runs at constant speeds of 50 and 195 km/h, respectively. The run at 50 km/h established the wheel load when aerodynamic downforce is not present, leaving only the static weight of the car. This figure can be compared with the weights measured when the car is placed on the corner weight scales as a sanity check for the suspension load cells. Taking the average over the time interval in which a speed of 50 km/h is maintained results in the vertical axle loads in Table 13.2.

Table 13.2 Average vertical wheel loads at 50 km/h	
Front static vertical load	8250 N
Rear static vertical load	8200 N
Total static vertical load	16450 N

Doing the same for the time spent at a speed of 195 km/h gives the total axle loads in Table 13.3.

Table 13.3 Average vertical wheel loads at 195 km/h	
Front vertical load	8775 N
Rear vertical load	9375 N
Total vertical load	18150 N

Subtracting the static loads from these figures results in the amount of downforce developed at a speed of 195 km/h at the tested front and rear ride heights (Table 13.4).

Table 13.4 Downforce at 195 km/h	
Front downforce L_F	525 N
Rear downforce L_R	1175 N
Total downforce L	1700 N

With a dynamic pressure 1740 Pa at these ride heights, the downforce coefficient $C_L A$ is

$$C_L \cdot A = \frac{1700}{1740} = 0.977$$

Finally, the aerodynamic center of pressure is located at $(525/1700) \times 100\% = 30.9\%$ of the vehicle's wheelbase from the front wheel centerline.

These tests should be repeated until the desired ride height interval is covered. When all the necessary data is collected, the following aero-maps then can be created:

- Downforce coefficient as a function of front and rear ride heights
- Center of pressure location as a function of front and rear ride heights

The more sophisticated analysis software packages can define lookup tables. Each aeromap is entered as a lookup table. Then a math channel is created that assumes the table value with front and rear ride heights as indices. As an example, Figure 13.15 graphs the aeromap of center-of-pressure location versus front and rear ride heights. The center-of-pressure location is expressed here as the distance in millimeters from the front axle centerline. Every value is stored in a spreadsheet, which then is imported into the analysis software as a lookup table. From this table, a math channel can be created that takes the front and rear ride height values and assumes the corresponding center-of-pressure location (Figure 13.16). This channel offers a good indication of the variation in the location of the center of pressure and allows the investigation of any abnormality in the aerodynamic balance of the vehicle.

The same can be done with the downforce coefficient table. With a measurement of dynamic pressure, the total aerodynamic downforce can be calculated at each point on the track. Combining this channel with the center-of-pressure channel indicates the absolute downforce on the front and rear axles. Alternatively, when the lookup table feature is not available in the analysis software, a lookup table can be generated using

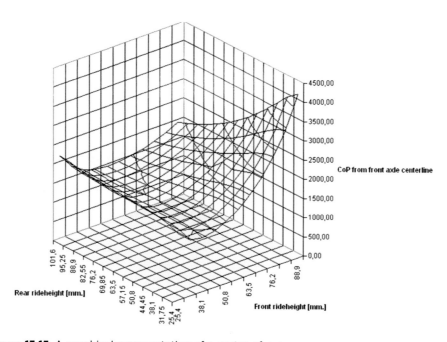

Figure 13.15 A graphical representation of a center-of-pressure aeromap

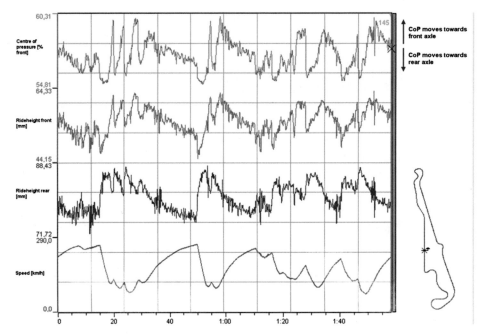

Figure 13.16 The center-of-pressure location math channel as a function of front and rear ride heights

a spreadsheet and the data export function in the analysis software. Front and rear ride height channels can be imported into the spreadsheet and associated with the corresponding location of the center of pressure and downforce coefficient.

As with coast-down testing, a constant velocity test requires a specific vehicle setup to maximize accuracy. The downforce produced by the vehicle depends on its ride height. Therefore, this is a very important parameter to control.

- Springs and damping should be as soft as possible to minimize vertical load variation resulting from bumps in the track.

- Any influence of packers or bump rubbers should be removed.

- Antiroll bars preferably are disconnected.

- Static ride height should be adjusted so that the target ride height is reached at the target speed. This is necessary to prepare aeromaps of different ride heights at different speeds (Figure 13.15).

- Tests should be performed in two opposite directions to minimize or remove the influence of wind direction and track gradient.

13.8   A Worked out Example of a Straight-Line Test

Straight-line aerodynamics testing will consist most of the times of

- Coast-down testing to measure vehicle drag
- Constant velocity testing to measure vehicle downforce and downforce distribution

For this kind of testing, attention to details and good preparation are of paramount importance. Especially putting together a vehicle's aeromaps is quite time consuming, and over the day the testing conditions may change. This can induce important errors in the measurement data.

This is a (nonexclusive) list of parameters that need to be checked constantly during a straight-line test:

- Air temperature
- Track temperature
- Air pressure
- Air humidity
- Wind speed and direction
- Vehicle weight (fuel load)
- Tire pressure
- Zero positions of the suspension potentiometers
- Suspension load cell calibration
- Ride height sensor calibration

In this section, some practical examples from a straight-line test with a GT3 car are discussed. The configuration of this car during the test is given in Table 13.5.

Table 13.5 GT3 car configuration at the start of the straight-line test	
Total vehicle weight M	1280 kg
Front spring rate SRf	420 N/mm
Rear spring rate SRr	180 N/mm
Front suspension motion ratio MRf	0.55
Rear suspension motion ratio MRr	0.75
Static front ride height $RH_{staticFRONT}$	60 mm
Static rear ride height $RH_{staticREAR}$	70 mm

The test was started with some coast-down tests from a very low speed with the clutch engaged (as this is also the case during the coast-downs from higher speed) to determine the vehicle's driveline friction and rolling resistance. One of these coast-downs is shown in Figure 13.17.

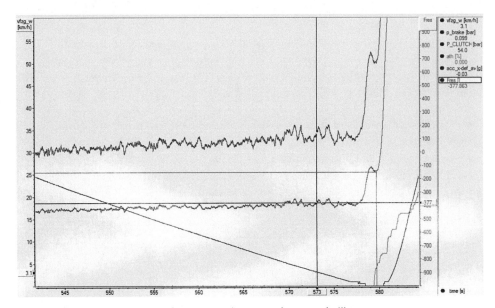

Figure 13.17 Coast-down test from a very low speed to standstill to measure rolling resistance

Figure 13.17 shows a math channel for the rolling resistance. At the cursor point, the car is being slowed down with a deceleration of −0.03 G. This means that the resisting force on the car is:

$$F_{res} = F_{rolling} = M \cdot G_{long} \cdot 9.81 = 1281 \cdot 0.03 \cdot 9.81 = 377 \text{ N}$$

In Figure 13.18 the overview of a straight-line run is pictured. The car is first accelerated to a speed of 60 km/h, which is then maintained for about 10 sec. This provides a reference point in the data to check the zero positions of the suspension potentiometers. As there is no aerodynamic downforce present at this speed, the potentiometer signals should be fluctuating around zero, as is the case in this example.

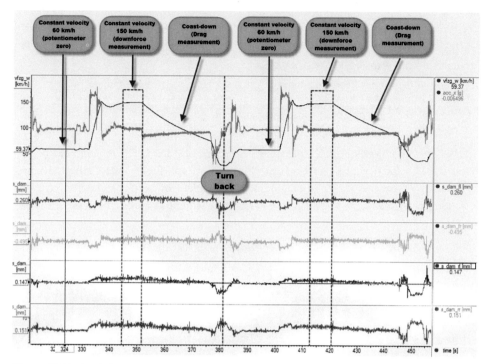

Figure 13.18 Straight-line run overview

Next, the car speeds up to 150 km/h, a speed which is also maintained for about 8 sec. This part of the run is used to establish the downforce levels in this configuration.

After this, the car is allowed to coast down until the driver runs out of road. The measured deceleration during this part of the run is used to calculate the aerodynamic drag.

To take into account any wind effects, the complete procedure is repeated in the opposite direction.

The weather data for this run is noted in Table 13.6.

Table 13.6 Weather data for straight line test	
Air temperature T_{air}	15 °C
Track temperature T_{track}	8 °C
Air pressure P_{air}	103–100 Pa
Air humidity	31%

From these data and Equation 13.5, the air density can be calculated:

Saturation vapor pressure at 15 °C = 1700 Pa
Actual vapor pressure = 1700 · 0.31 = 527 Pa

$$\rho = \frac{103100}{287.05 \cdot (15+273.15)} + \frac{527}{461.495 \cdot (15+273.15)} = 1.209 \ \text{kg/m}^3$$

First, let's have a closer look at the constant velocity runs at 150 km/h. A zoom of the first constant velocity run is given in Figure 13.19. The graph shows speed, longitudinal acceleration, suspension travel, front and rear ride height, front and rear downforce, and downforce coefficient $C_L A$. The following calculation is done at the cursor point.

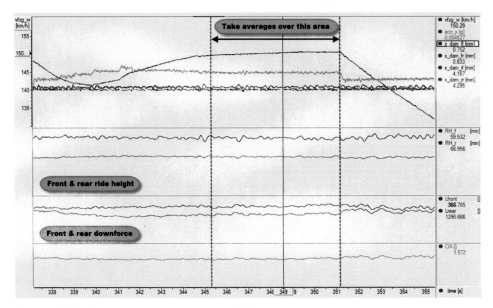

Figure 13.19 First constant velocity run at 150 km/h

First, the ride heights are calculated from the suspension travel signals:

$$RH_{\text{suspFRONT}} = 60 - \frac{0.752 + 0.833}{2} \cdot 0.55 = 59.5 \ \text{mm}$$

$$RH_{\text{suspREAR}} = 70 - \frac{4.167 + 4.295}{2} \cdot 0.85 = 66.4 \ \text{mm}$$

Then, the front and rear downforce is calculated:

$$L_F = 0.55 \cdot 420 \cdot (0.752 + 0.833) = 366 \text{ N}$$
$$L_R = 0.85 \cdot 180 \cdot (4.167 + 4.295) = 1295 \text{ N}$$

This results in a $C_L A$ of
$$C_L \cdot A = \frac{366 + 1295}{\frac{1}{2} \cdot 1.2085 \cdot \left(\frac{150.29}{3.6}\right)^2} = 1.577$$

To obtain uniformity, the data is averaged over the area indicated in Figure 13.19, giving the results in Table 13.7.

Table 13.7 Constant velocity measurement averages	
Front dynamic ride height	59.4 mm
Rear dynamic ride height	66.9 mm
Front downforce	480 N
Rear downforce	1199 N
Downforce coefficient CLA	1.593

Figure 13.20 shows the constant velocity run in the opposite direction. The averaged results over the indicated area are shown in Table 13.8.

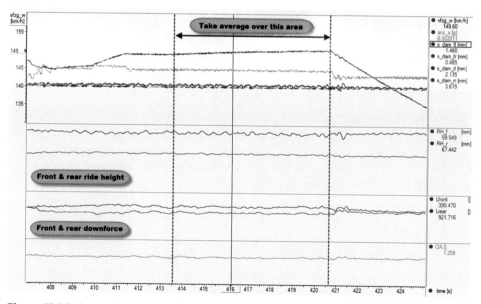

Figure 13.20 Second constant velocity run (in opposite direction) at 150 km/h

Table 13.8 Constant velocity measurement averages	
Front dynamic ride height	59.6 mm
Rear dynamic ride height	67.5 mm
Front downforce	372 N
Rear downforce	902 N
Downforce coefficient CLA	1.220

These results indicate that during the first run, the car was running in a headwind (higher $C_L A$) while in a tailwind coming back in the opposite direction. We can actually estimate the actual air speed from the measured downforce numbers and the average $C_L A$ of the two runs with Equation 13.23, although the fact that the ride heights are slightly different for both runs could induce a small error in this calculation.

$$V = \sqrt{\frac{L_F + L_R}{\frac{1}{2} \cdot \rho \cdot C_L \cdot A}}$$
(Eq. 13.23)

The average $C_L A$ is 1.4065. When we apply this equation to the results of both runs we get

$$V_1 = \sqrt{\frac{480 + 1199}{\frac{1}{2} \cdot 1.2085 \cdot 1.4065}} = 44.45 \text{ m/s} = 160.0 \text{ km/h}$$

$$V_2 = \sqrt{\frac{372 + 902}{\frac{1}{2} \cdot 1.2085 \cdot 1.4065}} = 38.72 \text{ m/s} = 139.4 \text{ km/h}$$

This means that the wind speed during this run was 10 km/h.

One of the coast-down runs is given in Figure 13.21, with channels for speed, longitudinal acceleration, drag force D, front and rear ride height, and the drag coefficient $C_D A$. We go over the calculations at the cursor point:

$$D = (M \cdot G_{\text{long}} \cdot 9.81) - F_{\text{rolling}} = (1280 \cdot 0.082 \cdot 9.81) - 377 = 653 \text{ N}$$

$$C_D \cdot A = \frac{653}{\frac{1}{2} \cdot 1.2085 \cdot \left(\frac{100}{3.6}\right)^2} = 1.398$$

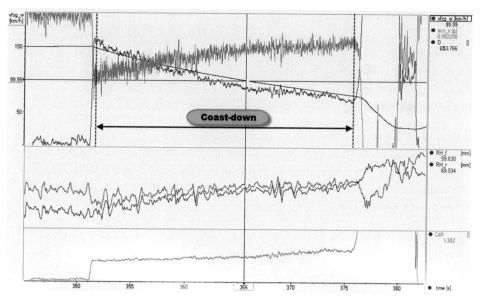

Figure 13.21 Coast-down run

With the larger variation in speed, there's now also a larger variation in ride heights compared with the constant velocity test. With multiple runs at different static ride heights, it becomes possible to populate the three aeromaps of the car (Figure 13.22):

- C_DA versus front and rear ride height
- C_LA versus front and rear ride height
- Aerobalance versus front and rear ride height

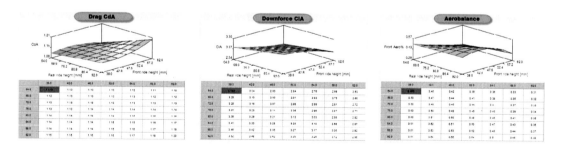

Figure 13.22 The three aeromaps

13.9   Airbox Efficiency

What determines the power potential of an engine? All power comes from the amount of fuel burned in the engine. The more fuel the engine can burn per time interval, the greater the power output is. However, to burn fuel, oxygen is required, and this comes straight from the atmosphere. The amount of air the engine can process depends primarily on the design of the cylinder head and the inlet manifold.

Atmospheric engines use the ambient atmospheric pressure to push air into the engine's cylinders. When regulations provide inlet restrictors, the air usually is guided through these restrictors into the inlet manifold and then into the engine. When the ambient air pressure is known and the absolute pressure in the inlet manifold is determined, this serves as a measure for the inlet system efficiency.

Figure 13.23 illustrates the manifold air pressure (MAP) signal of a GT car with the throttle position, engine RPM, and vehicle speed.

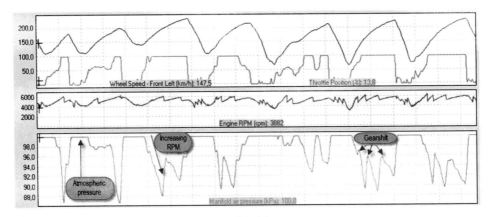

Figure 13.23 MAP signal for a GT car around Zolder

An approximate atmospheric pressure can be obtained from the graph by taking a point where the throttle is closed completely. In this case, it is 100 kPa. As soon as the throttle opens, the MAP drops proportional to the engine RPM. Shift points are indicated as upward spikes, when the throttle is closed momentarily. Note that these upward spikes are much more subtle when the car is equipped with a power-shift system that enables the driver to keep his foot down on the accelerator during upshifts.

A measure of how well the inlet system is performing is indicated when the minimum air pressure in the graph (which is approximately 87 kPa) is subtracted from the atmospheric pressure. As the throttle is opened, air flows into the engine cylinders, and the rise in RPM increases the flow velocity so air pressure drops. However, with increasing RPM, the engine literally asks for more air to be fed into the manifold. As vehicle speed increases, the dynamic pressure before the manifold increases quadratic to the vehicle velocity, which in this case is a good thing. The lower the pressure drop in the manifold, the better the air supply to the engine is. This is why engine builders try to design air inlets in such a way that the air pressure before the throttle is as close to the atmospheric pressure as possible.

Figure 13.23 shows a pressure drop of 100 − 87 = 13 kPa at an engine speed of 6100 RPM. To illustrate the effect of manifold pressure, a test was performed in which the air inlet restrictors were removed from the engine air inlet. The results are given in Figure 13.24.

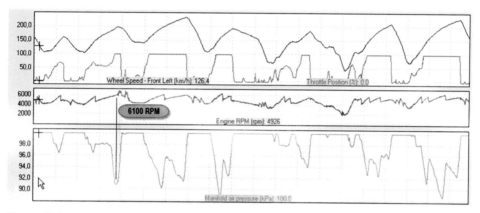

Figure 13.24 MAP signal for a GT car around Zolder, with no air inlet restrictors

Tests on the engine dyno resulted in a power increase of approximately 80 brake horse-power (bhp) by removing the restrictors. Figure 13.24 illustrates why this is the case. Atmospheric pressure is 100 kPa, and the MAP reading at 6100 RPM is 91 kPa, which means a drop of 9 kPa.

Chapter 14
Analyzing the Driver

Race car engineering is not limited to tuning a vehicle to its maximum dynamic performance. Race cars do not drive themselves; the driver is a very important part of the performance equation. Logging driver activities provides a detailed record of what is happening in the cockpit and furnishes the driver with tools that help improve performance.

14.1   Improving Driver Performance

When evaluating a driver, the data acquisition engineer must be aware of two significant pitfalls. The first is that driver activity and chassis balance are interrelated closely. Something diagnosed as driver deficiency may be the result of an unbalanced chassis. The opposite can be true as well, so the driver's comments should be interpreted in combination with detailed data analysis.

Realize that a race car driver is a human being with a finite tolerance to criticism. Even founded, well-intended, and tactfully offered suggestions are not accepted always in a graceful manner. In the worst-case scenario, pointing out to drivers what they are doing wrong can potentially undermine their self-confidence, something that should be avoided at all costs.

A solution that often works is letting drivers ascertain (to the best of their ability and in conjunction with subtle guidance from the engineer) what they are doing wrong. In addition, encourage them to utilize data analysis as a developmental tool. Drivers have everything they did on the track stored in their brain. Driver activity recordings made by the data logger should make sense to them. To ensure that this occurs, there are some conditions. First, drivers should know how to operate the analysis software. Second, they should be educated in the analysis techniques necessary to evaluate their performance. And third, they should possess some basic knowledge about the dynamics of the vehicle to correlate their performance with that of the vehicle. All of this depends on the willingness and motivation of drivers to learn and develop themselves. At the end of the day, this is nothing more than part of their job.

Practically, drivers should be able to analyze data independently on their own computer and should have access to the data quickly while everything is still fresh in their memory. Modern technology, such as USB storage devices and wireless pit box networks, can facilitate this accessibility.

In the cockpit, the driver has five main controls to help get the car around the track as quickly as possible: throttle pedal, brake pedal, steering wheel, clutch pedal, and gear lever. A driver's activities consist of acceleration, braking, cornering, and shifting gears. Figure 14.1 illustrates a display template that includes the important channels to begin the driver evaluation: (front) brake pressure, gear, engine RPM, vehicle speed, and throttle position. This screen template contains the basic information for evaluating driving style. Drivers usually want to compare their laps with previous outings or with the data of other drivers. The techniques for overlaying and comparing data from different laps were covered in chapter 3.

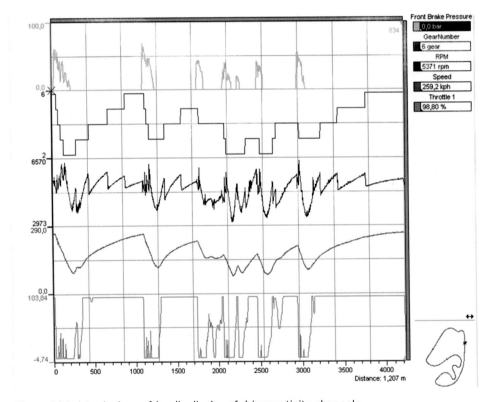

Figure 14.1 A typical user-friendly display of driver activity channels

Modern dashboard systems often allow the display of messages to the driver or output signals to be sent (e.g., to a lamp) once a condition is met. Different applications exist to assist drivers during their time on the track. Data logged on previous runs provides the information to program the dashboard. Here are some examples:

- Programmable shift lights, which are a series of LEDs placed on the dashboard to indicate when the driver should shift to a higher gear. For each gear, an independent shift RPM can be programmed in the dashboard.

- Brake balance indication on the dashboard.

- Visual indication on the dashboard when a wheel is blocking under braking or slipping under acceleration.

- Sector times from virtual beacons, which are placed at fixed distances from the infrared beacon indicating the start and finish of a lap. When the car reaches the respective distance of a virtual beacon, the sector time is displayed on the dashboard display. GPS integration has greatly improved the accuracy of this feature. Often, a reference lap can be programmed into the dashboard, enabling drivers to observe during their lap if they are faster or slower than the reference lap (Figure 14.2).

- Predictive lap time calculation in which a previously logged reference lap can be loaded into the dashboard. The time/distance data of the current lap is compared constantly with that of the reference lap; from the difference between the two, the lap time of the current lap can be predicted.

Figure 14.2 Virtual beacons compare the driver's current lap to a reference lap (Courtesy of Jean-Michel le Meur)

14.2 Driving Style Evaluation

For driver evaluation, the following characteristics should be investigated:

- Performance: This is a measure of achieved results. Performance improvement is the concept of measuring the output of a particular process and then modifying this process to increase its output, efficiency, or effectiveness. Examples of performance measurements are cornering speed, maximum lateral G during cornering, maximum longitudinal G during braking, and gearshift times. Lap time is also a performance measurement.

- Smoothness: *The American Heritage® Dictionary of the English Language* [14-1] defines *smooth* as "having a texture that lacks friction; not rough." A driver should maintain a certain degree of smoothness to avoid upsetting the car in transient phases. For instance, accelerating out of a corner with a fluctuating throttle pedal causes abrupt changes in longitudinal weight transfer, resulting in load fluctuations at the tire contact patches.

- Response: This is an output resulting from an input. Opposite steering lock can be a response to the rear end of the car stepping out during cornering. Response is also the time delay between two actions (e.g., the delay between coming off the throttle and applying the brakes).

- Consistency: This refers to the repeatability of performance factors (e.g., consistency in gearshift times, throttle blips, braking effort, and lap time consistency).

Driver improvements in smoothness, response, and consistency have a beneficial effect on overall performance. Some techniques for measuring and quantifying these driver characteristics are presented in Figure 14.3 and discussed in more detail in the following sections.

	Driver evaluation			
	Performance	Smoothness	Response	Consistency
Acceleration	Average throttle position Throttle histogram	Throttle speed	Full throttle point @ corner exit Coasting between coming of the brakes and going on the throttle	Evaluate performance, smoothness and response for different corners, laps or tracks
Braking	Max. total brake pressure Minimum Long. G Braking point location Braking length	Brake release smoothness	Braking aggression Coasting between off throttle and on brakes	Evaluate performance, smoothness and response for different corners, laps or tracks
Gearing	Shift point Upshift duration	Throttle blipping on downshifts		Evaluate performance and smoothness for different corners, laps or tracks
Steering	Driving line against laptime variance	Steering smoothness	Steering speed	Evaluate performance, smoothness and response for different corners, laps or tracks

Figure 14.3 Schematic presentation of driver analysis

14.3 Throttle Application

The accelerator pedal is the driver's primary interface with the vehicle. It has a simple function—to accelerate the vehicle. However, the driver can apply too little or too much throttle or apply it too slow or too fast. The more available engine power, the thinner this too much/too little line becomes.

Figure 14.4 shows an overlay of two drivers negotiating a corner. Driver A is the one that produced the colored data traces while Driver B provided the overlay in black. Driver B wants to start accelerating out of the corner a lot earlier, but eventually he needs to wait longer (35 m) before he reaches full throttle again. Although the minimum speed of Driver A is lower, the fact that he's at full acceleration earlier gives him a higher speed on the following straight. Driver B looks as if he's tap-dancing on the throttle pedal to modulate the grip of the driven tires. Driver A scores better in performance (higher average throttle position, more time at full throttle), smoothness (more fluent movement from zero to full throttle), and response (less time spent at part throttle). What Driver B is doing is a typical mistake for an inexperienced driver. He is braking early and too much (not keeping enough corner entry speed). As soon as he realizes this, he wants to correct it by going on the throttle, but at this phase in the corner the tires need to cope with maximum lateral force. This leaves very little tire grip for the longitudinal forces the driver is requesting to accelerate the car again. In the end, the driven wheels will spin and the driver needs to lift his foot off the throttle pedal.

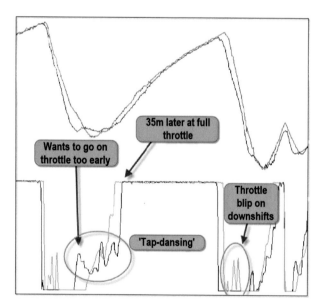

Figure 14.4 Throttle application comparison between two drivers negotiating the same corner

Another difference in driving style that catches the eye is the fact that driver A nicely blips the throttle on downshifting, whereas Driver B doesn't do this.

In the end, the lap time of driver A was 2 sec quicker than that of driver B.

14.3.1   The Throttle Histogram

The throttle histogram is a statistical tool that shows us how much time in a lap a driver is spending at different throttle positions. Ideally, the bin at full throttle should be as high as possible, keeping all the rest as low as possible.

In the following example, we consider the data from the laps that Figure 14.4 was taken from for both drivers. Figure 14.5 shows, besides the throttle histogram, a table with the average throttle position value for each lap. Driver A (red) has an average that is 4.3% higher than that of driver B. In general, the higher the average throttle value, the faster the lap time. The average throttle value per lap is a *performance* statistic.

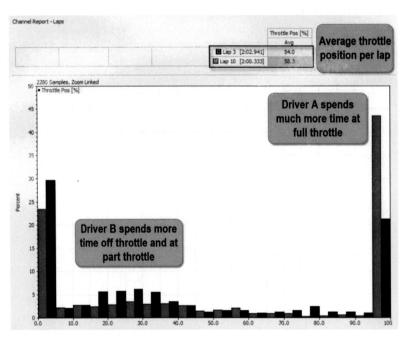

Figure 14.5 Throttle application comparison between two drivers negotiating the same corner

From the histogram we can draw the same conclusions as for the single corner section in Figure 14.4. Over one lap, driver A spends a much higher percentage at full throttle. The difference between the two drivers at 0% throttle is much smaller, and driver B's bins at part throttle are significantly higher, which indicates that driver A treats the throttle pedal more as an ON/OFF switch. The higher bins at part throttle confirm the tap-dancing on the pedal of driver B.

14.3.2 Full Throttle Time

Next to the average throttle position per lap, we can calculate another parameter, namely the time per lap spent at full throttle, which is simply the height of the last bin in the throttle histogram. It needs no explication that a better throttle application from the driver will result in a higher value of this channel at the end of the lap. A math channel for this could be defined as follows:

$$t_{100\%TP} = \int_{0}^{t_{Lap}} \frac{TP}{TP} \text{ when TP} > 95\% \qquad \text{(Eq. 14.1)}$$

With $t_{100\%TP}$ = Time spent at a throttle position higher than 95%
   t_{Lap} = Final lap time
   TP = Throttle position

This math channel is simply the integral of a channel with a constant value of 1, but only when the throttle position signal exceeds 95% (see chapter 17 for more information on the creation of conditional time counting channels). The result of this math channel is shown for a complete lap around Donington in Figure 14.6. This graph shows a comparison between two drivers. Although both drivers end the lap with full throttle time values that are really close, the graph shows some variation through the lap. To have any statistical meaning, we need to relate the maximum full throttle time for a lap to the lap time that the driver did or—in other words—express it as a percentage of lap time. For the two laps shown in Figure 14.6, the results are shown in Table 14.1.

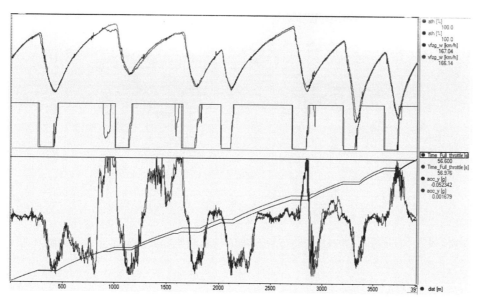

Figure 14.6 Full throttle time math channel for a complete lap around Donington

	Lap time [s]	Full throttle time [s]	Full throttle time [% of lap time]
	Table 14.1 Full throttle time values for Figure 14.6 expressed as percentage of lap time		
Red	89.230	56.976	$100 \cdot \dfrac{56.976}{89.230} = 63.85\%$
Blue	89.510	56.600	$100 \cdot \dfrac{56.600}{89.510} = 63.23\%$

Full throttle time is an effective statistic when displayed in a run chart, as in the example in Figure 14.7. This graph shows the lap-by-lap full throttle time values for two cars during a complete race. There are some extremely low values in the beginning and in the middle part of the race. This is caused by safety car situations. During the first half of the race, Driver A has a full throttle time which is about 5% lower than that of Driver B. This was intentional, as the driver was trying to save fuel in order to make it to the end of the race without making a pit stop for refueling. After the second safety car situation, Driver A is ensured about having enough fuel on board, and he gets to the same values as Driver B. Another point to note from this graph is that during the second half of the race, for both cars the full throttle time starts to decrease lap by lap. This is caused by tire degradation.

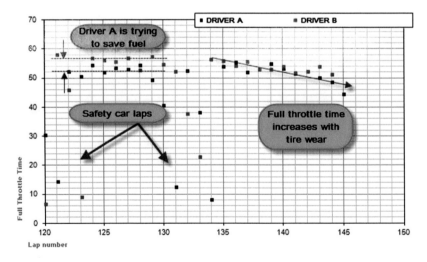

Figure 14.7 Full throttle time run chart for a complete race

14.3.3 Throttle Acceptance

When the driver exits a low- to medium-speed corner, the point where full throttle is reached should follow shortly after the G-peak. The value of the lateral acceleration channel at the full throttle point is a measure of the assertiveness of the driver. Figure 14.8 illustrates an early and late early throttle application, respectively, in two consecutive corners (the McLean's and Coppice corners at Donington Park).

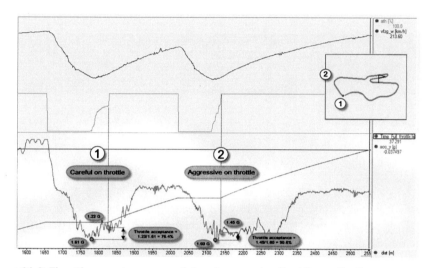

Figure 14.8 Throttle acceptance—careful and aggressive throttle application

In Figure 14.8, the driver exits McLean's corner at 118 km/h after a lateral acceleration maximum of 1.61 G was reached. At the point where the throttle is open fully, lateral acceleration has already decreased to 1.23 G. Throttle acceptance can be defined as the amount of lateral acceleration where the driver is able to reach full throttle. This value is expressed as a percentage of the maximum cornering Gs for the respective corner. For this example, the throttle acceptance is

$$100 \cdot \frac{1.23}{1.61} = 76.4\%$$

The next corner, Coppice, is a corner with the same cornering speed (115 km/h) and a maximum lateral acceleration of 1.60 G. Here the driver is able to go to full throttle before lateral acceleration has decreased to 1.45 G. This gives a throttle acceptance of

$$100 \cdot \frac{1.45}{1.60} = 90.6\%$$

Different cars produce different figures, and driver experience factors largely into this as well. However, it is safe to say that a throttle acceptance of 76.4% can be classified as being a bit careful on the gas if one corner later with the same cornering speed and lateral acceleration 90.6% is achieved.

Author Buddy Fey offers a target value for the percentage of lateral acceleration when the driver should be at full throttle [5-1]. These target values depend on how much power is available at the driven wheels (Table 14.2).

Table 14.2 Target values for percentage of lateral acceleration where the driver should be at full throttle	
Power output	% lateral G at 100% throttle
< 150 HP	95%
150–250 HP	90%
250–400 HP	85%
> 400 HP	80%

A late full throttle application is often observed when the car is excessively over- or understeering at the exit of a corner. Investigate other channels and talk to the driver to diagnose this. When there is no balance or traction problem, the driver is probably being too careful on the accelerator.

The driver also can apply full throttle too early. The result of this is probably the rear breaking out. The driver corrects with an opposite steering lock and backs off the throttle. Look for oversteer and traction problems here when the difference between the G-peak and lateral acceleration at the full throttle point becomes greater.

A worked out example of what kind of analysis can be done with the throttle acceptance as a statistical parameter is illustrated in Figures 14.9 to 14.11. In the analysis software, two math channels were created (see Figure 14.9). The first stores the absolute value of the maximum lateral acceleration it sees in a corner and keeps this value until the corner is finished. The second channel evaluates where the throttle reaches 100%, and at that point it stores the value of lateral acceleration. This channel is also reset when the corner is finished.

Next, the track map is divided into different sectors, and there are five corners for which throttle acceptances need to be evaluated. These sectors are shown in the track map in Figure 14.11. A tabular report is now created in the analysis software showing for the five required corners, the maximum lateral acceleration in the respective corner and the lateral acceleration value where the throttle reaches 100% (Figure 14.10). This table is exported into Excel, where the graphs seen in Figure 14.11 are plotted.

The data used in this example comes from a qualifying run at the Navarra racetrack. The radar plot in Figure 14.11 shows the range in which throttle acceptance was situated for each corner. The upper-right graph and the bar chart give mainly the same information. The bar chart has the advantage that the values per corner are plotted in chronological order. The main conclusion from this graph is that the fastest lap did not produce the highest throttle acceptance values except in corner two. The maximum values in each corner are somewhat distributed over the five different laps of the qualifying run, meaning that the driver probably did not put together the ideal lap.

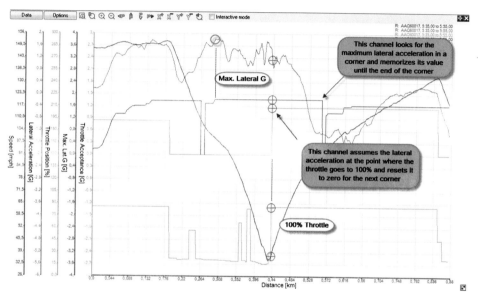

Figure 14.9 Math channels storing for each corner the maximum lateral acceleration and lateral acceleration at the full throttle point

Run "AAQ60017"	'AA' Maximum of MaxLatG [G] from Marker 2 to Marker 3	'AB' Maximum of MaxLatG [G] from Marker 4 to Marker 5	'AC' Maximum of MaxLatG [G] from Marker 6 to Marker 7	'AD' Maximum of MaxLatG [G] from Marker 8 to Marker 9	'AE' Maximum of MaxLatG [G] from Marker 12 to Marker 13	'AF' Maximum of Throttle acceptance [G] from Marker 2 to Marker 3	'AG' Maximum of Throttle acceptance [G] from Marker 4 to Marker 5	'AH' Maximum of Throttle acceptance [G] from Marker 6 to Marker 7	'AI' Maximum of Throttle acceptance [G] from Marker 8 to Marker 9	'AJ' Maximum of Throttle acceptance [G] from Marker 12 to Marker 13
Lap 1, 1:39.50	1,8294	1,9036	1,694	1,8959	1,681	1,4732	1,4339	1,426	1,4977	1,1641
Lap 2, 1:40.16	1,7578	1,875	1,7578	1,8346	1,6836	1,3104	0,97917	1,5982	1,1904	1,1581
Lap 3, 1:38.98	1,8242	1,8932	1,7839	1,737	1,724	1,1672	1,6135	1,4383	1,324	1,1305
Lap 4, 1:38.61	1,8307	1,8919	1,7539	1,8008	1,6419	1,3242	1,6234	1,4112	1,4112	1,2141
Lap 5, 1:39.05	1,918	1,8646	1,7005	1,7266	1,7005	1,3385	1,5292	1,0586	1,5086	1,3148
Lap 6, 1:45.74	1,9023	1,8646	1,7057	1,6224	1,6133	1,2958	0,9263	1,4367	0,0	1,3083

Maximum lateral acceleration per corner

Throttle acceptance per corner

Figure 14.10 Tabular report showing the maximum lateral acceleration and lateral acceleration at the full throttle point for five specific corners on the track

Chapter 14

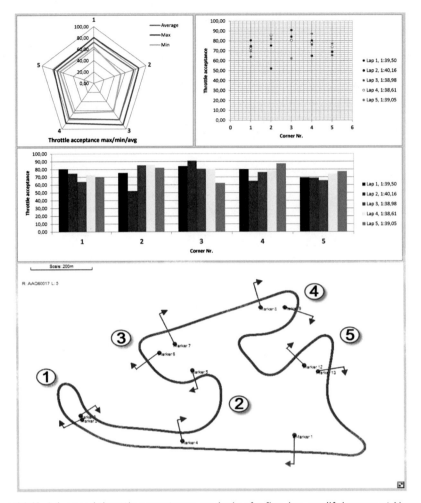

Figure 14.11 Advanced throttle acceptance analysis of a five-lap qualifying run at Navarra

14.3.4 Throttle Speed

Taking the first derivative of the throttle position channel gives us the instantaneous speed at which the pedal is being moved. Mathematically, this can be expressed as

$$v_{TP}(t) = TP(t) \cdot \frac{d}{dt}$$ (Eq. 14.2)

TP is the throttle position signal in this equation, and the channel is expressed in %/s. A throttle speed of 50% per second means the throttle pedal is being pushed to half of its maximum travel in 1 sec. To keep the accuracy high enough, the throttle position channel must be logged at a sufficient sampling rate. The absolute minimum is 20Hz; 50Hz is a good value.

The throttle speed channel gives us some information on the smoothness with which the driver applies the throttle. Figure 14.12 gives a comparison between two drivers. We see both drivers exiting a corner. The black trace shows that this respective driver was earlier at full throttle. However, the colored trace has a higher exit speed despite less throttle. The explanation for this can be found in the throttle speed channel. The black trace shows a lot more fluctuations than the red one. This puts unwanted pitch movement in the chassis, resulting in load variations at the tire contact patches. This will unsettle the car and prevent a good exit from this corner. The driver that produced the colored graphs is much smoother on the build-up to full throttle and has a better exit.

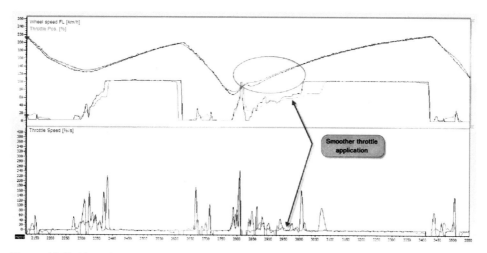

Figure 14.12 Throttle speed comparison between two drivers exiting a corner

When we now take the average of the throttle speed channel over a complete lap, this gives us another statistical value to investigate and track differences in driving styles. It is convenient to gate the throttle speed channel to exclude all negative throttle speed and values where the throttle is fully open before averaging. This takes away the speeds at which the driver comes off the throttle and the zero throttle speed at full throttle, which might wrongfully offset the average throttle speed values. This also makes it possible to compare throttle speed values from different tracks.

The example in Figure 14.13 shows the average throttle speed values per lap during a race with two drivers on the French Nogaro circuit. The average throttle speed value for Driver A is 20.89%/s, while Driver B scores a comparable 20.51%/s. Judging from those two values, both drivers have a similar throttle application. However, when we investigate Figure 14.13 we can conclude that the average values per lap are more scattered for Driver B. This driver has a higher average throttle speed in the first part of his stint, but his values decrease toward the end of the race. Probably, the driver tries to adapt to the changing grip as the tires get older. However, this driver got quicker near the end of the race. Driver A is much more consistent over his stint. He was an average 0.8 sec quicker per lap than Driver B. His average throttle speed is slightly increasing over the duration of his stint. He is trying to modulate the throttle pedal on corner exit as the tires are getting older and grip is decreasing. This is a different reaction to tire degradation compared with Driver B, and a typical difference between a professional and less-experienced driver.

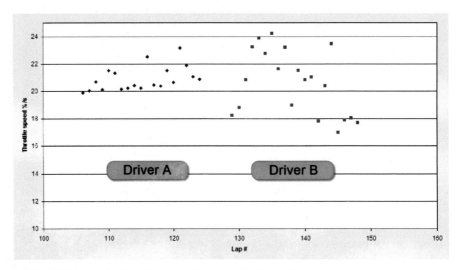

Figure 14.13 Lap-by-lap throttle speed average for two drivers

14.3.5 Coasting

Coasting is a period of time where the driver is neither on the throttle nor on the brakes. Theoretically, coasting is lost time that could have been used for acceleration (later braking, earlier acceleration). We can distinguish two types of coasting:

- Coasting between coming off the throttle and going on the brakes
- Coasting between coming off the brakes and going on the throttle

The first situation is always bad. Coasting after coming off the throttle and before hitting the brakes indicates that the driver could have braked later. This is a response issue that is often caused by inexperience or a lack of confidence in the car.

The second form of coasting is not necessarily bad. It can be part of a driving technique to enable the car to enter a corner without unwanted longitudinal load transfers affecting the attitude of the chassis. An example is discussed in Figure 14.14.

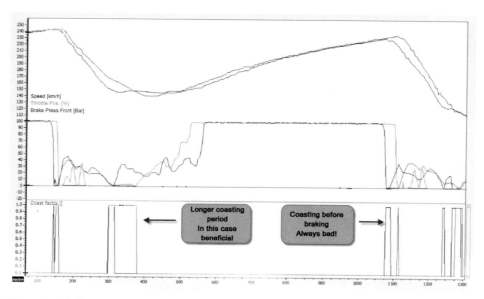

Figure 14.14 Coasting comparison between two drivers

A simple math channel can be created that gives a clear indication where the driver is coasting. To do this, a conditional channel is created that returns a value of one once the following two conditions are met:

$$Coasting = (TP < 5\%) \cdot (PBrake < 5\,bar) \qquad (Eq.\ 14.3)$$

This channel will assume a value of one whenever at the same time the throttle position is below 5% and brake pressure is less than 5 bars. In every other case the value of the channel will be zero.

The lower graph in Figure 14.14 shows the result of this channel for the displayed data. We are comparing two drivers again, driver A (color) and driver B (black). Driver A has a longer coasting period on corner entry compared with driver B. The entry speed of driver A is higher, and he is also able to reach full throttle sooner. This is a case where coasting on corner entry is beneficial. At the next braking zone, we see that driver B is coasting between coming off the throttle and going on the brakes. This is a definite loss of time.

It is very interesting to project the coast factor math channel on top of a track map (see Figure 14.15). This kind of visualization makes it easier to spot differences in driving styles.

Finally, when the coasting math channel is integrated against time over the duration of a lap, it will give the total time that the driver is coasting during that lap. This channel

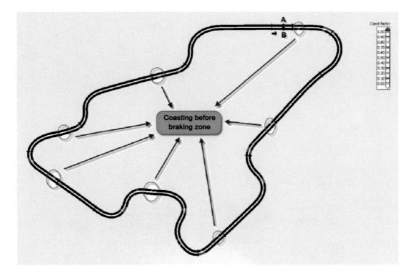

Figure 14.15 Coasting math channel displayed on a track map (Brno Grand Prix Circuit)

can be created similarly to the full throttle time channel discussed earlier in this chapter. Taking the maximum value from this channel and dividing it by the total lap time gives us another powerful statistical value to evaluate and track driving style over a longer period of time, from a race weekend to an entire season.

14.4   Braking

A driver's braking analysis should include the following:

- Braking point location and consistency

- Total braking distance and braking distance consistency

- Reaction time between the moment the driver comes off the throttle and steps on the brake

- Quickness in building up maximum deceleration

- How hard the driver is braking

- Brake pressure modulation to compensate for changes in friction between the tires and track surface

- Brake pressure variation during throttle blips for downshifting (driver footwork)

Time spent braking is time spent not accelerating the car. Braking performance is a question of braking late and as short as possible. Of course we need to slow down the car sufficiently to be able to make it into the corner in the first place, and during this time the driver will probably need to shift down the gears and get the car turned into the corner. We can conclude that it's easier said than done to brake late and short.

The logged data gives us the possibility to evaluate the braking techniques of the driver. We'll try to figure out if a driver brakes too early or too late, too hard or not hard enough, and how he handles the other actions he needs to perform while braking (downshifting, corner entry, and so forth).

Let's begin with an example. Figure 14.16 shows two drivers braking into a medium speed corner (ca. 110 km/h) from a straight where they reached a top speed of about 225 km/h. Driver A produced the colored traces, and driver B is the other one. Pictured channels are from the top down: speed, throttle, and front brake pressure.

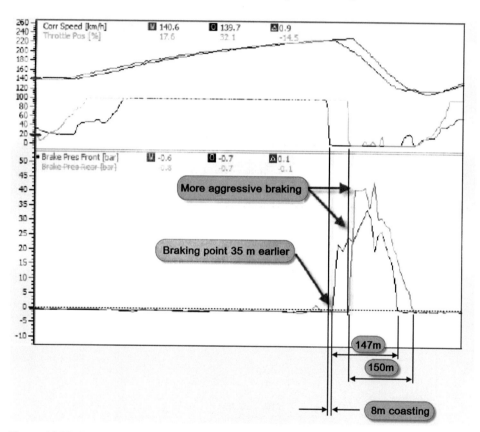

Figure 14.16 Comparison of braking techniques between two drivers

The biggest difference between the two drivers here is obviously the difference in braking point location. The black brake pressure trace jumps up 35 m before the pink one. The later braking point enables driver A to stay on the throttle longer, resulting in a higher top speed.

Driver B shows a coasting period of 8 m between coming off the throttle and going on the brakes.

Driver A peaks at 41 bars of front brake pressure or 7 bars more than driver B is achieving. He also builds up this pressure a lot quicker. Driver B reaches the maximum brake pressure in the middle of the corner.

The braking lengths are equal for both drivers but are offset due to the later braking point of driver A. The slope of the brake pressure trace where the drivers come off the brakes is steeper for driver B. Driver A is a bit gentler when he comes off the pedal, although he is blipping the throttle with his right foot where driver B is not. This is also the reason why the braking lengths are equal.

14.4.1 Braking Effort

To determine the amount of effort the driver uses to brake the vehicle, it suffices to look at two parameters:

- Maximum total brake pressure: We need to look at the sum of front and rear brake pressure as we do want to get a brake effort indication that is not influenced by changes in the front/rear brake balance. We therefore create a mathematical channel to give us the total brake pressure:

$$PBrake_{tot} = PBrake_{front} + PBrake_{rear} \qquad \text{(Eq. 14.4)}$$

- Minimum longitudinal acceleration: Maximum brake pressure normally should not necessarily result in the minimum peak of longitudinal acceleration but should at least be close to it (see the example in Figure 14.17). This is a measure of how much the vehicle is slowed down.

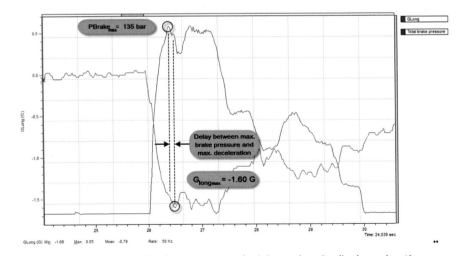

Figure 14.17 Maximum total brake pressure and minimum longitudinal acceleration

We need to keep in mind when interpreting minimum longitudinal G values that tire performance will have an influence on this. With total brake pressure remaining equal, a vehicle will be decelerated more on fresh tires than on old. Chances are that the driver will need to decrease the brake pressure in order to avoid locking up one or more wheels. So, maximum brake pressure and deceleration will be dependent from each other, so care must be taken when evaluating these values. Figure 14.18 shows an interesting comparison between three drivers in the same car. It concerns an *X-Y* plot of longitudinal acceleration (only braking, so negative G, is shown) against total brake pressure. The car in question is a 1350 kg GT3 car equipped with an ABS system.

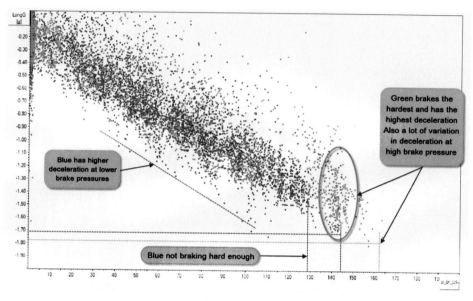

Figure 14.18 Maximum total brake pressure versus minimum longitudinal acceleration for three different drivers in an ABS-equipped GT3 car

The three drivers all have different styles when it comes to braking effort. The one that pushes the brake pedal the hardest is the one in green. He attains both the highest brake pressure and the highest deceleration, although the concentration of points around this maximum is not really high. However, at about 145 bars there is a very large variation in longitudinal Gs which might be an indication that he is braking too hard. The red data points seem to be a bit more consistent around the 145-bar mark.

Blue is clearly applying less pedal effort under braking. However, he has higher deceleration values at lower brake pressures, which might be because of a more efficient use of the ABS system. Although the graph gives a good indication of braking effort and how much the car is being slowed down, to find out why differences in braking style result in more efficient deceleration of the car should be investigated further using other analysis techniques available. Especially, the speed of brake pressure build-up and the smoothness applied when coming off the brakes are of vital importance.

14.4.2 Braking Point and Length

To visualize and evaluate braking points and length, look at the brake pressure channel versus distance (Figure 14.19) or put either a brake pressure channel on top of a track map (Figure 14.20). The following track map shows approximately equal brake lengths for both drivers, but driver A's braking points are consistently later than those of driver B.

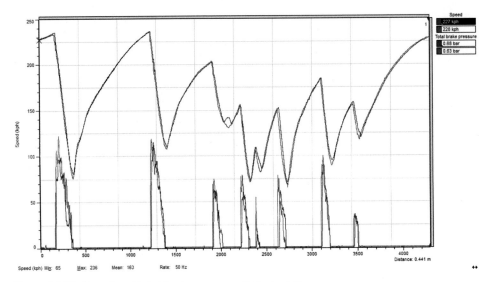

Figure 14.19 Speed and total brake pressure (Interlagos)

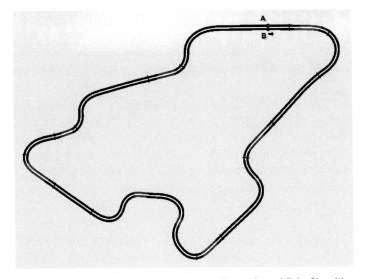

Figure 14.20 Braking zones projected on track map (Brno Grand Prix Circuit)

The technique to evaluate if a driver is braking too early has already been discussed in chapter 5. It involved comparing the magnitude of the combined acceleration signal when braking (only longitudinal deceleration present) and cornering (adding lateral acceleration). Another example of early braking is given in Figure 14.21.

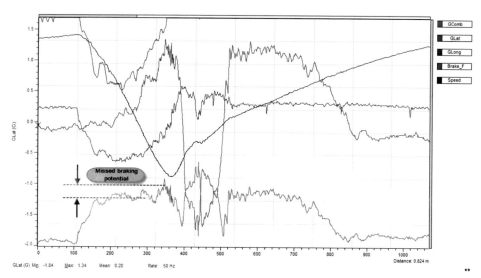

Figure 14.21 Braking too early

14.4.3 Braking Speed

Braking requires a fast build-up to maximum brake pressure and a certain degree of smoothness coming off the brakes. Too much brake pressure modulation upsets the chassis, making it even more difficult to stop the car in time. On the other hand, brake pressure modulation is necessary to compensate for changes in the traction between the tires and track surface, constantly at the limit of wheel lockup.

In the following example, three drivers are compared braking their way into Senna's S, the first (downhill) corner after start/finish on Brazil's Interlagos track. All three drivers were driving the same car model. A math channel is created to determine the brake application speed as the first derivative of the brake pressure signal (Equation 14.5). In this case, the braking speed is expressed in bar per second.

$$v_{\text{brake}}(t) = P\text{Brake}(t) \cdot \frac{d}{dt}$$

(Eq. 14.5)

Another way to do this is to differentiate the longitudinal G channel (see chapter 5, braking quickness). To analyze pedal work, however, use the channel that directly relates to the pedals, which in this case is the brake pressure channel.

The first driver's activities are indicated in Figure 14.22. The pictured channels are braking speed, (front) brake pressure, speed, and throttle position. The driver must reduce the speed of the car from 260 km/h to a minimum cornering speed of 88 km/h; this is achieved in a braking distance of 240 m (a performance measurement!). During this braking maneuver, the driver shifted from sixth to third gear, which does not help the situation.

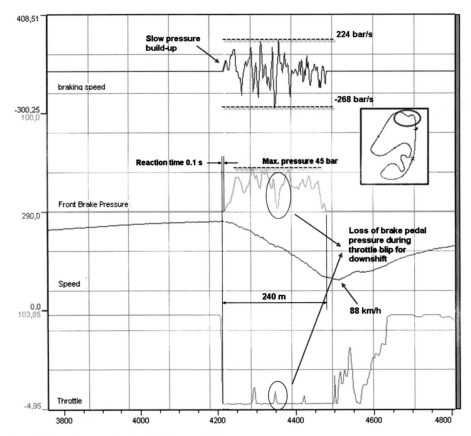

Figure 14.22 Driver 1 braking into Senna's S

The braking maneuver begins where the driver's right foot is removed from the throttle pedal and transferred to the brake pedal. This action takes the driver 0.1 seconds. The brake pressure channel and its derivative show that the brake pressure increases relatively slowly. Maximum brake pressure is 45 bars and is achieved only after one-third of the total braking distance is covered. The driver's footwork is rather sloppy, something that is indicated by a seriously fluctuating brake speed trace. During the driver's downshift from fifth to fourth gear, nearly all brake pressure is lost as the driver blips the throttle. The braking sequence ends abruptly as the driver's foot is removed from the pedal. This is followed by a short coasting period when the driver is not on the brake or the throttle.

Figure 14.23 provides an example of a much better braking maneuver performance, proven by a heroic braking distance of 195 meters and a braking point that is located 25 m farther down the track. The second driver takes Senna's S in second gear, so there is one downshift more than in the previous example. There is absolutely no delay between the moment the driver's foot is removed from the throttle and when the brake is engaged. A maximum brake pressure of 69 bars (at a speed of 301 bar/s) is reached instantaneously. From that moment, the driver gradually decreases pedal pressure to avoid wheel lock due to decreasing aerodynamic drag. This is achieved by neatly modulating the brake pressure below 90 bar/s. Peak speeds in this area are caused mainly by footwork during downshifting. This is how it should be done!

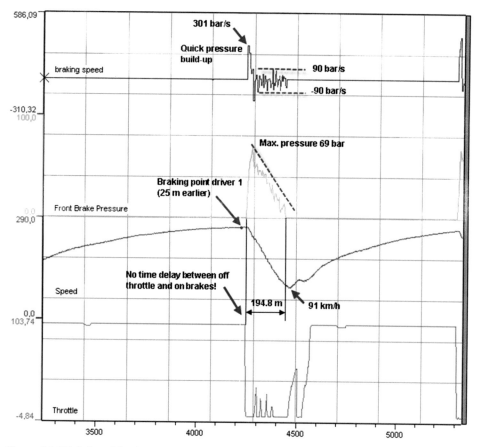

Figure 14.23 Driver 2 braking into Senna's S

The third driver is a left-foot braker, illustrated by the short transition period between coming off the throttle and engaging the brake in Figure 14.24. For a very short period, the driver is simultaneously on the throttle and building up brake pressure. Pressure is being increased to a maximum of 50 bars at a rate of 250 bar/s. The driver brakes 34 m earlier than the driver in Figure 14.22 and achieves a braking distance of 209 m. This driver also shifts down to second gear. After the first peak, the driver modulates the brakes at a rate below 70 bar/s, which is considerably lower than the drivers in the previous two examples. The third driver achieves this because his left foot is on the brakes, which keeps the right foot free to blip the throttle during downshifts. Here, the possible advantage of left-foot braking is illustrated. Although the driver's brake pressure modulation is better, this driver misses an opportunity in this braking zone for two reasons: selecting an early braking point and correcting pedal pressure halfway through the braking zone (see the indicated area in the brake pressure trace). The driver soon realizes here the pressure is decreasing at too high a rate and therefore increases pedal pressure.

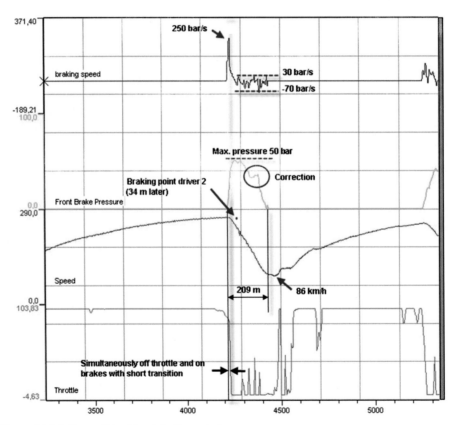

Figure 14.24 Driver 3 braking into Senna's S

The previous examples showed different techniques used in a very hard braking zone, where the primary goal was to slow the car down sufficiently in as short a distance as possible. However, the brake pedal is also a way for the driver to influence the vehicle's transient handling. The location of braking points, maximum braking effort and speed, and the way brake pressure is modulated determine at what rate longitudinal weight transfer takes place and the attitude of the car in the corner. A sudden reduction in brake pressure creates an instant forward longitudinal weight shift, momentarily providing more cornering grip to the front wheels. In addition, beginning to brake with less than maximum braking effort may allow a more predictable corner entry. Always observe all the variables and, more importantly, talk to the driver!

14.4.4 Braking Aggressiveness

As already mentioned in the previous section, assertive brake application is necessary at the beginning of the braking phase, especially in high-downforce cars. The driver will need to build up pressure in the system as quickly as possible. A significant peak at the beginning of the braking zone should always be present in the braking speed channel, as shown in Figure 14.25. This peak tells us how aggressive the driver applies the brakes and how fast brake pressure is being built up in the system.

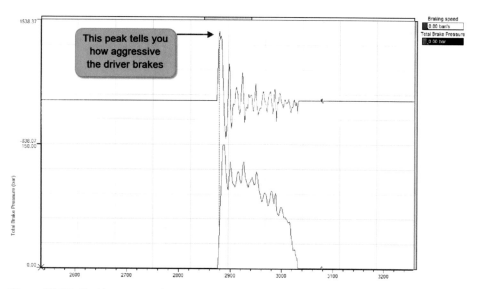

Figure 14.25 Braking aggressiveness

Similarly to the throttle speed channel, we need to log the brake pressure channel at a sufficiently high sampling rate. We are differentiating this channel, which is basically filtering it, so at a too low sampling rate the resulting math channel might not be accurate enough.

We can create a math channel for brake aggressiveness that shows the brake speed only when this channel exceeds a certain value. For example, we could define brake aggressiveness as a brake speed above 40 bar/s. This excludes all braking speed values not related to the initial driver aggressiveness and results in a channel that's ideally suited to calculate a lap statistic for braking aggressiveness. In Figure 14.26 the average brake aggressiveness is shown for two different drivers during a complete race weekend, clearly indicating the difference in initial brake application.

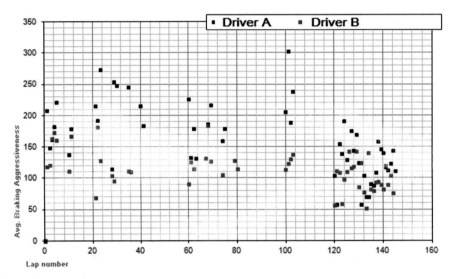

Figure 14.26 Average brake aggressiveness per lap for a complete race weekend

14.4.5 Brake Release Smoothness

Jackie Stewart was once quoted in an interview saying, *"It's not when you brake but when you take your foot off that counts. Most people don't understand that."* After the initial braking has been performed, the driver will need to decrease the pedal pressure in a smooth way in order not to upset the chassis by inducing unwanted sudden longitudinal weight transfers. And indeed, a good driver will be able to influence this weight transfer to his benefit by smoothly modulating the brake pedal. The way this is done can also be assessed using the braking speed channel.

Figures 14.22 and 14.23 showed the difference between terrible and smooth brake release. The driver in the first example modulates the brake pressure a lot (speeds between –268 and 224 bar/s). The brake pressure trace also stays reasonably flat, and the driver abruptly takes his foot off the pedal at the end of the braking phase.

The second driver shows a fast pressure build up (300 bar/s) followed by a smooth release phase where variations in braking speed are situated between ±90 bar/s. The brake pressure signal shows a steep brake application followed by a much less steep and nearly linear brake release.

Problems with brake release smoothness are very often caused by bad pedal work while downshifting. The fact that the driver needs to use his right foot to brake the car and at the same time blip the throttle pedal with it when he shifts to a lower gear often creates pressure variations in the brake system. Drivers that use their left foot to do the braking often show very little variation in brake release speed as illustrated in Figure 14.24. The braking speed when this driver comes off the throttle varies between –70 and 30 bar/s.

For a brake release smoothness channel that can serve for lap statistics, the brake speed channel can be gated to show only the absolute value of braking speed when this channel is smaller than a certain value. In the example in Figure 14.27, brake release smoothness was defined as braking speeds less than –5 bar/s. Average brake release smoothness is a useful lap statistic, as illustrated in the example in Figure 14.28. This graph shows average brake release smoothness for two drivers during a complete race weekend. There is a significant difference between the values of the two drivers, and the level of consistency of driver B indicates that he uses his left foot for braking instead of his right.

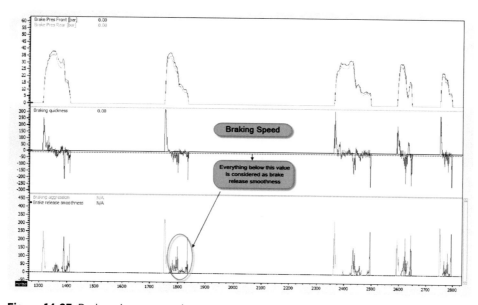

Figure 14.27 Brake release smoothness

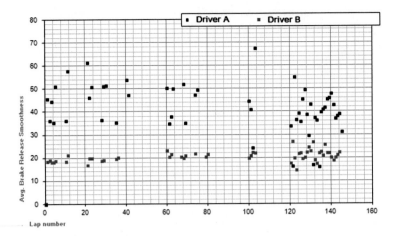

Figure 14.28 Average brake release smoothness per lap for a complete race weekend

14.5 Shifting Gears

Changing gears does not make the driver's life easier. Downshifting can be frustrating at times because it comes when the car must be slowed down into a corner over a very short distance. Concentrating on two different activities performed simultaneously requires skill.

Gear-change analysis focuses on the following points:

1. **Up-shift**
   - At which engine speed does the driver change to a higher gear?
   - Duration of the up-shift
2. **Downshift**
   - At which engine speed does the driver change to a lower gear?
   - Throttle blipping
   - Brake modulation during downshifting (i.e., the driver's footwork; see previous section)

The techniques used to analyze these issues are covered extensively in chapter 6.

14.6 Steering

The physics behind getting a race car around a corner are discussed in chapter 7. The traction circle is a tool used to determine the cornering potential of a car. The traction circle can also determine if the driver effectively uses the available cornering power.

Just like the throttle and the brake pedal, the steering wheel is a driver control that influences the dynamic attitude of the vehicle. Turning the wheel, therefore, requires the driver to exercise a degree of smoothness to not upset the chassis with unnecessary movements.

A rough steering angle signal results from steering feedback due to road irregularities and driver response to changes in the vehicle balance. The steering wheel gives a driver an indication of what is happening at the front tire contact patches. Any changes in the tires' self-aligning torque are felt by the driver's hands on the steering wheel and provide an idea of how much grip is available at the front axle. For the rear axle, the driver senses changes in the lateral acceleration to estimate the grip level.

These brain inputs result in a driver response at the steering wheel. This response should be of such magnitude that it keeps the car on its designated trajectory. Too much response upsets the chassis.

The way the driver reacts from the vehicle inputs he gets from the steering wheel will reflect on the speed with which he turns the wheel. Analogous to throttle and braking speed, we can create a math channel that tells us something about the steering smoothness of the driver. There are two ways to create this channel:

- Filter the steering angle channel and deduct the resulting channel from the original steering angle channel
- Differentiate the steering angle channel against time

In both cases, we take the absolute value of the result to account for left-hand and right-hand steering movement.

An example is provided in Figure 14.29. The steering wheel angle and steering speed traces are given for two different drivers going through Senna's S at Interlagos. The driver producing the black steering speed trace has a lower average amplitude, which also is proven by a smoother steering angle trace.

A car with handling problems requires more steering corrections from the driver and creates higher steering speed amplitudes. When a corner is taken at a lower speed, the steering speed amplitudes decrease. First find out from the driver if the corner is being approached at a maximum allowable speed and if the balance of the car is acceptable before thinking about steering smoothness.

Now we can take the lap average of the steering speed channel to give us a statistical value as a measure for steering smoothness. The lower the average value, the smoother the driver turns the steering wheel. Figure 14.30 gives a comparison between two drivers for a significant amount of laps. The chart shows lap time against average steering smoothness per lap. We can conclude from this graph that

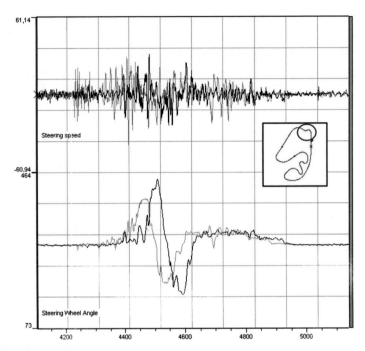

Figure 14.29 Steering wheel angle and steering speed for two drivers through Senna's S

- The two drivers turn the steering wheel differently
- In this case the smoothest driver produced the fastest lap times

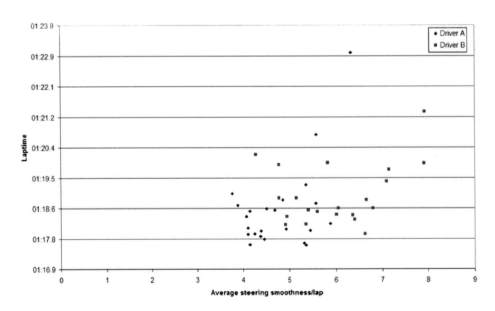

Figure 14.30 Lap time versus average steering smoothness for two drivers

When comparing steering smoothness values on different tracks and different conditions, you will find that the last conclusion is not a general truth. There will be situations where smoother steering doesn't translate into faster lap times.

14.7   The Driving Line

The line selected by the driver when negotiating the corner is determined by the maximum speed of a car being driven at the limit during cornering. To achieve the greatest possible cornering speed, the path through the corner should be an arc with the greatest possible radius. The speed maintained through the corner also determines the speed on the following straightaway. (However, it does not determine necessarily the top speed.) Because cornering speed and straightaway speed are the performance factors determining lap time, it is important to find out if the driver is locating the ideal path around the racetrack.

14.7.1   The Driving Line—Mathematical Definition

The corner radius gives us the line a driver took through a corner. Mathematically, corner radius is defined with the following equation:

$$R = \frac{V^2}{G_{\text{lat}}}$$

(Eq. 14.6)

With R = corner radius

V = vehicle speed

G_{lat} = lateral acceleration

For better display of the data, the following manipulation of Equation 14.6 is preferred:

$$R = \sqrt{\left(\frac{V^2}{G_{\text{lat}}}\right)^2}$$

(Eq. 14.7)

Sometimes the driving trajectory is also defined by the curvature r which is defined as the inverse of the corner radius (Equation 14.8). When Equations 14.7 and 14.8 are transformed into math channels in the analysis software, the result looks as illustrated in Figure 14.31.

$$r = \frac{1}{R}$$

(Eq. 14.8)

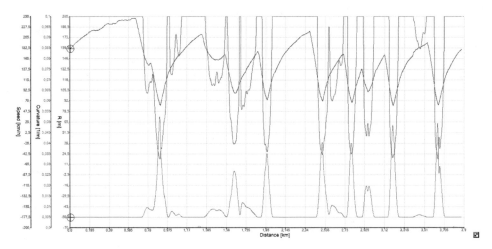

Figure 14.31 Speed, corner radius, and curvature for a lap around Navarra

According to Equation 14.7, the corner radius is the smallest where lateral acceleration reaches its maximum. With this in mind, the location of the apex can be determined from the corner radius graph. The apex is the point in the corner where the car is closest to the inside edge and is determined by the driving line chosen by the driver. We can distinguish three different situations:

- Mid-corner apex
- Early apex
- Late apex

Assuming that the track width at the corner entry and exit are the same, a constant radius line translates to an apex located in the middle of the corner. A mid-corner apex allows the driver to maintain a straight-line speed as long as possible without sacrificing corner exit speed.

Because the geometric location of the apex is the middle of the corner, the corner radius is at its minimum at this point. This results in a symmetrical corner radius trace, which is illustrated in Figure 14.32. Mid-corner apexes often show a flat, lateral G plateau in this section of the corner. An example of a mid-corner apex is shown in Figure 14.33. This is a 90° right-hand corner in which the maximum lateral acceleration is reached in the center of the corner. The lateral acceleration trace also shows the typical plateau.

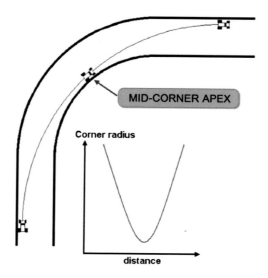

Figure 14.32 Mid-corner apex and the resulting shape of the corner radius graph

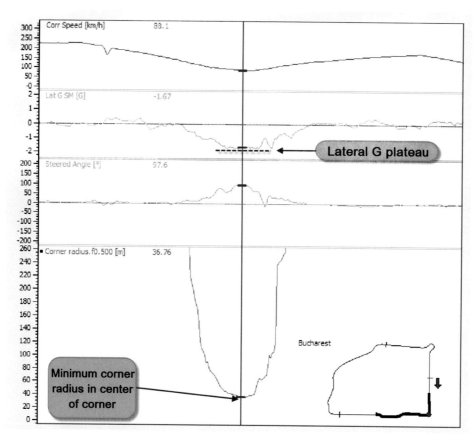

Figure 14.33 Mid-corner apex example

Late corner entry and late apex go hand in hand as indicated in Figure 14.34. This results in an excess amount of track left at the corner exit, which is not utilized when accelerating the car, and compromises speed on the following straight. In reality, the driver unwinds the steering wheel at this point to use all available grip for forward acceleration. Also, by performing the largest amount of turning at the corner entry, the car is in a better position for the exit, which makes it easier to accelerate out of the corner. However, the drawback of a late apex is sacrificing corner entry speed. Achieving a minimum corner radius in the early part of the corner gives away a late apex in the corner radius graph. Lateral Gs increase quickly, peaking early following corner entry, after which they decrease slowly until the driver starts to unwind the steering wheel (see the example in Figure 14.35).

Finally, an early corner entry results in an early apex. The driver turns the steering wheel more (to decrease the radius of the path) at the corner exit, which inevitably sacrifices the corner exit speed. In this case, the minimum corner radius is reached in the later stage of the corner, which creates a trace resembling Figure 14.36. As the steering angle increases, lateral acceleration increases to a late peak (see the example in Figure 14.37). Early apexing also results in a later throttle application point, as much of the cornering is done so late in the corner.

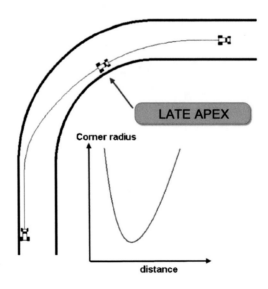

Figure 14.34 Late apex and the resulting shape of the corner radius graph

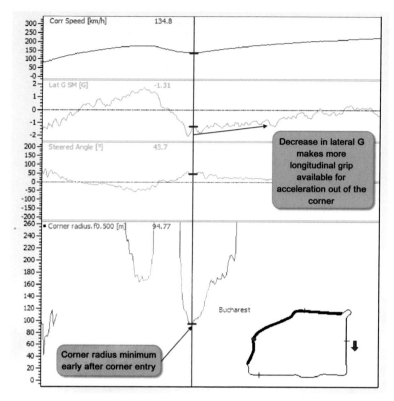

Figure 14.35 Late apex example

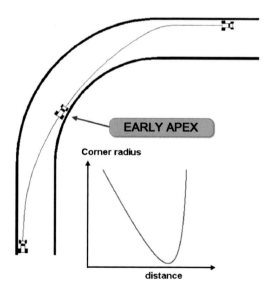

Figure 14.36 Early apex

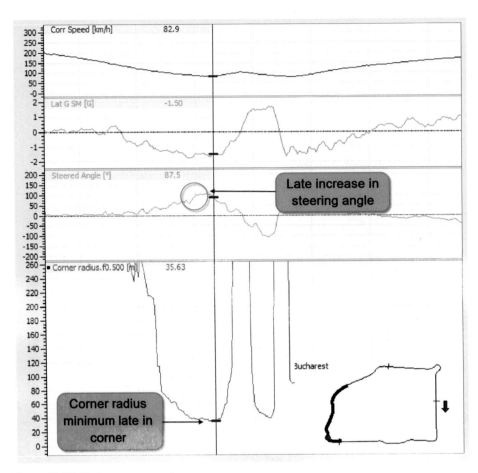

Figure 14.37 Early apex example

To determine where the driver places the apex, know what type of corner he is dealing with. A constant radius corner, one defined by one single radius, favors an apex placed close to the middle of the corner. A decreasing radius corner, where the latter part of the turn is tighter, normally requires a late apex, whereas in an increasing radius corner the apex is placed earlier.

Hairpins are corners exceeding 120 degrees and are special cases. These usually are tackled with a single, late apex to maximize corner exit speed, but an approach with a double apex is also possible. Much depends on the car and how it handles the mid-corner change of direction. To complicate the matter even more, grip level changes (for example rain conditions), banked corners, and bumps also influence apex placement.

14.7.2 How to Determine the Correct Driving Line

The data logging system reveals which trajectory was taken to get through a corner, but the driver and engineer must decide if it was the correct one. Look at the minimum cornering speed and corner exit speed to evaluate different lines. Always remember that a higher corner exit speed minimizes the time spent on the following straight. Therefore, driving line analysis should concentrate primarily on the corners that matter, the ones followed by a significant acceleration zone. Sector time analysis can be very helpful here as well.

In Equation 14.8 the curvature was defined as an alternative method of determining the driver's trajectory through a corner. In fact, plotting curvature in a time or distance graph has some visual advantages over the corner radius math channel. Curvature should be thought of as a measure of how much the car is turning. It is not a measure of how much the driver is turning the steering wheel, as this is influenced by the balance of the car. So whenever the curvature channel peaks, the car is turning at a maximum. The transition point from zero at corner entry tells us where the car starts turning, and the slope of the graph indicates the speed at which the car is being turned. The transition point to zero at corner exit tells us something about how the driver is straightening up the car. An example is given in Figure 14.38.

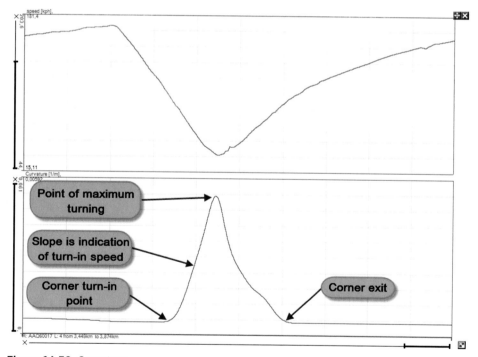

Figure 14.38 Curvature

The best line through a corner depends very much on what comes before and after it. However, when we look at a single corner in isolation we know that the line with the largest corner radius (or smallest curvature) is the fastest possible way through the corner. Indeed, Equation 14.7 tells us that for a fixed lateral acceleration the maximum speed is proportional to the square root of the corner radius. That means that for a specific corner a lower curvature peak will mean a faster driving line. A comparison of two drivers going through a corner is shown in Figure 14.39. The curvature channel shows clearly the two different techniques. The blue curvature trace indicates that this driver is turning into the corner later compared with the one in red and turns the car earlier on in the corner. This means that he needs to do less turning mid-corner, indicated by the lower peak in the curvature channel. The driver that produced the blue data has a higher mid-corner speed and takes a faster line through the corner. However, the total picture shows that he braked earlier (probably too early), which probably influenced the driving line he chose. The exit of the corner is the same for both drivers.

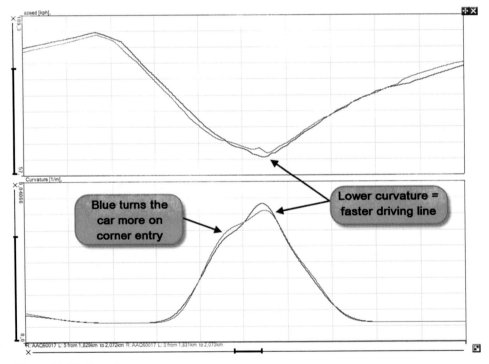

Figure 14.39 Curvature

Consistency of the driver in choosing a driving line can be investigated by looking at the variation in curvature peaks for specific corners. The average curvature per lap can also be very interesting to compare two different drivers. A lower average means that the respective driver is generally taking faster trajectories around the track. Figure 14.40

shows a run chart with the average curvature per lap for two drivers sharing the same car in an endurance race. There is clearly more scatter in the blue data, and the average is higher compared to the red data. This driver probably needs to work on his trajectories and improve consistency. Table 14.3 shows the average lap times of both drivers during the race and the standard deviation in lap time in order to give an idea about consistency.

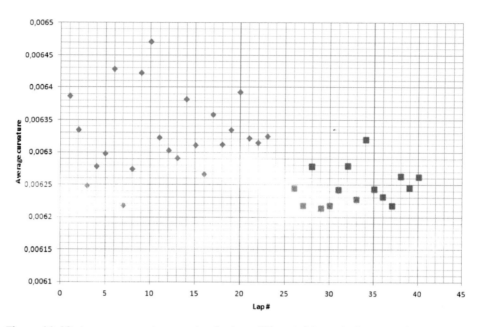

Figure 14.40 Average curvature per lap for two different drivers during an endurance race

Table 14.3 Lap time data of both drivers in Figure 14.40		
	Average lap time	Standard deviation lap time
Blue	2:07.800	0.8 s
Red	2:06.112	0.6 s

14.7.3 Driving Line Analysis Using GPS

GPS driving line analysis is a strongly marketed item, especially by the somewhat less expensive systems. Although it is very useful to use GPS for speed and distance calculation, the accuracy often depends largely on the post-processing of the data within the analysis software. Data recorded on different days might sometimes show offsets in positional data. This problem is caused by GPS satellite drift. With data that was recorded the same day, driving lines can be compared quite well.

For a good comparison, it is preferable to have some kind of indication of the track limits. The example in Figure 14.41 was taken from a rally-cross car. In the morning, the track perimeter was determined with a small GPS data logger strapped to the back of a bicycle. The data from the car was later overlaid on the bicycle run data to evaluate driving lines.

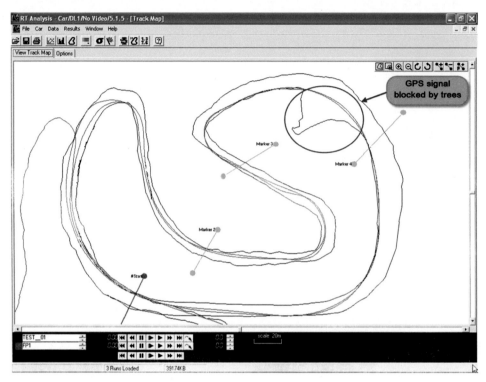

Figure 14.41 GPS track map of the Maasmechelen rally-cross circuit

The inside track boundary shows a region where the satellite coverage was lost. Normally the software will correct for this as long as the time that coverage is lost is limited. The software uses the signals of the internal accelerometers to correct the GPS signal. On the bicycle, however, there was not enough acceleration present to do a proper correction.

A lot of software packages offer the possibility to export GPS data in KML format so that it can be imported into Google Earth, as shown in Figure 14.42.

Figure 14.42 Driving lines in Google Earth™

14.7.4   Driving Line Analysis Using Video Feed

Video logging is the current hot item in data acquisition. Almost every manufacturer is including video in its range of products. Especially when synchronized with the logged data, video is also probably the best possible way to visualize what exactly is going on at the track. Audio is an added advantage. Some systems even have an extra audio input, which can, for example, be used to record the radio communication between the team and driver, all of this synchronized with the data.

Because we are more or less copying the driver's view, video systems are very suitable for the analysis of driving trajectories. Figure 14.43 shows a side-by-side comparison of a specific corner taken by a driver in two different laps. The curbstone reference shows that in the right-hand image the driver takes a wider line.

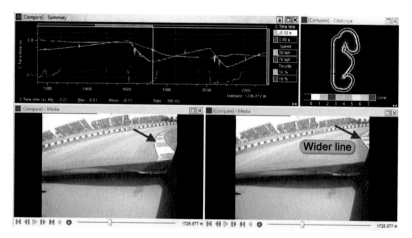

Figure 14.43 Video comparison of two different laps; the right video screen shows the driver taking a wider line through this corner

14.8   Driver Consistency over Multiple Laps

Driver consistency is easily assessable by observing lap times. Statistical calculations (e.g., average and standard deviation) can be performed to quantify consistency and used as measures for tactical decisions.

Sometimes, on short courses with many competitors on the track, it is difficult to determine how consistent the driver was from only the timesheets. In this case, rely on the sector time report.

Figure 14.44 shows a sector time report from the 12 first laps of a GT race on the Circuit Zolder racetrack. In this race, 45 competitors shared a 4-km circuit. The track was divided into 14 segments in which each corner and straight was defined as a separate segment.

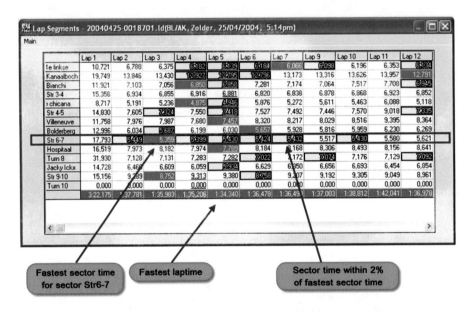

Figure 14.44 Sector time report of 12 laps during a GT race on the Zolder racetrack

In this report, the fastest segment time for each sector is indicated automatically with a black background, and every segment time coming within 2% of this time is highlighted in gray. The more gray area appearing in this report, the more consistent the driver is.

In sector Str6-7 over the 12 laps, a fastest sector time of 5.359 sec was reached. This means that every segment time within 5.359 sec × 1.02 = 5.466 sec is highlighted in gray. To be consistent, a driver needs to be within one-tenth of his fastest sector time every time.

Of course, this all depends on what one considers consistent. In this example, the driver is supposed to be within 2% of the best performance. The driver's fastest lap during the race was 94.344 sec. This means that a consistent lap time is anything within 94.344 sec × 1.02 = 96.227 sec, which is already a big difference in lap time.

Chapter 15
Simulation Tools

In all motor racing disciplines, track time is limited because race organizers must divide practice and race time among various classes to offer a suitable program to spectators. The testing time available between races is primarily a budget question. Because of this, race car behavior simulation is becoming more popular, and simulation software is now available to the wider public. This chapter offers a short introduction to simulation and how it can interact with the data acquisition system.

15.1   Introduction

When Timo Scheider won the 2009 DTM Championship for Audi, the team management made a remarkable statement [15-1]. One of the main reasons why the manufacturer had a competitive edge over its rival Mercedes was that the team had advanced in their lap time simulations up to the point where it determined up to 99% of the setup of the car. Instead of the drivers working toward a setup during the weekends that worked for them, they were expected to adapt themselves to the setup that was established through simulation. The team argued that this setup would provide the absolute maximum of vehicle performance and that the drivers should aim to get that performance out of the car.

Although this is a bold statement and a somewhat extreme approach, this story clearly illustrates where to put simulation nowadays within a racing organization. Mathematical modeling of a race car or any of its subsystems is exponentially growing in popularity, and as more and more software packages become available at affordable prices, simulation is working its way down to the "lower" racing categories in a comparable way that data acquisition has done in the last 15 years.

This chapter forms a short introduction to those simulation techniques that are closely linked to data acquisition and are a useful addition to the data engineer's toolbox. The two types of simulation software being introduced here are suspension kinematics simulations and lap time simulation. They are valuable expansions on the data acquisition system as they produce new data channels of parameters that are not directly measured (wheel loads, tire temperatures, dynamic roll center locations, camber angles, slip angles, and so on) or produce complete new datasets of the car in different configurations without the need to physically test these configurations on the racetrack.

The main advantages of using simulation tools are the following:

- We can create data channels of parameters that can't be measured directly, such as camber angles, roll center heights.

- We can then use these channels to increase the accuracy of other math channels (for example, weight transfer).

- Simulation can be used to determine or estimate certain vehicle parameters. This can be achieved by attempting to match data measured by the data acquisition system to the output of the simulation by tweaking the simulation's input parameters, a bit like solving an equation with more than one unknown variable.

- Simulation allows us to investigate the effects of changes in the car configuration without the need to actually drive the car.

- Simulation allows us to establish a base setup before we go to a racetrack and to intelligently prepare a schedule of setup modifications to try.

- We can compare real-world and simulated data to see if the car is performing as we expect.

- We can judge if the driver is using the complete potential of the vehicle.

- We can investigate how an individual change to the car influences the logged data to be better prepared when the change is actually tried on the car.

We should nevertheless always keep in mind that simulation is merely a tool and that it should be used as such. The results produced by the simulation software are as accurate as the accuracy of the modeled parameters. The following expression is an absolute reality when we apply simulation in the analysis of race car performance:

JUNK IN = JUNK OUT

The interaction between the data acquisition system and the applied simulations works in two directions. The simulation software requires input that in some cases must be measured on the track; the recorded data validates the model afterward. Once a reliable model is created, its output can be used not only to predict the effect of changes to the vehicle but also to calculate channels not directly measured on the car.

15.2 Suspension Kinematics Simulation

Suspension geometry simulation packages allow the user to input all relevant suspension pickup points, the three-dimensional coordinates, and other necessary vehicle dimensions. The software's output typically includes dynamic roll center location, camber change, wheel rates, and bump steer. This type of simulation is particularly useful for creating mathematical channels relating to suspension behavior for the data acquisition software.

The suspension kinematics describe the way that the sprung and unsprung mass of the vehicle relate to one another and to the relative motion of the various suspension and chassis components. A typical kinematics software package requires the three-dimensional coordinates of each suspension pickup point to be entered (Figure 15.1). The typical output parameters include the following:

- roll center height from the ground and offset from the axle centerline
- swing axle length and angle
- dynamic camber gain
- dynamic caster
- dynamic kingpin inclination
- tire scrub
- dynamic toe (bump steer)
- roll steer
- wheel movement versus shock absorber movement (motion ratio)
- antilift/antisquat
- dynamic track width
- Ackermann steering
- driveshaft angle and plunge

These parameters can be calculated as a function of ride height, wheel travel, roll angle, and steering angle. When the software allows vehicle dynamics parameters such as spring rates, corner weights, and center of gravity heights to be input, dynamic weight transfer and wheel loads can be calculated also.

When the location of the suspension pickup points are not supplied by the manufacturer, care must be taken when measuring them on the car. The output obtained from the software calculations is only as accurate as that of the coordinate measurements. Manufacturer drawings of the various suspension parts (e.g., hubs, uprights, wishbone,

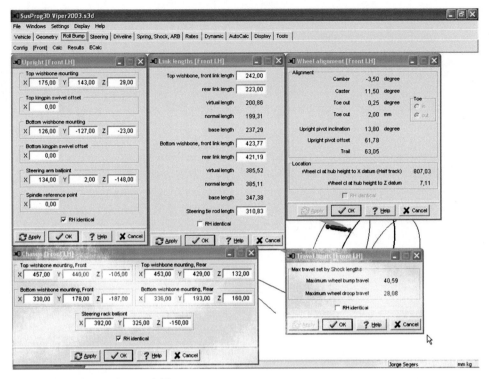

Figure 15.1 Kinematics model input screen

and chassis) are useful. Occasionally, parts must be disassembled to obtain a proper measurement. Typically, most of the time required to develop a good kinematics model goes toward measuring the suspension pickup points (if one is not designing the suspension from scratch). It is also necessary to ensure that the relative positions of the pickups are measured from a known ride height.

When an appropriate kinematics model has been created, the effect of modifying various suspension parameters can be investigated. In addition, the data acquisition engineer has access to more information to better understand the behavior of the vehicle. The output of the kinematics model can be input into the data analysis software through the use of math channels (Figure 15.2).

The following example explains how to create a math channel in the data analysis software for the front suspension motion ratio of a given car as a function of front suspension travel. Table 15.1 shows the output of the kinematics simulation. The second column gives the suspension travel (in a range of 28 mm bump to 28 mm of rebound), while the motion ratios corresponding to each suspension position are given in the third

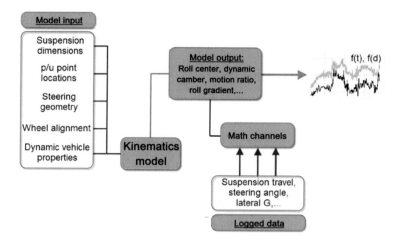

Figure 15.2 Linking the logged data to suspension kinematics simulations

column. These figures are then entered in a spreadsheet and from a plot of motion ratio versus shock absorber travel a trend line is determined (Figure 15.3). The equation of this line is used as a math channel for the motion ratio (Figure 15.4).

Table 15.1 Motion ratio versus shock absorber travel		
	Shock absorber travel	Motion ratio
Bump travel	28 mm	1.230
	24 mm	1.232
	20 mm	1.234
	16 mm	1.236
	12 mm	1.238
	8 mm	1.240
	4 mm	1.241
Static	0 mm	1.243
Rebound travel	−4 mm	1.245
	−8 mm	1.247
	−12 mm	1.250
	−16 mm	1.252
	−20	1.253
	−24	1.255
	−28	1.257

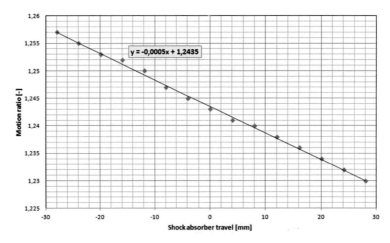

Figure 15.3 Motion ratio data plotted in spreadsheet with trend line

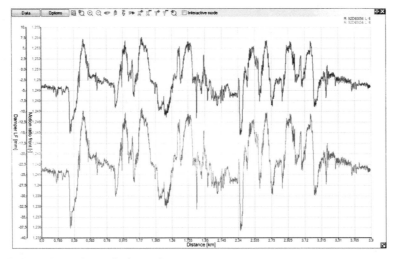

Figure 15.4 Motion ratio math channel

15.3 Lap Time Simulation

Lap time simulation is a useful tool for the engineer as it can increase his/her knowledge of the vehicle's performance and behavior on a specific track without the need to physically test the car on that track. Except for this knowledge it also enables the engineer to arrive at the track with a near to optimum setup, on the condition that the software is used correctly. By using lap time simulation, different car configurations can be tested and a good baseline setup determined with which to start a race weekend. More configurations can be tested in less time and at much lower cost, and run to run variations due to tire wear, fuel load, track grip, weather, and so on can be eliminated.

Very often when an individual modification is performed on a vehicle, more than one parameter is influenced (secondary effects). For example, a change in the vehicle's ride height has an influence on the aerodynamics but can also change the suspension roll center height. Lap time simulation allows us to easily isolate setup parameters and investigate the effects on vehicle performance.

Another added benefit of lap time simulation is that it allows us to investigate setups that are outside the physically available adjustment ranges of the car. This might open up perspectives for further development.

A good example of the effective application of lap time simulation software is found in the Balance of Performance concept used in GT racing by the FIA, which incorporates the use of the D.A.T.A.S. RaceSim package to predict cornering speeds, acceleration, and top speeds of the various cars in the championship. A mathematical model of each vehicle is created and validated using data recorded by the car during races and testing. Simulations are then made to determine the relative performance of each car model. Ballast, engine restrictors, or aerodynamic restrictions are determined from the simulation results to equalize performance of the different makes in the series.

15.3.1 Levels of Lap Time Simulation

We can distinguish between three main types of lap time simulation software:

- Steady-state simulation: This is the simplest form of lap time simulation, where the vehicle is assumed to be in one of the following three states: braking, accelerating, or cornering. The advantage of this type of simulation model is the ease of calculation and implementation. The limited amount of input parameters also means that complicated measurements are not necessary to create the model. The disadvantages are the limited accuracy and the fact that the influence of only a few parameters can be investigated.

- "Quasi"-steady-state simulation: In this type of simulation, the track is divided into a large number of corner segments defined by a length and constant corner radius, connected through a series of straights. In all these corner segments, the car is considered to be in steady state and subject to a lateral and longitudinal acceleration. The entry and exit speed of each segment can be worked out and therefore the time it takes the car to cover the segment. The sum of all segment times is the resulting lap time. Of course, a higher amount of segments will result in more accurate simulation results.

- Dynamic or transient simulation: In reality, when a vehicle goes through a corner it is never in a steady state. Dynamic simulation takes into account the response time of the vehicle in changing its attitude and direction of travel. The big difference of dynamic simulation compared to quasi-steady-state is that the effects of inertia and shock absorber configurations can be investigated.

The required level of simulation depends mainly on its complexity and the amount of input vehicle data. The accuracy of the simulation results goes together with the accuracy of the model, and in many cases it is better to keep things simple. Efficient use of simulation software requires a notion of the inherent inaccuracies of the chosen type of simulation.

To create a simulation of a car around a given track, the software needs to be provided with the following information (see Figure 15.5):

- The vehicle model: A mathematical description of the vehicle dynamics of the car.

- The tire model: Friction between tire and track surface is the major mechanism for generating forces on the vehicle, so the tire model should provide an accurate characterization of the magnitude and direction of the friction force generated at the tire contact patch.

- The track model: The mathematical definition of the driving line around the circuit. This is most of the time a data array of track curvature against covered distance.

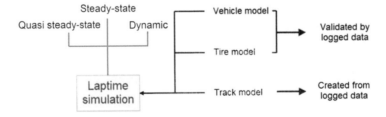

Figure 15.5 Lap time simulation concept

The track model is generally created from onboard recorded data, whereas the combination of vehicle and tire model is validated by comparison against the logged data. Once this validation is judged satisfactory, the model can be used to explore alternative vehicle configurations.

15.3.2 A Simple Point Mass Vehicle Model

The most simplified possible vehicle model is one where all mass components are grouped into one point, the vehicle's center of gravity. This point is assumed to be in contact with the road surface and able to develop a certain level of grip. The model might seem overly simplified, but in fact it can be used to gain some basic knowledge of the car in question. On this point mass, the following forces are applied:

- Vehicle mass
- Driving force from the engine
- Braking force
- Aerodynamic drag force
- Aerodynamic downforce
- Cornering force

The tire model for the single point mass is defined with a friction coefficient μ (Equation 15.1).

$$F_{\text{tire}} = \mu \cdot F_N \qquad \text{(Eq. 15.1)}$$

where F_{tire} is the friction force between the tire and the road surface, μ is the coefficient of friction, and F_N is the normal force. It is this force that keeps the car on the track. All forces acting on the center of gravity are illustrated in Figure 15.6.

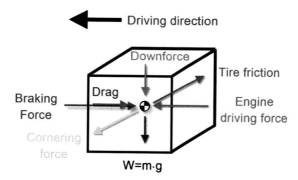

Figure 15.6 Single point mass model

The engine driving force is what thrusts the car forward. The maximum magnitude of this force is determined by the tire coefficient of friction and the normal load. The driving force is opposed by the aerodynamic drag, which is dependent on the speed of the car. The brakes provide the necessary force to slow the vehicle down. And finally, we have an aerodynamic downforce which is also dependent of the vehicle speed.

For example, the downforce is calculated of a 2010 Auto GP single-seater with a weight of 940 kg, including fuel and driver. First the tire's coefficient of friction is determined. Figure 15.7 shows the car in a 75 km/h corner, in which we assume that no aerodynamic downforce is present. The lateral acceleration at this point is 1.80 G.

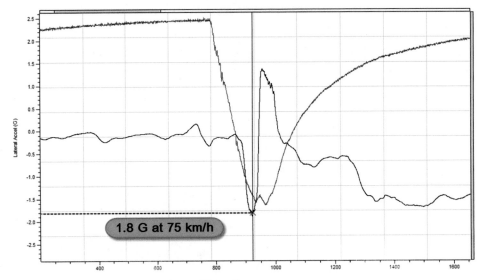

Figure 15.7 Auto GP car cornering at 75 km/h

In order for the car to accelerate at 1.8 G through this corner, the tires must produce a lateral friction force that is equal to the force due to lateral acceleration of the car mass M. This means that Equation 15.2 is true.

$$F_{\text{tire}} = M \cdot G_{\text{lat}} \cdot 9.81 \qquad \text{(Eq. 15.2)}$$

Or,

$$\mu \cdot F_N = M \cdot G_{\text{lat}} \cdot 9.81 \qquad \text{(Eq. 15.3)}$$

Without aerodynamic downforce, $F_N = M \cdot 9.81$, so the friction coefficient can simply be expressed as Equation 15.4.

$$\mu = G_{\text{lat}} \qquad \text{(Eq. 15.4)}$$

For the preceding example, the tire friction coefficient is thus 1.8 and F_{tire} equals

$$F_{\text{tire}} = 1.8 \cdot 940 \cdot 9.81 = 16599 \text{ N}$$

In Figure 15.8, the same car is now negotiating a corner at 215 km/h, now with a lateral acceleration of 2.38 G. Here, the following cornering force is required:

$$F_{\text{tire}} = 2.38 \cdot 940 \cdot 9.81 = 21947 \text{ N}$$

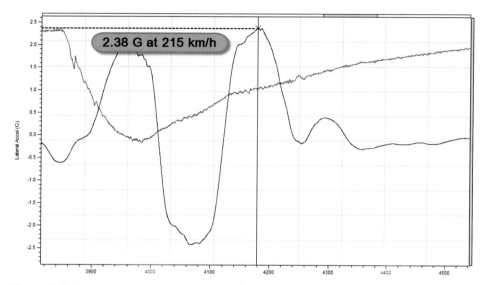

Figure 15.8 Auto GP car cornering at 215 km/h

With a friction coefficient of 1.8, the normal force acting on the tire is:

$$F_N = \frac{21947}{1.8} = 12193 \text{ N}$$

And finally, the downforce L produced by this car at 215 km/h is

$$L = 12193 - (940 \cdot 9.81) = 2972 \text{ N}$$

Using this very simple method, the vehicle's downforce coefficient can be estimated. This way the magnitude of aerodynamic downforce can be calculated for the complete speed range.

The next step in the simulation process is to create a representation of the track. To do this, the track is divided into a large number of small segments of a constant corner radius. This corner radius is either a specific length when the car is cornering or increases to infinity when the car is on a straight. Knowing the forces acting on the point mass (which were mentioned previously), the acceleration ($F = m \cdot a$) in each track segment can be calculated. From this follows the maximum segment speed, and as the segment length is known, the time that is spent in each sector can be calculated. Finally, the sum of all segment times is the lap time.

Although this mathematical model is a very simplistic representation of the race car, it is still quite useful to understand certain influences on performance. In Figure 15.9 a lap is shown of a GT3 car at the French Nogaro track. This graph was done using Race

Technology's Analysis software, which includes a very basic single mass model, of which the following parameters can be defined by the user (see Figure 15.10):

- Weight of the car
- Aerodynamic drag coefficient
- Rolling resistance
- Engine power curve
- Gear ratios
- Shift RPM and shift duration
- Lateral friction coefficient (optionally as a function of speed)
- Longitudinal friction coefficient (optionally as a function of speed)

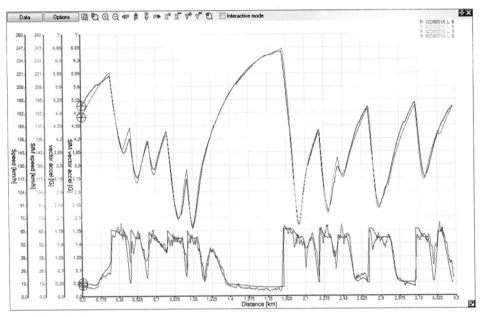

Figure 15.9 Real and simulated speed and combined acceleration of a GT3 car around Nogaro

The overlay of real and simulated speed and combined acceleration shows the correlation that is possible to achieve with a mathematical model with only a very limited amount of input parameters. In Table 15.2 the lap times are given for the real car and the simulation model. Using this configuration as a starting point for further simulations, the priority of lateral or longitudinal grip was investigated. Both the lateral and longitudinal grip was decreased with 2% to determine which of the two had the bigger effect on lap time at this track. The results in Table 15.2 clearly show that the effect of a 2% change in lateral grip is significantly larger than an equivalent change in longitudinal grip.

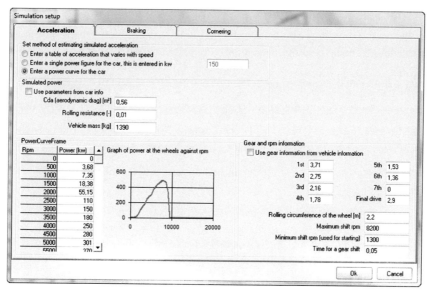

Figure 15.10 Simulation input parameters in Race Technology Analysis

Table 15.2 Lap time achieved by real car versus simulation model	
Real car	1'26.75
Simulation model—baseline	1'26.87
Simulation model— –2% braking grip	1'26.95
Simulation model— –2% lateral grip	1'27.46

This is only a simple example of what can be done with a pure steady-state vehicle model with only limited input parameters. Other possibilities include the following:

- Determining the optimal gear ratios for a given racetrack
- Analyzing the effect of shift RPM and up-shift duration on lap time
- Evaluating the compromise between aerodynamic downforce and drag and the effects on lap time and top speed
- Evaluating the effect of engine power on lap time and top speed
- Evaluating the effect of vehicle weight on lap time (ballast, fuel load)
- Determining the effect of a series of regulations on maximum vehicle performance (engine restrictor size versus vehicle weight, effect of penalty weight)
- Comparing the performance envelope of different cars
- Evaluating changes in grip levels (tire degradation, tire compounds, rain conditions)

15.3.3 Obtaining the Input Parameters for the Vehicle Model

Depending on the complexity of the simulation model, a number of vehicle parameters need to be determined. To obtain these parameters, there are different possibilities:

- Information can be obtained from the car, engine, or tire manufacturer.

- Some parameters can be measured (suspension geometry, center of gravity location)

- Specific tests can be organized to determine vehicle performance (wind tunnel or straight-line testing to obtain aero-data, engine dynamometer testing, tire rig testing).

- Parameters can be derived from the logged data (aerodynamic drag and downforce, tire grip).

- Some properties of the car can be estimated from experience numbers.

Table 15.3 gives a nonexclusive list of the vehicle parameters that need to be known to put together a decent mathematical model of a race car.

15.3.4 The Tire Model

The tire model is of vital importance in lap time simulation, as in this the interface is defined as how the vertical forces in the suspension/tire will be transformed into the horizontal tire contact patch forces that will keep the virtual car on the track. This transformation takes place through elastic deformation in the tire footprint. Mathematical modeling of this deformation is extremely complex and outside the scope of most lap time simulation packages. Instead, there needs to be a way to fit a mathematical function to measured tire data. Over the years, different solutions to this problem have been proposed, with Pacejka's Magic Formula [15-2] proving the most popular. In this section, the Pacejka tire model is briefly introduced.

The Pacejka is a semiempirical model to calculate steady-state tire force that is continuously being developed by TU Delft since the 1980s. We'll distinguish here a longitudinal and lateral force version of the tire model.

15.3.4.1 The Pacejka Longitudinal Tire Force Model

The general form of the longitudinal tire force (F_x) Magic formula (Pacejka 2006 version) is given in Equation 15.5:

$$F_x = D \cdot \sin\left[b_0 \cdot \arctan\left(S \cdot B + E(\arctan[S \cdot B] - S \cdot B) \right) \right] \qquad \text{(Eq. 15.5)}$$

In this equation, we have the following parameters:

$$D = \mu_p \cdot F_N \qquad \text{(Eq. 15.6)}$$

$$\mu_p = b_1 \cdot F_N + b_2 \qquad \text{(Eq. 15.7)}$$

Table 15.3 Vehicle parameters for lap time simulation	
Category	Parameter
General dimensions	Wheelbase
	Track width
Weight distribution	Corner weights
	Center of gravity height
	Sprung and unsprung weight
	Moment of inertia in pitch, roll, and yaw (in case of transient simulation)
Engine	Power/torque curve
	Driveline loss
	Engine RPM limit
Transmission	Gear ratios
	Shift points
	Differential limited slip properties
Suspension and Steering	Spring rates
	Antiroll bar rates
	Suspension motion ratios
	Packers/Bump rubber rates and dimensions
	Shock absorber force versus velocity curves (in case of transient simulation)
	Ride heights
	Wheel alignment (camber/caster/toe)
	Suspension geometry (roll center locations, dynamic camber gain, bump steer)
	Steering rack ratio
Aerodynamics	Drag coefficient (versus front and rear ride height)
	Downforce coefficient (versus front and rear ride height)
	Aerobalance (versus front and rear ride height)
Brakes	Maximum brake force
	Brake force distribution front/rear

$$B = \frac{\left(b_3 \cdot F_N + b_4\right) \cdot e^{\left(-b_5 \cdot F_N\right)}}{b_0 \cdot \mu_p} \qquad \text{(Eq. 15.8)}$$

$$S = \left[100 \cdot SR + b_9 \cdot F_N + b_{10}\right] \qquad \text{(Eq. 15.9)}$$

$$E = \left[b_6 \cdot F_N^2 + b_7 \cdot F_N + b_8\right] \qquad \text{(Eq. 15.10)}$$

In the preceding equations F_N is the normal load on the tire and SR is the tire's slip ratio. The trick is now to define the parameters $b_0, b_1, b_2 \ldots b_{10}$ in such a way that the resulting curve fits the measured tire data. Let's consider a typical Formula Ford tire with the coefficients given in Table 15.4.

Table 15.4 Longitudinal Pacejka coefficients for Formula Ford tire	
$b0$	1.5
$b1$	−90
$b2$	1545
$b3$	23.3
$b4$	400
$b5$	0
$b6$	0.0068
$b7$	0.055
$b8$	−0.024
$b9$	0
$b10$	0

Entering Equations 15.5 to 15.10 into Matlab and plotting the resulting longitudinal tire force F_x against slip ratio for a normal tire load F_N of 1000 N, 1500 N, and 2000 N results in the curves shown in Figure 15.11. We can see that the maximum tire forces are developed at a slip ratio of 8%, both in braking (negative slip ratio) and acceleration (positive slip ratio). A normal tire force of 2000 N gives a maximum longitudinal force of 2730 N at this slip ratio (again the same in braking and acceleration). The friction coefficient is 2730/2000 = 1.365.

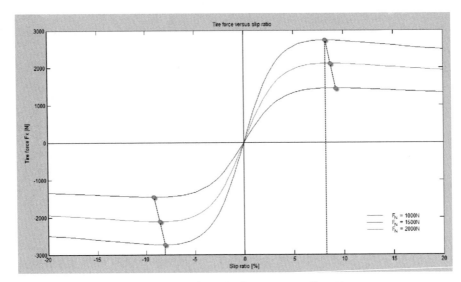

Figure 15.11 Formula Ford tire longitudinal tire force versus slip ratio

15.3.4.2 The Pacejka Lateral Tire Force Model

The lateral Pacejka model calculates the lateral tire forces from normal tire load and slip angle. The general form of the formula is very similar to the longitudinal version:

$$F_y = D \cdot \sin\left[a_0 \cdot \arctan\left(S \cdot B + E(\arctan[S \cdot B] - S \cdot B)\right)\right] + S_V \qquad \text{(Eq. 15.11)}$$

The individual subcomponents however are different to the longitudinal version:

$$D = \mu_{yp} \cdot F_N \qquad \text{(Eq. 15.12)}$$

$$\mu_{yp} = a_1 \cdot F_N + a_2 \qquad \text{(Eq. 15.13)}$$

$$S = \alpha + a_8 \cdot \gamma + a_9 \cdot F_N + a_{10} \qquad \text{(Eq. 15.14)}$$

$$B = \frac{a_3 \cdot \sin\left[2 \cdot \arctan\left(\dfrac{F_N}{a_4}\right)\right] \cdot \left[1 - a_5 \cdot |\gamma|\right]}{a_0 \cdot \mu_{yp} \cdot F_N} \qquad \text{(Eq. 15.15)}$$

$$E = a_6 \cdot F_N + a_7 \qquad \text{(Eq. 15.16)}$$

$$S_v = \left[(a_{11} \cdot F_N + a_{11}) \cdot \gamma + a_{13}\right] \cdot F_N + a_{14} \qquad \text{(Eq. 15.17)}$$

Again, F_N is the normal force, and α is the tire's slip angle. γ is the camber angle relative to the ground plane. Returning to the Formula Ford tire example, Table 15.5 gives the coefficients for the lateral tire force model. Figure 15.12 shows the results for lateral tire force versus slip angle for respective normal loads of 1000 N, 1500 N, and 2000 N.

Table 15.5 Lateral Pacejka coefficients for Formula Ford tire	
$a0$	1.4
$a1$	−32
$a2$	1625
$a3$	1875
$a4$	11
$a5$	0.013
$a6$	−0.14
$a7$	0.14
$a8$	0.019
$a9$	−0.019
$a10$	−0.18
$a11$	−11
$a12$	−0.021
$a13$	0.48
$a14$	10.2

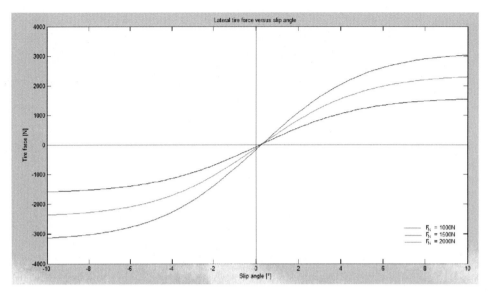

Figure 15.12 Formula Ford tire lateral tire force versus slip angle

The Pacejka model is only one version of the empirical tire force approximation. Over the years, the model has gone through a number of iterations. Most of the popular lap time simulation software packages use a Pacejka-style model to calculate the tire forces.

To obtain this kind of data for a specific tire to use in a simulation can be quite complicated. Tire manufacturers are often quite reluctant to provide accurate tire data to their customers, and indoor tire testing can take a big chunk out of a team's yearly budget. This is often used as an excuse not to integrate lap time simulation into the engineer's analysis toolbox. However, with some simple techniques it is possible to derive a first-cut tire model from the logged data.

The method to estimate a tire model from logged data was provided by Danny Nowlan [8-1]. In its most basic form a lateral tire model can be presented as in Equation 15.18. In this equation the lateral tire force is dependent of the tire slip angle and the normal load on the tire. As it is a first, rough approximation of the tire model, the influences of camber, pressure, temperature, and so on are neglected.

$$F_y = f(\alpha) \cdot f(F_N) \qquad \text{(Eq. 15.18)}$$

The first part of this equation $f(\alpha)$ describes the relationship between normalized lateral tire force and slip angle [4-2]. This function is bounded between –1 and 1 and is at zero when α is zero. Figure 15.13 shows the shape of this curve for a typical race car tire. Although this shape will differ from one tire to another, race car tires will generally achieve the peak of lateral tire force in a slip angle range of five to seven degrees. This function can be used later on to fine-tune the over-/understeer balance of the vehicle.

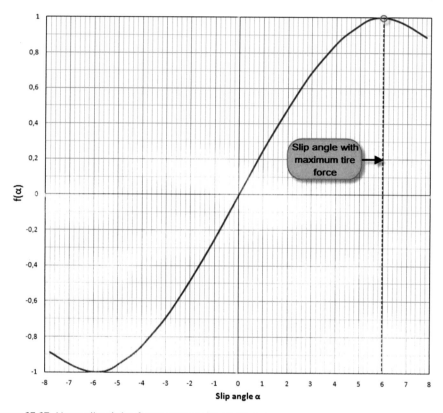

Figure 15.13 Normalized tire force versus slip angle curve

In Equation 15.18 $f(F_N)$ is what describes the maximum lateral tire force the tire can produce for a given vertical tire load. The method that will be described assumes a given $f(\alpha)$ function and distills the maximum lateral tire force at its respective slip angle. The first step in the calculation is to determine the maximum normal loads on the tires for which the calculation or measurement methods were discussed in chapter 10. Figure 15.14 shows an example of a lap around the Nurburgring in a GT3 car, including the calculated wheel loads. Table 15.6 gives the maximum wheel loads on any outside front and rear wheel and the load on the corresponding inside wheel.

Chapter 15

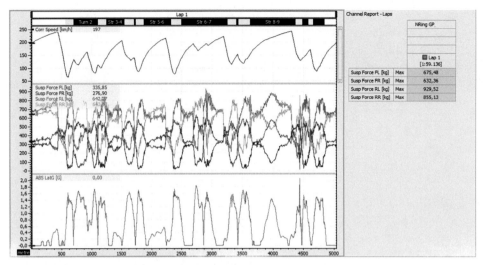

Figure 15.14 Calculated wheel loads for a GT3 car around Nurburgring

Table 15.6 Maximum wheel loads during Nurburgring lap	
Parameter	Value
Maximum wheel load on front outside tire	675.48 kg · 9.81 = 6626 N
Corresponding wheel load on front inside tire	62.74 kg · 9.81 = 615 N
Maximum wheel load on rear outside tire	929.52 kg · 9.81 = 9119 N
Corresponding wheel load on rear inside tire	279.01 kg · 9.81 = 2737 N

The maximum tire force curve will be estimated by performing a simple parabolic curve fit according to Equation 15.19.

$$F_{y\max} = k_a \cdot (1 - k_b \cdot F_N) \cdot F_N \qquad \text{(Eq. 15.19)}$$

In this equation, k_a represents the initial tire coefficient of friction without normal load on the tire and $k_b = \dfrac{1}{2 \cdot F_{N\max}}$. For the example shown the values of k_b are:

Front: $k_b = 7.55 \cdot 10^{-5}$

Rear: $k_b = 5.48 \cdot 10^{-5}$

Equations 15.20 and 15.21 estimate the total lateral tire force of both front and rear wheels, respectively, by applying a force equilibrium around the front and rear axles.

$$F_{N\,LF} + F_{N\,RF} = k_a \cdot \left((1 - k_b \cdot F_{N\,LF}) \cdot F_{N\,LF} + (1 - k_b \cdot F_{N\,RF}) \cdot F_{N\,RF} \right) \qquad \text{(Eq. 15.20)}$$

$$F_{N\,LR} + F_{N\,RR} = k_a \cdot \left((1 - k_b \cdot F_{N\,LR}) \cdot F_{N\,LR} + (1 - k_b \cdot F_{N\,RR}) \cdot F_{N\,RR} \right) \qquad \text{(Eq. 15.21)}$$

With the loads given in Table 15.6 and the k_b values calculated here, Equations 15.20 and 15.21 can be solved for k_a, giving the following results:

Front: $k_a = 1.86$

Rear: $k_a = 1.72$

Now that k_a and k_b are known, the lateral tire force versus normal load curve becomes as illustrated in Figure 15.15. This function multiplied by the chosen slip angle curve $f(\alpha)$ (Equation 15.18) is a good starting point for a tire model to use in lap time simulations. If the cornering speeds resulting from the simulation are too high compared with the logged data, the values for k_a should be lowered until good correlation is achieved. If the model lacks understeer compared with the logged data, the front k_a value needs to be dropped more than the rear (see the dotted lines in Figure 15.15). Another option to alter the model's balance is to shift the slip angle at which maximum lateral force is achieved forward or backward depending on the direction the balance needs to go. When the vehicle model is of adequate quality, achieving good correlation with the logged data should become a matter of fine-tuning the tire model.

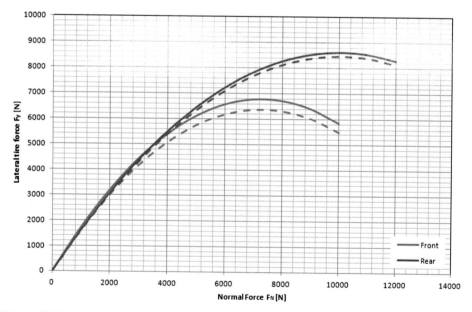

Figure 15.15 Modeled lateral tire force versus normal force curve

15.3.5   The Track Model

The primary task of the track model is to provide the simulated vehicle with a path to follow. Generally this is done by defining the corner radius or track curvature (inverse corner radius) as a function of distance. Corner radius can be defined as Equation 15.22.

$$R = \frac{V^2}{G_{Lat}}$$
(Eq. 15.22)

The track curvature then becomes

$$r = \frac{1}{R}$$
(Eq. 15.23)

Which of the two preceding equations is required depends on the simulation software used, but both can be created by exporting the respective math channel from the analysis software.

With this knowledge the driving line is defined around the track, assuming this is completely flat. In reality, this is rarely the case, and changes in track elevation can have a significant effect on the simulation results. The next step to refine the track model is to provide the track elevation versus distance. Some GPS systems are able to measure the elevation profile directly, but this is often inaccurate. A somewhat more laborious method is to use Google Earth to take height data (see Figures 15.16 and 15.17).

Figure 15.16 Taking elevation measurements in Google Earth

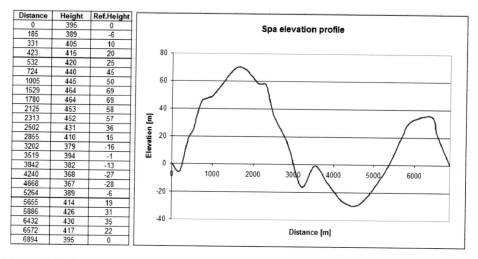

Distance	Height	Ref.Height
0	395	0
185	389	-6
331	405	10
423	415	20
532	420	25
724	440	45
1005	445	50
1529	464	69
1780	464	69
2125	453	58
2313	452	57
2502	431	36
2855	410	15
3202	379	-16
3519	394	-1
3842	382	-13
4240	368	-27
4668	367	-28
5264	389	-6
5655	414	19
5886	426	31
6432	430	35
6572	417	22
6894	395	0

Figure 15.17 Track elevation as a function of distance created from Google Earth elevation data

Another track property that can have a significant influence on the results is the banking of corners. If there is a banking angle present, this should be accounted for in the simulation. Banking angle can be determined from the logged data by creating a math channel from Equation 15.24.

$$\alpha = \operatorname{Arc}\tan\left[\frac{G_{vert} - 1}{G_{lat}}\right]$$

(Eq. 15.24)

In the case of a fully dynamic simulation, the asphalt profile and all the bumps present on the driving line should be defined. This is most of the time done by importing the suspension travel signals into the simulation software where the low speed content (inertial chassis movements) of the signals is filtered out, leaving only the high-speed movement from suspension movement due to bumps in the track surface.

A lot of simulation packages have the possibility to define local grip factors to account for differences in track surface, dirt on the track, and so on. These factors are often used to dial local correlation between simulation results and the logged data.

Finally, the environmental data such as air temperature, humidity, air pressure, and wind speed and direction are also an integral part of the track model. The wind speed and direction will mainly influence aerodynamic performance, while air temperature, humidity, and air pressure are necessary to calculate the air density, which influences available engine power as well as drag and downforce coefficients.

417

15.4   A Worked out Example

Once a vehicle model is created and validated to be sufficiently accurate, it can be used to perform simulations with the objective to learn more about the performance range of the specific vehicle. In this section, an example is given for a parameter study of a touring car model at the Interlagos track. These simulations were performed using the ChassisSim lap time simulation software. This is in fact a full dynamic simulation package, but for the sake of simplicity and because not all vehicle parameters were known, the simulations were performed assuming a completely flat track. The effect of elevation changes and road surface irregularities were not modeled. The correlation between the vehicle model and the real car is illustrated in Figure 15.18. Speed, lateral and longitudinal acceleration, and steering angle are judged to be accurate enough to be able to draw meaningful conclusions from the simulation results. The simulated data is displayed in color and the real data is in black.

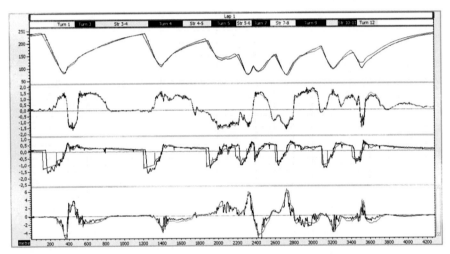

Figure 15.18 Overlay between real and simulated data showing the correlation between the real car and the simulation model

The first simulations were done with the purpose to get a feel of how lap time is influenced by the total amount of grip available from the track. For this, the tire grip factor was varied within a significant range. This kind of simulation gives the engineer an idea of what lap times to expect in, for example, rain conditions. Figure 15.19 shows the effects of this parameter on both lap time as top speed.

In the next simulation runs the effects of the vehicle weight, and the location of its center of gravity were investigated. The graphs in Figure 15.20 show a variation of just over 2 sec for a vehicle weight variation range of 150 kg. The top speed varies with 2 km/h within this range. The relationship of lap time versus vehicle weight is nearly linear within the chosen weight variation interval. The equation for this relationship is indicated in the graph. This dependency is useful knowledge for the race strategy, as it will

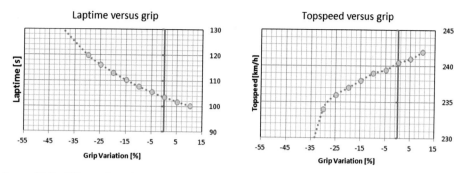

Figure 15.19 Effect of track grip on lap time and top speed

tell the engineer what gain in lap time performance will be possible when the fuel load of the car decreases (see chapter 16).

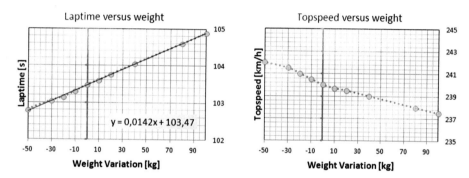

Figure 15.20 Effect of vehicle weight on lap time and top speed

The center of gravity height of the vehicle has an effect on the magnitude of total lateral and longitudinal weight transfer. Generally, a lower center of gravity will always be better for the performance. This effect is shown in Figure 15.21. A 40 mm variation of center of gravity height results in a lap time difference of about 0.8 sec or 0.02 sec per mm.

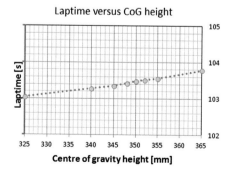

Figure 15.21 Effect of center of gravity height on lap time

To establish the ideal weight distribution for the vehicle at this particular track, some simulations were done to investigate the effect of front weight distribution and diagonal weight distribution (cross weight) on lap time performance. As can be seen in Figure 15.22, this car gets slower as more weight is put on the front axle and the effect seems to be very little for front weight percentages between 45 and 49%. For the cross weight balance there is a clear optimum at 49.5%. This value will vary for different tracks depending on track asymmetry (number of curves to the left/right) and how much time is spent in each of the traction circle quadrants (see chapter 18).

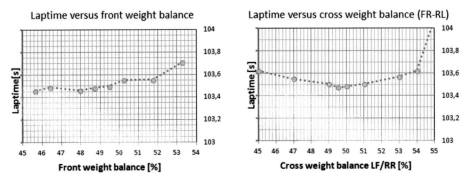

Figure 15.22 Effect front and diagonal weight distribution on lap time

These are some very basic parameter investigations that can give the engineer a good idea in which direction to go with the setup without specifying too many specifics. Table 15.7 shows the change in lap time when each of the given parameters is changed by 1% in relation to the initial vehicle model. This percentage changed was always applied in such a way that it had a negative effect on lap time. The results provide a means of determining which aspect of the vehicle configuration is important on a specific racetrack in order to optimize lap time.

Table 15.7 Parameter study from lap time simulation		
Parameter	Absolute change	Δ Lap time
General grip (lateral and longitudinal)	1%	0.382 s
Total vehicle weight	13 kg	0.173 s
Engine power	5 HP	0.062 s
Center of gravity height	3.5 mm	0.055 s
Front weight percentage	6.5 kg	0.035 s
Air density	0.01225 kg/m^3	0.035 s
Drag coefficient C_DA	0.02	0.035 s
Cross weight percentage	3.2 kg	0.023 s
Downforce coefficient C_LA	0.028	0.017 s
Aerobalance	1%	0.005 s

Of course, more specific investigations can be done. Figure 15.23 gives an example of the effect on front and rear ride heights of the car at the end of the track's main straight as the front spring ratio is decreased with 40 N/mm.

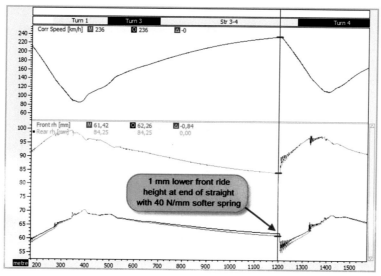

Figure 15.23 Difference in ride height at the end of the straight when the front spring rate is decreased

15.5 How to Integrate Lap Time Simulation in Daily Data Acquisition Tasks

15.5.1 Before the Meeting

The first step on fitting lap time simulation into the whole data analysis process is to create a model of the car and validate it against known data. This is an iterative process, and you'll find that you will keep fine-tuning the mathematical representation of the car. One of the main objectives of lap time simulation is that you'll learn more and more about the behavior of the vehicle, and fine-tuning the model is an integral part of that learning process.

Once a validated model is obtained, lap time simulation can be used to prepare for a meeting. Whenever lap time simulations are performed, it is as if the team would drive the car during a virtual test day. This means that the same methodology applies as if a real car were tested on a real track, with the significant benefit of being able to save much time and cost.

The first step is to plan a series of what-if scenarios and run them through the simulation model. Parameter studies such as discussed previously in this chapter are a good example of this. This is the procedure to follow relentlessly:

- Perform the setup change

- Run the simulation

- Obtain and analyze the simulated data

The results should always be critically analyzed, and one cannot rely exclusively on the resulting lap times. Testing the model outside of its boundaries doesn't make sense at this stage, as you're trying to establish a starting point for the test day/race weekend. A detailed log of what changes were done should be kept and the results documented for later reference.

The results obtained should be small, consistent changes. Large changes in the data often are the result of a problem with the vehicle model or a calculation issue within the software.

If your test plan is put together of items to test during the available track time, the simulation software can be used to go through the schedule and look at the effects in the recorded data. The simulation results can also lead to the conclusion that it's of no use to test a certain configuration on the track. The essence of track testing then becomes the validation of selected model solutions.

At the end of the virtual testing, the simulation model should be ready to be used at the track, and a database will be available of simulated data to be cross-referenced with reality.

15.5.2 During the Meeting

After the first outing of the car, when the first data is available, the first thing to do is to cross-reference this data with the simulated data (which should be readily available from the pre-meeting simulations). It is important to check first that the car is behaving as expected. Big discrepancies between the simulation and reality might indicate a technical problem, as the model was validated before. For example, roll stiffness distribution can be quickly checked by comparing simulated versus real roll gradient and roll angle ratio.

In most cases, when the car is working as expected, the cross-referencing should be not more than a simple sanity check. Between sessions, the simulation can help to validate the setup decisions of the engineer by performing what-if scenarios. During a test or race, meeting time is typically limited and the larger analysis work is done in the evening or on return in the workshop. The simulation software serves in these cases as a calculator for the engineer to help him make decisions concerning vehicle setup and take out a large part of the guesswork. A good log of the simulation runs and results should be kept for later reference.

15.5.3   After the Meeting

After the race or test, the engineer should go over the run sheets again and reevaluate the simulation results against the logged data. First of all, this will allow the engineer to investigate and explain any possible secondary effects on the changes that were performed (for example, a ride height change without camber compensation).

The final step is to use the real data to further improve the simulation model, especially in the following areas:

- Validation of aerodynamic performance and optimization of the aeromaps
- Reexamination of the track bump profile (sometimes this will already need to be done during the race weekend or test)
- Revalidate and fine-tune the tire model

Finally, setups can now be tested outside of the physically available adjustment range, and the results will motivate decisions to perform significant alterations to the vehicle.

15.6   Putting the Driver in the Simulation

Most simulations do not include a driver model and assume that the car is being driven at the grip limit at all times. It will inevitably occur from time to time that lap time simulation will result in a car setup that in theory will give the fastest lap time but in reality can't be handled by the driver. The way a driver perceives the car by force feedback in the steering wheel, visual cues, the perception of yaw rate through the back and bottom of his body, vibrations, sounds, and so on plays a big part of the equation that defines the ultimate performance of car and driver combination. If the car is giving the driver information that he is unable to process correctly, his resulting actions will have a negative effect on this performance and the effectiveness of the simulated setup will not be attained.

Technology is nowadays available to actually put the driver inside the simulation (driver-in-the-loop). The vehicle's subsystems (engine, driveline, aerodynamics) are all quite straightforward to model mathematically, and enough knowledge is available to come up with decent tire models. When this mathematical model can run with externally provided input parameters for driver activity (steering, throttle, brake, and gear change) the driver can actually "drive" the simulation model. In its most basic form, this is a video game.

However, current developments in driver-in-the-loop simulation are advancing rapidly. Most Formula One teams have at present a driving simulator in their factories and work relentlessly on validation of the car model against the real car. Professional drivers are actually hired for this purpose on a full-time basis. Drivers and teams have the possibility to rent driving time in a simulator at specialized companies. With the ever-increasing limitations on track testing, this kind of simulation is becoming more important as a substitute for teams to develop driver, car, and engineer.

This section attempts to give the reader an insight on two types of driver-in-the-loop simulation and shows how the techniques to analyze logged data that are covered in this book are one-to-one transferable to the virtual racetrack.

15.6.1 Sim Racing

Current auto racing simulations can hardly be considered as computer games anymore. Continuous development of the physics engine and hardware has made these applications come very close to reality. The mathematical models of the car have become increasingly detailed, complete with real-life variables such as tire wear, fuel consumption, and vehicle setup. Driving in a simulation requires an understanding from the driver of all the aspects of vehicle behavior seen in real-world racing. A lot of professional race drivers use this type of simulation with considerable success as a training aid to prepare for race weekends. They are joined by ten thousands of users all over the world in online communities organizing virtual racing leagues.

iRacing.com (Figure 15.24) is an example of an online subscription-based racing simulation that offers a realistic racing experience by offering exclusively cars that were licensed by their respective manufacturers and accurate laser-scanned track models. It was marketed from the start as both an entertainment service and as a training tool for real-world drivers. In July 2012 there were 35,000 active members [15-3].

Figure 15.24 Screenshot of the iRacing.com online racing simulation (Courtesy of iRacing.com)

A lot of sim racing providers offer the possibility to use telemetry and data-logging, and depending on the complexity of the physics engine there are generally a large amount of logged parameters available that would be very difficult or expensive to measure on a real race car.

In 2006 the Swedish company SimBin Development released GTR with data acquisition output that could be directly read in MoTeC's i2 analysis software. Nowadays it has become standard practice for serious racing simulations to provide data that can be read by professional analysis software. In 2011 iRacing.com partnered with McLaren Electronic Systems to incorporate their ATLAS Express analysis software into its system, meaning that their sim racing community now has access to the same data acquisition software as used in Formula One and NASCAR [15-4]. Table 15.8 gives an overview of the available channels in iRacing.com, which are all sampled at 60 Hz.

Table 15.8 iRacing.com data acquisition parameters	
Category	Parameter
General	Vehicle speed
	Running lap time
	Lap distance
Driver Activity	Braking force
	Clutch engagement
	Gear
	Throttle position
	Steering wheel angle
Inertial Signals	Lateral acceleration
	Longitudinal acceleration
	Vertical acceleration
	Yaw rate
	Yaw angle
Chassis and Suspension	Suspension movement
	Ride height
	Pitch angle (at vehicle's center of gravity)
	Pitch rate
	Roll angle (at vehicle's center of gravity)
	Roll rate
	Longitudinal velocity
	Lateral velocity
	Vertical velocity
	Steering wheel torque
Tires	Tire surface temperature inside/middle/outside
	Tire pressure
	Separate wheel speeds

Table 15.8 iRacing.com data acquisition parameters (Continued)	
Category	Parameter
GPS Variables	Latitude
	Longitude
	Altitude
Engine Parameters and Vital Signals	Fuel level
	Fuel pressure
	Engine manifold pressure
	Engine oil level
	Engine oil pressure
	Engine oil temperature
	Engine RPM
	Shift light indication
	Battery voltage
	Water level
	Water temperature

Figures 15.25 and 15.26 show logged data of a Williams FW31 Formula One car and a VW Jetta TDI, respectively, driven around Interlagos in iRacing.com. Figure 15.25 shows speed, yaw rate, steering angle, lateral and longitudinal acceleration, and the vehicle's velocity components in longitudinal and lateral direction for the FW31. In Figure 15.26 the tire surface temperatures of the Jetta are illustrated.

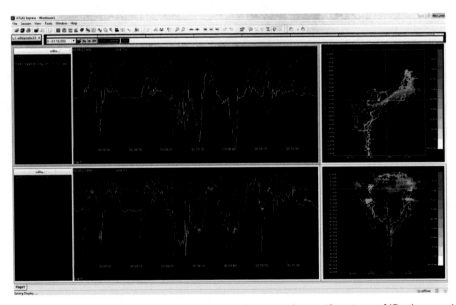

Figure 15.25 Simulated data of the Williams FW31 at Interlagos (Courtesy of iRacing.com)

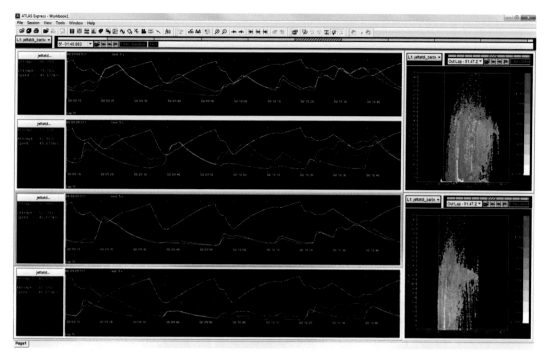

Figure 15.26 Simulated data of the VW Jetta TDI at Interlagos (Courtesy of iRacing.com)

It is self-explanatory that with this amount of data available to use in professional analysis software, all the techniques covered in this book are one-to-one applicable in racing simulations to the same extent they are in real-world racing.

For a racing team, this form of simulation does not allow them to profoundly manipulate the mathematical model of the car as with lap time simulation software. A large number of parameters needs to be considered as a given. However, this does not mean that there is no benefit to be had from sim racing, even for professional teams. Integration of sim racing activities in a professional racing environment can bring the following benefits:

- Advanced sensor signals are available in the simulation, which can be used to study vehicle behavior, create math channels, and so forth before investing in sensor hardware for the real car.

- Sim racing provides a training tool for engineers. Vehicle dynamics and data analysis techniques can be studied without the need for a real car to create the data. By putting the engineer behind the wheel, a feeling for setup changes can be developed.

- Racing simulations can be used to create the data necessary to develop track models for lap time simulation in cases where a new track is to be visited, of which no data is available.

An example of how good the correlation between the physics of a racing simulation and the corresponding real car can be is shown in Figure 15.27. These graphs show the vehicle speed and lateral acceleration traces of a Corvette C6R GT1 around the Brazilian Interlagos track. Although there are some discrepancies between the real data (in red) and the simulated data (in green), such as the cornering speed in low-speed corners, the simulated data can be useful for different types of analysis. Figure 15.28 shows a detailed

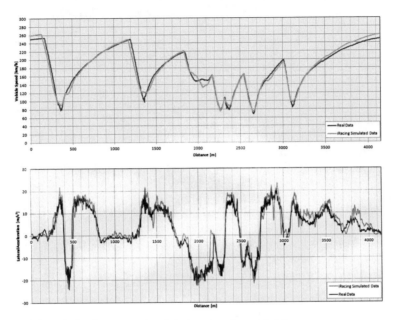

Figure 15.27 Correlation between simulated and real-world data

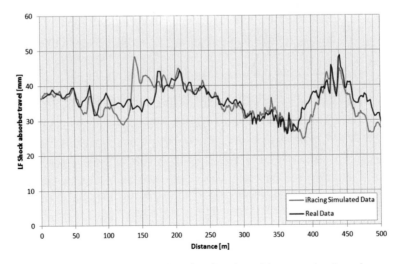

Figure 15.28 Correlation between simulated and real-world suspension travel

view of the left-front suspension travel signal in the first corner. Here again there are some differences, mainly in the suspension movement caused by inertial reactions of the chassis (including braking points and cornering force), but the high-speed correlation (bumps in the track surface) is remarkable.

15.6.2 Motion-Based Driver-in-the-Loop Simulation

Hardware and software developments, high-quality mathematical models of both the car and track, and good correlation with actual data will produce predictable results from simulation. However, in the middle of all this is the driver. To enhance the simulation experience, a driver needs to be subjected to the same feelings he has in a real race car. Visual and audio cues from the car are quite straightforward to provide to the driver, but the feeling of acceleration, cornering forces, yaw rate and angle, track surface condition, and so on are more complex to mimic. Motion platforms such as the one shown in Figure 15.29 are usually linked to the dynamic vehicle model, which gives the user the ability to feel how the vehicle would respond to control inputs. However, no motion platform can provide the full g-forces and torques that an actual vehicle can. A simulator must therefore "trick" the driver's brain.

Moving at a constant velocity is not perceived differently than sitting in a chair. Change of velocity, or acceleration, is perceived as force acting on the human body. The driver's vestibular system (inner ear) is manipulated by using the gravity acceleration vector as a replacement for the "real" acceleration by tilting the motion platform in combination with visual, audio, and vibration input.

Figure 15.29 Motion-based simulator (Courtesy of Bhai Tech Advanced Vehicle Science)

With the growing limitations on track testing in many series, this type of simulation is offering an increasingly accurate substitute for development. Driver-in-the-loop simulation is not only beneficial for driver and vehicle development but can also be used to evaluate the engineer's skills. Complete scenarios of test days or races including various strategy options can be simulated to train the engineer in making correct decisions when placed in a real event.

Chapter 16
Using the Data Acquisition System for Race Strategy

On race day, the engineer should be armed with enough knowledge to predetermine a race strategy. This knowledge also allows the engineer to be flexible when circumstances change during the race. Fuel consumption, tire wear, and driver consistency should be investigated to obtain the necessary knowledge. This chapter discusses methods for analyzing these parameters.

16.1   Fuel Consumption

During the practice sessions preceding a race, the engineer wants to address the following questions concerning the vehicle's fuel economy.

1. How much fuel is consumed per lap?
   In racing, fuel consumption commonly is not expressed in liters/100 km, as with road-going vehicles. On a racetrack, it is important to know what the consumption per lap will be.

2. How many laps can be completed on a tank?
   This number determines the amount of fuel that should be in the tank to complete the race. When refueling is necessary during the race, this figure determines the minimum amount of stops that must be made and establishes the pit stop window.

3. What is the weight penalty resulting from fuel load? What influence does this have on lap time?
   The performance potential of the vehicle changes as the fuel load changes during the race. A lighter load helps decrease lap times. As the fuel level drops, the car's center of gravity decreases in height. If the car does not have a centrally located fuel cell, it also changes longitudinally. This modifies the vehicle's balance.

It goes without saying that data acquisition can be a valuable tool that helps to answer these questions. Fuel consumption can be measured by the data acquisition system in several ways. The simplest solution is measuring the tank level. The quality of the sensor mounting in the fuel tank determines how useful this signal is.

Another way is to assess the fuel flow between the tank and the engine, both on the supply and return pipe. The difference between the two is the amount of fuel burned by the engine. Care should be taken with this measurement because the temperature of the fuel supplied to the engine may differ from that of the fuel returning to the tank in the return pipe. This modifies the fuel density; temperature compensation in the flow measurement is necessary to obtain an accurate result.

Most modern motor sport ECUs have a programmed algorithm for calculating fuel usage. The ECU software uses a three-dimensional fuel injection table as shown in Figure 16.1 to determine injector timing for every possible engine RPM and load. Every time an injector opens, the fuel passing through it equals the injector opening time multiplied by the flow rate of the injector. The sum of the amount of fuel for all injectors during a certain time period is the fuel consumed.

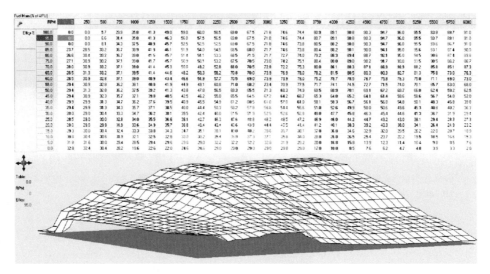

Figure 16.1 ECU fuel injection table

A variable containing total injector opening time as a function of elapsed time is stored primarily by the ECU, leaving it to the user to scale this variable to the liters used. Figure 16.2 shows an example of this in the MoTeC Dash Manager Software.

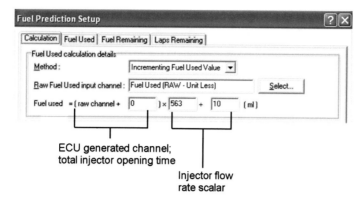

Figure 16.2 MoTeC Dash Manager fuel prediction calculation

From this, the following variables can be calculated by math channels:

• Amount of fuel used

• Amount of fuel left in the tank

• Amount of fuel used per lap

• Laps remaining on fuel tank

To make effective use of the fuel consumption data, the results have to be continuously checked against reality. This will not only guarantee the accuracy of the calculation, but it can also enable you to detect possible problems early enough (such as malfunctioning injector and faulty lambda regulation). There are two ways to do this:

• Measure the volume of fuel going in the tank before the start of and during a session and do the same for the fuel coming out at the end of the session

• Measure the weight and temperature of the fuel going in the tank before the start of and during a session and do the same for the fuel coming out at the end of the session. The used volume of fuel can then be calculated with the temperature dependent fuel density.

The first option is the least accurate method. The problem is that the fuel that goes in the tank before and during the session will often be at a different temperature compared with the fuel that comes out after the session. Fluids will change their volume according to their temperature, so merely measuring the volumes will not take this temperature dependency into account. When there is no difference in temperature between the fuel going in the tank and the fuel coming out, simply measuring the volume will not induce any additional error. However, when there is a temperature difference, the induced errors can become quite significant.

Therefore it's preferable to measure the weight of the fuel going in and coming out and at the same time measure the temperature of the fuel. Be sure to use a scale that's accurate to ±0.010 kg. Fuel temperature can be measured with a pyrometer or a fluid thermometer. By measuring the fuel temperature we can calculate the density of the fuel compared to standard conditions with Equation 16.1.

$$\frac{\Delta V}{V} = \left(\frac{1}{1 - a\frac{T_{fuel} - 15}{\rho_{15}}} \right) - 1 \qquad \text{(Eq. 16.1)}$$

Where V = Fuel volume [l]

    T_{fuel} = Fuel temperature [°C]

    ρ_{15} = Fuel density at 15 °C [kg/l]

    a = constant = 0.0008

To illustrate the magnitude of the temperature effect on fuel volume, Equation 16.1 is used to calculate the volume variation of 100 l of fuel across a temperature range of 50 °C. The initial conditions are the following:

Fuel volume = 100 l

Fuel temperature = 15 °C

Fuel density at 15 °C = 0.750 kg/l

The results are shown in Figure 16.3.

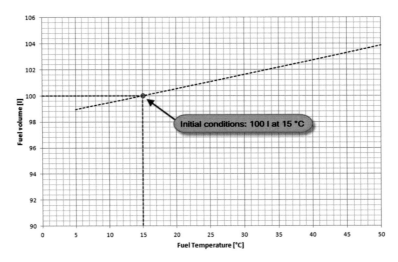

Figure 16.3 Volume variation of 100 l of fuel versus temperature

When the temperature effect on the fuel volume is taken into account, the fuel consumption can be estimated with much higher accuracy. The following example considers the fuel consumption of a GT1 car during a practice session. The measured values and consumption figures from the logged data are given in Table 16.1.

Table 16.1 Fuel drain and consumption figures from logged data for a GT1 free practice session	
Parameter	Value
Fuel density ρ_{15} at 15 °C	0.757 kg/l
Total fuel tank volume	96 l
Covered amount of laps during session	30
Fuel added before session	59.50 kg at 26 °C
Fuel added during session	45.23 kg at 32 °C
Fuel drained from car after session	24.48 kg at 41 °C
Fuel used calculation from data	106.16 l

The total amount of fuel used during the session is 59.50 kg + 45.23 kg – 24.48 kg = 80.25 kg.

The weight of the fuel is independent of its temperature, but to calculate the volume used, the temperature needs to be taken into account using Equation 16.1. The fuel that went into the tank at the start of the session was 59.50 kg with a temperature of 26° C. The volume correction factor is:

$$\frac{\Delta V}{V}+1=\frac{1}{1-0.0008\frac{(26-15)}{0.757}}=1.012$$

The volume of fuel is therefore:

$$\frac{59.50\,\text{kg}}{0.757\,\text{kg/l}}\cdot1.012=79.54\ \text{l}$$

During the session, 45.23 kg of fuel was added with a temperature of 32 °C.

$$\frac{\Delta V}{V}+1=\frac{1}{1-0.0008\frac{(32-15)}{0.757}}=1.018$$

$$\frac{45.23\,\text{kg}}{0.757\,\text{kg/L}}\cdot1.018=60.82\,\text{L}$$

The fuel that was drained from the tank after the session weighed 24.48 kg and the temperature measured at 41 °C.

$$\frac{\Delta V}{V} + 1 = \frac{1}{1 - 0.0008\dfrac{(41-15)}{0.757}} = 1.028$$

$$\frac{24.48\,\text{kg}}{0.757\,\text{kg/l}} \cdot 1.028 = 33.241$$

Finally, the used fuel volume becomes 79.54 + 60.82 − 33.24 = 107.12 l. The lap consumption is:

$$\frac{107.12}{30} = 3.57\ \text{l/Lap}$$

With a maximum fuel tank volume of 96 l, this lap consumption means that 96/3.57 = 26.89 laps can be done with a full tank. Practically, this number is rounded down to 26 laps as the car's fuel autonomy.

The logged data showed a total consumption of 106.16 l, which is 99.1% of the consumption determined from the drain figures. The fuel consumption calculation in the ECU was configured with the following parameters:

$$\text{Fuel Used} = \text{Total injection time} \cdot \frac{\text{Injector flow rate scalar}}{100}$$

In this example, for the injector flow rate scalar a value of 884 was chosen. To improve the accuracy of the fuel consumption calculation this value should be changed to:

$$884 \cdot \frac{1}{0.991} = 892$$

Keep in mind that in the preceding calculation, all laps entering and exiting the pit lane were taken into account. Generally, during these laps less fuel will be used compared to a lap at full speed. These laps can be taken out of the calculation only after the accuracy of the ECU calculated total fuel consumption is validated. If the accuracy of this volume is sufficient, the lap-by-lap consumption values can be taken from the data, as illustrated in Figure 16.4.

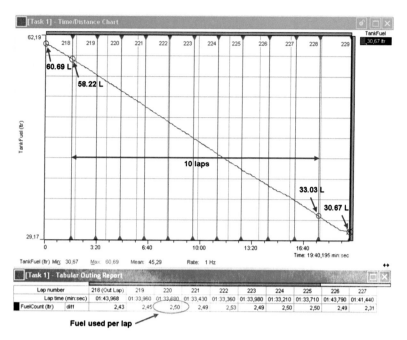

Figure 16.4 Fuel level of a GT1 car for a 12-lap run around Zhuhai

16.2 Lap Time Variation During a Race

Depending on various parameters such as the race duration, number of cars on the track, position in the field, and weather conditions, the lap times of a given race car can vary significantly during a race. Besides this, the ultimate performance of the car/driver combination will also change during a race, and this is mainly influenced by the following items:

- Grip decrease due to tire degradation

- Changing total vehicle weight due to fuel consumption and refueling during pit stops

- Driver condition and endurance

These parameters will have an important impact on the race strategy when it comes to pit stop planning, tire choice, and refueling amount, and the logged data can provide the strategist with useful information.

16.2.1 Fuel Load Variation

As explained earlier in this chapter, the variation of fuel load is directly connected to the total weight of the car, which will have a significant impact on the car's performance.

Because the location of the center of gravity changes, depending on the fuel tank location in the car, the variation in fuel load might also change the car's balance.

The question that needs to be answered is how much quicker will the car become as more fuel is being used. The easiest method to answer this question is to use lap time simulation and perform a parameter study of total vehicle weight versus lap time (see chapter 15). Depending on the complexity of the vehicle, model changes in the location of the center of gravity can be taken into account in the simulation as well. The result will generally be a linear function such as the one in Figure 16.5. These simulation results tell us that with an (almost) empty fuel tank the car is able to do a lap time of 103.47 sec. With a full tank the best possible lap time becomes 104.60 sec. Linear interpolation between these two values shows that every kilogram of fuel being used improves the lap time potential of the car with 0.0142 sec. Assuming a fuel density of 0.75 l/kg this value can be expressed in relation to used liters and becomes 0.0142 · 0.75 = 0.01 sec per liter.

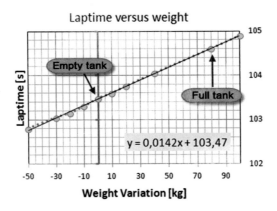

Figure 16.5 Simulation results for lap time against variations in total vehicle weight

16.2.2 Tire Wear

Tire wear is the second important factor for developing a race strategy. The performance of the tires over the race distance is not constant. The overall grip level decreases. If tire wear is greater on one axle, the car's balance changes as well.

To measure the effect of tire degradation, record longer runs during the practice sessions preceding the race. Grip and balance then can be investigated over the lifetime of a tire set. The following questions should be answered to obtain information on the lifetime of a set of tires.

- From the time they are new, how many laps are completed before the performance of the tires peak?

- In which lap are the highest grip levels recorded?

- From the performance peak, what is the drop-off in grip as a function of the lap number?

- What is the realistic maximum number of laps this tire set is going to last?

- In which direction is the balance of the car developing (oversteer or understeer)? Which axle produces the highest tire wear?

- What is the average possible lap time over the life of the tire set?

Figures 16.6 and 16.7 illustrate the performance of three drivers during a three-hour GT race on the Dubai Motodrom. The car in question was a 600-hp rear-wheel drive vehicle. The first illustration represents the lap times achieved by the three drivers. The race was split into three stints, each beginning with a full fuel tank and a new set of tires made of the same compound. The end of the second stint was interrupted by a safety car situation. The average lap times for each driver are given in Table 16.2. In and out laps and the laps completed under the safety car were not taken into account. The first driver is the fastest, with the slowest of the three tackling the middle stint. Assuming similar conditions, the second driver loses approximately 1.4 sec to the quickest driver, and the third driver limits this difference to 0.5 sec.

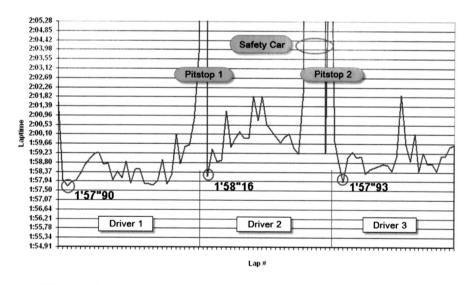

Figure 16.6 Lap time graph of a three-hour GT race in Dubai

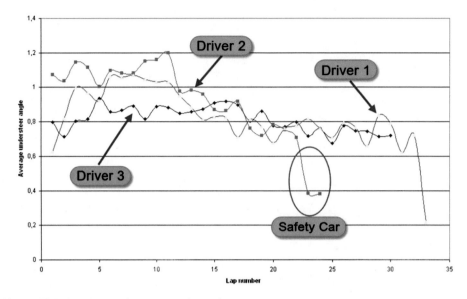

Figure 16.7 Average understeer angle per lap

	Table 16.2 Average race lap time and average understeer angle per driver	
	Average Lap Time	Average Understeer Angle
Driver 1	1'58"56	0.85 °
Driver 2	1'59"99	0.97 °
Driver 3	1'59"05	0.81 °

During the first stint, the driver complains about a diabolic understeer for the first 30% of the covered laps. The situation improves once the driver adjusts his driving style to the changing balance. This is evident in Figure 16.6. During the first ten laps of the race, there is a drop-off from the fastest lap (which was achieved in the third race lap) of 1.3 sec. After that, the times come down and the driver begins to record some high 57s again. During the last quarter of the stint (after approximately 24 laps), tire wear becomes noticeable as the lap times increase significantly.

The second stint shows a similar pattern. The difference here is that the stint generally is slower, and it takes until the middle of the stint before the tire set reaches its second life. The driver has more difficulty adapting to the changing situation. The third driver has the least difficulty coping with the understeering characteristic.

The first driver's comments are confirmed in Figure 16.7. Here the average understeer angle per lap is plotted. The higher the understeer angle, the more understeer the vehicle is developing. In Table 16.2, the average understeer angle for each driver's complete stint is calculated, illustrating that the second driver deals with the highest degree of understeer (or is inducing the most understeer through a specific driving style). This is confirmed in the graph.

All three drivers are confronted with increasing understeer for the first 10–15 laps in their stint. After that, the balance begins to develop into increasing oversteer, probably assisted by the decreasing fuel load on the rear axle. The third driver has the most consistent balance over a complete stint, but eventually the third driver's average lap time is 0.5 sec slower than that of the first driver.

The preceding example makes it clear that it is quite difficult to isolate the effects of tire wear on lap time from the fuel load effect and—more importantly—the performance of the driver. A good technique to get an idea about tire degradation before the race is to collect mileage information of all the tire sets used in the practice sessions, including qualifying. This way, generally data will be available from tires ranging from new to end of lifetime. Run charts can then be used to link them to the logged data. Examples are given in Figures 16.8 and 16.9 where overall grip factor (see chapter 8) and lap time are plotted against tire mileage (expressed in covered laps). The upper boundary for grip factor and lower boundary for lap time indicated by the dashed lines show a clear correlation to tire mileage. The scatter above and below these lines, respectively, include the side effects resulting from fuel load, traffic, track conditions, driver consistency, and so on.

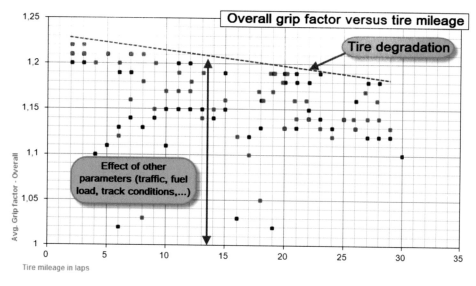

Figure 16.8 Overall grip factor as function of tire mileage

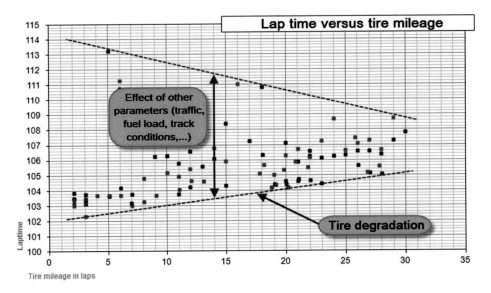

Figure 16.9 Lap time as function of tire mileage

16.2.3 Driver Consistency

The example in the previous section perfectly illustrates how drivers must adapt to changing situations. Driver consistency is the third important factor in a race strategy. A driver can be faster than the competition in a qualifying lap, but over a race distance a driver might have a greater degradation in lap times. Of course, the physical condition of the driver plays a major role in this. Problems with fitness and concentration often are indicated in the data as driver error. Gear-shifting mistakes, changes in throttle blipping, earlier-than-normal braking points, and other abnormalities can indicate a fatigued driver. See chapter 14 for more details on driver analysis.

Chapter 17
Data Analysis Using Metrics

These days it is easier to measure a large number of signals with a data logging system. This is obviously useless if the user is unable to analyze the resulting data, and the biggest problem is often a lack of time. Therefore a method is needed to present the data in such a way that important portions of it are quickly detectable and conclusions can be made fast and efficiently. Extracting metrics from the data and visualizing them in run charts are effective techniques when it comes to efficient data analysis. Throughout this book, many examples were given of run charts with lap metrics. In this chapter, the methods to create reliable statistics from the logged data are explained.

17.1   What Are Metrics?

Metrics can be compared to the concept of key performance indicators (KPIs) used to measure the progress made by an organization [17-1]. KPIs are quantifiable measurements, defined beforehand, that reflect the relative success of an organization compared with a predefined benchmark. Business examples of KPIs include deliveries made on time for a distribution company, telephone calls answered within a certain time in a call center, and graduation rates of students for schools.

The same principle can be applied in motor racing. A possible KPI could be the average season position on the starting grid of a car. The logged data inherently contains critical information about the performance of the car and driver, so it becomes possible to extract KPIs from the recorded information. For example, if it is known that a tire develops its maximum grip when the thread surface has a temperature between 70 and 80 degrees, a possible KPI is the time per lap that the tire temperature is within this range. More time spent within this range means better tire performance, so this KPI can be used to determine the effectiveness of setup options.

However, metrics are more than merely KPIs. Extracting statistics from the logged data provides us with a way to summarize very large amounts of data into meaningful numbers. By visualizing these statistics in run charts the data can be investigated through a bird's-eye perspective, and trends or potential problems can be quickly detected. This is a very effective method that points an engineer directly to those parts of the data that matter.

Metrics are typically statistical parameters that are related to the time or distance of one lap. Some examples are:

- Average throttle position per lap
- Percentage of lap distance spent braking
- Percentage of lap time that brake temperature exceeds a certain threshold

However, metrics can also be defined that are specific for a fixed location on the track. Some examples:

- Aerodynamic measurements on a straight, for example the calculation of front and rear downforce between distance a and b
- Minimum corner speed in a specific turn of the track

17.2   Why Use Metrics?

Typically, we will have one metric per completed lap. This makes metrics ideally suited to display them in run charts. A run chart is a time-based graph where time is expressed as lap number. By displaying data in a run chart, large amounts of data can be summarized into one simple graphic. Trends can be easily detected from this type of chart. Examples are given in Figures 17.1 and 17.2. The first figure shows a part of a ten-lap run with speed and understeer angle channels pictured. Although the information is present in the graph, it is very difficult to see from this type of visualization in which direction the balance of the car develops over time. Figure 17.2 shows a run chart in which

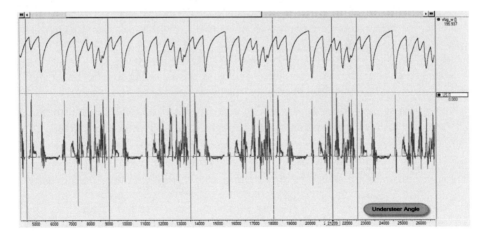

Figure 17.1 Distance graph of speed and understeer angle

the average value of the understeer angle channel is given for each completed lap. This graph makes it abundantly clear that the car is developing toward oversteer over the ten-lap distance.

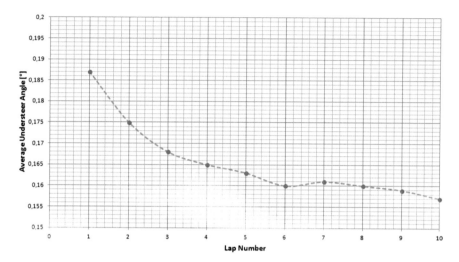

Figure 17.2 Run chart with the average value of understeer angle per lap

The example in Figure 17.2 covered a ten-lap period, but this can easily be increased to a complete race event, as illustrated in Figure 17.3.

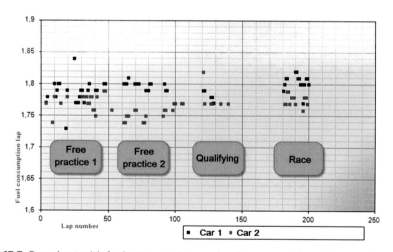

Figure 17.3 Run chart with fuel consumption per lap for a complete racing event

Another advantage of using metrics is that they can be plotted against lap time. This way, the effect of a specific parameter can be directly related to the car's ultimate performance. Figure 17.4 shows the integral of the steering angle plotted against lap time for five different cars for the duration of a complete race weekend. This graph indicates that more understeer (a higher steering angle integral) results in slower lap times for these cars.

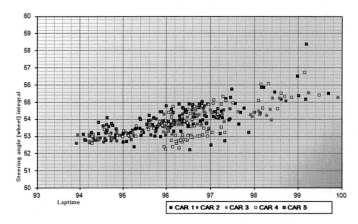

Figure 17.4 Steering angle integral for five different cars versus lap time

17.3   How to Create Metrics

The first step in metrics analysis is to determine which parameters we want to extract from the data. Metrics are basically statistical parameters, and in their simplest form the definition can be done quite straightforward in the analysis software. For example, the average, minimum, or maximum channel values normally do not require any manipulation by the user and can be defined in an outing report as pictured in Figure 17.5. This table can then be exported into an external software package capable of creating run charts (such as Excel or Matlab).

		Lap 1 [1:30.739]	Lap 2 [1:27.474]	Lap 3 [1:24.877]	Lap 4 [1:25.352]	Lap 5 [1:22.385]	Lap 6 [1:22.661]
	Avg	121.2	125.5	129.1	128.4	132.9	132.5
Ground Speed [km/h]	Min	58.4	58.7	60.0	57.4	57.0	56.8
	Max	212.4	218.4	219.9	222.8	223.9	222.9
RPM [rpm]	Min	2352	2502	2502	2484	2508	2412
	Max	6174	6354	6384	6372	6396	6270
Eng Oil Pres [bar]	Min	4.539	3.986	3.760	3.406	3.254	3.173
	Max	6.163	5.841	5.573	5.328	5.189	5.187
Eng Oil Temp [°C]	Min	82.0	61.9	97.1	101.6	105.2	103.9
	Max	90.4	97.2	101.9	105.5	108.7	109.6
Engine Temp [°C]	Min	76.9	81.1	84.6	87.0	88.8	89.7
	Max	81.1	84.6	87.0	89.0	89.7	91.3

Figure 17.5 Outing report with simple statistical values taken from raw signals

It becomes a bit more complicated when specific conditions are imposed on some lap statistics. Sometimes parts of the data need to be excluded from the signal before calculating a statistical value from it. For example, we attempt to determine a lap statistic that gives us the average lateral acceleration when a car is cornering to the left. Figure

17.6 shows a lap of a GT car around Interlagos. The lower trace is the lateral G signal where positive values mean that the car is in a left-hand corner. We want to determine the average of the lateral G signal on the positive side of the graph. This means that the negative values need to be ignored in the calculation. For this, a mathematical channel can be created that evaluates the sign of the signal, ignores the negative values, and only shows lateral acceleration when it's positive:

$$G_{lat}(+) = G_{lat} \cdot (G_{lat} > 0) \qquad \text{(Eq. 17.1)}$$

The result of this math channel is shown in Figure 17.7.

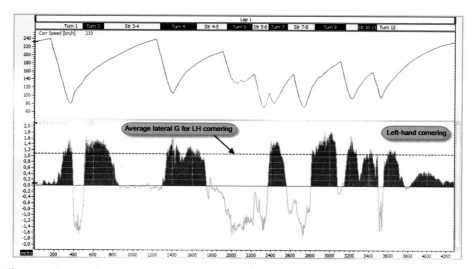

Figure 17.6 Speed and lateral acceleration for a lap around Interlagos

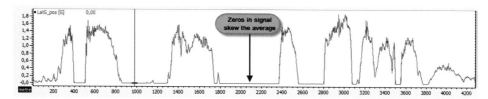

Figure 17.7 Math channel displaying lateral acceleration only when it is larger than zero

Although the negative acceleration values have now been removed from the original signal, another problem prevents us from taking an accurate average. Whenever the signal is not positive, it is replaced by the value zero. This means that depending on the sampling frequency of the original signal and the calculation rate of the math channel, a very large amount of zeros will skew the average to a lower value than expected. The original channel therefore needs to be manipulated differently in order to exclude data when the car is cornering to the right or not cornering at all. Some software packages

447

allow signal discontinuity (in other words, allow a channel to have no value). It is then possible to ignore data based on certain criteria and to replace these data with "nothing." This is called signal gating. In Figure 17.8 the lateral acceleration is gated for values above 0.1 G. Every data sample that doesn't exceed this value is deleted, causing areas of discontinuity in the channel. This math channel is well suited for taking the lap average.

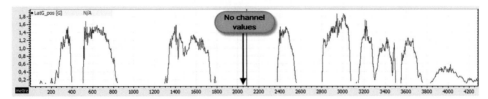

Figure 17.8 Gated lateral acceleration signal

Unfortunately, most of the data analysis software packages currently on the market do not allow channel discontinuities, so another solution needs to be proposed. As we want to calculate an average, we will first calculate the sum of all lateral acceleration values exceeding 0.1 G (Equation 17.2). Next, a second channel is created that calculates the amount of samples in the signal for which this condition is true. This can be done by taking the summation of each sample in a channel with a constant value of "one" when the correct condition is met according to Equation 17.3 (see Figure 17.9).

$$\mathrm{sigma}\left(G_{lat}\right) G_{lat} > 0.1 = \sum_{0}^{n}\left(G_{lat} \cdot (G_{lat} > 0.1)\right) \tag{Eq. 17.2}$$

$$\mathrm{samples}(n) \, G_{lat} > 0.1 = \sum_{0}^{n}\left(1 \cdot (G_{lat} > 0.1)\right) \tag{Eq. 17.3}$$

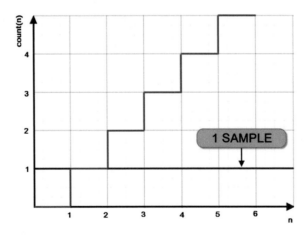

Figure 17.9 Sample counting by summation of a channel with a constant value of one

In these equations, n is the total amount of signal samples for the lateral G signal in a complete lap.

The average acceleration value is obtained by dividing the last value in the lap of the first channel by the last channel of the second. Both channels need to be reset to zero at the beginning of each lap to start the calculation of the average for the next lap. The syntax to obtain these math channels will vary from one software package to another. A flow chart explaining the different steps and conditions is given for each channel in Figures 17.10 and 17.11. If the analysis software math channel capabilities do not include sample-by-sample summation, the lateral acceleration channel can also be integrated against time during the correct conditions, and the result then multiplied by the sampling frequency. Care should be taken in this case that the calculation rate of the math channel is the same as the sampling frequency of the lateral G signal.

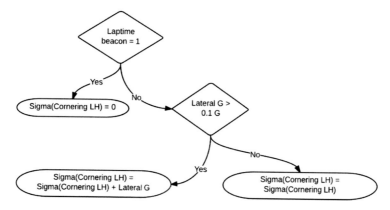

Figure 17.10 Flow chart for conditional summation of lateral G signal

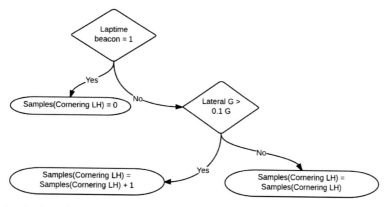

Figure 17.11 Flow chart for conditional sample counting of lateral G signal

Very often, lap statistics are time values such as the time per lap spent at full throttle or time per lap that tire temperature is in a specified range. A math channel for time can be easily created by integrating a channel with a constant value of one against time (Figure 17.12). To calculate the time at full throttle per lap, Equation 17.4 applies.

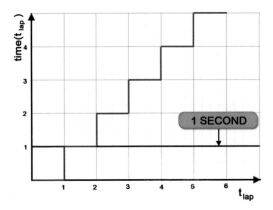

Figure 17.12 Calculation of a time signal by integrating a channel with a constant value of one against lap time

$$\text{time}\left(t_{\text{lap}}\right) TP > 98 = \int_{0}^{t_{\text{lap}}} \left(1 \cdot (TP > 98)\right) \qquad \text{(Eq. 17.4)}$$

In this equation t_{lap} is the running lap time and TP the throttle position signal. Figure 17.13 shows an example of this math channel. The last value in the lap is the full throttle time to be used in statistic reports.

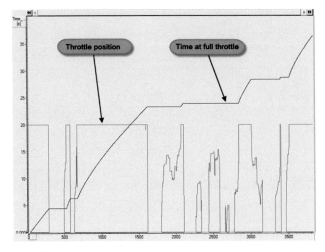

Figure 17.13 Full throttle time math channel

Similarly to time calculation, we can determine the distance during which a certain condition is true. Instead of integrating a constant value of one against time, we now integrate it against distance (Figure 17.14). For example, the braking distance per lap can be defined with Equation 17.5.

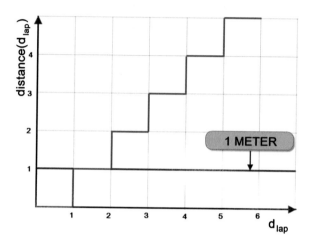

Figure 17.14 Calculation of a distance signal by integrating a channel with a constant value of one against lap distance

$$\text{distance}(d_{\text{lap}})\,P\text{Brake} > 5 = \int_{0}^{d_{\text{lap}}} \left(1 \cdot (P\text{Brake} > 5)\right) \qquad \text{(Eq. 17.5)}$$

Where d_{lap} = Lap distance
           $P\text{Brake}$ = Brake pressure

Time per lap or distance per lap that a specific condition is true is best presented in statistical tables as a percentage of the lap time or lap distance, respectively. As there will inevitably be some variation in lap time and distance, presenting it as a percentage keeps these statistics comparable from one lap to the other.

The metrics to extract from the data depend largely on what kind of analysis is being performed. Table 17.1 gives some examples of what is possible.

Table 17.1 Possible metrics to extract from logged data	
Metric	Remarks
Lap time	
Fuel consumption per lap	
Total brake pressure	Max/Average
Time on brakes	As percentage of lap time
Braking distance	As percentage of lap distance
Braking aggressiveness	Average
Brake release smoothness	Average
Brake balance	Min/Max/Average
Throttle position	Average
Time at full throttle	As percentage of lap time
Throttle speed	Average
Time coasting	As percentage of lap time
Time on brakes and on throttle	As percentage of lap time
Top speed	
Time in each gear	As percentage of lap time
Acceleration left-hand/right-hand	Max/Average
Acceleration/deceleration	Max/Average
Grip factor overall	Average
Grip factor cornering	Average
Grip factor braking	Average
Grip factor traction	Average
Grip factor aerodynamic	Average
Engine RPM	Min/Max/Average
Steering smoothness	Average
Curvature	Average
Tire air pressure	Max
Tire air temperature	Max
Tire surface temperature	Min/max /average
Tire surface temperature difference between left-hand and right-hand wheels	Average
Roll gradient front/rear	Average
Roll ratio	Average
Roll speed front/rear	Average
Shock absorber time spent at high/low speed bump/ rebound	As percentage of lap time
Understeer angle	Average
Steering angle	Lap integral

Chapter 18
Track Data

So far in this book, logged data was used to analyze driver, vehicle, and tire performance. These data can also be used to gain some information about the racetrack. Some interesting parameters that are extracted from the data can be used as references to compare different tracks.

18.1 What Can Be Learned from the Data about the Racetrack?

The setup of a race car will depend on what track is being raced and the answers to the following questions:

- Is it a fast or slow track (top speed, average speed, many slow or fast corners)?
- Will mechanical or aerodynamic grip be the dominating factor in finding performance?
- What is the ratio between left-hand and right-hand corners?
- Is the track heavy on the brakes?
- Is the track heavy on the tires?
- What gears are used the most often?
- Is it a smooth or bumpy track?

Some questions can probably be answered without the need to analyze the logged data. Figure 18.1 shows the French Nogaro track. The length of the track is 3.45 km, and it consists of 13 turns, of which 5 are to the left and 8 to the right. From the track layout it is also clear that 2 of the fastest turns (1 and 13) are to the left, while all the right-hand corners are generally slow, with the exception of turn 6. However, turn 6 is a turn where the car's speed is not limited by the grip of the tires.

A simple distance plot of the track with the speed, gear, and lateral and longitudinal acceleration will reveal simple things such as the top speed, average speed, and minimum speed, but also maximum lateral and longitudinal accelerations and the number of gear changes per lap. For the Nogaro track, the information in Table 18.1 was taken from a distance plot of lap from a GT3 car (Figure 18.2).

Figure 18.1 Nogaro

Table 18.1 Nogaro track data	
Parameter	Value
Top speed	256 km/h
Average speed	163 km/h
Minimum speed	67 km/h
Number of gearshifts	22
Maximum lateral G in left-hand corners	2.37 G
Maximum lateral G in right-hand corners	2.00 G
Maximum longitudinal acceleration	0.84 G
Maximum longitudinal deceleration	−1.95 G

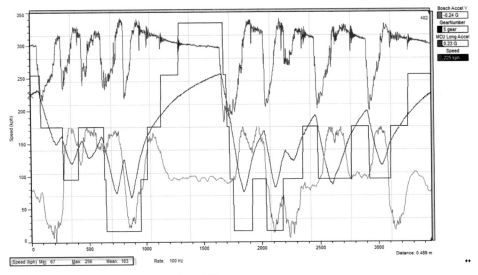

Figure 18.2 A lap around Nogaro in a GT3 car

18.2 Racetrack Metrics

Lap metrics such as the percentage of lap time that the brakes are applied or braking distance tells us if the track will be heavy on the brakes. The work W_{brakeTot} per lap can be calculated from Equations 18.1 and 18.2. The work of the brakes (expressed in Joule) is given by

$$W_{\text{brake}} = \left(\frac{1}{2} \cdot M \cdot V^2\right) \cdot (P\text{Brake} > 0) \qquad \text{(Eq. 18.1)}$$

In this equation, M is the total vehicle mass, V the car's velocity, and PBrake the brake pressure. For a complete lap, the total work done by the brakes becomes

$$W_{\text{brakeTot}} = \int_{0}^{t_{\text{lap}}} W_{\text{brake}} \cdot dt \qquad \text{(Eq. 18.2)}$$

The results of these math channels for the lap around Nogaro are shown in Figure 18.3. The last value of W_{brakeTot} is a lap metric that gives a good indication of how hard the brakes are being addressed. Obviously the total work done by the brakes depends on the type of car and the brake system configuration. For this particular car, the total work done by the brakes for a lap of Nogaro is 165.2 MJ.

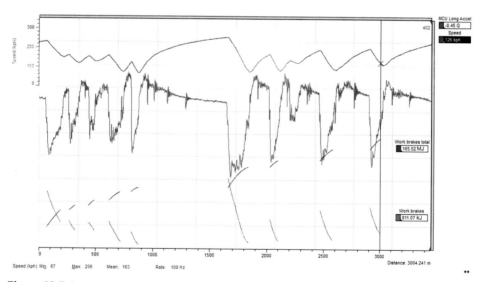

Figure 18.3 Instantaneous and total work of the brakes

The percentage of lap time spent at full throttle gives a good indication of how hard the engine will be stressed on a particular track. This car spends 26.1% of the lap time at full throttle. The back straight is where the engine is stressed the most as the car accelerates from 70 to 256 km/h.

18.3   Speed and Gear Histograms

The histograms in Figures 18.4 and 18.5 show how much each gear ratio is used during a lap and how much time is spent in different speed ranges. These two graphs can be useful in choosing the correct gear ratios. The speed histogram also gives a good indication of how important a role the aerodynamics will play at a specific track.

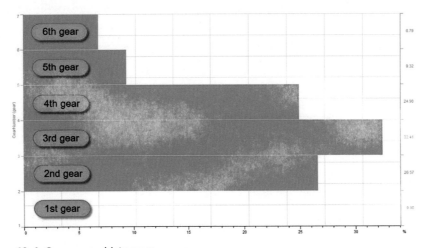

Figure 18.4 Gear usage histogram

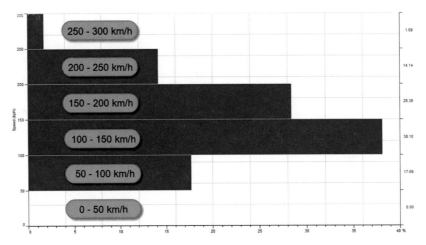

Figure 18.5 Speed histogram

18.4   The Friction Circle

The friction circle created from lateral and longitudinal acceleration data also contains significant information about the track characteristics. It shows quickly the maximum accelerations seen during cornering and acceleration or braking which were already calculated in Table 18.1. However, the density of data points in certain areas of the friction circle tells us something about how the tires are assessed. Figure 18.6 shows the friction circle for the lap around Nogaro. The lateral acceleration signal is positive for left-hand corners. In the graph, four sections are defined:

- Quadrant 1   Acceleration out of right-hand corners

- Quadrant 2   Acceleration out of left-hand corners

- Quadrant 3   Braking into right-hand corners

- Quadrant 4   Braking into left-hand corners

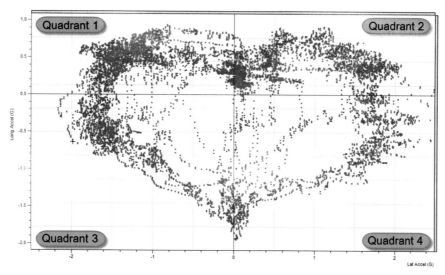

Figure 18.6 Friction circle for a lap of Nogaro

The density of data points in this friction circle is the highest in quadrant one. Which quadrant comes in second place is less clear, but it is either quadrant two or three. The density is the lowest in quadrant four.

Because of the fact that most friction is developed in quadrant one or while accelerating out of a right-hand corner, the left-rear tire is the one that is working the most of the four and will therefore probably show the highest wear rate. The necessary cold pressure with which this tire needs to be inflated to get to the correct hot pressure will probably be significantly less compared to the other three tires. More conclusions can be drawn from this information. A setup change that has a positive effect for braking into a left-hand corner will probably have less influence on the lap time compared with a setup change that helps acceleration out of right-hand corners, simply because there is less time spent in this condition. This means that the shape and distribution of points in the friction diagram can help the engineer decide about certain setup parameters. With the techniques explained in chapter 17, the time per lap that is spent in each quadrant of the friction circle can be calculated through Equations 18.3 to 18.6. For the Nogaro example, the results of these equations are presented in Table 18.2.

$$t_{Q1} = \left(\int_0^{t_{lap}} (1) \cdot (G_{lat} <= 0) \cdot (G_{long} > 0) \cdot dt \right) \cdot \frac{100}{t_{lap}} \qquad \text{(Eq. 18.3)}$$

$$t_{Q2} = \left(\int_0^{t_{lap}} (1) \cdot (G_{lat} > 0) \cdot (G_{long} > 0) \cdot dt \right) \cdot \frac{100}{t_{lap}} \qquad \text{(Eq. 18.4)}$$

$$t_{Q3} = \left(\int_0^{t_{lap}} (1) \cdot (G_{lat} <= 0) \cdot (G_{long} <= 0) \cdot dt \right) \cdot \frac{100}{t_{lap}} \qquad \text{(Eq. 18.5)}$$

$$t_{Q4} = \left(\int_0^{t_{lap}} (1) \cdot (G_{lat} > 0) \cdot (G_{long} <= 0) \cdot dt \right) \cdot \frac{100}{t_{lap}} \qquad \text{(Eq. 18.6)}$$

In these equations t_{lap} is the total lap time and t_{Q1-4} is the time spent in each quadrant expressed in percentage of total lap time.

Table 18.2 Percentage of total lap time spent in each quadrant of the friction diagram

Quadrant	Time percentage
Quadrant 1	34.29%
Quadrant 2	31.51%
Quadrant 3	22.02%
Quadrant 4	12.18%

18.5 How Bumpy Is the Track Surface?

To evaluate the bumpiness of a track shock absorber, speed should be observed. A track with more road surface irregularities will provide more high-speed spikes in the shock speed channels. For visualization purposes, it is useful to calculate the absolute value of the shock speed math channels, as shown in the lower graph in Figure 18.7. Even better for visualization is to overlay an absolute shock speed channel on a track map, as this clearly indicates which sections of the track are bumpier than others.

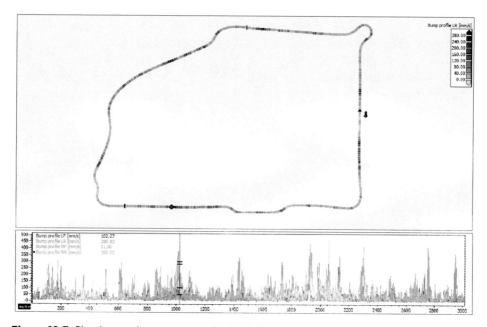

Figure 18.7 Shock speed as a measure for track bumpiness

The average value of the absolute shock speed is a metric that can be used to compare different tracks. However, in this case one should be confident that the suspension travel signals of the datasets being compared were recorded with the same sampling frequency and that the calculation rate for the shock speed math channels corresponds.

The math channel created to evaluate bumpiness of a track can now also be gated for specific conditions. For example, it might be useful to find out if a specific cornering phase is susceptible for bumps in the track surface. In Figure 18.8 the absolute value of shock speed is gated for two specific cases:

- Acceleration out of a corner: lateral Gs larger than 0.5 G and longitudinal Gs positive
- Braking: longitudinal Gs negative

459

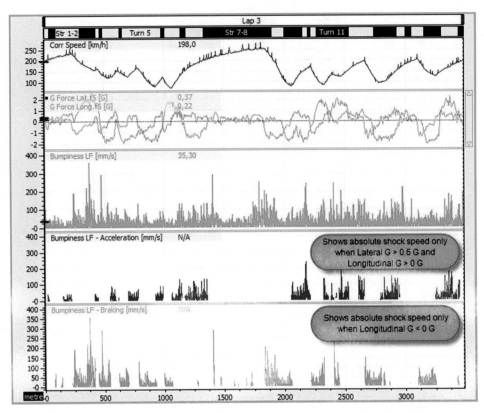

Figure 18.8 Gated shock speed to reveal influence of bumps on specific situations

Finally, the result of these channels can again be overlaid on a track map and the average channel values calculated as metrics to specify track bumpiness, as shown in Figure 18.9.

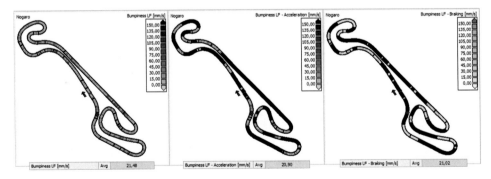

Figure 18.9 Gated shock speed signals displayed on track maps

Chapter 19
Introduction to Measurement

The previous chapters investigated how numerous sensor signals are analyzed to provide information about vehicle and driver performance. These signals so far were always taken for granted. However, when a physical phenomenon must be measured, it is necessary to understand how this is done. In addition, to draw the right conclusions from the data, the measurement must be evaluated to meet the necessary requirements. This chapter discusses the basics of sensor technology and metrology to arm the reader with the necessary knowledge to select and apply the correct sensors for obtaining measurements.

19.1   Introduction

Natural processes are by definition analog. They tend to vary smoothly over time. Measuring this kind of processes imposes a problem as the measuring device, the data logger, is basically a computer that can only think in binary numbers and detect discrete states (on and off). We therefore need a way to represent a continuous analog signal as a discrete series of numbers. This procedure is called analog to digital conversion (A/D conversion). The principle is graphically illustrated in Figure 19.1.

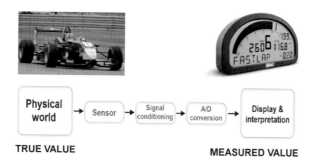

Figure 19.1 A/D conversion principle

Sensors are used as an interface between the physical process that needs to be measured (the "true" value) and the data logger. They generally output a continuously variable electrical output that represents the true value. In some cases this signal needs to be conditioned before being presented to the data logger. Examples of signal conditioning are filtering or use of a Wheatstone bridge for strain gauge measurements. Next, the analog signal must be translated to digital (binary) format before it can be saved to the data logger's memory. Once stored, we are talking about the "measured" value. Further in this chapter it will be argued that we can never be sure that the measured value equals the true value. Every measurement has some inherent inaccuracies, and the best that can be done is to do an estimation of these inaccuracies to define a confidence range within which we expect the true value to be situated.

19.2   Analog-Digital Conversion: Accuracy Implications

The data acquisition system is basically an extensive measurement tool with a memory. Like any other measurement tool, it has limitations regarding precision. The memory can store only data converted to digital form. This conversion takes a finite amount of time; as this process takes place, a change of magnitude in the signal goes undetected. One is forced to approximate a continuous signal by a succession of sampled points.

The digitizing process converts the analog values to a stream of data bits with values of zero or one. The resolution of the signal (the smallest change in signal that the system can detect) is limited to the voltage that corresponds to one bit of variation.

Consider a MoTeC ADL2 data logger that has two types of analog voltage inputs with different measurement ranges [19-1]. The user either has the option to choose a measurement input range of zero to 5.5 V or from zero to 15.3 V. Both types have a 12-bit resolution, which divides the input range in $2^{12} = 4096$ discrete steps. For the 5.5 V input, this means that the smallest detectable change in the input signal is 5500 mV/4096 = 1.343 mV. For the 15.3 V input this is 3.735 mV.

Consider that we want to connect a linear suspension potentiometer to this data logger. The measurement range of this sensor is given in Table 19.1.

Table 19.1 Output voltage for a typical linear potentiometer (with a range of 100 mm)	
Linear Distance	Output Voltage
0 mm	5.0 V
100 mm	0.0 V

If this potentiometer is connected to an input with a 5.5 V range, this means that we leave 0.5 V unused or 0.5/0.001343 = 372 discrete steps. Therefore, the smallest measurable linear distance in this situation will be 100/(4096 − 372) = 0.027 mm.

The input with the 15.3 V range leaves 10.3 V unused or 10.3/0.003735 = 2757 discrete steps. When the potentiometer is connected to such an input, the smallest measurable distance becomes 100/(4096 − 2757) = 0.075 mm.

One might argue the significance of measuring suspension travel with a resolution of 0.027 mm compared with 0.075 mm. However, this resolution becomes very significant if this signal is used to calculate the shock absorber speed. Let's assume that the potentiometer signal is logged with a sampling frequency of 100 Hz. This means that we will have a data sample for each 0.01 s, and the difference between two successive samples can't be less than 0.027 mm and 0.075 mm, depending on the type of input used. If the signal is now differentiated with a Δt of 0.01 s, it means that the minimum velocities that can be calculated are 0.027/0.01 = 2.7 mm/s and 0.075/0.01 = 7.5 mm/s. It is obvious that a minimum measurable shock speed of 7.5 mm/s is too high, as this velocity is well into the low-speed range of any shock absorber.

The regeneration of a signal is a succession of sampled points. Therefore, the preservation of the original signal depends on the number of sampled points per unit of time—the sampling frequency. Errors in signal recording can arise from a sampling frequency that is too low, a phenomenon known as aliasing.

The continuous line in Figure 19.2 represents a signal that needs to be measured, in this case a simple sine wave. The squares are the samples stored by the data logger. Everything happening between these points is ignored. The graph shows that the sampling frequency used was a bit lower than the frequency of the original sine wave. The signal produced by the data logger is a sine wave with a much lower frequency, an alias.

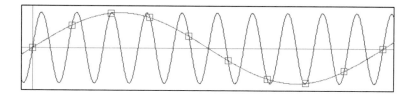

Figure 19.2 A too-slow sampling rate results in a false signal representation called aliasing

To avoid aliasing, the Nyquist-Shannon sampling theorem states that the frequency at which a signal is sampled must be greater than twice the highest frequency encountered in the signal. This means that to digitize a sine wave with a frequency of 20 Hz, the sampling frequency should be more than 40 Hz.

463

A sampling frequency that is too low can cause the data acquisition system to miss valuable events. Most systems allow sampling frequencies to be set according to specific needs. High sampling frequencies increase accuracy but require more memory, thus decreasing the available logging time.

The following sampling frequencies can be used as guidelines:

- Fluid and air temperatures   1–5 Hz
- Fluid and air pressures   10 Hz
- Chassis and driver activity   50 Hz
- Suspension motion and load   200–500 Hz
- GPS position   5–20 Hz

Sensor signals also are affected by noise resulting from vibration or electromagnetic fields from the ignition system. Noise is added to the measured signal when it exceeds the resolution of the analog-digital (A-D) conversion. Prevention of parasite signals is aided significantly by adequate wiring. Of course, the sensor itself also poses a question as to the accuracy of the measurement.

The required accuracy of a data acquisition system should be chosen carefully. Again, it comes down to the specific needs of the user. It is not necessary to log water temperature with an accuracy of 0.01 °C; this does not make you any smarter. For shock absorber motion, more accuracy is always better. Measuring the longitudinal g-force does not require a high sampling frequency, except when gearshift times must be derived from this signal. Think about what needs measuring and decide on the required accuracy.

19.3   Sensor Selection and Application

A sensor is a device that outputs an electrical signal in reaction to a physical phenomenon. For any imaginable measurement, a sensor probably exists. To justify the application of a given sensor, the requirements of the measurement must be determined first. Therefore, the following questions require answers:

- *What requires measuring?*

  The answer to this question often falls into one of the following categories: temperature, pressure, flow, displacement or position, velocity, acceleration, and force.

- *What is the expected measurement interval?*

  The minimum and maximum estimated measurement values need to be inside the sensor's range.

- *To what type of environmental circumstances will the sensor be exposed?*
  Because environmental effects can introduce errors into the measurement, this should be carefully considered when selecting a sensor. Temperature, pressure, and vibration can influence the output signal of the sensor. In addition, the mounting of the sensor and contamination by fluid, dirt, and similar contaminants can have an effect.

- *What kind of accuracy is required?*
  The highest possible accuracy for a sensor always is wanted, but there are economical factors to consider. In addition, using a sensor within a greater degree of accuracy than the data logger can record is not necessary. Signal conditioning and A-D conversion can cause inaccuracy in a highly accurate sensor signal.

- *What is the available budget?*
  Sensors come in different shapes and sizes, but there are also price differences between various sensors. A more expensive sensor usually has more functions than a cheaper one and scores better on the four points mentioned previously.

To evaluate these questions, one must understand the performance characteristics of the sensor mentioned on the sensor data sheet. It is absolutely necessary to grasp precisely what the data on the sensor data sheet means to appropriately evaluate a sensor. The important sensor properties are covered using the Texense ACC-5 capacitive accelerometer (http://www.texense.com) as an example.

1. Transfer Function
   This determines the relationship between physical input and electrical output. This often is illustrated in the data sheet as a graph showing this relationship. For the ACC-5, the linear function shown in Equation 19.1 applies.

$$V_{out}(a) = 2.5 + \left(a \cdot 0.4 \frac{V}{G} \right)$$ (Eq. 19.1)

With $V_{out}(a)$ = sensor output voltage at the measured acceleration value
         a = acceleration value measured by the sensor

2. Sensitivity
   This is the ratio between a small change in the electrical signal to a small change in physical input (i.e., the derivative of the transfer function). This means that for the ACC-5, the sensitivity equals 0.4 V/G.

3. Offset
   This is the value of the electrical signal at zero input. The ACC-5 measures 2.5 V at 0 G.

4. Measurement Range

The range of input signal that can be converted into an electrical signal. Signals outside the measurement range result in unacceptable inaccuracies. The measurement range of the Texense ACC-5 equals ±5.0 G.

These first four sensor properties allow the creation of a graphical representation of electrical output versus physical input. Figure 19.3 illustrates the transfer function calculated over the complete measurement range.

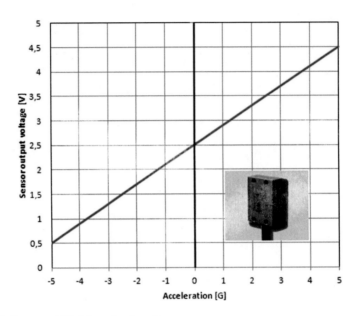

Figure 19.3 Texense ACC-5 transfer function

1. Uncertainty

Also called tolerance, uncertainty is the largest expected error between the actual and ideal output signal. On sensor data sheets, this usually is referred to as one of the following:

- Fraction of the full-scale output
- Fraction of the reading
- Fraction of the sensor's sensitivity

The acceleration sensor in this example has a quoted tolerance of ±1% of the sensor's sensitivity. Assuming that the sensor is exposed to an acceleration of 2.5 G, the ideal output voltage is

$$V_{out}(2.5\ G) = 2.5\ V + \left(2.5\ G \cdot 0.40\ \frac{V}{G}\right) = 3.5\ V$$

With a stated tolerance of ±1% of sensitivity, the range in which the sensitivity can vary is from 0.396 to 0.404 V. This means that the output voltage can vary from 3.490 to 3.510 V. For a real acceleration of 2.5 G, the value measured by the sensor can therefore range from 2.475 to 2.525 G.

2. Nonlinearity

   This is the maximum deviation from a linear transfer function over the specified measurement range. For the ACC-5, a nonlinearity of ±0.3% of sensitivity is stated, a value which is within the tolerance of the sensor.

3. Hysteresis

   This is the variation of the output value when the input value is cycled up and down. The ACC-5 data sheet does not mention hysteresis.

4. Noise

   All sensors produce some noise output, which must be considered in addition to the other electronic elements in the measurement system.

5. Resolution

   The sensor's resolution is the smallest detectable physical input factor. A sensor's resolution often is limited by the noise it produces.

The best possible sensor choice can still provide bad data if not properly applied. A sensor responds to its total environment, and therefore everything in this environment must be taken into account. This not only includes the external influences acting on the sensor but also the complete measurement system. Therefore, connectors, cables, power supply, signal conditioners, and logging unit all must work faultlessly together.

19.4   Measurement Uncertainty

Any measurement is valid only if accompanied by a consideration of the errors involved. Before taking a measurement, identify significant sources of error and eliminate them if possible. After the measurement is taken, maintain an impression of the probable remaining measurement error. Every time a sensor measurement is repeated, the results obtained will vary. Each measurement deviates by a certain amount from the true value for the following reasons:

- Inadequacies in the measurement object
- Inadequacies in the measuring instruments
- Inadequacies in the measurement method
- Environmental influences

- Influences by the person performing the measurements
- Changes over time

A quantity has a true value that one tries to calculate through measurement. However, recognizing that no measuring instrument is perfect and outside influences can never be eliminated completely, the best that can be achieved is an estimate of the true value. The difference between the measured value and the true value is called the error of the measurement, or accuracy. Because the true value of a quantity can never be determined, it is also impossible to know the exact accuracy of a measurement. However, estimating the effect that various errors have on the measured value is possible. When this effect is estimated, an uncertainty can be attached to the measured value, which indicates a range of values within which the true value is expected to be situated.

The total error in a measurement is comprised of the following components:

- Large errors
- Systematic errors
- Random errors

Large errors occur as a result of an improper measurement method, circuit errors, incorrect sensor application, and logging errors. They cannot be corrected for and only can be eliminated if detected before performing the measurement. When significant errors occur, the measurement is rendered obsolete; it serves no purpose incorporating them in any error quantification.

Systematic error, sometimes called statistical bias, is caused by deficiencies in the measured object, in the measurement method, and in the measuring instruments.

Statistical bias can be eliminated or reduced by calibrating the relevant instrument. Correcting the measurements to the results obtained with a reference instrument also reduces bias. For instance, an often-observed practice by race teams is comparing the output of tire pressure gauges to those used by the tire manufacturers to obtain the same measurement results. The difference between the two readings is the gauge's statistical bias.

Random errors occur because of factors beyond the engineer's control. Examples of these factors include the following:

- Environment (e.g., temperature, humidity, pressure, presence of magnetic fields, radiation)
- Aging of the measured object
- Aging of the measurement instruments

An example of a random error often occurs in the least significant digit in digital balances. Three measurements of a single object might be 0.567 g, 0.566 g, and 0.568 g.

Random error can be estimated statistically by attaching an uncertainty to the measurement result [19-2]. Random uncertainties generally follow a normal distribution, which basically means that small random deviations from the average measured value are much more probable than large ones.

In a series of measurements, if n single values $x_1, x_2, \ldots x_n$ are measured under comparable conditions, the average μ of these n values usually is considered an estimate of the true value. In a normal distribution, approximately 68% of all measured values fall within $\pm 1 \cdot \sigma$, and 95% fall within $\pm 1 \cdot \sigma$ (where σ is the standard deviation of the data). This is illustrated in Figure 19.4. The standard deviation determines the scatter in the data.

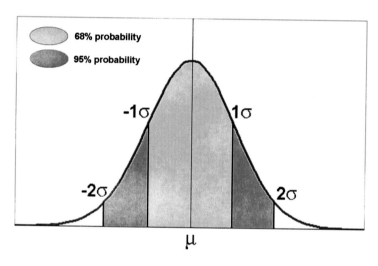

Figure 19.4 A normal distribution and its probability limits

Do not assume that μ is equal to the true value. When the series of measurements mentioned earlier is repeated, another result for μ might be obtained. The question that needs to be answered is, *what uncertainty can be assigned to the average value of the data?* For a normal distribution, the standard deviation of the average $\sigma_{average}$ is defined by Equation 19.2.

$$\sigma_{average} = \frac{\sigma}{\sqrt{n}} \qquad \text{(Eq. 19.2)}$$

With σ = standard deviation of the data

   n = number of data values

The standard deviation of the average, or in this context often called standard uncertainty, expresses the uncertainty of a measurement (Equation 19.3).

$$\text{Measurement result} = \mu \pm \frac{\sigma}{\sqrt{n}} \qquad \text{(Eq. 19.3)}$$

In practical terms, this means that there is a 68% probability that the true value lies within $\pm \frac{\sigma}{\sqrt{n}}$ of the average measured value and a 95% probability that it lies within twice this distance from the average.

As an example, the uncertainty of a measurement of a vehicle's roll angle ratio (see chapter 9) is evaluated. The roll ratio is calculated by dividing the rear roll angle by the front roll angle. These inputs are calculated in turn from the signals measured by suspension position sensors.

For this measurement, the data of a complete lap is evaluated, which resulted in 10,421 samples for the front and rear roll angles. For each sample, the roll ratio is calculated by dividing the rear roll angle by the front roll angle (assuming a linear relationship between the front and rear roll angle as Figure 19.5 suggests).

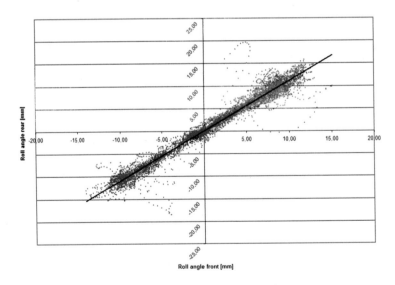

Figure 19.5 The relationship between front and rear roll angle

Following the theories explained earlier, the measured value of the roll ratio for the complete lap (the coefficient of direction of the straight line in Figure 19.5) is the average of all 10,421 roll ratio samples (Figure 19.6).

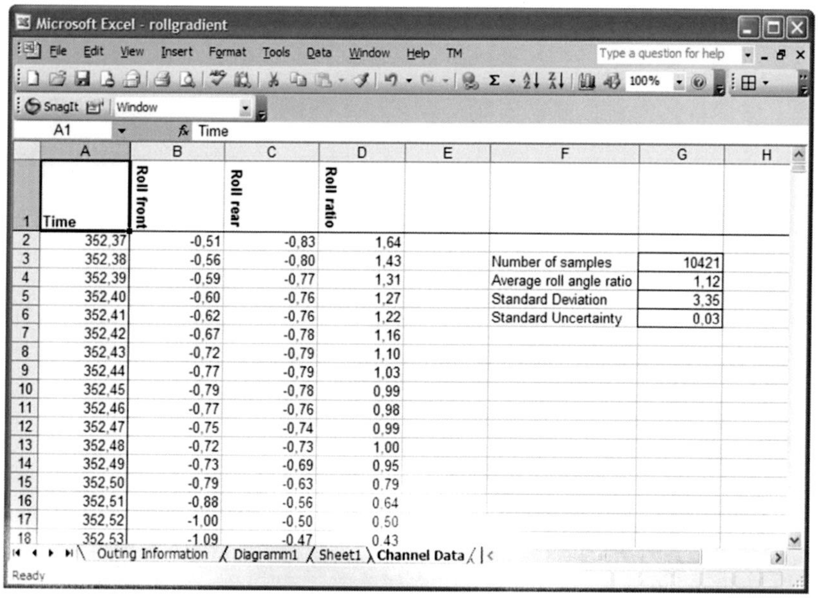

Figure 19.6 Roll ratio uncertainty calculation

The calculated average in this example equals 1.12. The standard deviation of the data is 3.35, which is a measure of the scatter of the data samples. This is quite high. Two main issues significantly influence the standard deviation of the data samples:

- When the car hits a curb, data also is incorporated into the calculation. This temporarily results in very large roll ratios.

- Data scatter around the y-axis in Figure 19.6 (where the front roll angle is zero) in theory causes the roll ratio to approach infinity. In reality, because of a finite sampling rate, it induces very high values for the roll ratio into the data.

The standard error is calculated using Equation 19.2 and equals 0.03. Therefore, it can be stated (with a confidence level of 68%) that the true value for the roll angle ratio is located within the following limits.

Lower confidence limit: $1.12 - 0.03 = 1.09$

Upper confidence limit: $1.12 - 0.03 = 1.15$

Or, with a 95% confidence level the true value is within these limits:

Lower confidence limit: $1.12 - (2 \cdot 0.03) = 1.06$

Upper confidence limit: $1.12 - (2 \cdot 0.03) = 1.18$

The measurement result now is expressed as follows:

$\zeta = 1.12 \pm 0.03$ with a confidence level of 68%

$\zeta = 1.12 \pm 0.06$ with a confidence level of 95%

19.5   Temperature Sensors

Most methods for measuring temperature rely on measuring some physical property of a metal that varies with temperature. In some cases, it is possible to determine temperature by measuring a target's thermal radiation. However, a temperature sensor's output always consists of an output voltage that corresponds to a temperature change. There are two basic types of temperature measurement:

1. Contact Temperature Measurement
   This requires the sensor to be in direct contact with the medium to be measured. Oil, water, and air temperature fall into this category. For these applications, thermocouples, thermistors, or resistive temperature detectors (RTDs) commonly are used.

2. Noncontact Temperature Measurement
   This is used for logging tire or brake disc temperatures with infrared (IR) sensors.

19.5.1   Thermocouple Temperature Sensors

A thermocouple temperature sensor consists of two wires of different materials welded together into a junction, called the measurement junction. At the other end of the signal wires is another junction, called the reference junction. A change in temperature within the measurement junction generates a current in the wires proportional to the temperature change. Temperature at the measurement junction then can be determined from the type of thermocouple used, the magnitude of the millivolt potential, and the temperature of the reference junction.

The big advantage of a thermocouple temperature measurement is the potential measurement range. Thermocouples may be rated from −270 to 1800 °C. Figure 19.7 shows an example of a thermocouple exhaust gas temperature sensor with a measurement range from zero to 1250 °C. They are also very reliable under vibration and shock because of their simple design. The disadvantage of using this sensor type is that it requires special extension wires and reference junction compensation.

Thermocouples are available in different combinations of metals or calibrations. The four most popular configurations are named J, K, E, and T. Each calibration has a different measurement range, although the maximum temperature varies with the diameter of the wire used in the thermocouple. Figure 19.8 shows the upper temperature limit of the four common thermocouple calibrations for different wire sizes [19-3].

Figure 19.7 Thermocouple exhaust gas temperature sensor (Courtesy of Texys International)

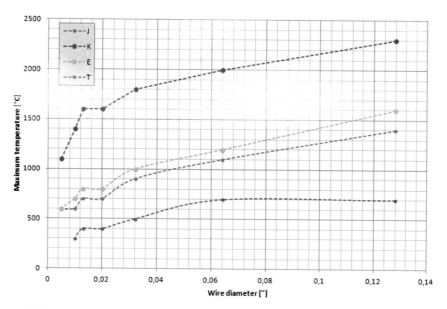

Figure 19.8 Upper temperature limits in degrees Celsius of protected bare wire thermocouples versus wire diameter

Thermocouple probes are available in three junction types: grounded, ungrounded, or exposed (Figure 19.9). With a grounded junction, the thermocouple wires are attached to the inside of the probe wall. In an ungrounded junction, the wires are detached from the probe wall. Therefore, the response time of an ungrounded junction is slower than that of a grounded junction. In an exposed junction, the thermocouple wires protrude from the probe wall and are in direct contact with their environment. This type of junction has the fastest response time but is limited in use to dry, noncorrosive, and nonpressurized environments. Thermocouples with exposed junctions often are used for air temperature measurement.

Grounded   Exposed   Ungrounded

Figure 19.9 Common thermocouple junctions

19.5.2 Thermistors

Thermistors (Figure 19.10) change their electrical resistance in relation to their temperature. They are typically composed of two metal oxides encapsulated in glass or epoxy. Thermistors are available in two types:

- Positive temperature coefficient (PTC): resistance increases with a rise in temperature

- Negative temperature coefficient (NTC): resistance decreases as temperature rises

Figure 19.10 Thermistor temperature sensor (Courtesy of Race Technology Ltd.)

The change in resistance of thermistors is generally quite large, resulting in high sensor sensitivity, but the measuring range is smaller than that of thermocouples (maximum a few hundred degrees Celsius). The relationship between temperature and resistance is not a linear one, but with external circuitry it can be made virtually linear. Thermistors are one of the most accurate types of temperature sensors.

19.5.3 Resistive Temperature Detectors

Resistive temperature detectors (RTDs) (Figure 19.11) work on the same principle as a thermistor. A change in electrical resistance is used to measure temperature. The sensing element consists of a wire coil or deposited film of pure metal, whose resistance has been documented at various temperatures. Common materials used in resistors are platinum (the most popular and accurate), nickel, or copper.

Figure 19.11 Platinum resistance temperature detector (Courtesy of Texys International)

An RTD can have a larger measurement range as a thermocouple, with a sensitivity located somewhere between that of a thermocouple and a thermistor. The resistance versus temperature characteristic of platinum RTDs is standardized, which ensures sensor interchangeability.

19.5.4 Infrared Temperature Measurement

Infrared (IR) technology is not a new phenomenon. It has been used in research and industrial applications for decades, but lately innovations have developed for noncontact IR sensors on race car applications. Especially popular are tire temperature (Figure 19.12) and brake disc temperature measurements, but possible applications include clutch temperature, alternator or electric motor temperature, or air box fire detection (Figure 19.13).

The following are the advantages of IR temperature measurement:

- Fast response times (in the ms range)
- Temperature measurement on moving targets
- Measuring physically inaccessible objects
- High measurement range
- No heat distortion (no heat energy lost from the target)

Figure 19.12 Installation of three IR temperature sensors on the front wheel of a GT3 car

Figure 19.13 IR temperature sensor for air box fire detection (Courtesy of Texys International)

Nevertheless, keep in mind the following disadvantages of IR measurements:

- The target must remain optically visible to the IR sensor. Dirt or dust can cause inaccuracies.
- Only surface temperatures can be measured.
- Emissivity of the surface material must be taken into account.

Every form of matter with a temperature above zero emits IR radiation proportional to its temperature. This is called characteristic radiation [19-4], and the spectrum of this radiation ranges from 0.7 to 1000 μm wavelength (Figure 19.14).

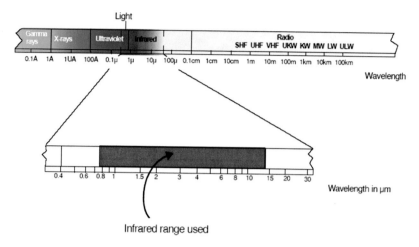

Figure 19.14 IR radiation spectrum

The functioning of IR sensors is complicated by the fact that surfaces other than so-called black-bodies emit less radiation at the same temperature. The relationship between the real emissive power and that of an ideal black-body is called emissivity (ε) and can have a maximum of one (for ideal black-bodies) and a minimum of zero. Bodies with an emissivity less than one are called gray bodies. Bodies where emissivity also depends on temperature and wavelength are called non-gray bodies.

Emissivity of the measured surface should be known to determine the correct wavelength in which the IR sensor needs to operate.

The IR sensor core converts the received radiation energy into an electrical signal. This core falls into one of two categories: quantum detectors or thermal detectors. Quantum detectors (or photodiodes) interact directly with the impacting photons, resulting in

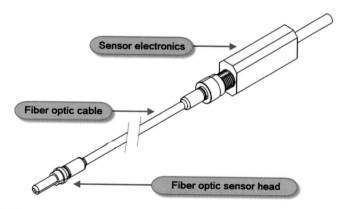

Figure 19.15 Fiber optic IR temperature sensor (Courtesy of Texys International)

electron pairs and ultimately an electrical signal. Thermal detectors change their temperature according to the impacting radiation. As with a thermocouple, this temperature change creates voltage.

The latest developments in IR temperature measurement technology involve the use of fiber optics. A fiber optic IR temperature sensor consists of three main parts (Figure 19.15):

- The sensor head: used to collect the target's radiance
- Fiber optic cable: for transfer of the signal
- Sensor electronics: microprocessor control unit

Fiber optics have the ability to carry optical signals over long distances around unavoidable obstructions, and the sensor head does not contain any electronic components. This makes it possible to place the electronics away from harsh environments, and the sensor can be subjected to much higher operating temperatures. The sensor head is not sensitive to electromagnetic fields, which make fiber optic IR sensors a good option for the measurement of temperature on electric motors.

19.6   Pressure Sensors

Pressure sensor applications on race cars include engine oil, brake line, coolant pressure, fuel, manifold air, and aerodynamic. Most pressure-sensing devices in automotive applications rely on piezo-resistive semiconductor technology. A piezo-resistive pressure sensor is essentially a strain gage. It contains a sensing element made up of a silicon chip with a thin silicon diaphragm and three or four piezo-resistors (Figure 19.16). The piezo-resistance of the semiconductor refers to the change in resistance by strain on the diaphragm, compared to a reference pressure. The resistor values change proportionally to the amount of pressure applied to the diaphragm. The thickness of the diaphragm determines the pressure range of the sensor.

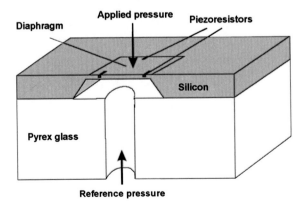

Figure 19.16 Piezo-resistive pressure sensing element

Depending on the reference pressure, piezo-resistive sensors can be divided into the following categories:

- Absolute pressure sensor in which the reference pressure is vacuum (Figure 19.17), for example, oil/fuel pressure sensor
- Differential pressure sensor, which has two ports for measuring two different pressures (Figure 19.18), for example, pitot tube sensor
- Gauge pressure sensor, which is a differential pressure measurement with atmospheric pressure as a reference (Figure 19.19), for example, engine inlet manifold pressure sensor

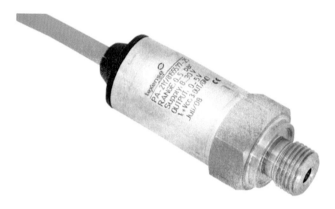

Figure 19.17 Absolute pressure sensor for fluid pressure measurement (Courtesy of Texys International)

Figure 19.18 Differential pressure sensor for aerodynamic applications (Courtesy of Texys International)

Figure 19.19 Gauge pressure sensor

The same principle of measurement is used in piezoelectric film sensors. This type of sensor consists of a thin sheet of piezo-resistive material connected to electrically conductive electrodes on each side. An electrical current is generated when a force is applied to the film which is amplified and converted to digital format. Some of the applications for which these sensors are suitable include the measurement of force, vibration, and impact. The piezo-resistive sheet can be produced in different sizes and shapes, and due to its thickness (25 to 120 µm) it can be placed between parts that are bolted together. Figure 19.20 shows an example of a piezoelectric film sensor mounted on the floor of a GP3 car to determine if the chassis is bottoming out at certain locations around the race track.

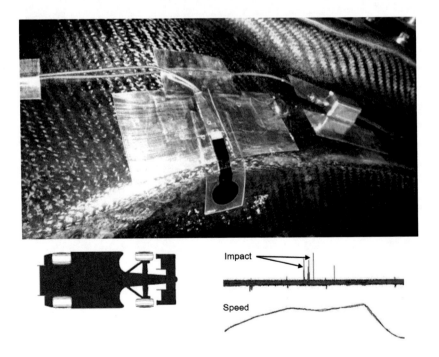

Figure 19.20 Bottoming sensor mounted on the floor of a GP3 car (Courtesy of Texys International)

19.7   Displacement Sensors

Displacement sensors are generally divided into two broad categories: linear motion and angular motion. The well-known linear potentiometer (Figure 19.21) and the string-potentiometer fall into the first category, while rotary potentiometers (Figure 19.22) measure angular motion.

Figure 19.21 Linear potentiometer

Figure 19.22 Rotary potentiometer

In race cars, linear and rotary potentiometers measure throttle position, gear position, suspension movement, steering angle, hydraulic level, and clutch or brake pedal position. They all work according to the principle illustrated in Figure 19.23. A potentiometer transforms a linear or rotary motion into a change in resistance. It is basically a voltage divider.

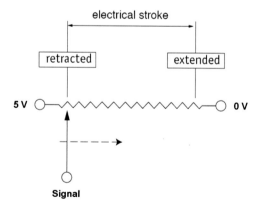

Figure 19.23 Operating principle of a potentiometer

The string potentiometer is a suitable sensor when size and mounting restrictions eliminate other choices. It can be used to measure multi-axis movements. The retractable cable allows for flexible mounting and can be routed around obstacles using pulleys and flexible guides.

19.8   Acceleration Sensors

Accelerometers have two main applications on race cars. The most popular is measuring the acceleration acting on the vehicle in lateral, longitudinal, or vertical direction. Second, they often measure vibration on various vehicle components (i.e., engine knock or track surface profiling by upright vibration measurements).

Based on their operation, accelerometers belong to either the capacitive or piezoelectric category.

19.8.1   Capacitive Accelerometers

Capacitive acceleration sensors measure a change in electrical capacitance, proportional to the acceleration acting on the sensor. Their operating principle is illustrated in Figure 19.24. A diaphragm with a known spring rate and mass is sandwiched between two fixed electrode plates. With these plates, the diaphragm forms two capacitors. As acceleration acts on the sensor, the diaphragm spring-mass experiences a force resulting in deflection. This deflection causes the distance between the spring-mass and the electrodes to vary, effectively changing the capacitor gaps.

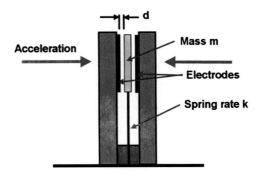

Figure 19.24 Capacitive accelerometer working principle

Capacitive accelerometers generally can measure smaller acceleration levels, making them more suitable for vehicle inertial measurements.

19.8.2   Piezoelectric Accelerometers

Piezoelectric accelerometers (Figure 19.25) use a piezoelectric material as a sensing element, which can output an electrical signal proportional to the stress applied to it. Most piezoelectric acceleration sensors are made of quartz crystal, piezoelectric ceramics, or tourmaline or lithium niobate. The piezoelectric elements in the sensor act as a spring, which is connected to the seismic masses. When acceleration acts on the sensor base, a force is created on the piezoelectric elements proportional to the applied acceleration and the size of the seismic mass (Newton's law of motion). Therefore, the more mass or acceleration there is, the higher the applied force and the more electrical output from the crystal.

Figure 19.25 Piezoelectric accelerometer

An important characteristic to keep in mind when selecting an acceleration sensor is the useful frequency range of a piezoelectric sensor, which is determined by its resonant frequency. This frequency can be estimated by Equation 19.4, where k is the spring rate of the piezoelectric element and m the size of the seismic mass.

$$\omega = \sqrt{\frac{k}{m}}$$

(Eq. 19.4)

A typical frequency response of a piezoelectric accelerometer is depicted in Figure 19.26.

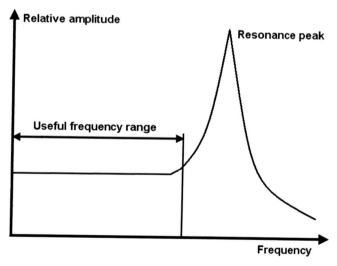

Figure 19.26 Typical frequency response of a piezoelectric accelerometer

Because of their wide dynamic measurement interval and frequency range and the fact that they can be made very small, piezoelectric accelerometers are found in applications where shock and vibration need mapping to understand the dynamic behavior of the object. Knock sensors and upright acceleration are the most common applications for race cars.

19.9   Speed Sensors

Measuring the speed of a rotating shaft finds multiple applications on a race car, of which engine RPM and wheel speed are the most common. Shaft speeds usually are measured using a Hall Effect sensor (Figure 19.27). If electric current flows through a conductor placed in a magnetic field, this field forces electrons to one side of the conductor, resulting in a voltage potential. This phenomenon is known as the Hall Effect, after the scientist who discovered it in 1879.

Figure 19.27 Hall Effect gear-tooth sensor (Courtesy of Texys International)

A Hall Effect sensor used with a ferrous trigger gear placed on the shaft (of which the speed needs to be determined) measures the variation in magnetic field between a magnet and the passing gear-teeth. The signal from the sensor then is converted into a digital block signal by external circuitry. This is illustrated in Figure 19.28.

To detect the trigger gear, it is necessary to provide a source of magnetic energy. Therefore, most Hall Effect sensors incorporate a permanent magnet with its axis of magnetization pointing toward the gear-teeth surface. When a tooth passes in front of the sensor, the flux density between the ferrous surface and the sensor face increases. When a valley passes before the sensor face, the flux density decreases.

Because Hall Effect sensors pick up the presence of a magnetic field, they essentially are immune to dust, oil, and other contaminants found on automotive components. The trigger for this kind of sensor is not necessarily a gear; other objects such as bolt heads or other metal profiles can be used.

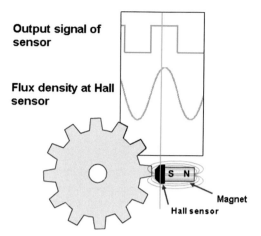

Figure 19.28 Working principle of a Hall Effect sensor

19.10 Strain Gages

When external forces are applied to an object, stress and strain result. Stress is the object's internal resisting forces. Strain is the deformation of the object that takes place because of these internal forces. Strain typically is measured by strain gages, which are designed to convert mechanical motion into an electrical signal. They rely on the fact that metallic conductors subjected to mechanical strain exhibit a change in electrical resistance.

Race car applications include suspension and steering loads, wheel forces, driveshaft torque, chassis loads, and ignition cut load cells. Strain gages also are used often as an integral part in (piezo-resistive) pressure transducers.

The operating principle of a strain gage is based on the relationship between strain and the resistance of electrical conductors. Strain is defined as the ratio between total deformation of the original length and the original length (Figure 19.29) and is expressed in Equation 19.5.

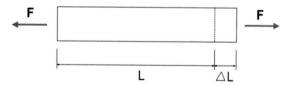

Figure 19.29 Definition of strain

$$\varepsilon = \frac{\Delta L}{L}$$

(Eq. 19.5)

Any electrical conductor changes its resistance with mechanical stress. This relationship is expressed with the gauge factor (GF) (Equation 19.6).

$$GF = \frac{\Delta R / R_0}{\Delta L / L} = \frac{\Delta R / R_0}{\varepsilon}$$

(Eq. 19.6)

In this equation, R_0 is the resistance of the electrical conductor when no mechanical stress is applied. ΔR is the difference in resistance from R_0 when the conductor experiences a strain equal to ε.

The strains measured with strain gages are normally very small. Consequently, the changes in electrical resistance also are very small. The strain gage must be included in a measurement system that can precisely determine this change in resistance. To measure relative changes in resistance around the order of 10^{-4} to 10^{-2} Ω/Ω, the strain gage should be integrated into a Wheatstone bridge (Figure 19.30).

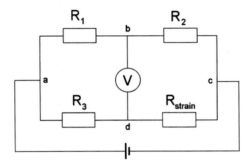

Figure 19.30 Strain gage measurement system using a Wheatstone bridge

In Figure 19.30, R_1, R_2, and R_3 are equal and R_{strain} is equal to this as well in an unstressed condition. A voltage (V_{in}) is applied between points a and c. As long as the strain gage does not experience a change in resistance, the output between points b and d exhibits no potential difference. However, when strain is applied, R_{strain} changes to a value unequal to R_1, R_2, and R_3. The bridge becomes unbalanced and an output voltage (V_{out}) exists between points b and d. V_{out} can be expressed with Equation 19.7.

$$V_{out} = V_{in} \cdot \left(\frac{R_3}{R_3 + R_{strain}} - \frac{R_1}{R_1 + R_2} \right)$$

(Eq. 19.7)

V_{out} typically fluctuates between zero and a couple of millivolts, so the sensor signal must be amplified before it can be directed into the data logger.

Strain-sensing materials change their structure at higher temperatures. Temperature also can alter the properties of the base material to which the strain gage is attached. This means that the gauge factor of the strain gage can change with varying temperature. Therefore, the manufacturer always should include temperature sensitivity data on the sensor's data sheet. If the temperature changes while strain is being measured, this should be compensated for.

Once measured, strain must be converted into an absolute value for the mechanical stress experienced by the object in question. This calculation can be done using Hooke's law, which applies to the elastic deformation range of linear elastic materials. In its simplest form, Hooke's law can be expressed as Equation 19.8.

$$\sigma = \varepsilon \cdot E \qquad \text{(Eq. 19.8)}$$

With σ = material stress

        ε = strain

        E = material's elasticity modulus

This version of Hooke's law only applies to uni-axial stress states (i.e., tension and compression bars). Multi-axial stress states require extended versions of Hooke's law [19-5].

19.11 Torque Sensors

Torque on a static part of the car can be measured with strain gages, but measuring the torque experienced by a rotating shaft presents a completely different problem as the signal measured by a shaft-mounted sensor needs to be transferred to the measurement electronics. The solution for this problem can be twofold:

- Slip rings provide a physical contact between axle and measurement electronics through which the power to the sensor is provided and the signal retrieved. The susceptibility of these rings to wear and packaging issues means this type of sensor solution is used less often in motor racing applications.

- The sensor signal and power is transferred wireless either by telemetry or magneto-elastic polarized band technology [19-6].

Traditionally, shaft torque is determined by measuring the strain of the shaft resulting from this torque with strain gauges. Magneto-elastic polarized band technology works on the principle that a change in the dimensions of an object causes a change of its magnetic state, a phenomenon called the Villari effect. This means that the effect of strain on the shaft can be used to produce a signal proportional to the applied torque and the shaft actually becomes the transducer. The change in magnetic field as torque is applied to the shaft is measured and converted to an electrical signal. Figure 19.31 shows an example of a drive shaft torque sensor.

Figure 19.31 Drive shaft torque sensor (Courtesy of NCTEngineering GmbH)

19.12   The Pitot Tube

Aerodynamic measurements (downforce, drag, and pressure distributions) often use a pitot tube as shown in Figure 19.32 to determine dynamic pressure (see chapter 13).

Figure 19.32 Pitot tube (Courtesy of Texys International)

As illustrated in Figure 19.33, a pitot tube consists of two concentric tubes, each with an inlet port. The outer tube measures the static air pressure, while the inner one is exposed to the sum of static and dynamic pressure. The tubes then are connected to a differential pressure sensor that outputs the dynamic air pressure to the data logger. To obtain good results, the pitot tube must be aligned with the flow velocity. Any misalignment should not exceed ±5 deg.

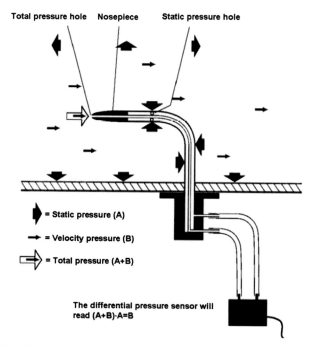

Figure 19.33 Working principle of a pitot tube

19.13   Oxygen Sensors

Oxygen sensors (or what automotive applications often refer to as lambda sensors) measure the volume of oxygen remaining in the engine's exhaust gas after combustion. With these sensors fitted to the exhaust manifold, the engineer and/or ECU can determine if the fuel-air mixture going into the engine is too rich (i.e., too much fuel) or too lean (i.e., too little fuel).

The sensor element consists of a ceramic cylinder plated inside and outside with porous platinum electrodes. It measures the difference in oxygen between the exhaust gas and the external air by generating a change in resistance proportional to the difference between the two.

Because lambda sensors (Figure 19.34) only work effectively when heated to approximately 300°C, most have heating elements incorporated in the ceramic to quickly raise the sensor tip to the correct temperature when the exhaust is still cold.

Figure 19.34 Lambda sensor

19.14   GPS

In previous chapters, the use of a GPS signal to measure location, distance, and speed was mentioned in numerous examples. GPS refers to a group of U.S. Department of Defense (DoD) satellites that constantly circle the Earth, making two complete orbits around the planet every 24 hours. These satellites transmit very low power radio signals, allowing a GPS receiver to determine its precise location on Earth.

GPS consists of three segments: space (satellites), control (ground stations), and user (GPS receiver).

The space segment is the heart of the system. It consists of at least 24 satellites, of which 21 are active. They orbit approximately 12 km above the Earth's surface and are arranged so that a GPS receiver always can receive at least 4 satellites at any given time. Civilian GPS receivers transmit a low-power radio signal at a frequency of 1575.42 MHz on the UHF band. This signal passes through clouds, glass, and plastic, but it does not penetrate solid objects such as trees and buildings.

Each satellite transmits a unique code, allowing a GPS receiver to identify the satellite. The main purpose of these signals is to calculate the travel time from the satellite to the receiver, also called time of arrival. The arrival time multiplied by the speed of light gives the distance between the satellite and the receiver. In addition to the satellite identification signal, a navigation message containing satellite orbital and clock information is sent to the GPS receiver.

The control segment, consisting of five Earth-based ground stations, tracks the GPS satellites and provides them with corrected orbital and time information.

The user segment is the GPS receiver. To establish its location, the receiver must know the exact location of the satellite in space and the distance to it. The navigational data transmitted by the satellites contain two types of information. The almanac data contains the approximate locations of the satellites. This data is transmitted continuously and stored in the memory of the GPS receiver so it knows the orbit in which every satellite is supposed to be. The almanac data is updated periodically as the satellites orbit.

The ground stations keep track of satellite orbit, altitude, location, and speed and send corrected data, called the ephemeris data, back to the satellites. Ephemeris data is valid for four to six hours.

The combination of almanac and ephemeris data tells the GPS receiver the exact location of the satellite in space. The distance between the receiver and respective satellite is calculated from the arrival time. The coded identification signal is a so-called "pseudo-random" signal because it looks like a noise signal. The GPS receiver generates the same signal and tries to match it to the satellite's signal. The receiver then compares the two to determine how much it needs to delay its signal to match the satellite signal. A radio wave travels at the speed of light ($2.99 \cdot 10^8$ m/s); multiplied with the delay time, the distance between receiver and satellite is determined.

The receiver needs at least four visible satellites to determine a three-dimensional location (longitude, latitude, and altitude) on Earth. The more satellites the receiver can see, the better the accuracy.

Most modern GPS receivers are parallel multicircuit receivers, with each circuit devoted to one particular satellite. In this way, strong locks can be maintained on all satellites at all times, even in difficult conditions such as blockage from trees, buildings, and other solid objects.

GPS signals can be logged by the race car data logging system to measure the position, speed, and heading of the vehicle. Standalone GPS position measurements are accurate to within 2 to 3 m. When corrections are applied using the data from lateral and longitudinal accelerometers, accuracy improves to 1 to 2 m [19-7]. GPS signals can be degraded by one or more of the following factors:

- Ionosphere or troposphere delay: As it passes through the atmosphere, the satellite signal slows down. The GPS uses a built-in model that partially corrects this type of error.

- Signal multipath: This occurs when the GPS signal is reflected off objects such as tall buildings before it reaches the receiver. This increases the signal travel time.

- Receiver clock error.

- Ephemeris error: This is the inaccuracy of the satellite's reported location.

- Number of satellites visible.

- Intentional degradation of the GPS signal: To prevent military adversaries using the highly accurate GPS signal the U.S. DoD intentionally degraded the signal prior to May 2000 (selective availability).

By combining high-accuracy GPS data with inertial measurements (acceleration and angular velocity) it is even possible to measure vehicle yaw and pitch (Figure 19.35). This system can be used to determine the vehicle's roll, pitch and slip angle [19-8].

Figure 19.35 Race Technology Speedbox INS GPS/inertial measurement system mounted on the roof of a GT3 car

19.15   Laser Distance Sensors

Laser distance sensors measure a race car's ride height or ground clearance. This sensor operates on the principle of triangulation. A laser emitter projects a beam onto an object (Figure 19.36). The reflection of this beam passes through a lens that focuses the beam onto a receiving photodiode element. A change in distance between sensor and target changes the angle of the reflected beam, thereby changing the location of the beam on the receiving element.

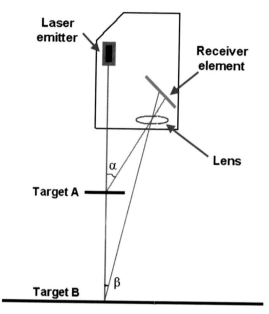

Figure 19.36 Principle of operation of a laser distance sensor

This receiving element is coupled to a microcontroller, which calculates the distance to the target from the reflected beam's location on the receiver and outputs a voltage proportional to the target distance.

Through the use of a microcontroller, a high linearity and accuracy is achieved. The signal can be filtered with user-determined rates to smooth the sensor's output signal. This is particularly useful for ride height measurements to filter out the roughness of the asphalt. Also, the emissivity of different target materials can be accounted for by the microcontroller.

Resolution and accuracy depend on the distance between the sensor and object. An object within close proximity to the sensor creates a significant difference in the angle between the emitted and reflected beam given a small change in distance. When the target is located farther from the sensor, a small change in distance results in a small difference in angle. Therefore, the highest resolution is achieved with laser distance sensors with a relatively small measurement range.

19.16 Surface Acoustic Wave Technology

Current sensor trends are definitely going toward MEMS devices (Micro-Electro-Mechanical Systems). This technology can be best described as miniaturized mechanical and electro-mechanical elements made through micro-fabrication, and the big potential is that multiple miniature sensors can be combined onto a common silicon substrate along with the necessary integrated circuits. Their method of production results in low production costs against excellent performance. The technology allows for grouping of multiple sensors in a single measurement device (e.g., three-dimensional acceleration and gyroscope measurements with a single sensor) or wireless signal transmission (e.g., in TPMS).

Among MEMS sensors perhaps the most interesting modern development is a class of sensors that makes use of surface acoustic wave technology (SAW). These sensors utilize the piezoelectric effect to convert an electrical signal into a mechanical wave. This wave is influenced by physical phenomena (including temperature, pressure, displacement, acceleration, torque, and chemical composition). The transducer then converts the wave back to an electrical signal. Changes in amplitude, phase, frequency, or time delay between the input and output electrical signals can be used to determine the magnitude of a desired physical phenomenon.

Surface acoustic waves are extremely versatile, and the technology is only beginning to realize its potential. They are low cost, rugged, sensitive, reliable, and suitable for a huge amount of applications. SAW sensors can be used to measure force, acceleration, angular rate, linear displacement, fluid level, flow rate, and even oil contamination. SAW sensors can be interrogated wirelessly and can operate without batteries, as in the example in Figure 19.37. This TPMS system uses wireless sensors mounted on wheels that do not require a battery.

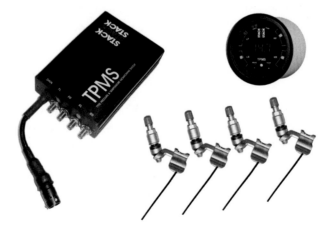

Figure 19.37 STACK tire pressure monitoring system using SAW technology (Courtesy of STACK Ltd.)

List of Symbols

This book contains a number of equations that use a variety of English letters and Greek symbols. The following list will help you better understand the equations.

English Letters

a	Acceleration
a_{yaw}	Yaw acceleration
a_{hub}	Hub vertical acceleration
$a_{suspension}$	Suspension vertical acceleration
a_{CP}	Tire contact patch vertical acceleration
a_{body}	Chassis vertical acceleration
A	Frontal vehicle surface
A	Skewness of a distribution
C	Damping rate
C_D	Aerodynamic drag coefficient
C_L	Aerodynamic downforce coefficient
C_p	Tire heat capacity
D	Aerodynamic drag force
E	Material elasticity modulus
f_s	Sampling frequency
F_{CP}	Tire contact patch force
F_{mass}	Acceleration force
F_{res}	Resistance force
$F_{rolling}$	Rolling resistance force
F_{spring}	Spring force
F_{shock}	Shock absorber force
$F_{suspension}$	Suspension force
F_{tire}	Friction force from tire
F_x	Longitudinal tire force

F_y	Lateral tire force
$F_{y\,max}$	Maximum lateral tire force
F_N	Normal force on tire
$F_{N\,max}$	Maximum normal tire force
F_{LF}	Left-front wheel load
F_{RF}	Right-front wheel load
F_{LR}	Left-rear wheel load
F_{RR}	Right-rear wheel load
g	Gravitational acceleration (g = 9.81 m/s²)
$G_{combined}$	Combined acceleration
G_{lat}	Lateral acceleration
G_{long}	Longitudinal acceleration
G_{vert}	Vertical acceleration
G_2	Kurtosis of a distribution
h_{roll}	Distance between vehicle center of gravity and roll center
h_{CoG}	Height of center of gravity from ground
h_{SCoG}	Height of center of gravity of the sprung mass
h_F	Front unsprung center of gravity height from ground
h_R	Rear unsprung center of gravity height from ground
h_{RCf}	Height of front roll center from ground
h_{RCr}	Height of rear roll center from ground
i	index
i_{total}	Total gear ratio
$K_{rolltot}$	Total vehicle roll stiffness
K_{rollf}	Front roll stiffness
K_{rollr}	Rear roll stiffness
$K_{rollfSPRINGS}$	Front spring roll stiffness
$K_{rollrSPRINGS}$	Rear spring roll stiffness
$K_{rollfARB}$	Front antiroll bar stiffness
$K_{rollrARB}$	Rear antiroll bar stiffness

K_H	Vehicle heave mode spring rate
K_P	Vehicle pitch mode spring rate
K_R	Vehicle roll mode spring rate
K_X	Vehicle warp mode spring rate
L	Length
L	Aerodynamic downforce
L_F	Front aerodynamic downforce
L_R	Rear aerodynamic downforce
m	Mass
m_{wheel}	Wheel mass
M	Total vehicle mass
M	Translational mass
M_f	Driveline inertia factor
M_r	Equivalent rotational mass
M_R	Wheel equivalent mass for roll
M_P	Wheel equivalent mass for pitch
MR_f	Front suspension motion ratio
MR_r	Rear suspension motion ratio
MR_{Rollf}	Front antiroll bar motion ratio
MR_{Rollr}	Rear antiroll bar motion ratio
M_{roll}	Roll moment
n	Number of samples
n_{engine}	Engine RPM
$n_{driveshaft}$	Drive shaft RPM
p_i	Percentile
P	Pressure
P_a	Pressure of dry air
P_{air}	Ambient air pressure
P_w	Pressure of water vapor
P_s	Water saturation vapor pressure

P_1	Cold tire pressure
P_2	Hot tire pressure
P_{engine}	Engine power
P_{mass}	Power left for acceleration
$Pbrake_{front}$	Front brake pressure
$Pbrake_{rear}$	Rear brake pressure
$Pbrake_{tot}$	Total brake pressure
PG	Pitch gradient
q	Roll stiffness distribution factor
q	Dynamic air pressure
r	Yaw rate
r	Curvature
$r_{rolling}$	Dynamic tire radius
$r_{StaticFRONT}$	Front static tire radius
$r_{StaticREAR}$	Rear static tire radius
R	Corner radius
R	Gas constant
R	Electrical resistance
R_a	Gas constant of dry air
R_w	Gas constant of water vapor
R_x	Tire rolling resistance coefficient
RG	Overall roll gradient
RG_F	Front roll gradient
RG_R	Rear roll gradient
$RH_{SuspFRONT}$	Front suspension ride height
$RH_{SuspREAR}$	Rear suspension ride height
$RH_{StaticFRONT}$	Front static ride height
$RH_{StaticREAR}$	Rear static ride height
$RH_{DynFRONT}$	Front dynamic ride height (suspension and tire)
$RH_{DynREAR}$	Rear dynamic ride height (suspension and tire)

s	Distance
s_{spring}	Spring compression
s_{shock}	Shock absorber travel
SR	Slip ratio
SR_{f}	Front spring rate
SR_{r}	Rear spring rate
SR_{rollf}	Front antiroll bar rate
SR_{rollr}	Rear antiroll bar rate
SR_{Tiref}	Front tire spring rate
SR_{Tirer}	Rear tire spring rate
SR_{Chassis}	Chassis torsion spring rate
t	Time
$t_{100\%TP}$	Time spent at full throttle
t_{Lap}	Lap time
TP	Throttle position
T	Temperature
T	Torque
t_{filter}	Filter interval
T_1	Tire temperature at cold pressure setting
T_2	Hot tire temperature
T	Track width
T_{F}	Front track width
T_{R}	Rear track width
T_{fuel}	Fuel temperature
T_{tire}	Tire temperature
T_{air}	Ambient air temperature
T_{track}	Track asphalt temperature
T_{ext}	Torque necessary to overcome external forces
T_{mass}	Acceleration torque
T_{wheel}	Wheel torque

$T\text{brake}_{\text{front}}$	Front brake disc temperature
$T\text{brake}_{\text{rear}}$	Rear brake disc temperature
V	Speed
V	Volume
V_0	Free rolling velocity
V_{slip}	Slip velocity
V_{out}	Sensor output voltage
v_{shock}	Shock absorber shaft speed
v_{TP}	Throttle speed
v_{brake}	Braking speed
W	Vehicle weight
W_{f1}	Front axle weight measured on level surface
W_{f2}	Front axle weight measured with raised rear axle
W_{L}	Left-hand side vehicle weight
W_{R}	Right-hand side vehicle weight
W_{LF}	Left-front corner weight
W_{RF}	Right-front corner weight
W_{LR}	Left-rear corner weight
W_{RR}	Right-rear corner weight
W_{s}	Total sprung weight
W_{sF}	Front sprung weight
W_{sR}	Rear sprung weight
W_{uF}	Front unsprung weight
W_{uR}	Rear unsprung weight
WB	Wheelbase
W_{brake}	Work of the brakes
WR_{f}	Front wheel rate
WR_{r}	Rear wheel rate
WR_{Rollf}	Front antiroll bar wheel rate
WR_{Rollr}	Rear antiroll bar wheel rate
W_{sF}	Static sprung weight of the front axle

W_{sR}	Static sprung weight of the rear axle
$WSPD_{FL}$	Wheel speed front left
$WSPD_{FR}$	Wheel speed front right
$WSPD_{RL}$	Wheel speed rear left
$WSPD_{RR}$	Wheel speed rear right
x_{wheel}	Wheel movement
x_{LF}	Left-front wheel movement
x_{RF}	Right-front wheel movement
x_{LR}	Left-rear wheel movement
x_{RR}	Right-rear wheel movement
$x_{suspensionLF}$	Front-left suspension movement
$x_{suspensionRF}$	Front-right suspension movement
$x_{suspensionLR}$	Rear-left suspension movement
$x_{suspensionRR}$	Rear-right suspension movement
x_H	Suspension heave movement
x_P	Suspension pitch movement
x_R	Suspension roll movement
x_W	Suspension warp movement
x_{CP}	Tire contact patch movement
x_{hub}	Hub displacement

Greek Symbols

α	Tire slip angle
α	Banking angle
α_{roll}	Overall vehicle roll angle
$\alpha_{RollSuspF}$	Front suspension roll angle
$\alpha_{RollSuspR}$	Rear suspension roll angle
$\alpha_{RollTiresF}$	Front tire roll angle
$\alpha_{RollTiresR}$	Rear tire roll angle
$\alpha_{torsion}$	Chassis torsion angle
β_{pitch}	Pitch angle

List of Symbols

δ	Steered angle at the wheel
δ_{SW}	Steered angle at the steering wheel
δ_{Acker}	Ackermann steering angle
δ_u	Understeer angle
ε	Strain
ζ	Roll angle ratio
ζ	Damping ratio
θ	Track slope angle
κ	Thermal conductivity between tire and air
κ_{track}	Thermal conductivity between tire and track surface
μ	Average of a data set
$\mu_{1/2}$	Median of a data set
μ	Friction coefficient
ω	Angular velocity
ω	Frequency
ω_{att}	Attitude velocity
ρ	Density of air
ρ_{15}	Fuel density at 15 °C
ρ_T	Tire compound density
σ	Standard deviation
$\sigma_{average}$	Standard deviation of the average

References

2-1. Tufte, Edward R., *The Visual Display of Quantitative Information*, Graphics Press LLC, Cheshire, Connecticut, 2001.

3-1. Mitchell, William C., *"A Method for Data Alignment,"* SAE paper No. 983087, SAE International, Warrendale, PA, 1998.

3-2. SAE International, *Vehicle Dynamics Terminology*, SAE Standard J670-2008-01, SAE International, Warrendale, PA, 2008.

4-1. Metz, Gregory L. and Metz, Daniel L., *"Deriving Wheel HP and Torque from Accelerometer Data,"* SAE Paper No. 2000-01-3544, SAE International, Warrendale, PA, 2000.

4-2. Milliken, William F. and Milliken, Douglas L., *Race Car Vehicle Dynamics*, SAE International, Warrendale, PA, 1995.

4-3. NHRA, *"Introduction to Drag Racing,"* www.nhra.com

5-1. Fey, Buddy, *Data Power—Using Racecar Data Acquisition*, Towery Publishing, London, UK, 1993.

5-2. Davison, Paul, *"Check Your Brake Balance Consistency,"* *Optimum G Newsletter*, Vol. 1, Issue 2, 2005 p. 4.

6-1. Van Valkenburg, Paul, *Race Car Engineering and Mechanics*, HP Books, Tucson, AZ, 1976.

8-1. Nowlan, Danny, *The Dynamics of the Race Car*, DNLEBooks, Sydney, Australia, 2011.

9-1. Rouelle, Claude, *"Race Car Vehicle Dynamic and Data Acquisition,"* Seminar binder, Race Car Dynamics and Data Acquisition Training Seminar, Denver, CO, 2001.

10-1. Fontdecaba, Josep I.B., *"Integral Suspension System for Motor Vehicles Based on Passive Components,"* SAE Paper No. 2002-01-3105, SAE International, Warrendale, PA, 2002.

13-1. SAE International, *Road Load Measurement and Dynamometer Simulation Using Coastdown Techniques*, SAE Standard J1263-201003, SAE International, Warrendale, PA, 2010.

13-2. Pi Research, *"Aerodynamics Application Note,"* Issue 1.0, Cosworth Electronics, Cambridge, UK, 1998.

14-1. Editors of The American Heritage Dictionaries, *The American Heritage Dictionary of the English Language*, Fourth Edition, Houghton Mifflin, Boston, MA 2006.

15-1. Autosport Magazine, *"DTM Review,"* Haymarket Publishing, November 12, 2009

15-2. Pacejka, Hans B., *Tire and Vehicle Dynamics, Second edition*, SAE International, Warrendale, PA, 2006.

15-3. *"iRacing.com,"* Wikipedia, The Free Encyclopedia, http://en.wikipedia.org/wiki/IRacing.com. Accessed February 21, 2013.

15-4. *"iRacing, McLaren Electronic Systems Partner in Online Racing Data Analysis,"* iRacing.com, http://www.iracing.com/inracingnews/iracing-news/iracing-mclaren-electronic-systems-partner-in-online-racing-data-analysis. Accessed February 21, 2013.

17-1. *"Performance indicator,"* Wikipedia, The Free Encyclopedia, http://en.wikipedia.org/wiki/Performance_indicator. Accessed December 18, 2012

19-1. Motec Pty Ltd., *"ADL2/EDL2 User's Manual,"* Motec Ltd., Victoria, Australia, 2005

19-2. Taylor, Barry N. and Kuyatt, Chris E., *"Guidelines for Evaluating and Expressing the Uncertainty of NIST Measurement Results,"* NIST Technical Note 1297, National Institute of Standards and Technology, Gaithersburg, MD, 1994.

19-3. *"Omega Engineering Technical Reference,"* http://www.omega.com/thermocouples.html. Accessed January 12, 2013

19-4. Gruner, Klaus-Dieter, *Principles of Non-contact Temperature Measurement*, Raytek GmbH, Berlin, Germany, 2003.

19-5. Hoffmann, Karl, *An Introduction to Measurements Using Strain Gages*, Hottinger Baldwin Messtechnik GmbH, Darmstadt, Germany, 1989.

19-6. Bitar, Sami, Probst, John S. and Garshelis, Ivan J., *"Development of a Magnetoelastic Torque Sensor for Formula One and CHAMP Car Racing Applications,"* SAE Paper No. 2000-01-0085, SAE International, Warrendale, PA, 2000.

19-7. Durant, Andrew J. and Hill, Martin J., *Technical Assessment of the DL2s GPS Data Quality*, Race Technology, Ltd., Nottingham, UK, 2005.

19-8. *"SPEEDBOX Overview and Features,"* Race Technology Ltd., http://www.race-technology.com/wiki/index.php/SPEEDBOX/OverviewAndFeatures, Accessed February 24, 2013

Bibliography

Bastow, Donald, Howard, Geoffrey and Whitehead, John, P., *Car Suspension and Handling—Fourth Edition*, SAE International, Warrendale, PA, 2004.

Bryden, Ray, *iRacing Paddock—Beginner's Guide to Road Racing on iRacing.com*, Bryden, Holden, MA, 2010.

Dixon, John C., *The Shock Absorber Handbook*, SAE International, Warrendale, PA, 1999.

Glimmerveen, John H., *Hands-on Race Car Engineer*, SAE International, Warrendale, PA, 2004.

Haney, Paul, *The Racing and High Performance Tire*, SAE International & TV Motorsports, Warrendale, PA, 2003.

Katz, Joseph, *New Directions in Race Car Aerodynamics—Second Edition*, Robert Bentley Inc., Cambridge, MA, 2006.

Kirkup, Les, *Calculating and Expressing Uncertainty in Measurement*, University of Technology Sydney, New South Wales, Australia, 2002.

Krumm, Michael, *Driving on the Edge—The Art and Science of Race Driving*, Icon Publishing Ltd., Worcestershire, UK, 2011.

Leuschen, Jason and Cooper, Kevin R., *"Effect of Ambient Conditions on the Measured Top Speed of a Winston Cup Car,"* SAE Paper No. 2004-01-3507, SAE International, Warrendale, PA, 2004.

Lopez, Carl, *Going Faster—Mastering the Art of Race Driving*, Robert Bentley Inc., Cambridge, MA, 1997.

Martin, B.T. and Law, Harry E., *"Development of an Expert System for Race Car Driver & Chassis Diagnostics,"* SAE Paper No. 2002-01-1574, SAE International, Warrendale, PA, 2002.

McBeath, Simon, *Competition Car Data Logging—A Practical Handbook*, Haynes Publishing, Newbury Park, CA, 2002.

Pi Research, *"Inertial Sensors Application Note,"* Issue 1.0, Pi Research, Cambridge, UK, 1997.

Puhn, Fred, *How to Make Your Car Handle*, HP Books, New York, 1981.

Searle, John, *"Equations for Speed, Time and Distance for Vehicles Under Maximum Acceleration,"* SAE Paper No. 1999-01-0078, SAE International, Warrendale, PA, 1999.

Smith, Carroll, *Tune To Win—The Art and Science of Race Car Development and Tuning*, Aero Publishers Inc., Fallbrook, CA, 1978.

Smith, Carroll, *Drive to Win*, Carroll Smith Consulting, Palos Verdes Estates, CA, 1996.

Vaduri, Sunder and Law, Harry E., *"Development of an Expert System for the Analysis of Track Test Data,"* SAE Paper No. 2000-01-1628, SAE International, Warrendale, PA, 2000.

Wilson, John S., *Sensor Technology Handbook*, Elsevier, Oxford, UK, 2005.

Index

About the Author

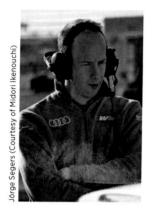

With an educational background in automotive engineering, Jörge Segers has been involved with racing disciplines such as GT and sports car racing, single-seaters, and touring cars since 1998. He started with an apprenticeship at GLPK Carsport, a Belgian team active in international GT racing. Mr. Segers became the team manager only three years later.

After finishing his studies, he was employed at BPR Competition Engineering as a track engineer in the International Sports Racing Series and later as a development manager at Eurotech Racing. At Eurotech, he was responsible for the GT racing activities of British sports car manufacturer Marcos Cars.

In 2001, Mr. Segers became the youngest team manager ever in an FIA organized championship. At GLPK Carsport, he was responsible for the team's activities and the FIA GT Championship. Subsequently, he has been working for other teams such as Henrik Roos Motorsports (FIA GT), Racing for Holland (Le Mans 24 Hours), DKR Engineering, Carsport Modena, and W-Racing Team. In 2010 Segers founded the consultancy company JS Engineering BVBA. The company specializes in providing engineering services to the motor racing industry as well as supplying data acquisition hardware to a multitude of organizations, both in- and outside the motorsport industry. Through JS Engineering, Segers tackled engineering projects in GT1 and GT3 racing to Stockcars and even bobsleigh competition. In 2013, he started working for the German team Phoenix Racing, where he is now active as an engineer in the DTM championship with Audi.

His interest in technical writing was triggered when he was asked to write part of the manual for a computer racing game for Simbin Development. A special interest in data acquisition and race car performance optimization led him to write this book. Since 2008, Segers has worked as a consultant for SAE International, organizing seminars on race car data acquisition.

Printed in the United States
By Bookmasters